GAO

Report to Congressional Addressees

September 2018

2017 HURRICANES AND WILDFIRES

Initial Observations on the Federal Response and Key Recovery Challenges

2017 Hurricanes & Wildfires: GAO's Initial Observations (9/2018)

GAO Highlights

Highlights of GAO-18-472, a report to congressional addressees

2017 HURRICANES AND WILDFIRES

Initial Observations on the Federal Response and Key Recovery Challenges

Why GAO Did This Study

In 2017, four sequential disasters—hurricanes Harvey, Irma, Maria, and the California wildfires—created an unprecedented demand for federal disaster response and recovery resources. According to FEMA, 2017 included three of the top five costliest hurricanes on record.

The National Oceanic and Atmospheric Administration estimated that the cumulative damages from weather and climate related disasters in the United States were over $300 billion in 2017 alone. As of June 2018, Congress had appropriated over $120 billion in supplemental funding for response and recovery related to the 2017 hurricanes and wildfires. Further, in October 2017, close to 14,000 federal employees were deployed in response to the disasters.

Given the scale and cost of these disasters, Congress and others have raised questions about the federal response and various recovery challenges that have arisen since the disasters. This report provides GAO's observations on: (1) federal and state preparedness and response coordination for hurricanes Harvey and Irma in Texas and Florida, and the California wildfires; (2) federal preparedness for and response to hurricanes Irma and Maria in Puerto Rico and the U.S. Virgin Islands; and (3) existing and emerging disaster recovery challenges highlighted by these disasters.

GAO analyzed FEMA policies, procedures, guidance, and data specific to disaster response and recovery programs. GAO focused on the busiest period of disaster response activity for the federal government—August 2017 through January 2018, with select updates on recovery efforts

What GAO Found

Federal and state preparedness and coordination efforts prior to and after the 2017 hurricane and wildfire disasters facilitated the response in Texas, Florida, and California. Specifically, the Federal Emergency Management Agency (FEMA) and state emergency management officials implemented various preparedness actions prior to landfall of the hurricanes and during the wildfires—such as predeploying federal personnel to support response efforts; colocating federal, state, and local emergency managers; and pre-staging and delivery of commodities like food and water. Further, according to FEMA and state officials, preexisting coordination mechanisms and relationships also facilitated response efforts in each state. For example, FEMA and each state had conducted numerous emergency exercises in the years prior to these disasters and had developed relationships during response to prior disasters that led to accelerated decision-making during the 2017 disasters. Federal and state officials emphasized that there were certainly unprecedented challenges during these disasters—such as deploying a sufficient and adequately-trained FEMA disaster workforce—and lessons learned, but prior response coordination efforts helped to quickly and effectively resolve many of these challenges.

The federal government provided significant support to Puerto Rico and the U.S. Virgin Islands in response to Hurricanes Irma and Maria, but faced numerous challenges that complicated response efforts. FEMA efforts in Puerto Rico alone were the largest and longest single response in the agency's history. As of April 2018, FEMA had obligated over $12 billion for response and recovery for Hurricane Maria (see figure below) reflecting the scale and complexity of efforts given the widespread damage. FEMA tasked federal agencies with over 1,000 response mission assignments for Hurricanes Maria and Irma in the territories at a cost of over $5 billion, compared to about 400 such assignments for Hurricanes Harvey and Irma and the California wildfires combined. For example, FEMA assigned the U.S. Army Corps of Engineers the mission to install over 1,700 emergency electricity generators in Puerto Rico, compared to the 310 for the response to Hurricane Katrina.

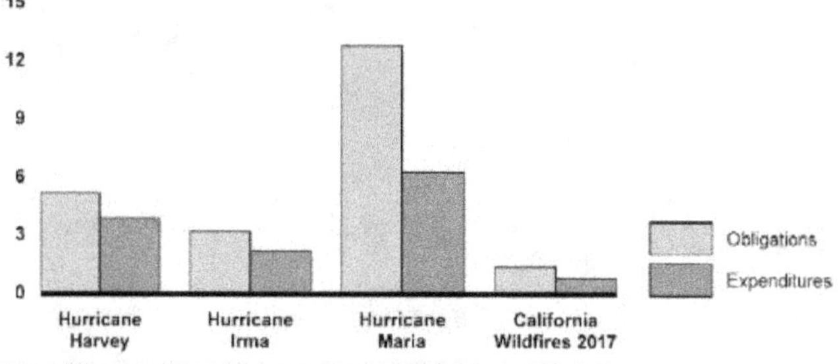
Federal Emergency Management Agency Disaster Relief Fund Obligations and Expenditures for Hurricanes Harvey, Irma, Maria, and California Wildfires through April 30, 2018

Source: GAO analysis of Federal Emergency Management Agency data | GAO-18-472

_______________________________ United States Government Accountability Office

and obtained updates through June 2018. In October and November 2017, GAO teams made site visits to hurricane damaged areas in Texas, Florida, Puerto Rico, and the U.S. Virgin Islands. At these locations, GAO visited FEMA joint field operation locations and interviewed FEMA, Department of Defense, and other federal officials about response and recovery operations, visited disaster recovery centers, and observed damage. GAO also interviewed FEMA officials responsible for wildfire response and recovery efforts in California.

Additionally, GAO interviewed state and territorial emergency management officials or their designee in Texas, Florida, California, Puerto Rico, and the U.S. Virgin Islands, as well as officials from eight cities and counties in Texas, Florida, and California (selected based on their proximity to the disaster impacted areas and their availability) to discuss their observations on the federal response in their respective jurisdictions. While the perspectives of these officials are not generalizable, they provided valuable insights into the federal response to the 2017 disasters.

This report includes 10 appendices that provide further details and data on federal response and recovery efforts. These areas cover key issues and challenges that GAO believes are critical for assessing the federal response and warrant continued Congressional and agency oversight during disaster recovery.

GAO is not making recommendations in this report, but has ongoing work that will address various response and recovery programs and challenges in more detail. GAO will make recommendations, as appropriate, once this work is completed.

In commenting on a draft of this report, DHS stated that the report highlighted the challenges of the complicated response and recovery efforts as well as provided insights into these efforts. DHS also noted that it is continuing to apply lessons learned from 2017 to improve its future program delivery and response efforts.

View GAO-18-472. For more information, contact Christopher Currie at (404) 679-1875 or curriec@gao.gov.

Note: An obligation is a definite commitment that creates a legal liability of the government for the payment of goods and services ordered or received. An expenditure is an amount paid by federal agencies by cash or cash equivalent, during the fiscal year to liquidate government obligations.

Nevertheless, GAO found that FEMA faced a number of challenges that slowed and complicated its response efforts to Hurricane Maria, particularly in Puerto Rico. Many of these challenges were also highlighted in FEMA's own 2017 hurricane after action report, including:

- the sequential and overlapping timing of the three hurricanes—with Maria being the last of the three—caused staffing shortages and required FEMA to shift staff to the territories that were already deployed to other disasters;
- logistical challenges complicated efforts to deploy federal resources and personnel quickly given the remote distance of both territories; and
- limited preparedness by the U.S. Virgin Islands and Puerto Rico for a Category 5 hurricane and incapacitation of local response functions due to widespread devastation and loss of power and communications led FEMA to assume response functions that territories would usually perform themselves.

The 2017 hurricanes and wildfires highlighted some longstanding issues and revealed other emerging response and recovery challenges. For example, the concurrent timing and scale of the disaster damages nationwide caused shortages in available debris removal contractors and delays in removing disaster debris—a key first step in recovery. In addition, FEMA's available workforce was overwhelmed by the response needs. For example, at the height of FEMA workforce deployments in October 2017, 54 percent of staff were serving in a capacity in which they did not hold the title of "Qualified"—according to FEMA's qualification system standards—a past challenge GAO has identified. FEMA officials noted that staff shortages, and lack of trained personnel with program expertise led to complications in its response efforts, particularly after Hurricane Maria.

Federal Disaster Workforce Deployed at the Height of 2017 Response Acivities

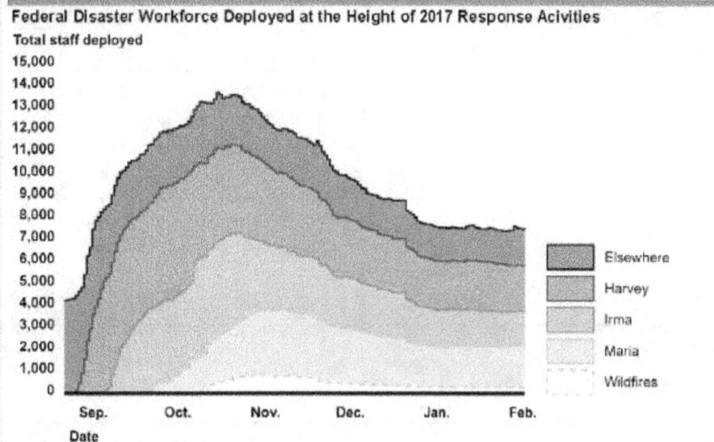

Source: GAO analysis of Department of Homeland Security data. | GAO-18-472

Further, federal, state, and local officials faced challenges finding temporary housing for disaster survivors given the extensive damage to available housing in each location. For example, given the widespread damage in Puerto Rico and lack of hotels and other temporary housing, FEMA transported survivors to the mainland United States to stay in hotels. FEMA also used new authorities and procedures to meet the need, such as providing Texas as much as $1 billion to manage its own housing program. However, this approach had not been used or tested in past disasters and state officials noted challenges in managing the program such as staffing shortfalls. State officials further noted challenges in coordinating with FEMA that led to delays in providing assistance to survivors. GAO will continue to monitor these programs.

_________________________ United States Government Accountability Office

Contents

2017 Hurricanes & Wildfires: GAO's Initial Observations (9/2018)

Table

2017 Hurricanes & Wildfires: GAO's Initial Observations (9/2018)

Figures

2017 Hurricanes & Wildfires: GAO's Initial Observations (9/2018)

2017 Hurricanes & Wildfires: GAO's Initial Observations (9/2018)

Abbreviations

DHS	Department of Homeland Security
DRF	Disaster Relief Fund
DOD	Department of Defense
EMAC	Emergency Management Assistance Compact
ESFs	emergency support functions
FCO	Federal Coordinating Officer
FEMA	Federal Emergency Management Agency
FQS	FEMA Qualification System
IA	Individual Assistance
IMAT	Incident Management Assistance Team
IT	information technology
JFO	joint field office
PA	Public Assistance
PREPA	Puerto Rico Electric Power Authority
PROMESA	Puerto Rico Oversight, Management, and Economic
SRIA	Sandy Recovery Improvement Act of 2013
USACE	U.S. Army Corps of Engineers

2017 Hurricanes & Wildfires: GAO's Initial Observations (9/2018)

441 G St. N.W.
Washington, DC 20548

September 4, 2018

Congressional Addressees

In 2017, four near-sequential disasters—Hurricane Harvey, Hurricane Irma, Hurricane Maria, and the California wildfires—created an unprecedented demand for federal disaster response and recovery resources.[1] According to the Federal Emergency Management Agency (FEMA), the 2017 hurricanes and wildfires collectively affected 47 million people—nearly 15 percent of the nation's population—with hurricanes Harvey, Irma, and Maria ranking among the top five costliest hurricanes on record.[2] See figure 1 for a timeline of these major disasters.[3]

---

[1]The focus of this report is on five geographic areas—Texas, Florida, Puerto Rico, the U.S. Virgin Islands, and California—affected by 4 out of the 137 presidentially disasters declared in 2017.

[2]According to FEMA, the five costliest hurricanes on record are Hurricane Katrina at $161 billion, Hurricane Harvey at $125 billion, Hurricane Maria at $90 billion, Hurricane Sandy at $71 billion, and Hurricane Irma at $50 billion.

[3]A major disaster is any natural catastrophe (including any hurricane, tornado, storm, high water, wind-driven water, tidal wave, tsunami, earthquake, volcanic eruption, landslide, mudslide, snowstorm, or drought), or, regardless of cause, any fire, flood, or explosion, in any part of the United States, which the president determines causes damage of sufficient severity and magnitude to warrant major disaster assistance to supplement the efforts and available resources of states, local governments, and disaster relief organizations in alleviating damage, loss, hardship, or suffering. See 42 U.S.C. § 5122(2).

Figure 1: Timeline of the 2017 Hurricanes and Wildfires

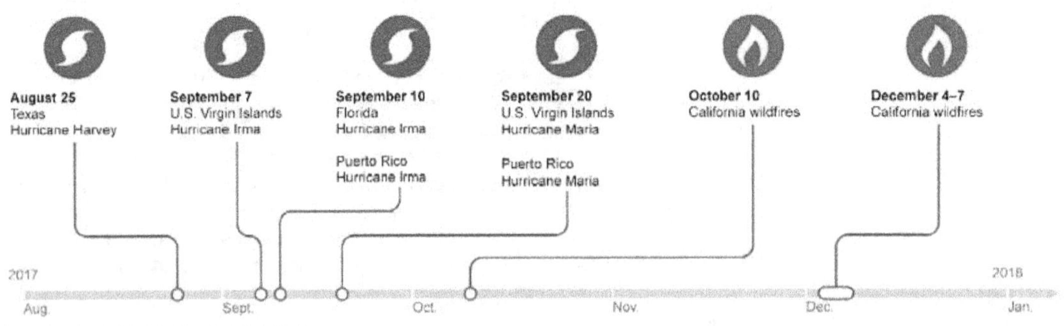

Source: Department of Homeland Security. | GAO-18-472

We have previously reported that the rising number and costs of disasters and the increasing reliance on the federal government for disaster assistance is a key source of federal fiscal exposure,[4] and that this cost will likely continue to rise as the climate changes.[5] In September 2016, we reported that from fiscal years 2005 through 2014, the federal government obligated over $277 billion for disaster assistance programs and activities. The National Oceanic and Atmospheric Administration estimated that the cumulative damages from weather- and climate-related disasters in 2017 alone cost the United States over $300 billion, making it the costliest year on record. As of June 2018, three supplemental appropriations bills have been enacted, providing over $120 billion in

[4]GAO, *Fiscal Exposures: Improving Cost Recognition in the Federal Budget*, GAO-14-28 (Washington, D.C.: Oct. 29, 2013).

[5]GAO, *Climate Change: Information on Potential Economic Effects Could Help Guide Federal Efforts to Reduce Fiscal Exposure*, GAO-17-720 (Washington, D.C.: Sept. 28, 2017). Managing fiscal exposure due to climate change has been on our high risk list since 2013, in part, because of concerns about the increasing costs of disaster response and recovery efforts. See GAO, *High-Risk Series: An Update*, GAO-15-290 (Washington, D.C.: Feb. 11, 2015); also
http://www.gao.gov/highrisk/limiting_federal_government_fiscal_exposure/why_did_study.

2017 Hurricanes & Wildfires: GAO's Initial Observations (9/2018)

supplemental federal funding for activities related to the 2017 hurricanes and wildfires.[6]

In 2005, Hurricane Katrina became the single largest, most destructive natural disaster in our nation's history causing over 1,800 deaths and an estimated $108 billion in damage. In the wake of Hurricane Katrina, we and others identified several issues of leadership and planning that plagued the response.[7] To address these critiques, Congress passed the Post-Katrina Emergency Management Reform Act of 2006 (Post-Katrina Act).[8] Among other things, the act clarified FEMA's roles and responsibilities as the primary federal agency responsible for disaster preparedness, response, and recovery, and provided additional authorities to federal agencies to address the shortcomings from Katrina.

Since the Post-Katrina Act was enacted in 2006, we have evaluated a range of emergency management issues including federal efforts to implement provisions of the act and improve national emergency preparedness, response, and recovery.[9] We have also evaluated the federal response to other major disasters since that time, most notably the response to and recovery from Hurricane Sandy in 2012. We have made numerous recommendations to FEMA and other federal agencies to strengthen their disaster response efforts, many of which have been

---

[6]This figure does not include transfers of unobligated balances from prior fiscal years or indefinite appropriations authorized to forgive any outstanding balance owed to the Department of Education under the Historically Black College and University Hurricane Supplemental Loan program. Also, the supplemental appropriations provided up to $78.5 million for oversight activities by nine Inspectors General and us related to the expenditure of these funds. Supplemental Appropriations for Disaster Relief Requirements Act, 2017, Pub. L. No. 115-56, div. B, 131 Stat. 1129, 1136 (2017); Additional Supplemental Appropriations for Disaster Relief Requirements Act, 2017 Pub. L. No. 115-72, div. A, 131 Stat. 1224, 1224 (2017); Supplemental Appropriations for Disaster Relief Requirements Act, 2018, Pub. L. No. 115-123, div. B, subdiv. 1, 132 Stat. 64, 65 (2018).

[7]See, for example GAO, *Hurricane Katrina: GAO's Preliminary Observations Regarding Preparedness, Response, and Recovery*, GAO-06-442T (Washington, DC: Mar. 8, 2006).

[8]Pub. L. No. 109-295, tit. VI, 120 Stat. 1355, 1394 (2006); see also 6 U.S.C. §§ 721, 722; 42 U.S.C. § 5144. The provisions of the Post-Katrina Act became effective upon enactment, October 4, 2006, with the exception of certain organizational changes related to FEMA, most of which took effect on March 31, 2007.

[9]Two reports focused specifically on the Post-Katrina Act; see GAO, *Actions Taken to Implement the Post-Katrina Emergency Management Reform Act of 2006*, GAO-09-59R, (Washington, D.C.: Nov. 21, 2008); and GAO, *National Preparedness: Actions Taken by FEMA to Implement Select Provisions of the Post-Katrina Emergency Management Reform Act of 2006*, GAO-14-99R (Washington, D.C.: Nov 26, 2013).

GAO-18-472 2017 Hurricanes and Wildfires

2017 Hurricanes & Wildfires: GAO's Initial Observations (9/2018)

implemented or are in the process of being implemented. We discuss some of these recommendations in more detail throughout this report.

Given the scale and cost of the 2017 disasters, Congress and others have raised questions about the federal response to these disasters and various recovery challenges that have arisen since these disasters. Under the authority of the U.S. Comptroller General to undertake reviews that help inform Congressional oversight, we initiated a review of the federal government's handling of the 2017 hurricanes and wildfires. Specifically, this report addresses:

1. our observations of federal and state preparedness and the response coordination for hurricanes Harvey and Irma in Texas and Florida, as well as for the California wildfires;

2. our observations of the federal preparedness and response to hurricanes Irma and Maria in Puerto Rico and the U.S. Virgin Islands; and

3. existing and emerging disaster recovery challenges highlighted by the 2017 hurricanes and wildfires.

In addition, this report includes 10 appendices that provide further details and data related to the federal response to the 2017 disasters and various recovery challenges. These appendices cover key issues and challenges that we believe are critical to the federal response and that warrant continued congressional and agency oversight during recovery. This work will include assessments of federal preparedness, planning, response, and recovery efforts. The appendices are:

- Appendix II: Federal Appropriations and FEMA Obligations for the 2017 Hurricanes and California Wildfires

- Appendix III: Federal Response Coordination during the 2017 Hurricanes and California Wildfires

- Appendix IV: Federal Contracting for the 2017 Hurricanes

- Appendix V: FEMA Disaster Workforce Capacity

- Appendix VI: FEMA's Individual Assistance Program

- Appendix VII: Fraud Risk Management in FEMA's Disaster Assistance Programs

- Appendix VIII: Payment Integrity and Prior Identified Requirements for Disaster Relief Funding

- Appendix IX: FEMA's Public Assistance Program

- Appendix X: Disaster Resilience and Hazard Mitigation

- Appendix XI: Department of Defense's Support of Civil Authorities during the 2017 Hurricanes and California Wildfires

To address all three objectives, we analyzed federal laws and FEMA policies, procedures, and guidance specific to emergency management. Specifically, we reviewed select sections of the Post-Katrina Act, including those associated with the establishment of (1) the *National Response Framework*, (2) the Federal Coordinating Officer (FCO) position—the lead federal official in charge of response, (3) Incident Management Assistance Teams (IMAT)—FEMA staff who rapidly deploy to an incident to provide leadership in the identification and provision of federal assistance and federal response capabilities, (4) the surge capacity force; and (5) the Sandy Recovery Improvement Act, particularly those sections associated with FEMA's public assistance program and debris removal responsibilities.[10] Additionally we reviewed the *National Response Framework*, National Disaster Recovery Framework, 2017 National Preparedness Report, and FEMA's 2014-2018 Strategic Plans. We also reviewed relevant information from our prior reports on FEMA's work.[11] Further, we analyzed key data from FEMA's financial management, workforce, and emergency operations systems for the

---

[10]The *National Response Framework* is the part of the National Preparedness System established in Presidential Policy Directive 8 that is to be used to manage any type of disaster or emergency response, regardless of scale, scope, and complexity. Specifically, this framework covers actions to save lives, protect property and the environment, stabilize communities, and meet basic human needs following an incident. Response also includes the execution of emergency plans and actions to support short-term recovery. Department of Homeland Security, Federal Emergency Management Agency, *National Response Framework, Third Edition* (Washington, D.C.: June 2016). The surge capacity force is a cadre of non-FEMA federal employees who augment FEMA's disaster response and recovery efforts.

[11]GAO-14-28; GAO-17-720; GAO-15-290; GAO-06-442T; GAO-09-59R; GAO-14-99R; *2017 Disaster Contracting: Observations on Federal Contracting for Response and Recovery Efforts*. GAO-18-335. (Washington, D.C.: Feb. 28, 2018); GAO, *Disaster Recovery: FEMA's Public Assistance Grant Program Experienced Challenges with Gulf Coast Rebuilding*, GAO-09-129 (Washington, D.C.: Dec. 18, 2008); GAO, *Hurricane Sandy: An Investment Strategy Could Help the Federal Government Enhance National Resilience for Future Disasters*, GAO-15-515 (Washington, D.C.: July 30, 2015); GAO, *Federal Emergency management Agency: Workforce Planning and Training Count be Enhanced by Incorporating Strategic Management Principles*, GAO-12-487 (Washington, D.C.: Apr. 26, 2012); GAO, *Federal Emergency Management Agency: Additional Planning and Data Collection Could Help Improve Workforce Management Efforts*, GAO-15-437 (Washington, D.C.: July, 8, 2015).

2017 Hurricanes & Wildfires: GAO's Initial Observations (9/2018)

period August 2017 through January 2018— the highest period of disaster response activity for the federal government—and obtained updates from FEMA through June 2018. We interviewed officials at FEMA headquarters about their data quality control procedures, reviewed existing information about data systems—particularly data definitions and data validation, conducted electronic testing and reviewed the data for obvious errors and omissions to ensure that all data were sufficiently reliable for the purposes of our reporting objectives, as described in appendix I.[12] See Related GAO Products for a full list of our products related to each appendix contained in this report.

Moreover, in October and November 2017, we conducted site visits to hurricane damaged areas in the greater Houston area, throughout southern Florida, in San Juan, Puerto Rico, and St. Croix, U.S. Virgin Islands, and visited FEMA's joint field offices (JFO) —multiagency coordination centers established near disaster sites for coordinating major disaster response and recovery efforts—for Hurricane Harvey, located in Austin Texas; Hurricane Irma, located in Orlando Florida; and hurricanes Irma and Maria, located in San Juan and St. Croix. At these locations, we interviewed FEMA's on-site leadership and conducted site visits to FEMA Disaster Response Centers. Further, we conducted interviews with FEMA's on-site leadership responsible for the response and recovery efforts in California. We also interviewed emergency management officials or their designees in each disaster-affected state and territory as well as local government officials from eight municipalities in Texas, Florida, and California to gain their insights and perspectives on the federal response to the hurricanes and wildfires in their respective states and territories. We selected the cities and counties whose officials we interviewed based on their geographic proximity to the disaster-affected sites we were already visiting, and their availability. The findings from these interviews cannot be generalized to all disaster-affected states, however, they provided valuable insights about their respective state's and the federal response to and recovery from the disasters. We also conducted interviews with Department of Defense officials who assisted FEMA in its response efforts. Further information on our scope and methodology can be found in appendix I.

---

[12]FEMA has 10 regional offices located across the continental United States See appendix XII for the location of each as well as the states each regional office is responsible for collaborating with to administer FEMA programs.

2017 Hurricanes & Wildfires: GAO's Initial Observations (9/2018)

We are not making recommendations in this report, but it is part of a body of work on related issues across federal departments as those discussed in appendix II through XI of this report, and we will further assess these issues moving forward, making recommendations, as appropriate, once this work is completed.

We conducted this performance audit from September 2017 to September 2018 in accordance with generally accepted government auditing standards. Those standards require that we plan and perform the audit to obtain sufficient, appropriate evidence to provide a reasonable basis for our findings and conclusions based on our audit objectives. We believe that the evidence obtained provides a reasonable basis for our findings and conclusions based on our audit objectives.

Background

Disaster Response Roles and Responsibilities

Disaster response can involve many federal, state, territorial, tribal, private sector, and nongovernmental entities. The *National Response Framework* describes how the federal government, states and localities, and other public and private sector institutions should respond to disasters and emergencies. For example, state, local, tribal and territorial governments are to play the lead roles in disaster response and recovery. Local emergency agencies—police, firefighters, and medical teams—are to be the first responders in a disaster or emergency.

2017 Hurricanes & Wildfires: GAO's Initial Observations (9/2018)

Federal agencies can become involved in responding to a disaster when effective response and recovery are beyond the capabilities of the state and affected local governments. In such cases, the Robert T. Stafford Disaster Relief and Emergency Assistance Act (Stafford Act), permits the President to declare a major disaster in response to a request by the governor of a state or territory or by the chief executive of a tribal government.[13] Such a declaration is the mechanism by which the federal government gets involved in funding and coordinating response and recovery activities.[14] Under the *National Response Framework*, the Department of Homeland Security (DHS) is the federal department with primary responsibility for coordinating disaster response, and within DHS, FEMA has lead responsibility. The Administrator of FEMA serves as the principal adviser to the President and the Secretary of Homeland Security regarding emergency management.[15]

Once a major disaster is declared, states, territories, and tribes may obtain federal assistance through the Disaster Relief Fund (DRF).[16] In general, response and recovery activities that FEMA coordinates under the Stafford Act are funded from the DRF. See appendix II for more information on DRF spending in response to the 2017 disasters.

In addition to DHS, at least 29 other federal agencies carry out disaster assistance programs and activities. The *National Response Framework* identifies 14 emergency support functions (ESFs)—such as communication, transportation, and energy—and designates a federal department or agency as the coordinating agency for each function. For example, provision of assets and services related to public works and

---

[13] 42 U.S.C. § 5170.

[14] *Presidential Policy Directive-8 National Preparedness* (PPD-8) establishes a national preparedness system made of an integrated set of guidance, programs, and processes designed to strengthen the security and resilience of the United States through systematic preparation for the natural and human-caused threats that pose the greatest risk. This system breaks preparedness activities into five different lines of effort—prevention, protection, mitigation, response, and recovery—each of which requires a separate planning framework.

[15] 6 U.S.C. § 313(c)(4).

[16] The DRF is the primary source of federal disaster assistance for state and local governments when a disaster is declared. The DRF is appropriated no-year funding, which allows FEMA to fund, direct, coordinate, and manage response and recovery efforts—including certain efforts by other federal agencies and state and local governments, among others—associated with domestic disasters and emergencies.

engineering, such as temporary roofing or power, are coordinated by the U.S. Army Corps of Engineers (USACE), a component of the Department of Defense (DOD). See appendix III for more information on the 14 ESFs and their assigned coordinating agencies.

Finally, the federal government also works with private-sector businesses and nongovernmental organizations such as the Red Cross, Salvation Army, and other voluntary organizations to provide food, shelter, and essential needs to survivors.

FEMA's Disaster Response Mechanisms

FEMA has multiple mechanisms by which to help coordinate and deliver the federal government's response to disasters. Among those are:

- **direct provision of assistance.** When a state, tribe, or territory that has received a major disaster declaration requests federal assistance, FEMA can provide that assistance directly in various forms, such as meals, water, or tarps.

- **mission assignment to other agencies.** FEMA coordinates disaster response efforts through mission assignments—work orders it issues that direct another federal agency to utilize its authorities and the resources granted to it under federal law in support of direct assistance to state, local, tribal, and territorial governments.[17] For example, FEMA often requests medical teams from the Department of Health and Human Services and logistical support from DOD.[18]

---

[17] 42 U.S.C. § 5192(a)(1). The Stafford Act authorizes the President to direct any federal agency, with or without reimbursement, to utilize its authorities and the resources granted to it under federal law in support of state and local response efforts for emergencies. This tasking authority, delegated to the FEMA Administrator, is carried out through a mission assignment.

[18] While DOD's primary mission is to defend the nation, the department is often asked to play a prominent role in supporting civil authorities and must be prepared to provide rapid response when called upon during disasters and declared emergencies (both natural and human-caused). DOD provides such support through its Defense Support of Civil Authorities mission.

- **distribution of donations.** FEMA can accept and distribute donations and gifts of services, money, or property to alleviate the suffering and damage caused by disasters.[19]

- **interagency agreements.** FEMA can also acquire supplies or services from other government agencies by executing an interagency agreement with those agencies.

- **procurement of supplies and services from contractors.** FEMA and other federal agencies support disaster response and recovery by procuring goods and services through contracts.

To provide disaster relief and recovery assistance, federal departments may have to solicit, award, and administer contracts. As of March 31, 2018, federal departments had obligated approximately $7.1 billion for contracts in support of hurricanes Harvey, Irma, and Maria.[20] The Post-Katrina Act, which addressed various shortcomings identified in the preparation for and response to Hurricane Katrina, included provisions to update FEMA's contracting practices.[21]

---

[19]See 42 U.S.C. § 5201(b). According to FEMA, acceptance of gifts is subject to ethical and operational constraints on a case-by-case basis. For example, FEMA Directive 112-13 establishes the process for accepting gifts from domestic sources and requires authorized agency officials to determine whether or not the gift reflects poorly on the agency, compromises the agency's integrity, attaches prohibited conditions on the gift or requires the agency to act outside its mission and duties, requires the expenditure of appropriated funds, provides the donor with some benefit, or creates a conflict of interest or the appearance of a conflict of interest.

[20]For the purposes of this report and appendix IV, contract obligations include obligations against what the Federal Procurement Data System-Next Generation (FPDS-NG) categorizes as definitive vehicles (definitive contracts and purchase orders that have a defined scope of work that do not allow for individual orders under them), and against what FPDS-NG categorizes as indefinite delivery vehicles (orders under the Federal Supply Schedule, orders/calls under blanket purchase agreements, orders under basic ordering agreements, orders under government-wide acquisition contracts, and orders under other indefinite delivery vehicles, such as indefinite delivery, indefinite quantity contracts).

[21]Pub. L. No. 109-295, §§ 601-699, 120 Stat. at 1394-1463. We have previously reported in 2015 that FEMA had not fully implemented the Post-Katrina Act's statutorily required contracting reforms following Hurricane Katrina; see GAO-15-783. We made eight recommendations to the FEMA Administrator and one recommendation to the Secretary of Homeland Security, three of which remain open.

2017 Hurricanes & Wildfires: GAO's Initial Observations (9/2018)

One of these provisions requires that FEMA identify and establish contracts prior to a disaster for goods and services that are typically needed during a disaster response—known as "advance" or "pre-positioned" contracts.[22] We are currently conducting more detailed reviews of federal contracting related to the 2017 disasters, including the wildfires. For more information on federal disaster contracting for the 2017 hurricanes, see appendix IV. Figure 2 shows the various mechanisms by which the federal government provides disaster response support.

Figure 2: Mechanisms Used by Federal Emergency Management Agency (FEMA) to Coordinate and Deliver Disaster Response

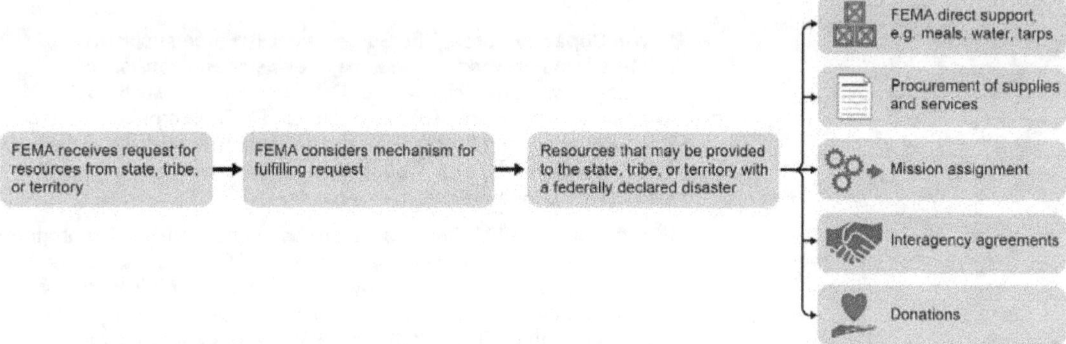

Source: Federal Emergency Management Agency. | GAO-18-472

Federal Disaster Workforce

The federal disaster workforce is designed to scale up or down depending on the timing and magnitude of disasters, and includes the following categories of employees:

- **Title 5 employees.**[23] These permanent and temporary employees make up FEMA's day-to-day workforce and are responsible for administering the agency's ongoing program activities. During

---

[22]In February 2018, we issued a report on our initial observations of federal contracting for response and recovery from the 2017 hurricanes. See GAO-18-335.

[23]Generally, Title 5 refers to the section of the United States Code that establishes the law for managing human resources in the federal government.

GAO-18-472 2017 Hurricanes and Wildfires

2017 Hurricanes & Wildfires: GAO's Initial Observations (9/2018)

- disasters, these employees can be deployed as needed. Examples of Title 5 employees include logistics specialists, contract officers, and budget analysts.

- **Stafford Act employees.**[24] Stafford Act employees provide support for disaster-related activities and augment FEMA's disaster workforce at facilities, regional offices, and headquarters. Stafford Act employees include a Cadre of On Call Response/Recovery Employees who are temporary employees with 2- to 4-year appointments and can be deployed to fulfill any role specifically related to the incident for which they are hired and qualified. IMAT staff are Cadre of On Call Response/Recovery Employees. They also include reservists, who work on an intermittent basis and are deployed as needed to fulfill incident management roles within their cadre function.[25]

- **Surge Capacity Force.** The Surge Capacity Force supplements FEMA's disaster workforce in a major disaster and consists of volunteers who are employees of DHS components, such as the Transportation Security Administration and U.S. Secret Service, as well as employees of other federal agencies, as authorized by the Post-Katrina Act.[26] Surge Capacity Force volunteers are deployed to disaster sites for a maximum of 3 months.

- **FEMA Corps.** FEMA Corps is a team-based national service program operated by AmeriCorps in partnership with FEMA. Members are not FEMA employees, but are deployed to augment FEMA's workforce for disaster readiness, preparedness, response, and recovery work under the supervision of FEMA staff. FEMA staff are responsible for developing projects for FEMA Corps members and providing technical supervision at project sites. FEMA Corps members are generally 18 to 24 years old and serve 10-month terms.

In addition to these four types of employees, FEMA hires locally and employs other personnel, such as contractors, to provide a variety of forms of assistance and services to meet disaster preparedness,

---

[24] See 42 U.S.C. § 5149(b)(1).

[25] Reservists' activities can include interviewing disaster survivors; conducting and verifying damage assessments; providing administrative, financial, and logistical support; and performing a wide variety of other tasks as identified by staffing needs and operational requirements.

[26] 6 U.S.C. § 711(b).

2017 Hurricanes & Wildfires: GAO's Initial Observations (9/2018)

response, and recovery needs, such as debris removal. Prior to Hurricane Harvey in August 2017, the federal disaster workforce, including Surge Capacity Force and FEMA Corps, was 24,040. As of January 2018, the federal disaster workforce had grown to 33,041, as shown in figure 3.[27] For more information on FEMA's disaster workforce, see appendix V.

[27]FEMA's disaster workforce, which is a component of the overall federal disaster workforce, was 11,213 prior to Hurricane Harvey, and had grown to 11,980 as of January 2018. According to FEMA officials, not all FEMA personnel can be deployed to a disaster. Those who cannot be deployed provide support to FEMA headquarters or regional offices, and the National Response Coordination Center. These personnel are part of FEMA's force strength, but not part of the disaster workforce. Additionally, several factors can affect the availability of the federal disaster workforce, including whether employees are on leave. Also, FEMA does not have direct oversight regarding the availability of the Surge Capacity Force, contractors, other federal agencies, or FEMA Corps as they are not FEMA employees.

2017 Hurricanes & Wildfires: GAO's Initial Observations (9/2018)

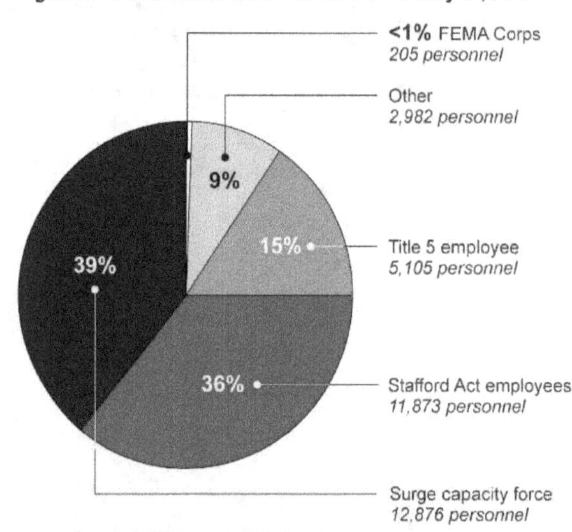

Figure 3: Federal Disaster Workforce As of January 31, 2018

Source: GAO analysis of Department of Homeland Security data. | GAO-18-472

Note: "Other" includes the following four workforce categories: permanent part-time, temporary part-time, temporary incident, and political appointees. Federal Emergency Management Agency (FEMA) Corps is a team-based national service program operated by AmeriCorps National Civilian Community Corps in partnership with FEMA. Members are not FEMA employees, but are deployed to augment FEMA's workforce for disaster readiness, preparedness, response, and recovery work under the supervision of FEMA staff. Title 5 employees are permanent and temporary employees who make up FEMA's day-to-day workforce and are responsible for administering the agency's ongoing program activities. Stafford Act employees include Cadre of On Call Response/Recovery Employees who are temporary employees with 2- to 4-year appointments who can be deployed to fulfill any role specifically related to the incident for which they are hired and qualified. The Surge Capacity Force supplements FEMA's disaster workforce in a major disaster and consists of volunteers who are employees of the Department of Homeland Security components and other federal agencies.

Overview of FEMA and Federal Disaster Recovery Programs

After a disaster strikes, the response phase typically lasts for days or weeks, depending on the impact and complexity of the disaster and eventually transitions into recovery operations. As with response, a number of federal departments and agencies may assist with various forms of disaster recovery assistance to individuals and state, local, tribal, and territorial governments. While this report focuses primarily on recovery programs that FEMA delivers, we are conducting work on other federal programs and issues, including use of the Community Development Block Grant and the National Flood Insurance Program for recovery from the disasters, as part of our collective body of work on the 2017 disasters.

FEMA provides three principal forms of disaster recovery funding assistance—Individual Assistance (IA), Public Assistance (PA) and Hazard Mitigation.[28]

Individual Assistance: FEMA's IA program provides financial assistance directly to survivors for the necessary expenses and serious needs that cannot be met through insurance or low-interest loans, such as temporary housing assistance, counseling, unemployment compensation, or medical expenses (for more information on FEMA's IA Program see appendix VI). Part of its mission is to provide this assistance quickly. In response to our previously identified weaknesses, FEMA has taken steps to improve its ability to do so while protecting government resources. For example, in March 2018, FEMA reported that the agency had collaborated with the Social Security Administration to assess the feasibility of a direct data exchange with the Administration for the purpose of identifying recipients using Social Security numbers that were ineligible or likely belonged to deceased individuals. It also reported that it had taken steps to more reliably determine eligibility for its Individuals and Households Program based on compliance with flood-insurance requirements. The agency took these actions in an effort to address recommendations we made in 2015 to help prevent improper payments.[29] See appendix VII for information on FEMA's actions to manage fraud risk related to its disaster assistance programs. Further, given the significant costs of these four disasters to the federal government, it is important that federal agencies tasked with response and recovery programs pay particular attention to internal controls and payment integrity issues related to disaster relief. See

---

[28] In addition to the three forms of funding assistance, the DRF also provides funding for (1) Fire Management Assistance grants to state, loca,l and tribal governments for the mitigation, management, and control of fires; (2) Mission Assignment which allows FEMA to issue task orders directing other federal agencies to provide direct assistance to disaster affected states, tribes, and territories; and (3) Administration to cover FEMA's costs for supporting the delivery of disaster assistance.

[29] GAO-15-15.

2017 Hurricanes & Wildfires: GAO's Initial Observations (9/2018)

appendix VIII for information on issues we identified in our prior work related to disaster relief payment integrity.[30]

Public Assistance: FEMA's PA program provides supplemental federal disaster grant assistance to state, local, tribal, and territorial governments, and certain types of private nonprofit organizations for debris removal, emergency protective measures, and the restoration of disaster-damaged, publicly-owned facilities and the facilities of certain private nonprofit organizations. The PA program also encourages protection of these damaged facilities from future events by providing assistance for hazard mitigation measures. The program—which represents the largest share of federal aid from the Disaster Relief Fund—is administered through a partnership between FEMA and the state, tribal or territorial grantee, which provides funding to local or tribal entities who are the subrecipients of a PA grant award. Thus, it entails an extensive paperwork and review process between FEMA and grantee officials based on specific eligibility rules that outline the types of damage that can be reimbursed by the federal government and steps that federal, state, and local governments must take in order to document eligibility. We have identified a number of past challenges affecting various aspects of the PA program. To address these various challenges, we made a number of recommendations, and FEMA has taken or is taking various actions to address them. For example, as of January 2018, FEMA officials had begun incorporating experiences and lessons learned from the 2017 hurricane season and planned to reevaluate the appropriate number of staff needed in the PA workforce, and present recommendations to senior leadership. Officials also reported completing activities to develop

---

[30]Effective fraud risk management can help ensure that federal disaster assistance programs serve their intended purpose, taxpayer dollars are spent effectively, and government assets are safeguarded. Since 2014, when we last reported on FEMA's implementation of controls to help prevent potentially improper or fraudulent payments in the IA program, we issued *A Framework for Managing Fraud Risks in Federal Programs* (Fraud Risk Framework). The Fraud Risk Framework provides a comprehensive set of leading practices that serve as a guide for agency managers to use when developing efforts to combat fraud in a strategic, risk-based way. In addition, the Fraud Reduction and Data Analytics Act of 2015, enacted in June 2016, requires the Office of Management and Budget to establish guidelines for agencies for implementing control activities to prevent, detect, and respond to fraud, including improper payments, and to incorporate the Fraud Risk Framework's leading practices into the guidelines. See GAO, *A Framework for Managing Fraud Risks in Federal Programs*, GAO-15-593SP (Washington, D.C.: July 28, 2015). Additionally, in April, 2018 we started a review focused on select agencies' design and implementation of key internal control activities related to preventing and detecting improper payments of disaster relief and recovery funding in response to the 2017 hurricanes and wildfires.

disaster-specific mitigation performance measures that align with
strategic goals, and analyzed available data to identify the drivers of
mitigation in events of various sizes. The agency took these actions in
response to recommendations we made in 2018 to complete a workforce
staffing assessment that identifies the appropriate number of staff to
implement a new PA delivery model nationwide, and to develop
performance measures for the new delivery model that better align with
the agency's strategic goal for hazard mitigation.[31]

The Sandy Recovery Improvement Act of 2013 (SRIA) authorized the use
of alternative procedures in administering the PA program, thereby
providing new flexibilities to FEMA, states, and local governments for
debris removal, infrastructure repair, and rebuilding projects using funds
from this program.[32] The stated goals of the alternative procedures are to
reduce the costs to the federal government, increase flexibility in the
administration of the PA program, expedite the provision of assistance
under the program, and provide financial incentives for

---

[31]GAO-18-30.

[32]SRIA amended the Stafford Act by adding Section 428, which authorized FEMA to
approve Public Assistance program projects under the alternative procedures provided by
that section for any presidentially-declared major disaster or emergency. This section
further authorized FEMA to carry out the alternative procedures as a pilot program until
FEMA promulgates regulations to implement this section. Pub. L. No. 113-2, div. B, §
1102(2), 127 Stat. 39, amending Pub. L. No. 93-288, tit. IV, § 428 (codified at 42 U.S.C. §
5189f).

recipients of the program for the timely and cost-effective completion of projects.[33] Alternative procedures for permanent work are designed to give jurisdictions more flexibility in determining how, where, and what to rebuild, particularly after incurring significant damage. Applicants may choose to combine multiple critical facilities and rebuild them in a manner that makes them less likely to incur future disaster damages. In 2013 FEMA began a pilot program to utilize the alternative procedures for debris removal and permanent work projects in the recovery from Hurricane Sandy in New York and New Jersey, as of April 2018, FEMA reported that 29 percent of New York's permanent work projects are under the alternate procedures—approximately $8.6 billion. However, no state or territory has used alternative procedures for 100 percent of their permanent work projects. According to Puerto Rico's Draft Recovery Plan issued in July 2018, the Commonwealth estimated costs for permanent work projects ranges from $26.7 billion to $37.4 billion.[34]

In 2015, FEMA awarded a contract for program support to help implement a redesigned PA program. FEMA officials told us that the redesigning effort was primarily focused on specializing roles, segmenting the work, standardizing processes, and consolidating resources. It also included developing a new information system (PA Grants Manager and Grants Portal) to better maintain and share grant documentation. Taken together, according to officials, these efforts represent FEMA's "new delivery model" for the PA program, and, represents a significant process and

---

[33] See 42 U.S.C. § 5189f(c).

[34] DHS, Preliminary Draft: *"Transformation and Innovation in the Wake of Devastation: An Economic and Disaster Recovery Plan for Puerto Rico."* July 9, 2018.

cultural shift towards a streamlined and standardized way of delivering PA.[35]

In September 2017, FEMA decided to begin using the new delivery model nationwide for all subsequent declared disasters, including hurricanes Harvey and Irma in Texas and Florida and the wildfires in California. However, for hurricanes Irma and Maria in Puerto Rico and the U.S. Virgin Islands, FEMA is utilizing the PA alternative procedures model. According to FEMA officials, Puerto Rico was already in the process of implementing this model in response to prior disaster events. See appendix IX for more information on FEMA's PA Program.

Hazard Mitigation Grant Program: This program is designed to improve community resilience—the ability to prepare and plan for, absorb, recover from, and more successfully adapt to disasters—to future disasters during recovery. The program funds a wide range of projects, such as purchasing properties in flood-prone areas, adding shutters to windows to prevent future damage from hurricane winds and rains, and rebuilding culverts in drainage ditches to prevent future flooding damage. In light of our identification of the rise in the number—and the increase in severity—of disasters as a key source of federal fiscal exposure, we and others have advocated hazard mitigation and resiliency to help limit the nation's fiscal exposure.[36] In 2015, we identified challenges in effectively incorporating mitigation into PA projects and grant guidance during the

---

[35] According to FEMA officials, the new delivery model is a re-engineering of the previous process, given that the laws, regulations, and policies underlying the PA program were not changed. In addition to creating a new online information system—Grants Portal—for applicants to develop and submit their grant applications and associated documents, key changes brought about by the re-engineering effort included (1) identifying opportunities for hazard mitigation earlier in the process; creating consolidated resource centers to standardize and centralize PA staff responsible for managing grant applications; and creating new specialized positions, such as hazard mitigation liaisons, program delivery managers, and site inspectors, to ensure more consistent guidance to applicants. Other changes to the process included enhancing outreach to applicants during the "exploratory call"—the first contact between FEMA and local officials—and during the first in-person meeting, called the "recovery scoping meeting." FEMA also revised decision points during the process when program officials can request more information from applicants, and applicants can review and approve the completion of project development steps.

[36] GAO-15-515. Hazard mitigation is any sustained action taken to reduce or eliminate long-term risk to people and property from natural hazards and their effects. In addition to the Hazard Mitigation Grant Program, FEMA may also fund hazard mitigation projects related to the damaged facilities receiving PA funding pursuant to section 406 of the Stafford Act, as amended. 42 U.S.C. § 5172; 44 C.F.R. § 206.226.

2017 Hurricanes & Wildfires: GAO's Initial Observations (9/2018)

recovery from Hurricane Sandy in the northeastern United States.[37] We recommended that FEMA assess the challenges and implement corrective actions as needed, and that the Mitigation Framework Leadership Group—created to help coordinate hazard mitigation efforts of relevant federal, state, local, territorial, and tribal organizations—establish an investment strategy to identify, prioritize, and implement federal investments in disaster resilience. FEMA concurred with our recommendations and is taking steps to implement them. In appendix X we identify several challenges the communities impacted by the 2017 disasters face and opportunities for resiliency. We have plans to examine these challenges and opportunities more broadly in an upcoming review.

Federal and State Coordination Efforts Facilitated Preparedness and Response to the 2017 Disasters in Texas, Florida, and California

FEMA coordinated closely with Texas, Florida, and California emergency management officials and other federal, local, and volunteer emergency partners to implement various emergency preparedness actions prior to the 2017 disasters, in each state, and to respond to these disasters. According to FEMA and state officials, these actions helped overcome a number of challenges they faced such as deploying a sufficient and adequately-trained disaster workforce and removing debris in a timely manner after the hurricanes and wildfires. These efforts also show progress made since the 2006 Post-Katrina Act, which reflected various themes we identified when reviewing the 2005 federal response to Hurricane Katrina, such as the importance of clear procedures for national response activities, advance planning, and robust training and exercise programs.[38]

Preparedness Activities in Texas, Florida, and California Helped Strengthen the Response

FEMA and state officials in Texas, Florida, and California took certain key actions in advance of the 2017 disasters that enabled them to more effectively provide assistance following each disaster. Specifically, according to FEMA's FCO for Hurricane Harvey, Texas had learned from its experience with prior disasters to ensure that personnel and resources were in place before the hurricane arrived. In accordance with the Post-Katrina Act, Texas requested that FEMA deploy IMAT staff prior to hurricane landfall. Subsequently, the IMAT set up centers to distribute meals and water and prepared federal agencies so that response teams and resources were ready to go upon landfall. Before landfall, there were

---

[37]GAO-15-515.

[38]See Pub. L. No. 109-295, tit. VI, 120 Stat. 1355, 1394 (2006).

four regional IMAT teams and a national IMAT team already in place. FEMA also dispensed mission assignments to DOD and the U.S. Coast Guard, among other agencies, with ESF responsibilities to carry out missions as needed.

Similarly, Florida's governor requested, and the President approved, a pre-landfall emergency declaration on September 5, 2017, for all 67 counties in Florida. The pre-declaration authorized FEMA to set up emergency berms, pre-position supplies, and take other key preparation steps such as sheltering and evacuation support, according to Florida emergency management officials. Florida, like Texas, also requested the pre-positioning of FEMA IMAT response teams. According to FEMA officials, Florida set up an incident operations center in Tallahassee and response personnel were located there before the hurricane made landfall.

In addition, prior to landfall, FEMA set up state-driven task forces in Texas for sheltering, family reunification, and feeding, among other things, to provide support at the local level. For example, the feeding task force coordinated with Feeding America and other nonprofits that provided food and nutrition while the reunification task force worked with the National Center for Missing and Exploited Children to reunite family members who were separated.

According to IMAT officials, they conducted regular emergency response exercises with the states leading up to the hurricanes which better trained and prepared them to coordinate during actual response efforts.

In California, FEMA and state Office of Emergency Services officials credited the ability to quickly and effectively coordinate with federal partners and respond to the wildfires to the state's past emergency preparedness experience and capacity.

Coordination Systems and Activities Helped Build Relationships That Facilitated Response in Texas, Florida, and California	FEMA and state officials in Texas, Florida, and California all described response coordination systems and activities that helped build relationships among federal, state, and local partners that are crucial to an effective response. The emergency management community has long recognized the importance of building relationships before a disaster. As a former FEMA Administrator stated, the worst time to exchange business cards is during a disaster. For example, in Texas and California, those relationships were primarily formed from regular meetings and the exercises that FEMA conducts with state emergency response partners.

    GAO-18-472 2017 Hurricanes and Wildfires

Specifically, FEMA officials at the Joint Field Office in Austin, Texas told us that all emergency response entities in Texas work together via an interagency coordination group, which they credited for enhancing the relationship between these entities.

Texas, Florida and California officials also described that having state agency staff embedded in FEMA's organization, and vice versa, was helpful. In each state, FEMA employees were embedded in state offices prior to the disasters, and in doing so had developed a close working relationship with state emergency management personnel. In Texas, embedded state emergency staff provided training, emergency exercises, and advice to local jurisdictions. Texas Division of Emergency Management staff told us that they are in daily contact with local officials year-round, which enhances coordination in times of disaster. According to the California Office of Emergency Services (OES) Director, the pre-existing relationship between California OES, the California governor's office, and FEMA's Region IX office—the FEMA regional office with oversight for the state of California—allowed California to approach the response to the wildfires as a team, with clear roles and responsibilities among the state, the FEMA region and other partners like the National Guard. According to FEMA officials, Region IX staff were members embedded with the state of California for almost 60 days following the start of the wildfires. By colocating from the start, FEMA and California's OES were able to work collaboratively in decision making and setting priorities, according to the California OES director. The California OES director agreed with FEMA officials at the Joint Field Office in Austin who said that co-location facilitated decision-making by reducing the bureaucracy that would typically be involved in reaching out to partners spread out in different regions of the state and country.[39]

In addition to forming a close working relationship with FEMA, officials from all three states described close preexisting working relationships with volunteer organizations that play a significant role in disaster response in their states. For example, a FEMA official with responsibility for coordinating volunteer partnerships stated that in Texas, volunteer organizations are treated as full and equal partners, which facilitated volunteer partners' contribution to the response and recovery. Similarly, officials from California and FEMA officials in Florida told us that

---

[39]In April 2018, we initiated a separate review of the California wildfires that will more fully examine the federal response to the wildfires, including the role played by FEMA and other relevant federal agencies.

  GAO-18-472 2017 Hurricanes and Wildfires

nonprofits have made significant contributions to response and recovery. Figure 4 shows an example of such contributions following Hurricane Irma.

Figure 4: Nonprofit Volunteer Team Clearing Debris in Big Pine Key, Florida after Hurricane Irma

Source: GAO. | GAO-18-472

Although state and FEMA officials largely described a well-coordinated and successful response to the hurricanes and wildfires, all three states experienced a number of challenges—most notably with deployment of a sufficient and adequately-trained FEMA disaster workforce and delays with debris removal—which we describe later in this report.[40]

---

[40]We began a review in the spring of 2018 of temporary sheltering challenges experienced during the 2017 disasters that will more fully examine the role of voluntary organizations in disasters.

2017 Hurricanes & Wildfires: GAO's Initial Observations (9/2018)

<table>
<tr><td>

The Federal Government Provided Support for Puerto Rico and the U.S. Virgin Islands, but Faced Multiple Challenges in Its Response

</td><td>

The federal government provided logistical support and conducted various preparedness actions in Puerto Rico and the U.S. Virgin Islands in advance of the hurricanes, as well as provided a high volume of response support to both territories after the hurricanes hit. Hurricane Maria made landfall on Puerto Rico as a category 4 hurricane, causing widespread infrastructural damages that left 3.7 million of the island's residents without electricity and 95 percent of cell towers out of service, and forced every airport and seaport on the territory to be closed. FEMA's response to Puerto Rico and the U.S. Virgin Islands included resources from dozens of federal agencies bringing unique capabilities to the response effort through 1,093 mission assignments totaling more than $5.5 billion, as of January 29, 2018. Forty-one percent of the mission assignments in Puerto Rico and the U.S. Virgin Islands were executed by the Department of Defense, resulting in more than $2 billion in obligations. However, FEMA faced challenges specific to Puerto Rico and the U.S. Virgin Islands that complicated its response efforts. As a result, FEMA has taken some action to incorporate lessons learned in preparation for the next hurricane season.

</td></tr>
<tr><td>

The Federal Government Provided Logistical Support and Conducted Various Preparedness Activities in Puerto Rico and the U.S. Virgin Islands in Advance of the Hurricanes

</td><td>

The federal government provided logistical support, deployed key incident management staff, and conducted numerous planning exercises prior to hurricanes Irma and Maria making landfall in Puerto Rico and the U.S. Virgin Islands in 2017. Specifically, FEMA shipped meals, delivered other commodities and activated contracts and mission assignments for additional federal support to the territories in advance of the hurricanes. Further, FEMA had conducted various planning and response exercises from 2009 to 2017. These efforts included nine exercises that FEMA Region II—the FEMA regional office with oversight for both territories—conducted in 2017 for incident types with catastrophic impacts, such as tropical cyclones and tsunamis, in Puerto Rico and the U.S. Virgin Islands prior to hurricanes Irma and Maria. The agency also conducted an exercise in 2016 which, according to FEMA officials, allowed the regional and national IMATs the opportunity to integrate as one FEMA response team in preparation for a catastrophic disaster. According to FEMA officials, the exercise worked to enhance the capability and integration of the IMAT teams and the Regional Response Coordination Center—which coordinates federal response efforts during a disaster— to provide an effective response and resource support to Puerto Rico in the event of a catastrophic hurricane. DOD also conducted several events prior to the hurricanes that, according to FEMA officials, aided the response to hurricanes Irma and Maria, such as the DOD Annual Joint Interagency

</td></tr>
</table>

Figure 5: The Federal Government's Logistical Support to Puerto Rico and the U.S. Virgin Islands In Advance of Hurricane Irma and Hurricane Maria

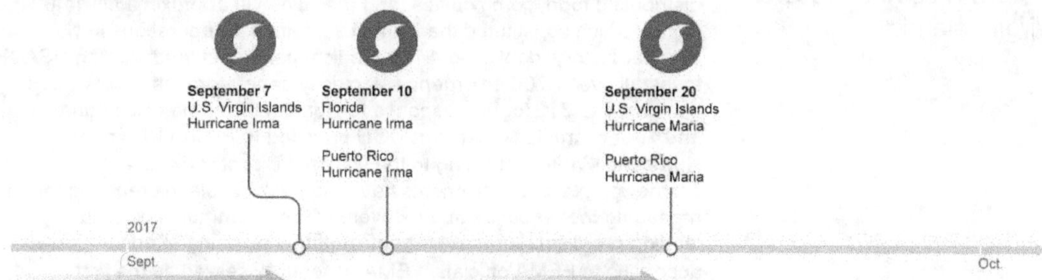

Prior to Hurricane Irma

- The Federal Emergency Management Agency (FEMA) shipped 250,000 meals to the U.S. Virgin Islands from the Distribution Center (DC) in Puerto Rico.

- FEMA activated contracts and mission assignments to provide another 2.8 million meals per day for the U.S. Virgin Islands and Puerto Rico for 30 days.

- FEMA activated contracts to provide 3.7 million liters of bottled water per day for the U.S. Virgin Islands and Puerto Rico for 30 days.

- FEMA had a pre-positioned communications caches staged in Puerto Rico at all times.

- FEMA deployed 1,430 Urban Search and Rescue Personnel; 2 regional Incident Management Assistance Teams; 2,257 federal workforce personnel; 1 disaster medical assistance team; 24 generators; 1 million meals, and 2 million liters of water.

Prior to Hurricane Maria

- Containers of commodities from FEMA's Caribbean DC were already stocked in the Port in St. Thomas in response to Irma 14 days earlier.

- The *USS Wright* and the Crowley Barge *El Conquistador* were holding at sea south of Puerto Rico in a safe area as the storm transited.

- FEMA had pre-positioned communications caches staged in the U.S. Virgin Islands.

- FEMA deployed 276 Urban Search and Rescue Personnel: 1 national and 2 regional Incident Management Assistance Teams (IMAT); 2,763 federal workforce personnel; 4 generators; 1.6 million meals, and approximately 700,000 liters of water.

Source: Department of Homeland Security. | GAO-18-472

---

[41]According to FEMA, this event which was attended by multiple local and federal agencies, was focused on a hypothetical hurricane impacting the U.S. Virgin Islands and included a site survey of the Port of Ponce and local airport in the event of a Defense Support of Civil Authorities response.

2017 Hurricanes & Wildfires: GAO's Initial Observations (9/2018)

<table>
<tr><td>

The Federal Government Provided a High Volume of Response Support to Puerto Rico and the U.S. Virgin Islands

</td><td>

According to FEMA's Office of Response and Recovery Assistant Administrator for Field Operations, FEMA's response to Puerto Rico was one of the largest recovery efforts in its history and included, among other things, bringing in food and supplies valued at approximately $1 billion; distributing food, commodities, and medicine via approximately 1,400 flights, which constituted the longest sustained air operations in U.S. disaster history; deploying 4,700 medical personnel; and utilizing USACE to install over 1,700 emergency electricity generators, as of May 2018, compared to 310 for the response to Hurricane Katrina. See figures 6 and 7 for examples of support DOD provided to Puerto Rico after Hurricane Maria. According to the National Disaster Recovery Framework, local governments have the primary role in preparing for and managing the response and recovery of their communities, including leading pre-disaster recovery and mitigation planning efforts.[42] However, according to FEMA officials, FEMA essentially served as the first responder in the early response efforts in Puerto Rico. FEMA officials said that many services they provided—such as power restoration, debris removal, and commodity distribution—are typically provided by territorial or local governments.[43]

</td></tr>
</table>

---

[42]Department of Homeland Security, *National Disaster Recovery Framework*, Second Edition (June 2016).

[43]Debris removal services are generally provided by vendors that are contracted by local and territorial governments. While FEMA provides funding assistance for removal of debris from publicly and privately-owned lands and waters through the PA program, the respective state or local governmental entity generally has the responsibility to execute and manage debris removal operations.

2017 Hurricanes & Wildfires: GAO's Initial Observations (9/2018)

Figure 6: DOD Assigned USNS Comfort for Puerto Rico Response in November 2017 after Hurricane Maria

2017 Hurricanes & Wildfires: GAO's Initial Observations (9/2018)

Figure 7: Temporary Blue Roofs in Puerto Rico Installed by the U.S. Army Corps of Engineers after Hurricane Maria in February 2018

Source: Federal Emergency Management Agency. | GAO-18-472

In the U.S. Virgin Islands, recent disaster training and the pre-positioning of supplies due to the anticipated impact of Hurricane Irma facilitated the response efforts following Hurricane Maria, according to DOD officials. FEMA partnered well with local officials, according to the U.S. Virgin Islands Territorial Emergency Management Agency Director. According to FEMA's FCO for the U.S. Virgin Islands, the federal government deployed assets, including IMATs, urban search and rescue teams, and medical assistance teams. FEMA and USACE colocated with the U.S. Virgin Islands Territorial Emergency Management Agency in downtown St. Croix from the onset. In addition, due to the sequence of Hurricane Irma hitting the U.S. Virgin Islands immediately before Hurricane Maria, DOD already had personnel and resources (i.e., ships) deployed to the area, according to DOD officials, which enabled DOD to respond to Hurricane Maria faster than it otherwise would have.

In both Puerto Rico and the U.S. Virgin Islands, DOD was also asked by FEMA to provide support that the department has not typically provided for prior hurricanes (e.g. air operations, mortuary affairs, and power grid restoration). According to DOD officials, active duty military personnel and reservists also provided life-sustaining commodities such as food and water. Additionally, USACE members provided services such as installing generators and tarp roofs. See appendix XI for a summary of DOD's role in the response effort and appendix III for more information on the full scale of federal support provided to Puerto Rico and the U. S. Virgin Islands, as well as the states affected by the 2017 hurricanes and wildfires.

FEMA Response Efforts Were Complicated By Factors Specific to Puerto Rico and the U.S. Virgin Islands

Major Factors that Affected Response to Hurricanes Irma and Maria

100 percent of Puerto Rico Electric Power Agency (PREPA) clients without electric power service

80 percent of all PREPA Infrastructure was destroyed

80 percent of Puerto Rico Aqueduct and Sewer Authority clients without water service

80 to 85 percent of communication towers not operational

Large numbers of roads with landslides and several dozen bridges collapsed

Maritime ports and airports closed for at least 5 days after Maria hit Puerto Rico

Satellite phones not working

Emergency Operations Plan not built for catastrophic levels nor 100 percent loss of communication

Ample fuel but not enough personnel and fuel tankers for transportation throughout the island

Source: Federal Emergency Management Agency |
GAO-18-472

FEMA's response efforts in Puerto Rico and the U.S. Virgin Islands were complicated by a number of factors including (1) the remote distance of the territories, (2) limited local preparedness for a major hurricane, (3) outdated local infrastructure, (4) workforce capacity constraints, and (5) additional challenges in Puerto Rico.

These challenges were compounded by FEMA's previous deployment of personnel and assets to support the response for Hurricane Harvey in Texas and Hurricane Irma in Florida due to the unprecedented near-sequential disasters of 2017. As a result of lessons learned from these challenges, FEMA has taken a number of steps to plan for the next hurricane season.

Remote Distance of Territories. Given Puerto Rico's and the U.S. Virgin Islands' remote distance from the U.S. mainland, FEMA faced challenges in getting key personnel and resources to the territories before and after the hurricanes made landfall, and with distributing those resources to survivors. Both Puerto Rico and the U.S. Virgin Islands are located approximately 1,000 nautical miles from the U.S. mainland where personnel, equipment, and other key resources had to be moved from, as depicted in figure 8.

2017 Hurricanes & Wildfires: GAO's Initial Observations (9/2018)

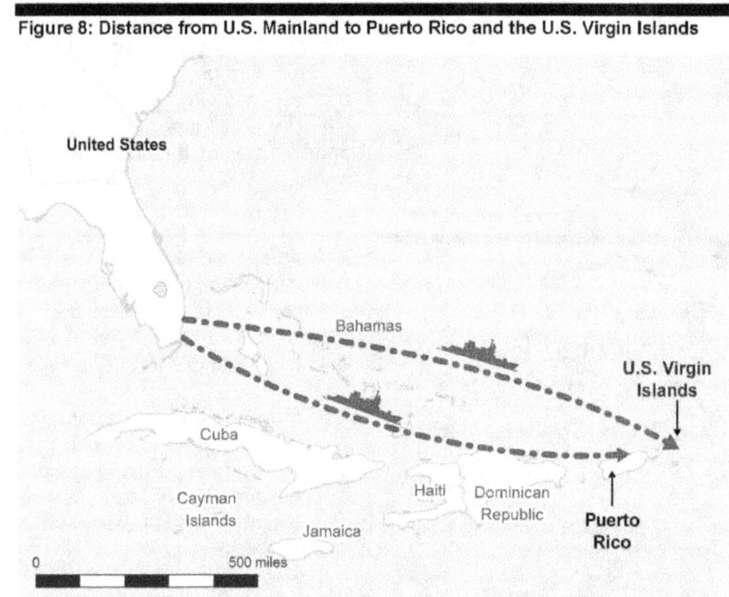

Source: Map Resources. | GAO-18-472

Under typical disaster operations, responders are moved to the disaster response area via commercial travel options—or as in Texas and Florida, on roadways from nearby states, according to FEMA officials. However, limitations on air travel due to capacity constraints and power outages meant that FEMA had to coordinate and mobilize agency partners to provide chartered air transportation until commercial travel options resumed. Further, the destruction of major transportation routes made the deployment of these personnel and distribution of the commodities even more challenging according to FEMA officials. For example, in Puerto Rico, FEMA officials said food, commodities, and medicine had to be distributed by helicopter drop for several weeks because of landslides or destroyed bridges.

Limited Local Preparedness. Puerto Rico and the U.S. Virgin Islands had engaged in disaster preparedness exercises prior to Hurricane Maria; however, neither had recently experienced nor stockpiled the resources necessary for a hurricane of that magnitude. For example, Puerto Rico officials said their emergency plans allowed the local government to

2017 Hurricanes & Wildfires: GAO's Initial Observations (9/2018)

respond effectively to Hurricane Irma (e.g., evacuating residents, purchasing food, and securing their homes). However, their plans were insufficient for the magnitude of Hurricane Maria which made landfall 2 weeks later. Specifically, Puerto Rico officials had not considered that a hurricane would cause a loss of power for as long as Hurricane Maria did.

Hurricane Maria was the strongest hurricane to make landfall in Puerto Rico since a Category 5 hurricane in 1928, according to the National Oceanic and Atmospheric Administration.[44] Puerto Rico officials explained that local preparation for a Category 5 hurricane is limited by physical space and financial resources needed to stockpile necessary supplies to respond to a hurricane of that magnitude and also because such hurricanes occur infrequently. According to FEMA officials, FEMA took on a more active role in the response to Hurricane Maria due to preparedness challenges in Puerto Rico.

In the U.S. Virgin Islands, the local government had conducted preparedness exercises and local officials had a grasp of the emergency management process, according to DOD officials.[45] According to FEMA officials, these preparedness exercises were for tropical cyclones and other incident types such as an earthquake and a tsunami which have catastrophic impacts similar to hurricanes Irma and Maria. However, according to FEMA's *2017 Hurricane Season FEMA After-Action Report*, FEMA could have better leveraged information from these and other prior exercises in the Caribbean, including a 2011 exercise after-action report for Puerto Rico which indicated that the territory would require extensive federal support in moving commodities, including from the mainland to the territory, and to distribution points throughout the territory. In contrast, FEMA's leverage of information from prior exercises in Florida proved to be critical in that state's ability to efficiently execute mutual aid agreements in response to Hurricane Irma.

---

[44] National Oceanic and Atmospheric Administration (NOAA) measures hurricanes on a scale from 1 to 5 with a Category 1 being the least intense and a Category 5 being the most intense. NOAA defines a Category 4 hurricane as one with winds 130-156 miles per hour and Category 5 with winds above 157 miles per hour. Hurricane Maria made landfall on the U.S. Virgin Islands as a Category 5 hurricane and Puerto Rico as a high end Category 4 hurricane.

[45] Exercises are a useful tool for jurisdictions to identify emergency preparedness capability strengths and shortfalls which can be used to inform future preparedness efforts and response operations.

FEMA officials said they have encouraged both Puerto Rico and the U.S. Virgin Islands to develop planning timelines and formal Emergency Management Assistance Compacts (EMAC)—mutual aid agreements that allow states to support one another during a disaster response—which play a critical role in managing risk to communities and infrastructure. Although an EMAC supported requests for assistance to Puerto Rico, getting interstate mutual aid and assistance through the EMAC process was more difficult because there are no other states or territories adjacent to Puerto Rico and the U.S. Virgin Islands, according to DOD officials.[46]

Outdated Local Infrastructure. Hurricane Maria devastated the already fragile and outdated infrastructure in Puerto Rico and the U.S. Virgin Islands, which complicated response efforts according to the FEMA Administrator and Puerto Rico officials. Specifically, Hurricane Maria crippled the power grid, communication systems, and transportation infrastructure throughout both territories, hindering communication and delaying emergency response activities. See figures 9 and 10 for photographs of damage sustained in the U.S. Virgin Islands and Puerto Rico.

---

[46]We are currently conducting a separate review on Puerto Rico and the U.S. Virgin Islands' disaster recovery plans, which we plan on issuing in spring 2019.

Figure 9: Damaged Power Pole in the U.S. Virgin Islands after Hurricane Maria in November 2017

Source: GAO. | GAO-18-472

The damage was more extensive in Puerto Rico. Three months after Hurricane Maria hit, Puerto Rico had 65 percent of its power restored while the U.S. Virgin Islands had closer to 90 percent, according to FEMA officials. The U.S. Virgin Islands was quicker to restore power in part due to previous infrastructure investments and mitigation efforts implemented by the government, according to FEMA officials.

Source: Federal Emergency Management Agency. | GAO-18-472

According to Puerto Rico officials, much of the territory's infrastructure (e.g., roads, sewage systems, and bridges) is more than 50 years old. As a result, some replacement parts were no longer available and had to be specially manufactured, delaying power restoration. Moreover, many of the power lines connecting the large power stations in southern Puerto Rico through the mountains to the north—where the majority of the island's residents reside—were destroyed by the storm according to officials from the Puerto Rico Electric Power Authority (PREPA).

According to FEMA and Puerto Rico Aqueduct and Sewer Authority officials, Puerto Rico had limited access to federal funds to renew and

2017 Hurricanes & Wildfires: GAO's Initial Observations (9/2018)

replace infrastructure prior to hurricanes Irma and Maria due to its outstanding public debt.[47] Specifically, PREPA officials told us that their ability to prepare for the hurricane season was impacted by Puerto Rico's financial situation due to vendor concerns with reimbursement for services and goods.[48] Moreover, previous hazard mitigation efforts to strengthen the island's infrastructure were not enough to withstand the force of Hurricane Maria, according to FEMA officials. For example, Puerto Rico's construction codes called for buildings to withstand winds of 145 miles per hour, but Hurricane Maria's winds exceeded 175 miles per hour causing massive wind and flood damage to housing and office space, including the Puerto Rico Emergency Management Agency office, further delaying hurricane response efforts. We also provide more details about both territories' challenges as well as goals for incorporating resilience after the 2017 disasters in appendix X.[49]

Workforce Capacity Constraints. Given that FEMA was confronted with concurrently responding to four large and complex disasters, this exacerbated FEMA workforce capacity constraints and training deficits for deployed workers according to FEMA officials. This was especially true for Hurricane Maria, which was the last of the three major hurricanes in

---

[47] Puerto Rico has roughly $70 billion in outstanding debt and $50 billion in unfunded pension liabilities, and since August 2015 has defaulted on over $1.5 billion in debt. The effects of hurricanes Irma and Maria will further affect Puerto Rico's ability to repay its debt, as well as its overall economic condition. For more on Puerto Rico's public debt see GAO, *Puerto Rico: Factors Contributing to the Debt Crisis and Potential Federal Actions to Address Them*, GAO-18-387 (Washington, D.C.: May 9, 2018).

[48] Congress passed the Puerto Rico Oversight, Management, and Economic Stability Act (PROMESA) in June 2016. See Pub. L. No. 114-187, 130 Stat. 549 (2016). PROMESA temporarily prevented creditors from suing Puerto Rico over missed debt payments. PROMESA established a Financial Management and Oversight Board with broad powers of budgetary and financial control over Puerto Rico. In addition, it created procedures for adjusting debts accumulated by the Puerto Rico government and its component units. On May 3, 2017, after the termination of the original stay preventing creditors from suing the territory, the board filed a petition under Title III of PROMESA beginning a broad-based debt restructuring process.

[49] We are also currently conducting a more detailed review of the power grid restoration and resilience efforts in Puerto Rico and the U.S. Virgin Islands, as well as USACE power restoration capacity and efforts in Puerto Rico, which we plan to issue in spring 2019.

2017.[50] FEMA leadership and the FCO in the U.S. Virgin Islands said that some of FEMA's disaster staff deployed to Puerto Rico and the U.S. Virgin Islands were not physically able to handle the extreme or austere environment of the territories, which detracted from mission needs. According to FEMA officials, the physical fitness of staff could be assessed prior to deploying staff.

Similar to Texas and Florida, federal and local response agencies were colocated at the JFO in Puerto Rico and the U.S. Virgin Islands to facilitate coordination and response. However, according to the IMAT leader in the U.S. Virgin Islands, the U.S. Virgin Islands IMAT team needs more exercises alongside the national IMAT teams in order to build response skills and strong relationships.

In addition, with much of the housing destroyed in both Puerto Rico and the U.S. Virgin Islands, locating accommodations for the nearly 15,000 federal government employees—including military personnel—deployed to assist in response activities became a major challenge, according to FEMA officials. We discuss more of the workforce challenges FEMA faced in the wake of the 2017 disasters later in this report. See appendix V for a summary of FEMA's workforce capacity and related challenges during the 2017 disaster response.[51]

Other Challenges in Puerto Rico. Prior to Hurricane Maria's landfall, FEMA identified some factors unique to Puerto Rico that could affect response efforts. Specifically, FEMA's Region II Hurricane Annex for Puerto Rico and the U.S. Virgin Islands, dated June 2014, outlines the territories' emergency response policies, procedures, and responsibilities, including communication, transportation, and mass evacuation in the

---

[50]According to FEMA officials, FEMA employed use of a force package for the first time to Hurricane Harvey. A force package is a set of force modules with time-phased deployment dates and each force module within a package provides a capability for disaster response. The force package provides the personnel to support an event based on the incident size and scope. Field leadership is provided with an initial deployment of time-phased personnel (supervisors and management personnel arriving first) allowing them to better manage further deployments and staffing requests on the margins or as the operation changes over time.

[51]We are currently conducting a separate review focused on FEMA's workforce management challenges.

event of a disaster.[52] According to FEMA's Region II Hurricane Annex, information in Puerto Rico must be conveyed in Spanish—which is the main spoken and written language. However, in the aftermath of Hurricane Maria, FEMA did not have enough bilingual employees to communicate with local residents or translate documents. According to FEMA officials, this resulted in further delays while staff were reshuffled from other disasters to Puerto Rico. In addition, unlike in the continental United States where individuals mostly apply for IA at disaster recovery centers or online, in Puerto Rico, officials needed to conduct more door-to-door visits to reach disaster survivors and conduct assessments, according to FEMA officials. Locating addresses and individuals was challenging, according to FEMA officials, because many affected areas did not have posted addresses, many individuals use nicknames instead of their given names, and often several families were located on a single property. Additionally, we are conducting work on how states and territories account for disaster-related deaths and injuries, and the impact on disaster assistance.

FEMA Has Taken Some Action to Incorporate Lessons Learned in Preparation for the Next Hurricane Season

Following the 2017 hurricane season, FEMA has taken a number of steps to help prepare for the 2018 season. For example, in July 2018, FEMA issued an after-action review of the agency's preparations for, immediate response to, and initial recovery operations for hurricanes Harvey, Irma, and Maria. The after-action report identifies 18 key findings across five focus areas and offers targeted, agency-wide recommendations for improvements as well as broader lessons for the emergency management community.[53] FEMA officials reported that they have already taken several actions in preparation for the 2018 hurricane season. These include:

- updating hurricane plans, annexes, and procedures for all U.S. states and territories;

---

[52] According to FEMA, the purpose of FEMA's Region II Hurricane Annex for Puerto Rico and the U.S. Virgin Islands is to support the expedited jurisdictional response to tropical and subtropical systems, including catastrophic hurricanes, as well as tropical depressions, tropical storms, and hurricanes, and their secondary and cascading impacts on locations in Puerto Rico and the U.S. Virgin Islands. FEMA Region II Hurricane Annex for Puerto Rico & the U.S. Virgin Islands. June 1, 2014.

[53] The five focus areas of the 2017 Hurricane Season FEMA After-Action Report include: (1) scaling a response for concurrent complex incidents; (2) staffing for concurrent complex incidents; (3) sustaining whole community logistics operations; (4) responding during long-term Infrastructure outages; and (5) mass care to initial housing operations.

2017 Hurricanes & Wildfires: GAO's Initial Observations (9/2018)

- improving staff skills and readiness including by creating a Standard Operating Procedure for a central location for equipping and training staff prior to disaster deployments;

- improving logistics operations such as by increasing disaster supplies for all U.S. territories for items including meals, water, tarps; and generators, specifically for Puerto Rico and the U.S. Virgin Islands. FEMA is also adding 360 new emergency generators to its inventory and has pre-positioned 630 generators in the Caribbean for the 2018 hurricane season; and

- updating communications systems from land-based radios to satellite-based technology; refining tactical and long-haul communications, from land mobile radios to satellite communications.

In addition to these efforts, FEMA conducted a National Level Exercise to assess and enhance its response and initial recovery capability during the first 2 weeks of May 2018, which focused on issues identified in its 2017 hurricane season after-action review.[54] The findings and recommendations of the after-action report influenced the development of FEMA's 2018-2022 Strategic Plan, released in March 2018, according to FEMA officials.

While FEMA described actions it has taken in response to the 2017 disasters, it was too soon to assess the adequacy of these actions as part of this review and whether the actions will have the intended impact.[55]

---

[54] According to FEMA, the National Level Exercise as a whole is a large exercise series running from January through the summer of 2018, which includes seminars, workshops, and tabletop exercises, as well as a functional exercise in May focused on thematic areas identified from ongoing real-world continuous improvement efforts. The 2018 National Level Exercise examined the ability of all levels of government, private industry, and nongovernmental organizations to protect against, respond to, and recover from a major Mid-Atlantic hurricane, and allowed the whole community to examine lessons observed following the storms of the 2017 Atlantic hurricane season.

[55] We are conducting a comprehensive review of the federal government's national preparedness capabilities, training, and funding to assist communities in responding to and recovering from major disasters, which we plan to issue in the summer of 2019.

2017 Hurricanes & Wildfires: GAO's Initial Observations (9/2018)

The 2017 Hurricanes and Wildfires Highlighted Challenges FEMA Faces in Meeting Its Response and Recovery Missions

The 2017 hurricanes and wildfires reaffirmed the existence of some long-standing response and recovery challenges, but also highlighted several new challenges related to (1) the near-sequential timing of the disasters, (2) housing assistance, (3) workforce management, and (4) public assistance.

The Timing of the Four Near-Sequential Major Disasters and Unique Circumstances in Each Location Presented Challenges for Debris Removal in 2017

Debris removal is an important first step in the disaster recovery process, allowing communities to expedite the recovery process by restoring accessibility to public services and space, while ensuring public health and safety in the aftermath of a disaster. The PA Program provides funding assistance for the removal of debris and wreckage from publicly and privately-owned lands and waters resulting from a major disaster, when such removal is in the public interest.[56] For example, debris removal is in the public interest if it would eliminate an immediate threat to lives, public health and safety, or property. In addition to funding, FEMA can provide a range of assistance and guidance to help PA applicants mitigate associated difficulties with debris removal. For example, FEMA can provide Direct Federal Assistance for debris removal if the event exceeds state and local capability and if the recipient requests such support. When local jurisdictions do not have the capacity for debris removal, FEMA can assign the USACE or other federal agencies to conduct the removal, or other agencies may support these efforts through various authorities. However, the respective state or local governmental entity has the responsibility to execute and manage debris removal operations.

Officials in Texas, Florida, Puerto Rico, and California reported challenges with debris removal operations following each disaster in 2017, for example, clearing trees and other vegetative debris, as well as residential, commercial, and construction goods, including hazardous materials. The officials said these challenges arose from a shortage of

---

[56] See 42 U.S.C. § 5173; 44 C.F.R. 206.224.

debris removal contractors, inadequate debris contract provisions, and disputes over responsibility for marine debris removal.

Shortage of debris removal contractors. Some Texas and Florida jurisdictions experienced challenges with the availability of debris removal contractors, given the large demand throughout the regions, and in some cases, even when contracts were in place, contractors did not honor them. For example, according to the FEMA FCO in Florida, contractors are primarily located in the Gulf Coast area and serve a national market. Because many debris contractors were already engaged in Texas, the contractors were not available to provide services in Florida even if they had prior contracts in place. Additionally, some officials from local jurisdictions reported that they had existing contracts for debris removal that had been in place up to 5 years ago. However, because newer contracts were offering more money per cubic yard, some vendors, despite being under contract in a given jurisdiction, prioritized work in another jurisdiction that offered higher rates, according to local officials. Florida officials said that in such cases there was not much they could do except to urge fulfillment of the contract terms.

According to local officials in one Texas jurisdiction, their debris removal contracts are awarded based on price, with preference given to the lowest bids, which can make it difficult for them to get debris removal services in a timely manner in times of high demand as happened in 2017, because contractors inevitably prioritize jurisdictions that pay more. In this case, the officials asked FEMA to issue one regional contract at a higher bid price to ensure all jurisdictions had the opportunity to access debris removal services. According to FEMA's Policy Branch Chief, the magnitude of debris across very large geographic areas, the lack of proximity of debris removal contractors to certain areas, and the limited number of debris removal contractors providing such services resulted in much of the difficulty related to debris removal experienced after the 2017 hurricanes. It also resulted in the inability of multiple states and municipalities to quickly procure a debris removal contactor at a reasonable rate. See figure 11 for an example of a debris pile awaiting pick up in a Texas residential neighborhood following Hurricane Harvey.

2017 Hurricanes & Wildfires: GAO's Initial Observations (9/2018)

Source: GAO. | GAO-18-472

In addition to the funding assistance that FEMA can provide for debris removal operations, FEMA officials said that the agency also has an online debris contractor registry to assist PA applicants in identifying and contacting contractor resources. Additionally, through its regional counsel at Joint Field Offices and through its Procurement Disaster Assistance Team, FEMA proactively engages with communities to provide technical assistance and guidance to PA applicants for debris removal contracting. However, FEMA officials stated that greater readiness and preparedness at the state level may be able to address some of the issues states and municipalities experienced with debris removal in 2017. FEMA PA officials told us that they are exploring potential opportunities to provide additional guidance to applicants on federal procurement rules to assist preparedness efforts. FEMA is also considering the potential utility of new debris removal estimating methodologies and technologies to serve as a basis for providing debris removal funding based on estimates as opposed to actual costs under the PA alternative procedures.

2017 Hurricanes & Wildfires: GAO's Initial Observations (9/2018)

Inadequate debris contract provisions. In California, the state's primary debris contractor did not have the capacity to handle all of the debris removal after the 2017 wildfires. Therefore, California OES coordinated with FEMA, which directed USACE to provide debris removal services. According to the California OES director, the state experienced challenges with meeting the requirements for a federal contract and the lack of flexibility resulted in delays with the debris removal process. Moreover, according to FEMA Region IX officials in California, because wildfires create ash debris, asbestos, and other toxic chemicals, debris removal contracts must have specific provisions to address fire debris. However, the region's advance contracts with USACE for debris removal did not have a task order for fire debris because this was the first time FEMA requested USACE support for fire debris removal. This caused issues in the debris removal process.

Disputes over responsibility for marine debris removal. In the Florida Keys, determining responsibility for marine debris removal from the canals was a challenge after Hurricane Irma, according to the Monroe County emergency management director. County officials estimated that there were between 1,300 and 1,800 sunken or derelict boats for which neither the private owners who use the water canals nor the Coast Guard nor the county would claim responsibility for debris removal.[57] In the absence of available contractors, some jurisdictions opted to use their own staff and equipment to remove debris. However, these jurisdictions faced fiscal challenges because of FEMA delays processing reimbursements.

Responsibility for marine debris removal has been a longstanding issue with parties reaching different solutions at different times, according to Monroe County officials in Florida. See figure 12 for an example of marine

---

[57]We reported in 2017 that abandoned and derelict vessels can block navigable U.S. waterways and pose threats to the environment, public health and safety, as fuel and hazardous material can leak into the water as the vessels deteriorate. See GAO, *Maritime Environment: Federal and State Actions, Expenditures and Challenges to Addressing Abandoned and Derelict Vessels*, GAO-17-202 (Washington, D.C.: Mar. 28, 2017). Federal agencies respond to abandoned and derelict vessels in accordance with federal law, interagency agreements, and funding availability. Federal laws and the National Contingency Plan—the government's blueprint for responding to oil and hazardous substance releases—establish federal agency roles for leading a response to an abandoned and derelict vessels-related incident based on various factors, such as the type of abandoned and derelict vessels threat posed and its location. Interagency agreements have also helped to guide federal abandoned and derelict vessels response efforts.

debris in the Florida Keys, responsibility for the removal of which was in
dispute at the time of our November 2017 visit there.

Figure 12: Marine Debris in Florida Keys Canal Following Hurricane Irma in 2017

Source: GAO. | GAO-18-472

According to FEMA officials, the agency offers PA applicants financial
incentives through its PA Alternative Procedures Debris Removal Pilot
Program to establish Debris Management Plans, written procedures, and
guidance for managing debris removal in an expeditious, efficient, and
environmentally sound manner. FEMA also provides PA applicants with a
job aid to assist applicants in developing the Debris Management Plans,
according to FEMA's Policy Branch Chief. Applicants that develop and
have the plan in place prior to a declaration and meet other program
requirements can take advantage of a one-time 2 percent federal cost
share increase on debris removal operations for 90-days following the 1st
day of the incident period. Additionally, FEMA reviews the plan and
informs applicants of deficiencies and how such deficiencies could be

2017 Hurricanes & Wildfires: GAO's Initial Observations (9/2018)

remedied, which could result in faster processing of their project and therefore reimbursement, if action is taken to address the deficiencies.[58]

FEMA, States, and Territories Are Using a Variety of Existing and New Short-Term Housing Options for Disaster Survivors, but Challenges Persist

According to DHS's 2017 National Preparedness Report, providing effective and affordable short-term housing for disaster survivors has been a longstanding and continuing challenge.[59] For example, according to the report, many states and territories expect the federal government to take on the responsibility of addressing housing gaps, as states often face shortages in effective housing options following a large-scale disaster. Moreover, short-term housing options that might work in one location may not be suitable for another for various reasons, according to the report, hence the need for FEMA to be flexible in its implementation of potential housing solutions. The FEMA Administrator has also highlighted these challenges, noting that state and local officials, not FEMA, are in the best position to determine the necessary housing options for their citizens, with support from the federal government. The Administrator cited the various federal housing models states used after the 2017 hurricanes and wildfires. These models included Direct Lease, Multifamily Lease and Repair, Manufactured Housing Units and Recreational Vehicles, Permanent Housing Construction Repair Program, Sheltering and Temporary Essential Power, and Transitional Sheltering Assistance. According to FEMA officials, these alternative housing models were identified as a result of lessons learned from recent major disasters such as the 2016 flooding in Louisiana and Hurricane Matthew as well as insights leveraged from a housing summit the agency held in February 2017—FEMA's Housing Assistance Initiative.[60]

- **Direct Lease.** FEMA provides temporary housing units directly to survivors when rental resources are unavailable. FEMA and the state

---

[58]We have initiated two reviews examining advance and post-disaster contracting, which will include contracts that were used for debris removal, and the DHS Office of Inspector General plans to conduct future reviews of disaster debris removal contracts.

[59]Department of Homeland Security, *National Preparedness Report* (Washington, D.C.: Aug. 28, 2017).

[60]FEMA's Housing Assistance Initiative integrated the efforts of 13 working groups and ongoing housing initiatives to develop an implementation plan that outlines short-term and long-term changes to how FEMA provides disaster housing and that outlines a new strategic vision that engages states, other federal agencies, and industry to grow national disaster housing capabilities.

of Florida are prioritizing use of this approach for housing recovery in the state, according to FEMA officials.

- **Multifamily Lease and Repair.** According to FEMA, FEMA repairs existing multi-family housing units, such as apartments, to use as temporary housing for eligible applicants who are unable to use Rental Assistance—a grant in the form of a check to enable survivors, both homeowners and renters, to rent temporary replacement housing—due to a lack of available resources.

- **Manufactured Housing Units and Recreational Vehicles.** These are manufactured homes or other readily fabricated dwellings owned by FEMA and provided to eligible applicants for use as temporary housing for a limited time. Recreational vehicles have been approved for use in response to hurricanes Harvey and Irma. This form of assistance is being implemented in Texas and Florida.

- **Permanent Housing Construction.** FEMA may provide financial assistance or direct assistance to individuals and households in insular areas outside the continental United States, or in other locations where no alternative housing resources are available and where temporary housing assistance is unavailable, infeasible, or not cost-effective. Assistance may be authorized for direct repairs or new home construction; however, FEMA has only authorized Permanent Housing Construction. This is one element of the new approach to housing recovery utilized in Texas, Puerto Rico, and the U.S. Virgin Islands, according to FEMA officials.

- **Sheltering and Temporary Essential Power.** FEMA uses Sheltering and Temporary Essential Power to assist state, territorial and tribal governments in performing work and services essential to saving lives, protecting public health and safety, and protecting property to enable survivors to shelter at home, according to FEMA officials.

- **Transitional Sheltering Assistance.** FEMA may provide Transitional Sheltering Assistance services to applicants who are unable to return to their pre-disaster primary residence because their home is either uninhabitable or inaccessible. The goal of this program is to reduce the number of disaster survivors in congregate shelters by transitioning survivors into short-term accommodations through direct payments to lodging providers, such as hotels. Puerto Rico used this approach despite initial concerns that this would have a negative effect on migration away from the island territory, according to FEMA officials.

See table 1 for the number of eligible and approved applicants for each of these housing and sheltering assistance options for each disaster location, and appendix VI for more information on how and where these sheltering and housing approaches were implemented in response to the 2017 disasters.

Table 1: Number of Registrations and Approved Applicants for Each Type of Housing and Sheltering Assistance Provided by Disaster Location, as of June 22, 2018

Disaster	Total Registrations	Multifamily Lease Repair	Manufactured Housing Units and Recreational Vehicles	Permanent Housing Construction Repair Program	Direct Lease	Sheltering and Temporary Essential Power Program	Transitional Sheltering Assistance
Hurricane Harvey in Texas	895,528	0	2,848	247	131	15,578	53,894
Hurricane Irma in Florida	2,644,403	0	257	0	63	129	26,633
Hurricane Irma and Hurricane Maria in Puerto Rico	1,138,444	16	0	33	237	33,016	6,907
Hurricane Irma and Hurricane Maria in U.S. Virgin Islands	39,415	0	0	0	61	1,920	0
California wildfires	25,425	0	154	0	94	0	618
Total	4,743,215	16	3,259	280	586	50,643	88,052

Source: Federal Emergency Management Agency | GAO-18-472

Note: Total registrations represent the total number of survivors considered for disaster assistance at each of the disaster locations specified. However, the number of registrations for the Sheltering and Temporary Essential Power Program may be different because the Sheltering and Temporary Essential Power Program is separate from FEMA's Individuals and Households Program and is not included in the registration process. Disaster survivors interested in the Sheltering and Temporary Essential Power Program must first apply for FEMA's Individuals and Households Program assistance and then apply directly to the State, Territorial, or Tribal entity administering the Sheltering and Temporary Essential Power Program.

These alternative approaches for housing recovery—primarily funded through FEMA's IA program—reflect the agency's efforts to support recovery efforts that are responsive to local needs and available resources, and that address previously identified challenges facing their programs. However, despite successes, in each of the disaster-affected

2017 Hurricanes & Wildfires: GAO's Initial Observations (9/2018)

areas, officials noted complex and ongoing housing concerns, as discussed below.

Texas: In September 2017, FEMA entered into an agreement with the Texas General Land Office to provide for housing recovery, marking the first time the agency has coordinated with a nonfederal agency to provide this housing service, according to FEMA officials. FEMA estimates these costs will reach approximately $1 billion. State officials in Texas plan to implement the new housing model to manage the delivery of direct housing to more than 6,600 applicants.[61] However, the officials cited staffing shortfalls at the state level, and information sharing challenges among FEMA, state, and local officials, which may result in delays in granting housing relief to applicants.

Florida: Housing shortages already existed in Florida prior to Hurricane Irma, and locating adequate housing subsequent to the disasters has been a major challenge, according to state and local officials. In Florida, officials told us that that zoning laws restrict the number of housing units based on the capacity for evacuation from the area. As a result, state officials said they preferred to utilize the direct lease option for the first time to leverage the high volume of vacation rentals, particularly in Lee, Collier, and Monroe Counties. However, local officials said in December 2017 that housing shortages existed in areas of the Florida Keys, and that there were concerns about the timeliness of providing housing units to disaster survivors.

U.S. Virgin Islands: Significant wind damage from Hurricane Irma followed by significant water damage from Hurricane Maria severely depleted the housing available for disaster survivors. Local officials stated that they are addressing the shortage and challenges through a combination of direct temporary housing—direct lease and multifamily lease and repair, and potentially permanent housing construction repairs. However, FEMA officials noted challenges in providing housing to

---

[61]Under the new model developed immediately after Hurricane Harvey, the General Land Office—a Texas state agency—acts as the program administrator, while local government officials each individually run the program, which provides a range of housing options to applicants, including permanent housing construction and direct lease. According to FEMA officials, after-action reviews which highlighted challenges experienced in the Baton Rouge flooding of 2017 drove this model of contracting with the state to provide housing assistance. As part of that review, FEMA captured lessons learned from the flooding event that recommended, among other changes, giving grant authority to enable states to develop capability in advance of a disaster.

   GAO-18-472 2017 Hurricanes and Wildfires

2017 Hurricanes & Wildfires: GAO's Initial Observations (9/2018)

disaster survivors and local officials due to staff shortages for inspections and inexperienced FEMA staff who are not prepared to support the housing mission. According to FEMA's Housing Inspection Services officials, to expedite availability of trained inspectors, FEMA pursued and received a waiver of the standard background check process for inspectors during recruitment efforts following Hurricane Harvey and throughout the 2017 hurricane season. The process, which normally takes about 2 weeks, was abbreviated to approximately 2 to 3 days. It also initiated innovations for the inspection process that included streamlining the scope of field inspection to more readily allow third party representatives to meet with the inspector and a self-declaration process as a last resort to verify either occupancy or ownership.

Puerto Rico: FEMA and territorial officials are offering multiple programs to address the unique challenges to long-term housing for survivors on the island. For example, the governor considered the shortage of hotel space available on the island and ultimately decided to request Transitional Sheltering Assistance, despite concerns that it would encourage middle class, professional residents to leave the island, according to FEMA officials.[62] The governor also requested transportation assistance for the first time to assist people who wish to relocate, including those in nursing homes and hospitals, FEMA officials added.[63]

California: Even before the 2017 disasters, critical housing shortages existed in California. According to FEMA officials, Sonoma County, California had 144 available housing units prior to the wildfires, which burned 5,098 homes in Sonoma and another 5,031 homes in Mendocino County, creating a large housing deficit. Locating adequate housing subsequent to the disasters has been a major challenge, according to

---

[62] See 42 U.S.C. § 5189c (authorizing the provisions of transportation assistance to relocate individuals displaced from their predisaster primary residences as a result of a declared major disaster or to return an individual or household to their pre-disaster primary residence or alternative location). According to FEMA, the 2017 disaster season was the largest implementation of Transitional Sheltering Assistance in the agency's history. In addition to Puerto Rico, this type of assistance was applied in Texas, Florida, and California in response to the 2017 hurricanes and wildfires.

[63] According to FEMA, a mission assignment was approved for National Disaster Medical System to provide a medical evacuation of dialysis patients from both the US Virgin Islands and Puerto Rico to the Continental United States. Officials said that transportation assistance was not approved or used to assist Puerto Rico survivors in leaving the island. Transportation assistance was approved on May 3, 2018, however, to assist survivors that were checked into Transitional Sheltering Assistance (TSA) hotels within the Continental United States in returning to Puerto Rico. This assistance was provided from May 3, 2018 through August 30, 2018.

2017 Hurricanes & Wildfires: GAO's Initial Observations (9/2018)

California state officials. These officials reported that local ordinances have compounded the complexity of finding housing solutions, and local officials navigate alterations to rules for temporary situations (e.g. prohibiting mobile homes in certain areas).

Federal, state, and local officials formed housing task forces to inform the state and FEMA of local challenges as well as opportunities to provide shelter. According to state officials, the pre-existing relationship with FEMA along with California's more centralized emergency management decision-making structure has facilitated this joint decision-making approach. While this approach has enabled the state to meet its most pressing short-term housing needs, according to FEMA officials, the state faces other challenges in the long term. For example, FEMA officials estimated that Direct Temporary Housing, which should be occupied by disaster survivors no more than 18 months, will be needed for a period of at least 36 months by survivors of the wildfires since that is how long it is estimated that survivors will take to rebuild.[64]

Although FEMA and state officials acknowledge the potential of the alternative approaches to meet local needs, early implementation challenges raise concerns about the effectiveness and management of these approaches for long-term recovery. We describe these challenges and approaches for each location further in appendix VI.[65]

---

[64] According to FEMA's Individuals and Households Program Unified Guidance, FEMA may extend Direct Temporary Housing Assistance beyond the 18-month period of assistance when the affected state, territorial, or tribal government requests an extension in writing. See also 42 U.S.C. § 5174(c)(1)(B)(iii).

[65] We are initiating a comprehensive review of FEMA's Individual Assistance Program—including FEMA housing assistance—that will examine challenges and lessons learned from the 2017 disasters, which we plan to issue in 2019.

2017 Hurricanes & Wildfires: GAO's Initial Observations (9/2018)

FEMA Faced Workforce Challenges With Deploying Enough Personnel, Providing Training, and Retaining Staff

FEMA's workforce allocations and plans were overwhelmed by the 2017 disaster response needs and long-standing workforce challenges we have identified in prior work were exacerbated by the need to provide a concurrent response to the disasters. Based on its internal workforce analyses, FEMA faced a staff shortage of more than 30 percent as of September 1, 2017.[66] Among other things, the Post-Katrina Act required FEMA to develop a strategic human capital plan that includes an assessment of the critical skills and competencies of FEMA's workforce and provide an action plan that includes workforce planning strategies and program objectives to train employees.[67] We have previously found that FEMA has faced challenges developing workforce strategies and ensuring adequate training that affects FEMA's ability to ensure workforce capacity to respond to and recover from large-scale disasters.[68] In our prior reports, we have recommended, among other things, that FEMA incorporate certain principles, including goals and performance measures, into its workforce planning and training efforts. FEMA concurred, and has taken steps to address some of our recommendations. However, FEMA officials said that the agency does not expect to address all of our recommendations until 2020.

Deploying Personnel

Prior to the 2017 disasters, one of FEMA's strategic goals was to maintain a FEMA disaster workforce that is capable of responding to two concurrent large-scale disasters. Following the 2017 disasters, FEMA officials told us that their experience responding to four near-simultaneous disasters made them realize that they will need to continue to improve their workforce planning to be prepared to simultaneously support multiple disasters. FEMA relies on both permanent and disaster-related temporary employees to respond to presidentially-declared disasters. See figure 13 for the total federal disaster workforce, including the FEMA disaster workforce, deployed to the various disasters in 2017.

---

[66] FEMA's workforce analysis only represented FEMA employees and did not include local hires, FEMA Corps, Surge Capacity Force, contractors or employees from other federal agencies.

[67] See 5 U.S.C. § 10102.

[68] GAO-12-487.

Figure 13: Federal Disaster Workforce Deployed in Response to the 2017 Disasters in September 2017 through February 2018

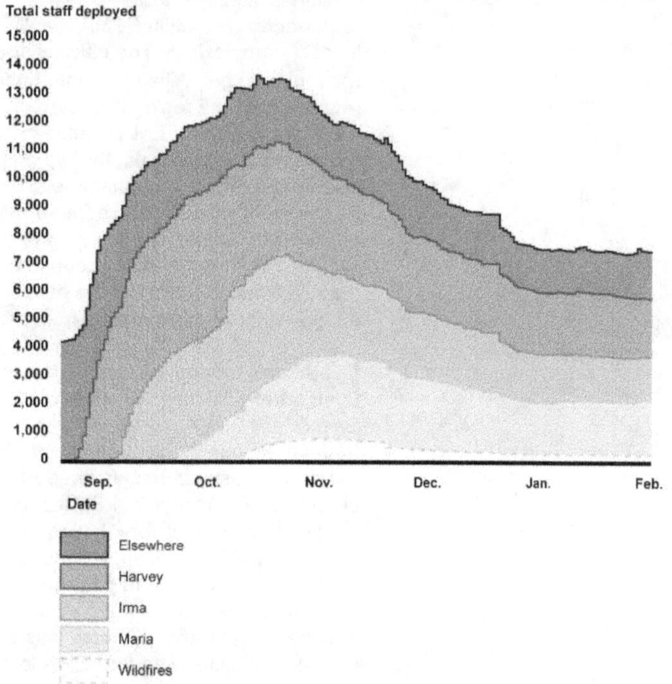

Source: GAO analysis of Department of Homeland Security data. | GAO-18-472

Note: Data include Federal Emergency Management Agency (FEMA) workforce and non-FEMA employees that FEMA can deploy during a disaster response such as the Surge Capacity Force, FEMA Corps and contractors. Data do not represent local hires or employee types such as permanent part-time, temporary part-time, and temporary incident employees.

According to FEMA officials, the near-sequential disasters in 2017 required FEMA management to redeploy response personnel from one disaster to the next. For example, FEMA initially deployed a national IMAT team of 32 personnel to Texas following Hurricane Harvey, after hurricanes Irma and Maria hit, FEMA replaced this team with a regional IMAT team of 12 personnel, according to Harris County officials in Texas. Also, according to the FEMA deputy FCO in California, FEMA had already deployed the majority of its workforce to support the hurricanes when the wildfires began and so there was some delay in initially

2017 Hurricanes & Wildfires: GAO's Initial Observations (9/2018)

deploying an adequate number of staff to support the wildfires response. According to FEMA Region IX officials responsible for responding to the California wildfires, FEMA classified the hurricanes as the most complex level of disaster, while FEMA initially classified the wildfires at a lower level of complexity.[69] The officials added that as a result, it was difficult for the region to get skilled staff into positions that were crucial for the response, so the region accepted employees who could only deploy for a week or two when FEMA would normally deploy them for 30 days. According to the officials, the region had retained some staff in California and was able to use contractors to backfill positions in cases where FEMA redeployed staff to support the hurricane response. Region IX officials added that as the region requested more staff, it sometimes received staff who had not been in the field for a while and lacked up-to-date knowledge to handle the mission needs, or staff who were coming off of long-term deployments from the hurricanes and were exhausted.

FEMA took several actions to address this shortfall in personnel by calling upon non-FEMA employees to deploy to the 2017 disaster areas. Specifically FEMA deployed more staff from other federal agencies through the use of the Surge Capacity Force, moved available staff between disaster zones as needed, hired locally, and used contractor personnel. For example, FEMA expanded the Surge Capacity Force for the first time in its history. Leveraging the Surge Capacity Force, the agency rapidly mobilized, trained, and equipped personnel from 34 non-DHS federal agencies to perform a variety of missions in support of the 2017 disasters, according to FEMA officials. FEMA officials in Florida said that the Surge Capacity Force was invaluable. One of our prior workforce recommendations was for FEMA to develop recruitment plans to address staff shortages in two new workforce elements, including the Surge Capacity Force.[70] FEMA concurred with this recommendation and has fully implemented it. However, FEMA officials said that they observed challenges with shifting personnel as conditions changed and said that the Surge Capacity Force still did not provide enough people, primarily due to the unanticipated staff demand created by the concurrent response to four major disasters.

---

[69]FEMA defines disasters by incident types. A Type 1 event is the most complex, requiring national resources to safely and effectively manage and operate. Other levels of disaster do not call for the same level of national resources.

[70]GAO-15-437. FEMA has implemented activities to address all recommendations in this report, including those related to the Surge Capacity Force.

2017 Hurricanes & Wildfires: GAO's Initial Observations (9/2018)

Providing Training

FEMA recruited a large number of employees to meet the unprecedented demand for staffing resources in response to the 2017 disasters. According to FEMA officials, the large influx of new employees added to challenges conducting timely, program-specific training. More than half of FEMA personnel were serving in a capacity in which they did not hold the title of "Qualified"—during the peak of deployments to the 2017 disasters, according to our analysis of data from FEMA's Deployment Tracking System.[71] According to FEMA officials, an individual's qualification in the tracking system does not necessarily correlate to incomplete tasks and training. Officials added that there is no feasible way to provide the training required to fulfill all requirements for qualification because although some courses could be offered in the field, many staff positions require more than one training, not all of which can be delivered in a field environment.

According to the FCO for Hurricane Harvey, limited funding dedicated to training also hampered the agency's ability to meet basic training needs. This resulted in FEMA delivering aspects of the training even as the Surge Capacity Force actively responded to the disasters. FEMA officials stated that in the absence of required training, they developed just-in-time training, as well as hiring contractors to provide training locally. According to a FEMA official in Florida, FEMA should ideally provide training before a disaster so that the agency knows who is volunteering and can tailor training for tasks that fit their skills.

Retaining Staff

FEMA officials reported multiple challenges in retaining staff, including IMAT staff who play a key role in supporting the response to major disasters. According to FEMA officials, low pay and difficulty maintaining

---

[71] According to FEMA officials, "Qualified" or "FQS qualification" is an official designation that refers to the fulfillment of criteria established by the FEMA Qualification System (FQS). The term is applied to FEMA personnel who, following an evaluation and validation of cadre-specific tasks and training requirements, are capable of independently executing their incident-based roles. The proportion of staff serving in a capacity in which they did not hold the title of "qualified" does not include non-FEMA disaster workforce components, such as the Surge Capacity Force and contractors. The qualification of these non-FEMA disaster workforce personnel is not tracked in FQS. For example, according to FEMA officials, Surge Capacity Force personnel are expected to self-report their skills when they arrive at their assigned location and receive training for roles that fit their self-assessment, prior to being deployed to the field to perform that role. If they are assigned a new role once they get to their duty station, they receive training for their new role. FEMA contractors as well as USACE members and local hires also receive program specific training before they begin working.

2017 Hurricanes & Wildfires: GAO's Initial Observations (9/2018)

work-life balance have been identified as contributing to retention challenges on national Type I and regional Type II IMATs. According to the IMAT chief for Hurricane Harvey, attrition was high among IMAT staff because of the demanding nature of the job and low pay. FEMA officials in Florida also said that they faced challenges in hiring and retaining specialists such as engineers. According to these officials, the hiring process is lengthy and the pay is not competitive. Challenges revising and delivering training in a timely fashion may have also contributed to high turnover among reservists and other staff, according to the FCO in Texas. This is consistent with issues we had found in 2016 when we reported that the IMAT program had experienced high attrition across national and regional IMATs—since its implementation in fiscal year 2013—and that FEMA had not developed a strategy to address this challenge.[72] We recommended that FEMA develop a plan and workforce strategy for retention of IMAT staff. However, FEMA had not completed actions to respond to this recommendation as of July 2018. Nonetheless, FEMA officials said that the agency is examining its workforce challenges and has taken a number of actions to address staff retention. For example, officials told us they are working to expedite hiring decisions for IMAT personnel and increase the readiness of IMAT teams. According to FEMA officials, the agency has also made changes to ensure the composition of IMATs better reflect response priorities and foster greater team cohesion. Finally, it has established working groups to examine critical long-standing issues, such as training and equipment, that impact the team's ability to deploy and perform, in an effort to improve morale and retain personnel. We provide more details on the disaster workforce and related challenges in appendix V.

Use of Alternative Procedures and New Approaches to Service Delivery Offer Opportunities to Enhance Recovery Efforts but Also Present Challenges for the Public Assistance Program

Use of the alternative procedures and redesigned PA delivery model offers FEMA opportunities to help address some challenges experienced in past disasters and enhance overall recovery efforts. However, the relative lack of experience in administering disaster assistance using these approaches coupled with the magnitude of expertise and resource shortages presented by the response to multiple large-scale disasters also presents challenges.

---

[72]GAO-16-87.

2017 Hurricanes & Wildfires: GAO's Initial Observations (9/2018)

Local officials told us that, in consultation with FEMA, they are considering the extent to which they will use the Public Assistance Program alternative procedures to support their infrastructure recovery goals. As shown in figure 14, the alternative procedures offer a modified approach to estimating and funding debris removal and permanent work under the Public Assistance programs in ways that can offer substantial benefits to disaster-affected communities.

Figure 14: Summary of Alternative Procedures for Federal Emergency Management Agency's (FEMA) Public Assistance Program, Authorized in 2013

Debris removals

- Provide grants on the basis of fixed estimates to provide financial incentives for governments with FEMA-approved debris removal plan and one or more pre-qualified debris removal contracts prior to a disaster.
- Uses a sliding scale for determining the federal cost share for debris removal based on the time it takes to complete debris and wreckage removal.
- Allow applicants to recycle debris and use the proceeds from recycling without reducing the award amount.
- Reimburse for the base and overtime wages for employed staff performing debris removal-related activities.
- Incentivize local governments to have FEMA-approved debris management plans.
- If actual costs are less than estimated costs, allow grantee to use all or part of remaining funds for specifed purposes, such as debris managment planning.

Permanent work

- Allows for the consolidation of multiple individual facilities into a single project to the extent determined appropriate by the Administrator.
- Issue PA grants to applicants based on fixed estimates of their total public assistance eligibility if the applicant agrees to be responsible for any actual costs that exceed the estimate.
- Provide an option for applicants to receive an in-lieu contribution, without reduction, on the basis of estimates of certain costs and providing guidance on cost estimating procedures and dealing with differences between estimates and actual final costs.

Source: GAO analysis of FEMA information. | GAO-18-472

Note: See Pub. L. No. 113-2, div. B, § 1102(2), 127 Stat. 39, amending Pub. L. No. 93-288, tit. IV, § 428 (codified at 42 U.S.C. § 5189f). Following both Hurricane Katrina and Sandy, Congress authorized similar pilot programs to provide similar flexibilities in the Public Assistance Program, in an effort to reduce challenges and costs associated with the program, and incentivize states to speed the recovery process. FEMA operated that pilot program from June 2007 through December 2008 when authority for the pilot program expired.

According to FEMA officials, in the U.S. Virgin Islands and in the states, participation in the pilot program for permanent work alternative procedures will occur for select projects, by applicant request. These projects are to be administered using existing guidance that FEMA previously developed for its pilot program to implement the permanent work alternative procedures.[73] In contrast, for permanent work projects in Puerto Rico, alternative procedures will be used for all large permanent work projects.[74] On April 11, 2018, FEMA issued the *Public Assistance Alternative Procedures (Section 428) Guide for Permanent Work* to guide recovery from Hurricane Maria in Puerto Rico after the Puerto Rico governor requested the use of alternative procedures for all large permanent work projects due to the unique circumstances in the territory (i.e., the magnitude of impacts and Puerto Rico's fiscal circumstances). They added that this approach will provide the flexibility Puerto Rico requires to achieve its post-disaster recovery goals while limiting risk to the federal government.[75] According to FEMA and Puerto Rico officials, use of the alternative procedures is appropriate to support the large-scale rebuilding effort there. However, it is unclear whether such flexibilities will eliminate other challenges associated with the PA program, such as reducing delays from challenges to eligibility determinations and supporting a timely recovery. According to FEMA officials, although the front end of the PA alternative procedures pilot program may take longer than the standard PA procedures, once project formulation (including any identified hazard mitigation measures) and cost agreements are made,

---

[73] FEMA updated this guide in 2016 and is applicable to all disasters declared on or after March 29, 2016. This guide is available at www.fema.gov/media-library/assets/documents/115868.

[74] Due to the extraordinary level of infrastructure damage caused by Hurricane Maria, as well as the financial status of Puerto Rico, officials chose to use the alternative procedures for all large project funding for Public Assistance categories C through G pursuant to section 428 of the Stafford Act. Puerto Rico; Amendment No. 5 to Notice of a Major Disaster Declaration, 82 Fed. Reg. 53,514 (Nov. 16, 2017). For fiscal year 2018, the large project threshold is $125,500.

[75] According to FEMA, any permanent work started before 12:00 am on September 17, 2017 will be attributed to Disaster Declaration 4336 in Puerto Rico, using the traditional PA procedures, and any work started after that time, regardless of whether the work was required by Hurricane Irma or Hurricane Maria, will be attributed to Disaster Declaration 4339 in Puerto Rico and will follow the procedures established in the disaster-specific guide. This guide describes the scope and limitations of the alternative procedures, the changes to the aspects of the PA Program to which these procedures apply, and identifies responsibilities for certain activities, as well as timelines for key actions and decisions. Where appropriate, FEMA may develop additional guidance and tools for implementation.

2017 Hurricanes & Wildfires: GAO's Initial Observations (9/2018)

the entire sum of the agreed-upon funding level is obligated and made available to the recipient at a quicker rate due to the entire amount of the project being obligated from the outset. Additionally, the ability of an applicant to share funds between consolidated projects under alternative procedures reduces delays that occur when managing multiple complex projects coming in at higher or lower than anticipated costs, thus making for a smoother and more efficient recovery, according to FEMA officials. FEMA continues to develop a robust data collection and evaluation plan to perform substantive analysis of the pilot program and to better position itself to provide data on increased or decreased recovery timeframes, according to agency officials.

As of April 1, 2018, FEMA had approved 52 alternative procedures subawards in 30 states. Officials stated that the 52 awards likely represent large numbers of projects under the normal PA procedures, and therefore do not accurately reflect the frequency of FEMA and the states' use of the procedures. However, none of these projects were for recovery from a disaster the scale of the 2017 hurricanes and wildfires. Nonetheless, according to FEMA officials, the projects have provided valuable lessons learned which the agency has incorporated into its alternative procedures program guidance for Puerto Rico. We provide more details on the implementation of the PA program, including use of the alternative procedures, in appendix IX.

New Delivery Model

In recent years, FEMA has taken steps to redesign the PA program to address past challenges and make the program easier for FEMA and grantee officials to manage. As part of this effort, FEMA redesigned processes for developing, reviewing, and approving grant applications. The redesign also involves hiring for new PA staff positions, a standardized grant processing approach, and a new information system to better maintain and share grant documentation.

FEMA's original intention was to implement the new PA delivery model for all future disasters beginning in January 2018. However, in September 2017, FEMA expedited full implementation of the new model shortly after Hurricane Harvey made landfall. In a November 2017 report, we reviewed early implementation of the new delivery model in disasters that occurred prior to the four large-scale disasters of 2017 and found that FEMA needed to do more to assess the workforce needed to fully implement the model, such as the number of staff needed to fill certain new positions, or achieve staffing goals for supporting hazard mitigation on PA projects.[76]

---

[76]GAO-18-30.

We also found that FEMA had developed a new information-sharing system (now known as PA Grants Manager and Grants Portal) to address past information-sharing challenges, such as difficulties in sharing grant documentation among FEMA, state, and local officials and tracking the status of PA projects, but had not fully addressed two of four key information technology (IT) management controls—requirements development and systems testing and integration—that are necessary to ensure systems work effectively and meet user needs. In our report, we recommended that FEMA assess the workforce needed for the new delivery model and improve the key IT management controls for Grants Portal. The agency concurred with our recommendations and according to officials, is taking steps to implement them. Our early observations about the workforce challenges experienced using the new delivery model in Texas, Florida, and California are similar to the challenges we cited in our prior work.[77] Although we saw some of the intended benefits of the redesign, officials in all eight municipalities we met with also cited one or more challenges with training and customer service, the new information system, or the incorporation of hazard mitigation into PA Projects, that have not yet been fully addressed.

Training and Customer Service. We interviewed local government officials from eight Texas, Florida, and California municipalities about their experiences using the new delivery model and officials from four of the municipalities said that they had positive experiences with the customer service provided by PA staff. For example, officials with a Texas municipality said that they have good communication with FEMA PA personnel whom they said are responsive to questions about Grants Portal. Officials from a Florida county said that under the old model they were forced to submit documents multiple times as a result of FEMA staff losing them, whereas with the new model, they can submit documents just once by uploading them directly into Grants Portal. However, local officials also noted challenges with the new delivery model. Specifically, officials with one California county said that they experienced staff turnover, and after about a month without any PA Program Delivery

---

[77]In our previous report, we found that officials who were testing the new delivery model for PA delivery experienced a variety of challenges. FEMA managers and PA applicants at the state and local level cited insufficient staff levels and problems with poorly trained staff, which affected customer service and the timely processing of PA grant applications from the states. Furthermore, we found deficiencies in how FEMA developed its new information system, which affected how well the system's capabilities would meet user needs and insufficiently addressed integration of the system with other internal and external information systems. See GAO-18-30.

2017 Hurricanes & Wildfires: GAO's Initial Observations (9/2018)

Manager, FEMA assigned a new official who was untrained and inexperienced in the new process, and therefore unable to provide guidance on using the new IT system or answer questions about the process. Additionally, local officials in a Texas jurisdiction said that they received better customer service under the old model because the project manager writing the project worksheet could provide the applicant some information immediately to help gauge eligibility, and inform local fiscal decisions. Texas officials added that with the new process, all of the information is passed to centralized staff to write up the project while the Program Delivery Manager only collects project information, leaving the applicant unaware of next steps or reimbursement eligibility.

Speaking about their experiences using the new delivery model, officials in four municipalities we interviewed noted that they had little or no prior knowledge of these changes before using the new process for recovery from their 2017 disasters. Further, the officials stated that FEMA did not provide sufficient information about the new process. Texas, Florida, and California county officials we interviewed also expressed frustration with the lack of consistency in the implementation guidance FEMA provides and with project eligibility determination. According to officials from three of the eight jurisdictions, FEMA's process and decision-making is not clear and this is further complicated by the inability of FEMA staff to fully articulate the new process, due in part to limited training. FEMA officials acknowledged the challenge of training a large number of new employees on the new delivery model and stated that the agency has taken a number of steps to address these challenges and provide training to applicants and FEMA employees. For example, as part of its initial rollout of the new model, FEMA participated in "listening sessions" with state and local stakeholders. FEMA has also established and advertised a mechanism (the Change Control Tool) by which users of Grants Manager and Grants Portal can suggest a process improvement. Submissions to the tool are evaluated and prioritized on a monthly basis, according to FEMA officials. Additionally, officials said that FEMA is working to improve and expand its capacity to deliver training to applicants and FEMA employees. For example, in addition to hiring additional trainers, the agency is expanding the length and content of program training for field personnel, according to FEMA officials.

New Information System. Local government officials from two of the eight Texas, Florida, and California municipalities we interviewed about their experiences using Grants Portal commended the new PA information system for its transparency, however, officials from four jurisdictions expressed concerns about delays, not having sufficient

                    GAO-18-472 2017 Hurricanes and Wildfires

2017 Hurricanes & Wildfires: GAO's Initial Observations (9/2018)

guidance on how to use the new system, and how the system interfaces with their own state systems. Also, local officials from Texas, Florida and California expressed concerns about experiencing delays with FEMA's processing of their projects, and subsequent obligation of the necessary funds. Further, officials from three municipalities said it is unclear what happens once applicants submit their project applications to Grants Portal. For example, county officials in Florida said that under the old PA model, a FEMA project manager was available to walk applicants through the process of developing and submitting a project application; however, with the new model, applicants are required to develop and submit project applications without any assistance. Texas, Florida, and California officials said that after submitting their applications, they typically receive little information from FEMA about the processing of their application. According to FEMA officials, FEMA operates a hotline that FEMA staff and PA Program applicants can call to obtain answers to questions regarding use of the Grants Portal. FEMA is also working on further improving the functionalities of Grants Manager and Grants Portal to meet the needs of all of its users and to interface with the various federal and non-federal systems that track and manage PA grants. Additionally, expanding training will help improve both applicants' understanding of the process and FEMA employees' ability to work with applicants, according to FEMA officials.

Although it is too early to determine the effects of challenges with customer service and use of the information system under the new delivery model, local officials we met with have noted delays in processing PA applications. We provide more details on the experiences of each state using the new delivery model in appendix IX.

Incorporating Hazard Mitigation. The new delivery model under PA offers opportunities to better integrate hazard mitigation into recovery projects. Initial estimates indicate that the cost of damages from the 2017 hurricanes and wildfires will be far greater than the cost of damages for both hurricanes Katrina and Sandy. We have previously reported that using hazard mitigation and climate adaptation to enhance disaster resilience is critical to help address the federal fiscal exposure to disaster losses.[78] We also observed that although most funding for resilience activities is provided in the wake of a disaster, there are several aspects of incorporating resilience into post-disaster rebuilding efforts that may

---

[78]GAO-15-515.

                    GAO-18-472 2017 Hurricanes and Wildfires

create barriers to its effectiveness. For example, in our prior work on Hurricane Sandy, we found that in some states, officials with primary responsibility for hazard mitigation noted that they wore other hats in the emergency operations center in the initial hours to days and were too focused on response functions to think about hazard mitigation.[79]

FEMA designed the new PA delivery model to help state and local officials interact with FEMA experts to identify opportunities to incorporate hazard mitigation into PA projects early and throughout the process. Officials from 3 of the 6 municipalities we interviewed in Texas and Florida that are implementing the new delivery model confirmed that FEMA has provided mitigation experts to assist local officials with incorporating hazard mitigation on PA projects.[80] However, these officials also noted limitations in the extent to which mitigation experts were able to provide support on project development, echoing FEMA's broad workforce training challenges already discussed. According to officials with FEMA's PA Program Delivery Branch, FEMA is currently in the process of conducting a comprehensive workforce review through which PA is assessing the size and composition of the deployable workforce. As part of this effort, FEMA is assessing the way it uses all available resources, including FEMA staff and technical assistance contractors to meet the demands of variable disaster cycles.

On site visits to Texas and Florida, we observed how instances of previous investments in disaster resilience reduced the damages from the storms, and may have lowered associated disaster costs. Both states and California have efforts underway that demonstrate their commitment to a resilient recovery. For example, Texas has a systematic approach to solicit hazard mitigation projects from local governments through Rebuild Texas—a commission set up by the Texas governor to marshal statewide resources and effort to rebuild public infrastructure damaged by Hurricane Harvey. Nevertheless, officials in Texas and Florida raised concerns about challenges to building disaster resilience during recovery, which were similar to the challenges we previously found reported by state and local officials affected by Hurricane Sandy.[81] These include the

---

[79]GAO-15-515.

[80]According to state officials in California, while disaster mitigation is a goal generally, due to the nature of the damages from these fires, the officials do not expect many opportunities for mitigation. California officials we spoke to did not state any challenges with hazard mitigation related to their PA recovery efforts.

[81]GAO-15-515.

2017 Hurricanes & Wildfires: GAO's Initial Observations (9/2018)

challenges with incorporating hazard mitigation that we previously discussed, and also challenges that go beyond PA projects, such as coordinating federal aid from multiple programs and local barriers to investment in resilience efforts. For example, Texas and Florida officials each described difficulties finding adequate funding to carry out key projects to make communities more resilient to flooding.

We provide more details on how each state plans to incorporate disaster resilience, and their challenges, in appendix X.[82]

Agency Comments

We provided a draft of this report to DHS and DOD for their review and comment. DHS provided a comment letter that is reprinted in appendix XIII and technical comments that we incorporated, as appropriate. DOD provided only technical comments that we incorporated, as appropriate.

In its comment letter, DHS acknowledged the challenges it faced conducting concurrent response operations for three major hurricanes—Harvey, Irma, and Maria—while preparing to take action on two more (hurricanes Jose and Nate) during the 2017 hurricane season. DHS also listed various actions it has taken since 2017 that are intended to expedite affected jurisdictions' recovery from the 2017 disasters, prepare for the 2018 hurricane season, and incorporate lessons learned to better prepare the nation for future disasters.

---

[82]We plan to conduct future work on states' experiences incorporating resilience enhancements in response to and recovery from the 2017 disasters.

We will send copies of this report to the secretaries of Defense and Homeland Security, the FEMA Administrator, and appropriate congressional committees. If you or your staff have any questions about this report, please contact me at (404) 679-1875 or curriec@gao.gov. Contact points for our Offices of Congressional Relations and Public Affairs may be found on the last page of this report. Other key contributors to this report are listed in appendix XV.

Chris P. Currie
Director
Homeland Security and Justice

Congressional Addressees

The Honorable Richard Shelby
Chairman
The Honorable Patrick Leahy
Vice Chairman
Committee on Appropriations
United States Senate

The Honorable Susan M. Collins
Chairman
The Honorable Robert P. Casey, Jr.
Ranking Member
Special Committee on Aging
United States Senate

The Honorable Mike Enzi
Chairman
Committee on the Budget
United States Senate

The Honorable Lisa Murkowski
Chairman
The Honorable Maria Cantwell
Ranking Member
Committee on Energy and Natural Resources
United States Senate

The Honorable Ron Johnson
Chairman
The Honorable Claire McCaskill
Ranking Member
Committee on Homeland Security and Governmental Affairs
United States Senate

The Honorable Rand Paul
Chairman
The Honorable Gary Peters
Ranking Member
Subcommittee on Federal Spending, Oversight and Emergency
Management
Committee on Homeland Security and Governmental Affairs
United States Senate

The Honorable Bill Nelson
United States Senate

The Honorable Marco Rubio
United States Senate

The Honorable Rodney Frelinghuysen
Chairman
The Honorable Nita Lowey
Ranking Member
Committee on Appropriations
House of Representatives

The Honorable Greg Walden
Chairman
The Honorable Joe Barton
Vice Chairman
The Honorable Frank Pallone, Jr
Ranking Member
Committee on Energy and Commerce
House of Representatives

The Honorable Jeb Hensarling
Chairman
The Honorable Maxine Waters
Ranking Member
Committee on Financial Services
House of Representatives

The Honorable Ann Wagner
Chairwoman
The Honorable Al Green
Ranking Member
Subcommittee on Oversight Investigations
Committee on Financial Services
House of Representatives

The Honorable Sean Duffy
Chairman
The Honorable Emanuel Cleaver
Ranking Member
Subcommittee on Housing and Insurance
Committee on Financial Services
House of Representatives

The Honorable Michael McCaul
Chairman
The Honorable Bennie Thompson
Ranking Member
Committee on Homeland Security
House of Representatives

The Honorable Dan Donovan
Chairman
The Honorable Donald Payne Jr.
Ranking Member
Subcommittee on Emergency Preparedness, Response, and
Communications
Committee on Homeland Security
House of Representatives

The Honorable Trey Gowdy
Chairman
The Honorable Elijah Cummings
Ranking Member
Committee on Oversight and Government Reform
House of Representatives

The Honorable Gary Palmer
Chairman
Subcommittee on Intergovernmental Affairs
Committee on Oversight and Government Reform
House of Representatives

The Honorable Greg Gianforte
Chairman
Subcommittee on the Interior, Energy, and Environment
Committee on Oversight and Government Reform
House of Representatives

The Honorable Bill Shuster
Chairman
The Honorable Peter DeFazio
Ranking Member
Committee on Transportation and Infrastructure
House of Representatives

Resident Commissioner Jenniffer González-Colón
House of Representatives

The Honorable John Culberson
House of Representatives

The Honorable Jeff Denham
House of Representatives

The Honorable Ron DeSantis
House of Representatives

The Honorable Alcee L. Hastings
House of Representatives

The Honorable Jared Huffman
House of Representatives

The Honorable Zoe Lofgren
House of Representatives

The Honorable Mike Thompson
House of Representatives

The Honorable Debbie Wasserman Schultz
House of Representatives

The Honorable Nydia Velázquez
House of Representatives

Appendix I: Objectives, Scope, and Methodology

This report addresses the following: (1) our observations of the federal response coordination for hurricanes Harvey and Irma, in Texas and Florida, as well as for the California wildfires; (2) our observations of the federal response to hurricanes Irma and Maria in Puerto Rico and the U.S. Virgin Islands; and (3) existing and emerging disaster recovery challenges as well as opportunities highlighted by the 2017 hurricanes and wildfires.

To address all three objectives, we analyzed federal laws and FEMA policies, procedures, and guidance specific to emergency management. Specifically, we reviewed select sections of the Post-Katrina Act, including those associated with the establishment of (1) the *National Response Framework*, (2) the Federal Coordinating Officer (FCO) position—the lead federal official in charge of response, (3) Incident Management Assistance Teams (IMAT)—FEMA staff who rapidly deploy to an incident to provide leadership in the identification and provision of federal assistance and federal response capabilities, (4) the surge capacity force; and (5) the Sandy Recovery Improvement Act, particularly those sections associated with FEMA's public assistance program and debris removal responsibilities.[1] We also reviewed the *National Response Framework; the National Disaster Recovery Framework;* the 2017 *National Preparedness Report;* FEMA's 2014-2018 Strategic Plan, and the 2017 Hurricane Season FEMA After-Action Report. We included relevant information from our prior reports. Additionally, we obtained and analyzed key data from FEMA's financial management, workforce, emergency operations systems, and the federal procurement system. We focused on the highest period of disaster response activity for the federal government—August 2017 to January 2018, and we updated information provided as available in the subsequent months through June 2018. To ensure the reliability of the updated data, we interviewed officials at FEMA headquarters about their data quality control procedures, reviewed existing information about data systems—particularly data definitions and

---

[1] The *National Response Framework* is the part of the National Preparedness System established in Presidential Policy Directive 8 that is to be used to manage any type of disaster or emergency response, regardless of scale, scope, and complexity. Specifically, this framework covers actions to save lives, protect property and the environment, stabilize communities, and meet basic human needs following an incident. Response also includes the execution of emergency plans and actions to support short-term recovery. Department of Homeland Security, Federal Emergency Management Agency, *National Response Framework, Third Edition* (Washington, D.C.: June 2016). The surge capacity force is a cadre of non-FEMA federal employees who augment FEMA's disaster response and recovery efforts.

data validation, conducted electronic testing, and reviewed the data for
obvious errors and omissions. We found the data to be sufficiently reliable
for the purposes of this report.

Moreover, in October and November 2017, we visited hurricane-damaged
areas in the greater Houston area, throughout the southern part of
Florida, in San Juan, Puerto Rico, and St. Croix, U.S. Virgin Islands.
Further, we interviewed state emergency management officials or their
designees in each disaster-affected state and territory as well as local
government officials from eight municipalities in Texas, Florida, and
California to gain their insights and perspectives on the federal response
to the hurricanes and wildfires in their respective states and territories.
We selected the cities and counties whose officials we interviewed based
on their geographic proximity to the disaster affected sites we were
already visiting, as well as their availability. The findings from these
interviews cannot be generalized to all disaster-affected states; however,
they provided insights to the respective states' response to and recovery
from the disasters along with the federal government's role. We visited
FEMA's joint field offices for: Hurricane Harvey, located in Austin Texas;
Hurricane Irma, located in Orlando Florida; and hurricanes Irma and
Maria, located in San Juan and St. Croix. We interviewed FEMA's on-site
leadership in all of these locations, and conducted telephone interviews
with FEMA's on-site leadership responsible for the response and recovery
efforts in California. In addition, we conducted site visits to various FEMA
branch offices and Disaster Response Centers (DRC) in Houston, Texas;
Bonita Springs and Marathon, Florida; San Juan, Puerto Rico; and St.
Croix, U.S. Virgin Islands.

To address our first objective of the federal response coordination for
hurricanes Harvey and Irma, in Texas and Florida, as well as for the
California wildfires, we:

- Conducted site visits to hurricane-impacted areas of Florida and
  Texas.

- Conducted interviews with: emergency management officials from
  California, Florida, and Texas; FEMA leadership from Regions IV, VI,
  and IX; officials from Houston, Texas, Harris County, Texas,
  Marathon, Florida, and Monroe County, Florida.

- Analyzed the implementation of the National Response Framework for
  hurricanes Harvey and Irma, and the California wildfires.

2017 Hurricanes & Wildfires: GAO's Initial Observations (9/2018)

To address our second objective on the federal response to Hurricanes Irma and Maria in Puerto Rico and the U.S. Virgin Islands, we:

- Conducted site visits to hurricane impacted areas of Puerto Rico and U.S. Virgin Islands.

- Conducted interviews with officials from: the Puerto Rico Emergency Management Agency, the Puerto Rico Aqueduct and Sewer Authority, the Puerto Rico Electric Power Authority; the U.S. Virgin Islands Emergency Management Office; FEMA Region II; the Department of Defense (DOD) U.S. Northern Command (NORTHCOM); the U.S. Transportation Command (TRANSCOM); and the National Guard Bureau.

- Obtained information provided by DOD and FEMA on federal resources pre-positioned and provided in response to hurricanes Irma and Maria.

To address our third objective, existing and emerging disaster recovery challenges as well as opportunities highlighted by the 2017 hurricanes and wildfires; we:

- Conducted interviews with: emergency management officials from California, Florida, and Texas; FEMA leadership from Regions IV, VI, and IX; officials from Houston, Texas, Harris County, Texas, Marathon, Florida, and Monroe County, Florida..

- We obtained and analyzed data from FEMA's Deployment Tracking System (DTS)—FEMA's system for maintaining information on their workforce, including managing deployments of workforce elements to respond to declared disasters, and maintaining information on staff skills, qualifications, and training. To ensure that the data were sufficiently reliable for our purposes, we interviewed officials at FEMA headquarters and regional offices about their data quality control procedures, reviewed existing information about data systems—particularly data dictionary and data validation, conducted electronic testing, and reviewed the data for obvious errors and omissions.

- We obtained and analyzed DHS and FEMA guidance related to federal response and recovery from major disasters. These include the 2017 *National Preparedness Report*; select DHS OIG Reports; our relevant prior reports; FEMA's *2014 – 2018 Strategic Plan; the National Disaster Recovery Framework*; FEMA's Alternative Procedures for Public Assistance Authorized in 2013 by the Sandy Recovery Improvement Act.

2017 Hurricanes & Wildfires: GAO's Initial Observations (9/2018)

In addition, we undertook the following for the detailed information included in our appendices:

Appendix II: Federal Appropriations and FEMA Obligations for the 2017 Hurricanes and California Wildfires

- We obtained and analyzed data from FEMA's Integrated Financial Management Information System (IFMIS) on the amount of Disaster Relief Fund obligations and spend plans for the hurricanes and wildfires for fiscal years 2017 and 2018. IFMIS is FEMA's official accounting and financial management system that pulls all of FEMA's financial data from other FEMA, DHS, and government-wide systems (subsystems), and is the source of data for both internal and external financial reporting. The system records and tracks all financial transactions. To assess the reliability of these data, we reviewed the data and discussed data quality control procedures with FEMA officials. We determined that the data we used from these systems were sufficiently reliable for the purposes of this report.

  We also obtained and analyzed disaster-related supplemental appropriations acts which provided additional direct funding for the 2017 hurricanes and wildfires included in our review.

Appendix III: Federal Response Coordination during the 2017 Hurricanes and Wildfires

- We obtained and analyzed FEMA's third edition of the National Response Framework (NRF). The NRF is a guide to how the nation responds to all types of disasters and emergencies. It establishes the federal response structure for disaster response that includes 14 core capabilities. We used the NRF to assess the FEMA-led federal response to the 2017 hurricanes and wildfires included in our review.

- We obtained and analyzed data from FEMA's web-based Emergency Operations Command (Web EOC)—the database used for submitting and tracking the disposition of resource requests from state and local officials to the federal government following a presidentially-declared disaster, among other things. To assess the reliability of these data, we reviewed the data for errors and discussed data quality control procedures with FEMA officials. We determined that the data we used from this system were sufficiently reliable for the purposes of this report.

2017 Hurricanes & Wildfires: GAO's Initial Observations (9/2018)

Appendix IV: Federal Contracting for the 2017 Disasters

- We obtained and analyzed data from FEMA, the U.S. Army Corps of Engineers, and the Federal Procurement Data System-Next Generation (FPDS-NG) through January 31, 2018, to determine federal contract obligations for each hurricane, the types of products and services procured, and rates of competition. We assessed the reliability of FPDS-NG data by reviewing existing information about the FPDS-NG system and the data it collects— specifically, the data dictionary and data validation rules—and performed electronic testing. We determined the FPDS-NG data were sufficiently reliable for the purposes of this report.

Appendix V: FEMA Disaster Workforce Capacity

- We obtained and analyzed data from DTS. To assess the reliability of these data, we reviewed the data and discussed data quality control procedures with FEMA officials. We determined that the data we used from these systems were sufficiently reliable for the purposes of this report.

- We obtained and analyzed FEMA's Human Capital Strategic Plan 2016-2020. The plan outlines FEMA's focus on five strategic goals specific to their workforce, and establishes goals for retention, training, recruitment, and capabilities gaps, among other things.

Appendix VI: FEMA's Individual Assistance Program

- We obtained and analyzed FEMA's Individuals and Households Programs Unified Guidance –September 2016, which documents FEMA's policies and procedures for its Individual Assistance program—to include FEMA's housing program for individuals.

- Further, we obtained data from FEMA's Emergency Management Mission Integrated Environment (EMMIE)—on the number of individual Assistance (IA) applicants for the hurricanes and wildfires in our review; and we obtained and analyzed data from FEMA's IFMIS on the amounts obligated towards IA by FEMA as of February 28, 2018.

- We also obtained aggregated data from FEMA on the number of survivors who registered for disaster assistance as well as the number who were approved for each type of housing and sheltering assistance, by disaster location as of June 22, 2018.

Appendix VII: Fraud Risk Management in FEMA's Disaster Assistance Programs

- We obtained and analyzed information relevant to fraud risk management in FEMA's disaster-assistance programs. Specifically, we interviewed officials from FEMA's Fraud and Internal Investigations Division and obtained and analyzed relevant documentation including FEMA's Fraud Prevention and Investigation Directive. In addition, we reviewed information on FEMA's antifraud efforts reported in the DHS Fiscal Year 2017 Agency Financial Report. We also reviewed our relevant prior work and DHS Office of the Inspector General reports.

Appendix VIII: Payment Integrity Related to Disaster Relief Funding

- We analyzed information from our prior work on payment integrity and internal controls.

Appendix IX: FEMA's Public Assistance Program

- We obtained PA obligation amounts from FEMA derived from EMMIE for California, Florida, Puerto Rico, Texas, and the U. S. Virgin Islands as of February 15, 2018.

Appendix X: Disaster Resilience and Hazard Mitigation

- We reviewed information from our prior work on the costs of natural disasters and the impact of hazard mitigation efforts. We obtained and analyzed information from FEMA and local officials on previous hazard mitigation efforts and future mitigation projects.

- We obtained and analyzed information from the draft National Mitigation Investment Strategy in 2018. The National Mitigation Investment Strategy provides a national approach to investments in mitigation activities and risk management across the United States.

- We obtained and analyzed information from FEMA's and HUD's guidance on hazard mitigation grant programs. This information details for what purpose and when hazard mitigation funding is available to states, tribes or territories.

2017 Hurricanes & Wildfires: GAO's Initial Observations (9/2018)

Appendix XI: Department of Defense's Support of Civil Authorities during the 2017 Hurricanes and Wildfires

- We conducted interviews with the following DOD components—Office of the Undersecretary for Defense Policy, Defense Support of Civilian Authorities (DSCA), NORTHCOM, TRANSCOM, Defense Logistics Agency, Army North, and Defense Coordinating Officers—who are the lead DOD representatives to FEMA during a major disaster declaration for FEMA Regions II, IV, VI, and IX. We also interviewed and collected data from the U.S. Army Corps of Engineers on their response efforts. We interviewed National Guard Bureau officials who provided personnel and logistical support for the 2017 disaster response efforts. During these interviews, we obtained information on their efforts to assist in the response to the 2017 hurricanes and wildfires. We also obtained summary data from these components on their response efforts. However, we did not verify the reliability of their data, although DOD officials noted that most of the data was also provided to external parties or made publicly available.

2017 Hurricanes & Wildfires: GAO's Initial Observations (9/2018)

Appendix II: Federal Appropriations and FEMA Obligations for the 2017 Hurricanes and California Wildfires

Overview

The Federal Emergency Management Agency's (FEMA) Disaster Relief Fund (DRF) is the primary source of federal disaster assistance for state and local governments. Congress appropriates no-year funding for the DRF, which allows FEMA to fund, direct, coordinate, and manage response and recovery efforts associated with domestic disasters and emergencies.

In addition to DHS, at least 29 other agencies carry out disaster assistance programs and activities. Some of these programs exist for the express purpose of supporting disaster response efforts and others are disaster-eligible—not specifically designated for disasters but able to be used for this purpose.

Federal Appropriations

Since the 2017 hurricanes and California wildfires, Congress and the President have provided the Department of Homeland Security (DHS) and 18 other federal agencies with at least $120 billion in supplemental appropriations for activities related to these disasters.[1] Table 2 summarizes these appropriations by agency.

Table 2: Supplemental Appropriations For 2017 Hurricanes and California Wildfires

Agency	Purpose	Amount appropriated (in billions of dollars)[a]
Department of Homeland Security	For the Federal Emergency Management Agency Disaster Relief Fund, among other disaster-related purposes	50.7
Department of Housing and Urban Development	For restoration of infrastructure and housing and economic revitalization in impacted areas, among other disaster-related purposes	35.4
Department of Defense	For Army, Navy, Air Force and Marine Corps, expenses related to the 2017 hurricanes and Army Corps of Engineers construction of flood and storm damage reduction projects, among other disaster-related purposes	18.6[b]
Department of Agriculture	For expenses related to crops, trees, bushes, and vine losses; nutrition assistance; and wildland fire suppression operations, among other disaster-related purposes	5.5
Department of Education	For assisting in meeting the educational needs of individuals affected by a covered disaster or emergency, among other disaster-related purposes	2.7[c]
Small Business Administration	For direct loans to small businesses and associated expenses	2.1
Department of Transportation	For aviation, highway, and transit system expenses related to the consequences of the 2017 hurricanes, among other disaster-related purposes	1.8
Department of Health and Human Services	For Centers for Disease Control and Prevention expenses directly related to the consequences of the 2017 hurricanes, among other disaster-related purposes	1.1
Department of Commerce	For expenses related to flood mitigation, disaster relief, long-term recovery, and restoration of infrastructure in areas affected by the 2017 hurricanes, among other disaster-related purposes	1.0

---

[1] Supplemental Appropriations for Disaster Relief Requirements Act, 2017, Pub. L. No. 115-56, div. B, 131 Stat. 1129, 1136 (2017); Additional Supplemental Appropriations for Disaster Relief Requirements Act, 2017 Pub. L. No. 115-72, div. A, 131 Stat. 1224, 1224 (2017); Further Additional Supplemental Appropriations for Disaster Relief Requirements Act, 2018, Pub. L. No. 115-123, div. Supplemental Appropriations for Disaster Relief Requirements Act, 2018, Pub. L. No. 115-123, div. B, subdiv. 1, 132 Stat. 64, 65 (2018).

2017 Hurricanes & Wildfires: GAO's Initial Observations (9/2018)

| 10 other federal departments and agencies receiving less than $1 billion | 1.2 |
| Total | 120.0[d] |

Source: GAO analysis of disaster-related supplemental appropriations acts. | GAO-18-472

Note: The supplemental appropriations provided up to $78.5 million for GAO and nine Inspectors General for oversight activities related to the expenditure of these funds.

[a]Some of the funds included in this table are no-year funds while others are available for specific periods of time. We do not include conditions, requirements, or authorities related to the use of funds.

[b]Does not include transfers of unobligated balances from prior fiscal years.

[c]Does not include indefinite appropriations authorized to forgive any outstanding balance owed to the Department of Education under the Historically Black College and University Hurricane Supplemental Loan program.

[d]Column does not sum to total due to rounding.

FEMA Disaster Relief Fund Obligations and Expenditures

FEMA reports monthly to Congress on its obligation and expenditure of DRF funds.[2] As of April 30, 2018, FEMA reports having obligated approximately $22.6 billion from the DRF for response and recovery efforts for the 2017 hurricanes and California wildfires, of which FEMA reports having expended a little over half—approximately $13.2 billion. FEMA projects obligating a total of about $30 billion by the end of fiscal year 2018.

Thus far, Hurricane Maria accounts for the highest amount of DRF obligations—$12.8 billion—followed by hurricanes Harvey and Irma. The 2017 California wildfires account for the smallest amount—approximately $1.4 billion obligated through April 30, 2018. See figure 15.

Figure 15: Disaster Relief Fund Obligations and Expenditures for Hurricanes Harvey, Irma, Maria, and California Wildfires, Through April 30, 2018

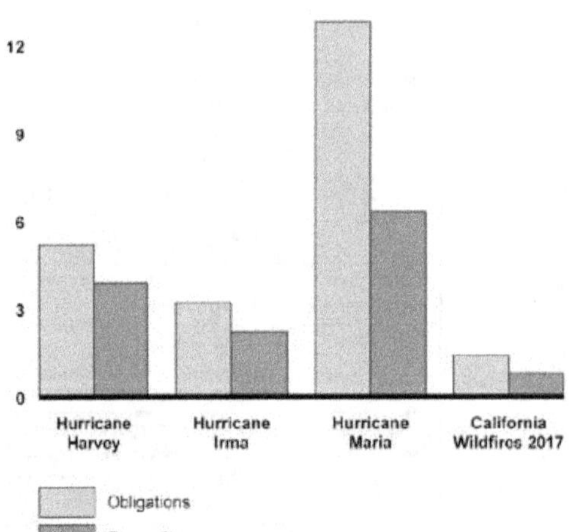

Source: GAO analysis of Federal Emergency Management Agency data. | GAO-18-472

---

[2]An obligation is a definite commitment that creates a legal liability of the government for the payment of goods and services ordered or received. An expenditure is an amount paid by federal agencies, by cash or cash equivalent, during the fiscal year to liquidate government obligations. Whereas appropriations may, among other things, stipulate a federal agency's discretionary budget authority, obligations and expenditures are generally a better measure of the actual federal commitment (spending) of dollars on the provision of goods and services.

FEMA tracks its DRF obligations in five categories—called programs:

(1) **Individual Assistance**: The Individual Assistance Program provides financial assistance directly to disaster victims for the necessary expenses and serious needs that cannot be met through insurance or low-interest Small Business Administration loans, such as temporary housing assistance, counseling, unemployment compensation, or medical expenses.

(2) **Mission Assignment**: Work orders FEMA issues that direct another federal agency to utilize its authorities and the resources granted to it under federal law in support of direct assistance to state, local, tribal, and territorial governments.

(3) **Public Assistance**: The Public Assistance program provides financial assistance to state, tribal, territorial, and local governments for activities including debris removal; emergency protective measures; and the repair, replacement, or restoration of disaster-damaged, publicly-owned facilities.

(4) **Administration**: Costs for FEMA's delivery of disaster assistance including the salary and travel costs for the disaster workforce, rent and security expenses associated with field operation locations, and supplies and information technology for field operation staff, among other things.

(5) **Hazard Mitigation**: The Hazard Mitigation Program provides funds to state, tribal, territorial, and local governments, among other entities, to assist communities in implementing long-term measures to help reduce the potential risk of future damages to facilities.

The proportion of funding obligated for each type of program varies as the disaster moves from more immediate response efforts to longer term response and recovery efforts. According to FEMA officials, soon after a disaster, Individual Assistance costs are typically the first to be obligated over a period of about 18 months. FEMA officials stated that mission assignment funds are also generally obligated during the response phase of a disaster, though the exact timing depends on how long it takes FEMA to receive and validate invoices from other federal agencies. Public assistance funds generally take longer to obligate—up to 10 years following a disaster—due to the complexity of funding for large public infrastructure projects, according to FEMA officials. Finally, FEMA officials stated that hazard mitigation funding is typically the last to be obligated, often many years after the disaster, as the response and recovery efforts abate.

The proportion of funding obligated for each type of program also varies due to other characteristics of the disaster. For example, mission assignment obligations comprised 60 percent of all actual and projected DRF obligations for the California wildfires and 4 percent of all such obligations for Hurricane Harvey. According to FEMA officials, neither the state of California nor the local counties had the capability or capacity to immediately take on the task of debris removal in response to the 2017 California wildfires, so FEMA funded this through a U.S. Army Corps of Engineers mission assignment. In another example, the administration costs are projected to be highest for Hurricane Irma—31 percent—and lowest for the California wildfires—3 percent. FEMA officials explained that the administrative costs for the 2017 California wildfires are much less because the majority of the wildfire costs were funded through mission assignments to the U.S. Army Corps of

     GAO-18-472 2017 Hurricanes and Wildfires

Engineers. These officials also stated that they expect the administrative costs for Hurricane Irma to decrease when program delivery levels off. See figure 16 for the actual and projected DRF obligations by program.

Figure 16: Actual and Projected Disaster Relief Fund Obligations For 2017 Hurricanes and California Wildfires, By Program and Disaster

Program and purpose	Actual and projected obligations for each program as percentages of total obligations for that disaster (dollars in millions)			
	Hurricane Harvey	Hurricane Irma	Hurricane Maria	California wildfires
Individual Assistance Provides financial assistance directly to disaster victims for the necessary expenses and serious needs that cannot be met through insurance or low-interest Small Business Administration loans, such as temporary housing assistance, counseling, unemployment compensation, or medical expenses.	47% $2,969	32% $1,371	17% $2,966	4% $60
Mission Assignment Federal Emergency Management Administration (FEMA) work orders that direct another federal agency to utilize its authorities and the resources granted to it under federal law in support of direct assistance to state, local, tribal, and territorial governments.	4% $264	12% $503	30% $5,233	60% $1,031
Public Assistance Provides financial assistance to state, tribal, territorial, and local governments for activities including debris removal; emergency protective measures; and the repair, replacement, or restoration of disaster-damaged, publicly-owned facilities.	20% $1,269	24% $1,039	33% $5,800	34% $586
Administration Costs for FEMA's delivery of disaster assistance including the salary and travel costs for the disaster workforce, rent and security expenses associated with field operation locations, and supplies and information technology for field operation staff, among other things.	28% $1,806	31% $1,342	17% $3,040	3% $48
Hazard Mitigation Provides funds to state, tribal, territorial, and local governments, among other entities, to assist communities in implementing long-term measures to help reduce the potential risk of future damages to facilities.	1% $43	2% $68	2% $380	0% $0

Source: GAO analysis of FEMA data. | GAO-18-472

Note: These cost figures reflect obligations incurred as of April 30, 2018, and obligations projected through September 30, 2018. Mission assignment obligations include obligations for Urban Search and Rescue.

Prior Relevant GAO Reports on Disaster Costs

Federal Disaster Assistance: Federal Departments and Agencies Obligated at Least $277.6 Billion during Fiscal Years 2005 through 2014. GAO-16-797. Washington, D.C.: September 22, 2016.

Federal Emergency Management Agency: Opportunities Exist to Strengthen Oversight of Administrative Costs for Major Disasters. GAO-15-65. Washington, D.C.: December 17, 2014.

Federal Disaster Assistance: Improved Criteria Needed to Assess a Jurisdiction's Capability to Respond and Recover on Its Own. GAO-12-838. Washington, D.C.: September 12, 2012.

2017 Hurricanes & Wildfires: GAO's Initial Observations (9/2018)

Appendix III: Federal Response Coordination during the 2017 Hurricanes and California Wildfires

Overview

Major disasters such as the sequence of historically powerful hurricanes and damaging wildfires experienced in 2017, pose a challenge to national emergency preparedness.

The *National Response Framework* (NRF) states that the Secretary of Homeland Security is to ensure that preparedness actions are coordinated to prevent gaps in the federal government's efforts to respond to all hazards. Further, the NRF identifies Emergency Support Functions (ESF) that serve as the federal government's primary coordinating structure for building, sustaining, and delivering response capabilities. The ESFs define specific functional areas—such as communication, transportation, and energy—for the most frequently needed capabilities during an emergency to help coordinate the provision of assets and services by departments and agencies.

FEMA executes these support functions through "mission assignments," directing another federal agency to complete a specific task and citing funding, managerial controls, and guidance.

Federal Preparedness Activities Prior to Each Hurricane

Response activity for major disasters relies on coordination among federal, state, local and territorial governments, as well as on preparedness activities at all levels. The Federal Emergency Management Agency (FEMA), in coordination with the states and territories, took several actions in advance of the hurricanes in Texas, Florida, Puerto Rico and the U.S. Virgin Islands to help prepare for the disasters, as shown in table 3.

Table 3: Examples of Federal Disaster Preparedness Activities Undertaken Prior to the 2017 Hurricanes, By Location

Preparedness Activity	Hurricane Harvey in Texas as of August 25, 2017	Hurricane Irma in Florida as of September 9, 2017	Hurricane Irma in Puerto Rico and the U.S. Virgin Islands as of September 6, 2017	Hurricane Maria in Puerto Rico and the U.S. Virgin Islands as of September 19, 2017
Urban Search and Rescue Personnel Deployed	6 task forces	1,303	1,430	276
Incident Management Assistance Teams Deployed[a]	1 national 3 regional	0 national 1 regional	2 regional	1 national 2 regional
Federal Workforce Deployed	784	16,639	2,257	2,763
Disaster Medical Assistance Teams Deployed	0	13	1	0
Number of Generators Delivered	35	0	24	4
Commodities Delivered	306,966 Meals and 96,978 liters of water delivered	4.8million meals and 9.9M liters of water delivered	1 million meals, and 2 million liters of water delivered	1,617,241 meals, and 698,570 liters of water delivered
Open Shelters	7 shelters open in a with population of 91	249 shelters open with a population of 48,739	26 shelters open with a population of 388	8 shelters open with a population of 306
Number of Emergency Support Functions Activated[b]	13 of 14	13 of 14	12 of 14	13 of 14

Source: GAO Analysis of Federal Emergency Management Agency's Senior Leadership Briefing and Recovery Snapshots for the 2017 disasters. | GAO-18-472

2017 Hurricanes & Wildfires: GAO's Initial Observations (9/2018)

Federal Response Activity for Each Disaster

There were 1,515 mission assignments—that is, an order from FEMA directing another federal agency to complete a specific task—for the 2017 hurricanes and California wildfires, and total obligations for these mission assignments was more than $7.8 billion, as of January 2018. Moreover, while all four incidents were declared major disasters—requiring Emergency Support Function (ESF) support that serve as the federal government's primary coordinating structure for building, sustaining, and delivering response capabilities, through mission assignments—the unique scale of the response activity in the territories is evident, as shown in figure 17.

Figure 17: Federal Government Response Activity and Obligations through Mission Assignments for Each 2017 Disaster, as of January 2018

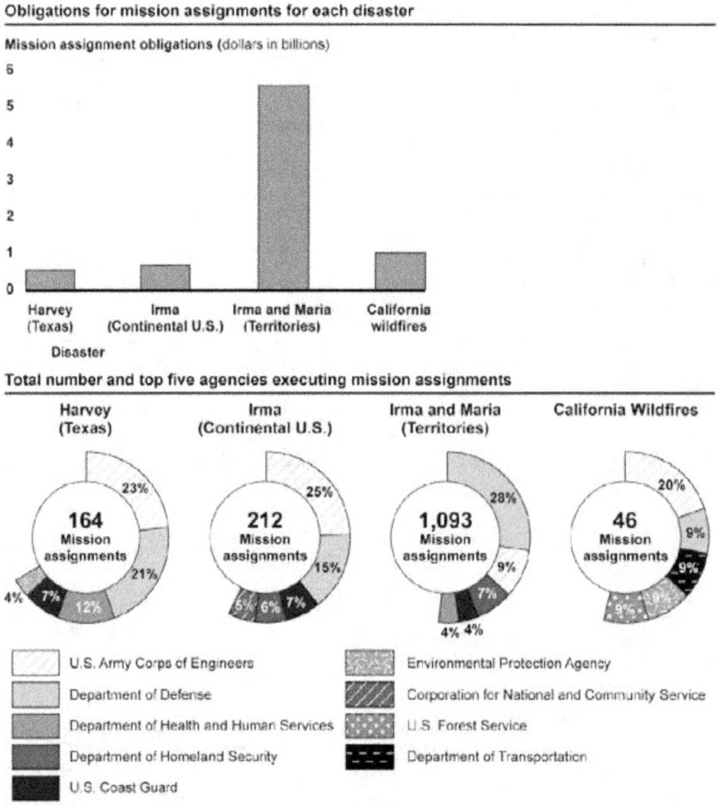

Obligations for mission assignments for each disaster

Total number and top five agencies executing mission assignments

Note: Mission assignment—that is, an order from the Federal Emergency Management Agency (FEMA) directing another federal agency to complete a specific task— totals and percentages for each agency reflect data entered into FEMA's Web-based Emergency Operations Center (WebEOC) system of approved resource requests by response officials. Data presented reflect totals and percentages where data are available. This does not include 1,285 request records (out of 3,339 total) for which data are not available to determine whether FEMA sourced the request through a

As of January 2018, the territorial response for hurricanes Irma and Maria alone resulted in more than 1,000 mission assignments and over $5.5 billion in obligations. Dozens of federal agencies provided support to FEMA and the states affected by the four disasters, but for all events, the Department of Defense (DOD) and the U.S. Army Corps of Engineers (USACE) were leading partners executing mission assignments from FEMA to support response activities. When requested, and approved by the Secretary of Defense, DOD provides Defense Support of Civil Authorities during domestic incidents and is therefore considered a support agency to all ESFs. In some cases, DOD received a greater percentage of requests under the ESF than the lead coordinating agencies. For example, in response to hurricanes Irma and Maria in the territories, FEMA assigned DOD 35 requests and USACE one request for ESF 8, for which the Department of Health and Human Services (HHS) is the lead coordinating agency; whereas FEMA assigned HHS 32 requests for ESF 8. According to FEMA Office of Response and Recovery officials, the 2017 disasters challenged FEMA in many ways, necessitating a larger role for DOD due to its specialized capabilities. Further, the response efforts followed the FEMA Region II Puerto Rico and U.S. Virgin Islands Hurricane Annex planning considerations, which identifies DOD for several mission responsibilities due to the unique considerations of the Islands' location. In addition, DOD was needed for missions deemed "uncommon" such as airfield assessments and opening. For each ESF— there is a lead federal agency designated as the coordinator. The ESF coordinators oversee the preparedness activities for a particular ESF and coordinate with its primary and support agencies. See table 4 for selected examples of ESF delivered in support of all four 2017 disasters.

Table 4: Number of Mission Assignments Received By Emergency Support Function (ESF) Agencies in Response to the 2017 Disasters and Selected Examples of Support, as of January 29, 2018

ESF #1: Transportation
Coordinator: Department of Transportation

Harvey	3	In response to Hurricane Harvey in Texas, the Department of Transportation and the Federal Transit Administration received a mission assignment from the Federal Emergency Management Agency (FEMA) deploying personnel to assist with assessing the damages to public transit systems and associated costs.
Irma in the Mainland	4	
Irma and Maria in the territories	51	
California Wildfires	4	

ESF #2: Communications
Coordinator: DHS /National Communications System

Harvey	2	In response to Hurricane Irma in Florida, the General Services Administration received a mission assignment from FEMA deploying personnel to assist with disaster response operations at various locations.
Irma in the Mainland	2	
Irma and Maria in the territories	14	
California Wildfires	2	

ESF #3: Public Works and Engineering
Coordinator: U.S. Army Corps of Engineers

Harvey	35	In response to the hurricanes in the U.S. Virgin Islands, the U. S. Army Corps of Engineers received a mission assignment from FEMA to provide temporary roofing for the territory in support of response operations. This included deploying the temporary roofing team and implementing contracting processes to provide temporary support.
Irma in the Mainland	44	
Irma and Maria in the territories	96	

   GAO-18-472 2017 Hurricanes and Wildfires

2017 Hurricanes & Wildfires: GAO's Initial Observations (9/2018)

California Wildfires	8	

		In response to the California wildfires, the U.S. Forest Service and the Department of Interior received a mission assignment from FEMA to provide fire assistance and suppression implementation planning.
Harvey	4	
Irma in the Mainland	3	
Irma and Maria in the territories	31	
California Wildfires	5	

		In response to the flooding related to Hurricane Harvey, the U.S. Geological Survey received a mission assignment from FEMA to provide advance support, real-time field measurements, and daily reporting of water heights for counties along the Gulf of Mexico coast.
Harvey	4	
Irma in the Mainland	1	
Irma and Maria in the territories	74	
California Wildfires	1	

		In response to Hurricane Irma in Florida, the Department of Housing and Urban Development received a mission assignment from FEMA to support multiple programs providing shelter to disaster survivors. For example, assessing and coordinating assistance to elderly populations in the Transitional Shelter Assistance Program, coordinating with public housing authorities on timelines for repairs to damaged units; and efforts to ensure Fair Housing Act compliance.
Harvey	4	
Irma in the Mainland	5	
Irma and Maria in the territories	20	
California Wildfires	0	

		In response to hurricanes Irma and Maria in Puerto Rico, the Defense Logistics Agency received a mission assignment from FEMA to provide 82 million commercial "meals ready to eat" in support of response operations.
Harvey	5	
Irma in the Mainland	5	
Irma and Maria in the territories	122	
California Wildfires	3	

		In response to damages from Hurricane Maria on the island of St. Croix, in the U.S. Virgin Islands, the DOD received a mission assignment from FEMA to provide deployable temporary medical facilities to the island.
Harvey	18	
Irma in the Mainland	7	
Irma and Maria in the territories	70	
California Wildfires	2	

		In response to the historic flooding caused by Hurricane Harvey in Texas, multiple agencies—including U.S. Customs and Border Protection, U.S. Coast Guard, and the Department of Fish and Wildlife—received mission assignments from FEMA to provide boating equipment to move up to 20,000 survivors.
Harvey	13	
Irma in the Mainland	5	
Irma and Maria in the territories	15	

2017 Hurricanes & Wildfires: GAO's Initial Observations (9/2018)

California Wildfires	1	
ESF #10: Oil and Hazardous Materials Coordinator: Environmental Protection Agency		
Harvey	7	In response to Hurricane Irma in Florida, the Environmental Protection Agency received a mission assignment from FEMA to support the assessment and response operations to actual or threatened hazardous substances and oil releases to remove the threat of danger or contamination to the public.
Irma in the Mainland	14	
Irma and Maria in the territories	27	
California Wildfires	4	
ESF #11: Agricultural and Natural Resources Coordinator: Department of Agriculture		
Harvey	2	In response to hurricanes Irma and Maria, the U.S. Department of Agriculture received a mission assignment from FEMA to provide personnel with technical expertise in responding to animal and agricultural health issues, agricultural emergency management, and nutrition assistance in support of response operations in Puerto Rico.
Irma in the Mainland	4	
Irma and Maria in the territories	15	
California Wildfires	3	
ESF #12: Energy Coordinator: Department of Energy		
Harvey	1	The U.S. Department of Energy received a mission assignment from FEMA to provide subject matter experts in electrical distribution, transmission, generation, energy efficiency, renewable energy and related topics to advise the U.S. Army Corps of Engineers on the assessment, planning and reconstruction of the electrical grid in Puerto Rico following Hurricane Maria.
Irma in the Mainland	3	
Irma and Maria in the territories	32	
California Wildfires	3	
ESF #13: Public Safety and Security Coordinator: Department of Justice		
Harvey	7	The Federal Protective Services received a mission assignment from FEMA to provide security guard service at FEMA facilities in Southern California, following the 2017 wildfires.
Irma	3	
Maria	39	
Wildfires	4	
ESF #15: External Affairs Coordinator: DHS		
Harvey	0	DOD received a mission assignment from FEMA to provide support to distribute emergency messages in support of Hurricane Irma response operations in the U.S. Virgin Islands.
Irma	0	
Maria	49	
Wildfires	0	

Source: FEMA. | GAO-18-472

Note: Mission assignment data for each ESF and disaster reflect data entered into FEMA's Web-based Emergency Operations Center (WebEOC) system of approved resource requests by response officials. This does not include 591 records for which data are not available to determine which ESF response officials identified for the mission assignment. ESF data for Maria includes obligations that stemmed from Hurricane Irma's impact on the U.S. Virgin Islands and Puerto Rico. ESF 14 is no longer in use as of 2011. When requested, and approved by the Secretary of Defense, DOD provides Defense Support of Civil Authorities during domestic incidents and is therefore considered a support agency to all ESFs. In some cases, DOD received a greater percentage of requests under the ESF than the lead coordinating agencies. According to FEMA Office of Response and Recovery officials, the 2017 disasters challenged FEMA in many ways, necessitating a larger role for DOD due to its specialized capabilities. Further, the response efforts followed the FEMA Region II Puerto Rico and U.S. Virgin Islands Hurricane Annex planning considerations, which identifies DOD for several mission responsibilities due to the unique considerations of the Islands' location. In addition, DOD was needed for missions deemed "uncommon" such as airfield assessments and opening.

Prior Relevant GAO Reports on Federal Coordination in Disaster Response

Emergency Preparedness: Opportunities Exist to Strengthen Interagency Assessments and Accountability for Closing Capability Gaps. GAO-15-20. Washington, D.C.: Published December 4, 2014 and reissued December 9, 2015.

Federal Emergency Management Agency: Progress and Continuing Challenges in National Preparedness Efforts. GAO-16-560T. Washington, D.C.: April 12, 2016.

Disaster Response: FEMA Has Made Progress Implementing Key Programs, but Opportunities for Improvement Exist. GAO-16-87. Washington, D.C.: February 5, 2016.

Appendix IV: Federal Contracting for the 2017 Hurricanes

Historically, federal contracts comprise a large share of federal expenditures for hurricane response and recovery efforts. It can take years to fully account for federal contract obligations resulting from a hurricane. For example, federal agencies are still making contract obligations as part of the recovery efforts as far back as hurricanes Sandy and Katrina, which occurred in 2012 and 2005, respectively. According to early estimates, the 2017 hurricanes are among the most expensive hurricanes in terms of federal contract obligations since 2005, when agencies began tracking information by hurricane.

Advance Contracting

To facilitate a faster response, FEMA and USACE identify goods and services that are typically needed for disaster response and establish contracts for them—known as advance contracts—prior to the disasters. As of January 31, 2018, FEMA reported that it had obligated over $2.4 billion through advance contracts for products and services such as prefabricated buildings, food, and inspection services, in response to hurricanes Harvey, Irma, and Maria. As of the same date, USACE reported that it obligated about $555 million through its advance contracts for services such as temporary power, temporary roofing, and debris removal.

Competition

Across all three hurricanes, we found that as of January 31, 2018, the overall competition rate—the percentage of total obligations reported under competitive contracts—was 81 percent.

Total Contract Obligations for Hurricanes Harvey, Irma, and Maria

A number of federal departments procured goods and services in response to the three 2017 hurricanes. As of January 31, 2018, the Department of Homeland Security (DHS), which includes the Federal Emergency Management Agency (FEMA), and the Department of Defense (DOD), which include the U.S. Army Corps of Engineers (USACE), accounted for approximately 96 percent of total contract obligations[3] across 21 federal departments.[4] As of January 31, 2018, federal departments had obligated over $6.2 billion for contracts in support of the response and recovery efforts for hurricanes Harvey, Irma, and Maria. Figure 18 provides details on agencies' contract obligations in support of the three hurricanes.

Figure 18: Contract Obligations in Support of Hurricanes Harvey, Irma, and Maria Response Efforts, by Agency, through January 31, 2018

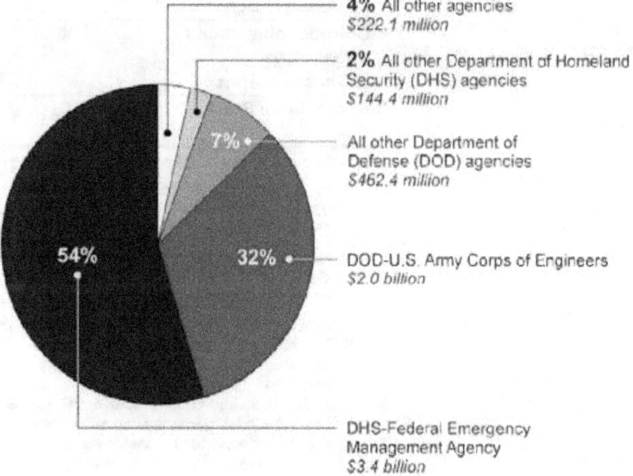

Source: GAO analysis of Federal Procurement Data System-Next Generation data. | GAO-18-472

[3] For the purposes of this appendix, contract obligations include obligations against what the General Services Administration's Federal Procurement Data System-Next Generation (FPDS-NG) categorizes as definitive vehicles (definitive contracts and purchase orders that have a defined scope of work that do not allow for individual orders under them), and against what FPDS-NG categorizes as indefinite delivery vehicles (orders under the Federal Supply Schedule, orders/calls under blanket purchase agreements, orders under basic ordering agreements, orders under government-wide acquisition contracts, and orders under other indefinite delivery vehicles, such as indefinite delivery, indefinite quantity contracts).

[4] In addition to DOD and DHS, the following departments had contract obligations in support of hurricanes Harvey, Irma, and Maria response efforts: the departments of Agriculture, Commerce, Energy, Health and Human Services, Housing and Urban Development, Interior, Justice, State, Transportation, Treasury, and Veterans Affairs; the Agency for International Development; the Broadcasting Board of Governors; the Corporation for National and Community Service; the Environmental Protection Agency; the General Services Administration; the National Aeronautics and Space Administration; the Social Security Administration; and the Small Business Administration.

Each of the three 2017 hurricanes hit different geographic locations and caused varying degrees of destruction, from flooding and wind damage to massive power outages. As such, contract obligations varied by hurricane in terms of amount and whether they were for products or services, as shown in table 5.

Table 5: Contracting Information by 2017 Hurricane through January 31, 2018

	Harvey	Irma	Maria
Total Contract Obligations (Dollars in millions)	1,364	1,026	3,826
Percent obligated by Federal Emergency Management Agency (%)	79	71	41
Percent obligated by U.S. Army Corps of Engineers(%)	4	3	50
Contract obligations for products (Dollars in millions)	649	213	1,259
Contract obligations for services (Dollars in millions)	715	813	2,567
Competition Rate (%)	82	7%	81

Source: GAO analysis of Federal Procurement Data System-Next Generation data I GAO-18-472

Note: For the purposes of this appendix, competition rate is the percentage of total obligations associated with contracts awarded competitively. We calculated competition rates as the percentage of obligations on competitive contracts over all obligations on contracts annually.

Numbers may not add due to rounding. Examples of products procured through contracts include food, water, and shelter; while examples of services include power restoration and the repair or alteration of damaged buildings.

Competitive contracts included contracts and orders coded in the Federal Procurement Data System-Next Generation (FPDS-NG) as "full and open competition," "full and open after exclusion of sources," and "competed under simplified acquisition procedures," as well as orders coded as "subject to fair opportunity" and as "fair opportunity given," and "competitive set aside." Noncompetitive contracts included contracts and orders coded in FPDS-NG as "not competed," "not available for competition," and "not competed under simplified acquisition procedures," as well as orders coded as an exception to "subject to fair opportunity," including "urgency," "only one source," "minimum guarantee," "follow-on action following competitive initial action," "other statutory authority," and "sole source."

Approximately $3 billion of the $6.2 billion in contracts obligated for the three hurricanes as of January 31, 2018, was obligated through advance contracts. Table 6 provides additional details on FEMA and USACE obligations on advance contracts.

2017 Hurricanes & Wildfires: GAO's Initial Observations (9/2018)

	Harvey	Irma	Maria
Obligations on Advance Contracts (Dollars in millions)	948	566	1,493
Federal Emergency Management Agency (Dollars in millions)	940	536	975
U.S. Army Corps of Engineers (Dollars in millions)	7	30	518

Source: GAO analysis of Department of Homeland Security and Department of Defense data. | GAO-18-472

Note: Numbers may not add due to rounding. Advance contracts are contracts identified and established prior to a disaster, for goods and services that are typically needed during a disaster response.

Federal agencies procured a variety of products and services through contracts in response to the hurricanes, obligating more than $2.1 billion for products and about $4.1 billion for services. Figure 19 identifies the top five product groups in terms of contract obligations, and the proportion of obligations for each hurricane. These contracts include life-sustaining products such as food, water, and power for survivors.

Figure 19: Top Five Product Groups in Terms of Contract Obligations through January 31, 2018, and Proportion of Obligations by Hurricane

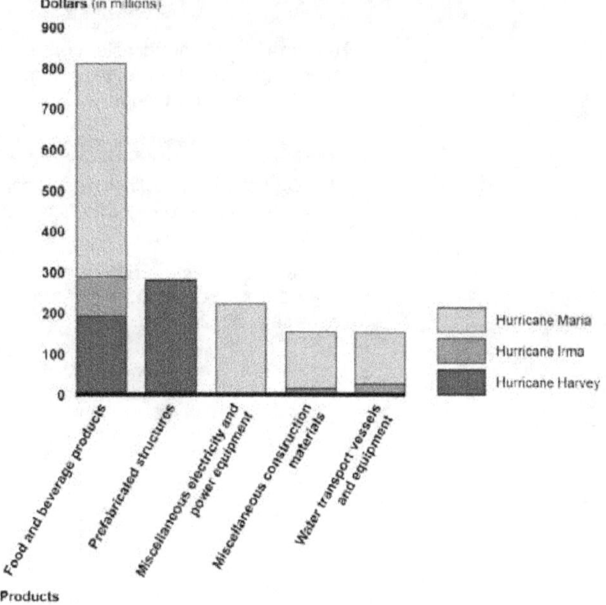

Source: GAO analysis of Federal Procurement Data System-Next Generation data. | GAO-18-472

Figure 20 identifies the top five service groups in terms of contract obligations, and the proportion of obligations for each hurricane. For example, these contracts include inspection services, such as housing inspections, and professional support services, such as support for FEMA's housing and feeding missions in the affected areas.

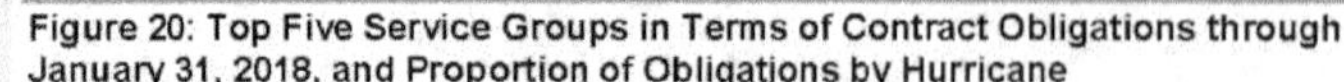

Figure 20: Top Five Service Groups in Terms of Contract Obligations through January 31, 2018, and Proportion of Obligations by Hurricane

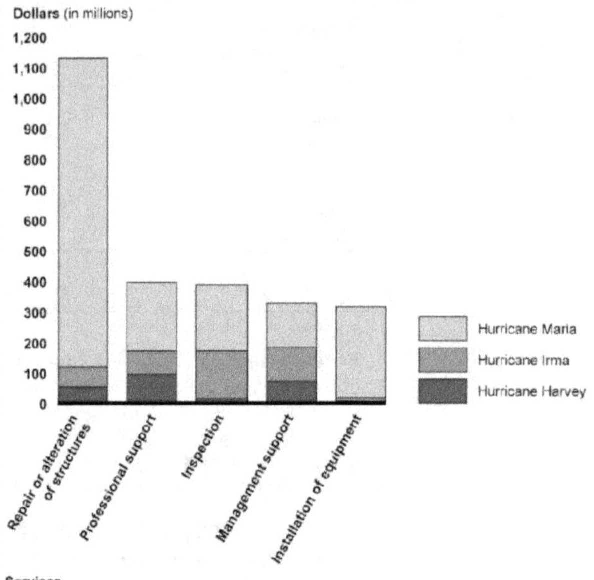

Source: GAO analysis of Federal Procurement Data System-Next Generation data. | GAO-18-472

Additional details on disaster contracting and on obligations for products and services procured for the three hurricanes can be found in our prior work on 2017 disaster contracting.

Prior Relevant GAO Reports on Disaster Contracting

2017 Disaster Contracting: Observations on Federal Contracting for Response and Recovery Efforts. GAO-18-335. Washington, D.C.: February 28, 2018.

Disaster Contracting: FEMA Needs to Cohesively Manage Its Workforce and Fully Address Post-Katrina Reforms. GAO-15-783. Washington, D.C.: September 29, 2015.

Contact

View GAO-18-472. For more information, contact Marie Mak at (202) 512-4841 or makm@gao.gov.

Appendix V: FEMA Disaster Workforce Capacity

Under the Stafford Act, FEMA has the authority to augment its permanent full-time staff with temporary personnel when needed. Additionally, during a disaster response, FEMA deploys non-FEMA employees from two workforce components—the Surge Capacity Force and the FEMA Corps. FEMA also hires locally and employs other personnel, such as contractors, to provide a variety of products and services, such as debris removal.

According to FEMA's 2014-2018 Strategic Plan, the agency's goal is to develop and manage its disaster workforce to respond to two concurrent catastrophic disasters. Although the federal disaster workforce FEMA can deploy has expanded in recent years, to over 24,000 as of August 20, 2017, the agency faced challenges training employees and maintaining staffing levels across four concurrent disasters.

In September 2017, in response to staffing shortfalls, FEMA expanded its Surge Capacity Force program to include not only volunteers from the Department of Homeland Security (DHS), but all federal employees. As of January 2018, the program had enrolled over 12,000 employees, compared to 4,033 in 2015.

FEMA Faced Challenges Responding to Sequential Disasters in Late 2017

The Federal Emergency Management Agency (FEMA) experienced challenges in recruiting and maintaining its workforce to support the hurricanes and wildfires response in 2017. Prior to landfall of Hurricane Harvey in August 2017, FEMA had already deployed staff to other long-term recovery operations. In addition, based on its internal workforce analyses, FEMA faced a staff shortage of 37 percent as of September 1, 2017. Figure 21 shows the deployment of the federal disaster personnel across the 2017 disasters.

Figure 21: Federal Disaster Workforce Deployed In Response to the 2017 Disasters from September 2017 through February 2018

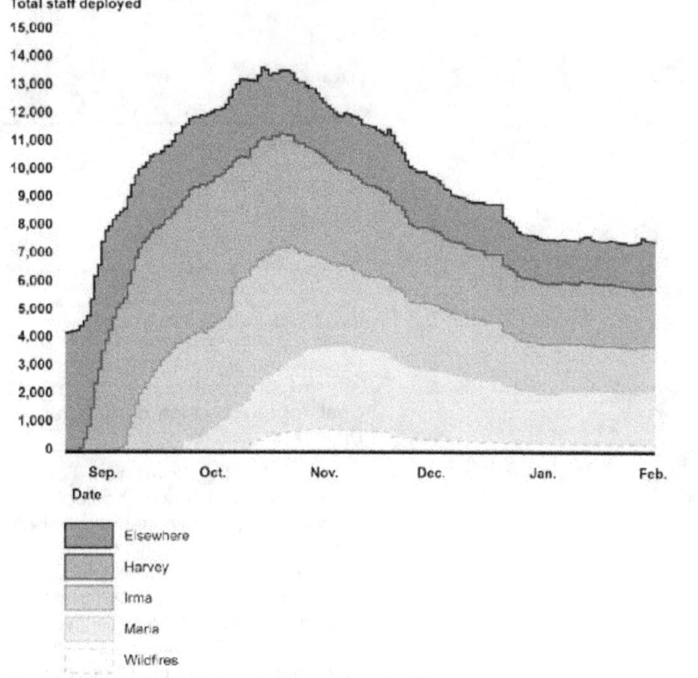

Source: GAO analysis of Department of Homeland Security data. | GAO-18-472

Note: Data include Federal Emergency Management Agency (FEMA) workforce and non-FEMA employees that FEMA can deploy during a disaster response such as the Surge Capacity Force, FEMA Corps and contractors. Data do not represent local hires or employee types such as permanent part-time, temporary part-time, and temporary incident employees.

Less than Half of FEMA's Deployed Workforce Held a Qualified Title During 2017 Disasters

FEMA faced challenges maintaining a "Qualified" workforce—a FEMA

2017 Hurricanes & Wildfires: GAO's Initial Observations (9/2018)

Qualification System designation that refers to personnel who, following an evaluation and validation of specific tasks and training requirements, are capable of independently executing their specific roles—across concurrent disasters. As shown in figure 22, at the height of workforce deployments in mid-October 2017, 54 percent of staff were serving in a capacity in which they did not hold the title of "Qualified."

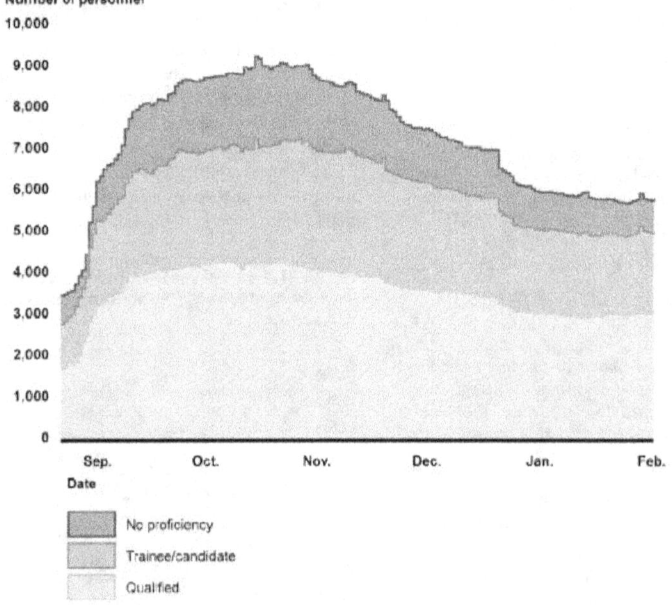

Figure 22: Federal Emergency Management Agency Qualification Levels for Deployed Staff During the 2017 Disaster Response

Source: GAO analysis of Department of Homeland Security data | GAO-18-472
Note: Data only represent FEMA employees and do not include local hires, FEMA Corps, Surge Capacity Force, contractors or employees from other federal agencies.

Observations from Affected States and Territories

Challenges Reported by Officials in Responding to Sequence of 2017 Disasters

Local and FEMA officials from Texas and California—the two states that experienced disasters at the beginning and end of the 2017 disasters season—expressed concern over FEMA's workforce capacity in responding to concurrent catastrophic disasters. FEMA and local officials in Texas said that staff were initially deployed when Hurricane Harvey landed, but some staff were re-deployed once hurricanes Irma and Maria hit. Local officials in California described the difficulty in responding to wildfires with a shortage of staff, while FEMA officials noted the exhaustion of staff re-deployed to California after returning from deployments in the areas impacted by the hurricanes—often with only a 1- or 2-day break in between. As a result, many staff were not in a state to best serve mission needs according to officials. An employee serving at the start of the 2017 hurricane season is shown in figure 23.

2017 Hurricanes & Wildfires: GAO's Initial Observations (9/2018)

Source: FEMA. | GAO-18-472

Mixed Results in Matching Surge Capacity Force Skills to Job Assignments

The Surge Capacity Force comprises DHS and other federal employees who volunteer to deploy in the event of a disaster for a maximum of 45 days of service.[5]

- Available staff as of August 2017: 6,537

- Peak deployed during 2017 disasters: 3,102

Hurricane Harvey (Texas): FEMA officials reported successes with utilizing the expertise of the Surge Capacity Force to match disaster needs by pre-collecting data on skill sets.

Hurricane Irma (Florida): FEMA officials noted the value of the Surge Capacity Force, but cited challenges with understaffing and identifying tasks that best match their skill sets (e.g. a NASA engineer could be better used to help with planning rather than loading copy paper into printers). Figure 24 shows a volunteer in Florida.

Hurricane Maria and Hurricane Irma (Puerto Rico): FEMA officials noted the success of the Surge Capacity Force, but volunteers cited concerns in matching their skill sets to disaster recovery tasks in Puerto Rico as well as disconnects between information given during training and the job requirements.

Hurricane Maria and Hurricane Irma (U.S. Virgin Islands): FEMA officials in the U.S. Virgin Islands noted the positive attitude and integration of members of the Surge Capacity Force.

California Wildfires: FEMA officials said that although the Surge Capacity Force staff were well trained in individual assistance, they were not always capable of leading teams in austere environments.

---

[5]On October 6, 2017 the Acting Secretary of DHS extended the deployment cap for voluntary extensions for 45 additional days and encouraged volunteers to speak with their supervisors regarding deployment durations.

Source: FEMA. | GAO-18-472

Concerns Raised About Reservists without Qualified Titles and Who Refused to Deploy

Reservists are FEMA first responders who are available on an on-call basis during an emergency or disaster. They must be available to deploy within 24-48 hours, and will be deployed for 30 or more days.

- Available reservists as of August 2017: 6,708

- Peak deployed during 2017 disasters: 4,645

As of May 2017, 46 percent of all FEMA reservists did not hold the title of "Qualified" for their job function and from August to November 2017 over 15 percent of eligible reservists refused at least one deployment, according to FEMA data, for medical reasons or other concerns.

Hurricane Harvey (Texas): Officials from the Joint Field Office—a multiagency coordination center established near a disaster site for coordinating major disaster response and recovery efforts—voiced concern over the deployment of unqualified reservists because training was outdated or unavailable prior to deployment.

Hurricane Irma (Florida): The FEMA Federal Coordinating Officer in Florida—who coordinates federal activities in support of the state—and Florida Division of Emergency Management officials said morale for some reservists (who made up one-third of staff in Florida during peak deployment) was low due to lengthy deployments, pay cuts, and a shortage of role models. State officials also expressed concern over the number of refusals from deployable reservists who cited medical and scheduling concerns.

Hurricane Maria and Hurricane Irma (U.S. Virgin Islands): The Federal Coordinating Officer in the U.S. Virgin Islands said many reservists were not physically fit to handle conditions on the island and a fitness test should have been required before they were eligible to deploy.

GAO-18-472 2017 Hurricanes and Wildfires

2017 Hurricanes & Wildfires: GAO's Initial Observations (9/2018)

Concerns with Turnover of Some IMAT Staff and Need for Additional Training

Hurricane Harvey (Texas): FEMA officials expressed concerns with the high turnover rate of Incident Management Assistance Team (IMAT) staff—the first FEMA emergency management staff deployed to a major disaster site— which they attributed to low pay and the challenging nature of the work.

Hurricane Maria and Hurricane Irma (U.S. Virgin Islands): FEMA officials noted that attrition is high among IMAT staff and the pay does not incentivize staff to stay. Officials also stressed the need for additional training for Region II IMAT employees alongside national IMAT teams.

Prior Relevant GAO Reports on FEMA's Workforce

Disaster Contracting: FEMA Needs to Cohesively Manage Its Workforce and Fully Address Post-Katrina Reforms. GAO-15-783. Washington, D.C.: September 29, 2015.

Federal Emergency Management Agency: Additional Planning and Data Collection Could Help Improve Workforce Management Efforts. GAO-15-437. Washington, D.C.: July 9, 2015.

Emergency Preparedness: Opportunities Exist to Strengthen Interagency Assessments and Accountability for Closing Capability Gaps. GAO-15-20. Washington, D.C.: December 4, 2014.

FEMA Reservists: Training Could Benefit from Examination of Practices at Other Agencies. GAO-13-250R. Washington, D.C.: March 22, 2013.

Disaster Assistance Workforce: FEMA Could Enhance Human Capital Management and Training. GAO-12-538. Washington, D.C.: May 25, 2012.

Federal Emergency Management Agency: Workforce Planning and Training Could Be Enhanced by Incorporating Strategic Management Principles. GAO-12-487. Washington, D.C.: April 26, 2012.

Contact

View GAO-18-472. For more information, contact Chris Currie at (404) 679-1875 or curriec@gao.gov.

2017 Hurricanes & Wildfires: GAO's Initial Observations (9/2018)

Appendix VI: FEMA's Individual Assistance Program

FEMA's IA Program aims to provide individual applicants resources to help meet their sustenance, shelter, and medical needs in the wake of a disaster. FEMA provides substantial assistance through the Individuals and Households Program (IHP)—one of five support programs under IA. The IHP includes two categories of aid:

- **Housing Assistance** which can include financial or direct assistance for temporary housing, home repairs, replacement of a primary home, and in limited locations, permanent housing construction when needed due to disaster effects.

- **Other Needs Assistance** which can include financial assistance for uninsured or underinsured, disaster-related needs, such as transportation, funeral, medical, and child care assistance. Some types of assistance are dependent on an applicant's ability to secure a Small Business Administration disaster loan.

As part of the IHP, individuals affected by disasters declared in fiscal year 2017 may be eligible for up to $33,300 in assistance. Those affected by disasters declared in fiscal year 2018 may be eligible for up to $34,000 in assistance.

In addition to the IHP, FEMA may provide assistance essential to meet immediate threats to life and property resulting from a major disaster, including emergency shelter.

FEMA Individual Assistance Program Activity to Support State Goals for Housing Recovery

The Federal Emergency Management's (FEMA) Individual Assistance (IA) program provides financial assistance and direct services to eligible individuals and households who have uninsured or underinsured necessary expenses and serious needs. In response to the unprecedented 2017 hurricane season, FEMA officials have collaborated with state, territorial and tribal governments to craft new approaches to delivering housing assistance and leverage the broad scope of available authorities under the Stafford Act to meet local needs for housing recovery. These approaches include both financial and direct housing assistance, such as:

- **Direct Lease:** FEMA provides temporary housing units directly to survivors when rental resources are unavailable. FEMA and the state of Florida are prioritizing use of this approach for housing recovery in the state.

- **Multifamily Lease and Repair:** FEMA repairs existing multi-family housing units, such as apartments, to use as temporary housing for eligible applicants who are unable to use Rental Assistance—a financial grant provided to homeowners and renters whose homes were made uninhabitable or inaccessible by the disaster, to assist with expenses to rent temporary housing—due to a lack of available resources. According to FEMA officials, this approach is among the range of options territorial officials intend to leverage to address local conditions.

- **Manufactured Housing Units and Recreational Vehicles:** These are manufactured homes or other readily fabricated dwellings (e.g., a pre-fabricated dwelling) owned by FEMA and provided to eligible applicants for use as temporary housing. Recreational Vehicles have been approved for use in response to hurricanes Harvey and Irma. This form of assistance is being implemented in Texas and Florida.

- **Permanent Housing Construction:** FEMA may provide financial assistance or direct assistance to individuals and households in insular areas outside the continental United States or in other locations where no alternative housing resources are available and where temporary housing assistance is unavailable, infeasible, or not cost-effective. Under this program, repairs can be made to ensure that a home is habitable, such as repairs to heating, ventilation, and air conditioning systems, walls, floors, and ceilings, but is not intended to restore the home to the pre-disaster condition. According to FEMA officials, this assistance was authorized in Texas, Puerto Rico, and the U.S. Virgin Islands.

- **Sheltering and Temporary Essential Power (STEP):** According to FEMA guidance, STEP was designed to assist state, territorial, and tribal governments in performing work and services essential to saving lives, protecting public health and safety, and protecting property to enable survivors to shelter at home. This approach is among the options state, territorial, and tribal officials told us that they may leverage to address local conditions.

- **Transitional Sheltering Assistance (TSA):** FEMA may provide TSA to

GAO-18-472 2017 Hurricanes and Wildfires

applicants who are unable to return to their pre-disaster primary
residence because their home is either uninhabitable or inaccessible.
The goal of TSA is to reduce the number of disaster survivors in
congregate shelters by transitioning survivors into short-term
accommodations through direct payments to lodging providers, such as
hotels. Puerto Rico used this approach despite initial concerns that this
would have a negative effect on migration away from the island territory,
according to FEMA officials.

As of February 2018, FEMA approved more than 1.6 million applications for
IHP, resulting in obligations of over $2.5 billion for Housing Assistance and
$1.1 billion for Other Needs Assistance (i.e., financial assistance for
uninsured or underinsured, disaster-related needs, such as medical), as
shown in figure 25 below. See table 7 for the number of approved applicants
for each FEMA housing and sheltering assistance type for the 2017 disasters
as of June 2018.

**Figure 25: Total Number of Applicants and Funds Awarded through FEMA's
Individuals and Households Program by 2017 Hurricane or Wildfire, as of February
28, 2018**

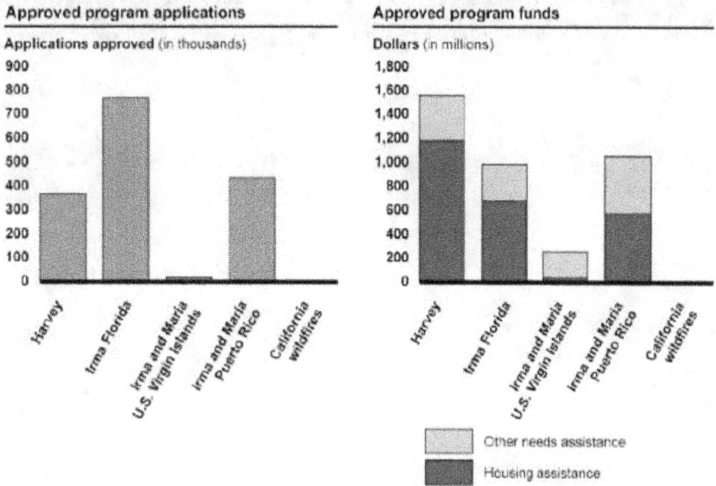

Source: Federal Emergency Management Agency's National Emergency Management Information System. | GAO-18-472

GAO-18-472 2017 Hurricanes and Wildfires

2017 Hurricanes & Wildfires: GAO's Initial Observations (9/2018)

Table 7: Number of Individual and Households Program Registrations and Approved Applicants for Each Type of Housing and Sheltering Assistance Provided by Disaster Location, as of June 22, 2018

Disaster	Total Registrations	Multifamily Lease Repair	Manufactured Housing Units and Recreational Vehicles	Permanent Housing Construction Repair Program	Direct Lease	Sheltering and Temporary Essential Power Program	Transitional Sheltering Assistance
Hurricane Harvey in Texas	895,528	0	2,848	247	131	15,578	53,894
Hurricane Irma in Florida	2,644,403	0	257	0	63	129	26,633
Hurricane Irma and Hurricane Maria in Puerto Rico	1,138,444	16	0	33	237	33,016	6,907
Hurricane Irma and Hurricane Maria in U.S. Virgin Islands	39,415	0	0	0	61	1,920	0
California wildfires	25,425	0	154	0	94	0	618
Total	4,743,215	16	3,259	280	586	50,643	88,052

Note: Total registrations represent the number of survivors who applied for disaster assistance at each disaster location. However, the number of registrations for the Sheltering and Temporary Essential Power Program may be different because the Sheltering and Temporary Essential Power Program is separate from FEMA's Individuals and Households Program and is not included in the registration process. Disaster survivors interested in the Sheltering and Temporary Essential Power Program must first apply for FEMA's Individuals and Households Program assistance and then apply directly to the State, Territorial, or Tribal entity administering the Sheltering and Temporary Essential Power Program.

2017 Hurricanes & Wildfires: GAO's Initial Observations (9/2018)

Texas – Hurricane Harvey

FEMA entered into an agreement with the Texas General Land Office to
provide for housing recovery, marking the first time the agency has
coordinated with a non-federal agency to provide this housing service,
according to FEMA officials. State officials in Texas will be implementing the
new housing approach to manage the delivery of direct housing to more than
6,600 applicants whom FEMA has determined are eligible for direct
assistance. FEMA has approved the following direct housing options for
eligible applicants in Texas: Permanent Housing Construction Repairs, Direct
Lease, Multifamily Lease and Repair, Manufactured Housing Units, and
Recreational Vehicles. Local officials cited several advantages to the new
housing approach such as the ability to keep homeowners and families in
their district thereby sustaining a jurisdiction's tax revenue, supporting
businesses, and maintaining public education funding.

Florida – Hurricane Irma

In Florida, state officials preferred to utilize the Direct Lease option to
leverage the high volume of vacation rentals, particularly in Lee, Collier, and
Monroe counties. FEMA authorized the use of recreational vehicles,
purchased directly from commercial dealers, for use as temporary housing, in
addition to manufactured homes, as shown in figure 26. FEMA officials
estimated that manufactured homes can cost up to $113,000 while the travel
trailers are about $60,000. According to FEMA officials, the decision whether
to use the manufactured home, travel trailer or Direct Lease housing options
depends on the availability of feasible sites. A FEMA official visits each
resident in FEMA housing monthly to check on their progress in transitioning
out to their own housing, according to FEMA officials.

2017 Hurricanes & Wildfires: GAO's Initial Observations (9/2018)

Source: GAO. | GAO-18-472

Puerto Rico – Hurricane Irma and Hurricane Maria

In Puerto Rico, all five IA programs are approved—the Individuals and Households Program, Crisis Counseling, Disaster Legal Services, Disaster Case Management, and Disaster Unemployment Assistance. As of December 2017, more than 1 million residents had applied for IA and FEMA officials extended the deadline to apply through March 2018. FEMA officials told us that they anticipated needing to assist residents in taking next steps to follow up on their applications and collect funds.

According to FEMA officials, they are also using multiple programs and authorities to provide aid to residents with housing needs, including the Direct Lease and the Multifamily Lease and Repair Programs, and the Permanent Housing Construction Repair Program. FEMA is also providing sheltering and emergency assistance through the TSA program, and the STEP program (known as Tu Hogar Renace - Your Home Reborn in Puerto Rico), among others. For example, under STEP, repairs can be done while homeowners remain in place, and the program may provide up to $20,000 for repairs (although the Federal Coordinating Officer—the lead federal official in charge of response—has the discretion to approve greater costs to accommodate a household's access and functional needs or when the home requires a generator). FEMA estimates that STEP assistance may be provided for 80,000 homes or more. As of June 22, 2018, FEMA had approved 33,016 survivors to use the program in Puerto Rico.

U.S. Virgin Islands – Hurricane Irma and Hurricane Maria

Local officials said they plan to address a shortage of housing through unique housing routes—for example, structured tents, which are used in military operations and are built to withstand 140 mph winds.

2017 Hurricanes & Wildfires: GAO's Initial Observations (9/2018)

California Wildfires

According to California officials, in partnership with FEMA, they established a Housing Task Force to determine how to provide direct housing assistance to thousands of applicants in a timely manner, and incorporate lessons learned from prior wildfire disaster experiences in the state. The task force is also examining options to convert campgrounds into temporary housing.

Prior Relevant GAO Reports on FEMA's Individual Assistance Program

Federal Disaster Assistance: Individual Assistance Requests Often Granted, but FEMA Could Better Document Factors Considered. GAO-18-366. Washington, D.C: May 31, 2018.

2017 Hurricanes & Wildfires: GAO's Initial Observations (9/2018)

Appendix VII: Fraud Risk Management in FEMA's Disaster Assistance Programs

Overview

Effective fraud risk management, including controls to prevent, detect, and respond to fraud, can help ensure that federal disaster assistance programs serve their intended purpose, taxpayer dollars are spent effectively, and government assets are safeguarded.

Our Fraud Risk Framework provides a guide for federal program managers to use when developing or enhancing efforts to combat fraud in a strategic, risk-based manner. The framework includes leading practices in four components: (1) Commit to combating fraud; (2) Assess fraud risks; (3) Design and implement a strategy with specific control activities; and (4) Evaluate and adapt fraud risk management activities.

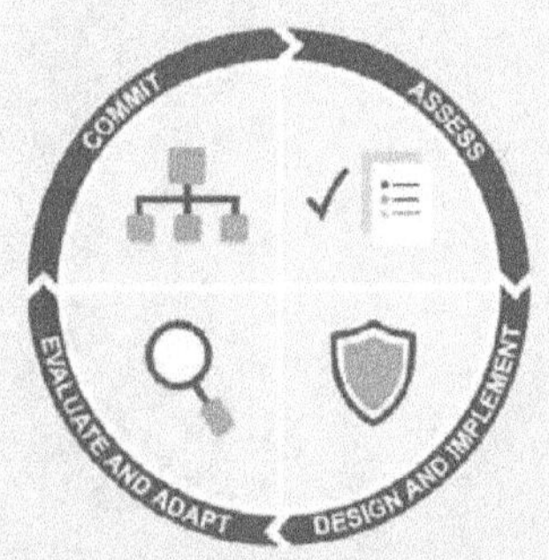

Source: GAO. | GAO-18-472

Further, the Fraud Reduction and Data Analytics Act of 2015 requires agencies to establish financial and administrative controls that incorporate the Fraud Risk Framework's leading practices.

Observations from Prior Work and Affected States and Territories

The size and scope of the 2017 hurricanes and California wildfires raises questions about the ability of Federal Emergency Management Agency (FEMA) program managers to balance the need to quickly deliver benefits and services while minimizing the risk of fraud, waste, and abuse. Balancing these goals is particularly important given the amount of funds involved—as of June 2018, at least $120 billion had been appropriated to the Department of Homeland Security (DHS), including FEMA, and 18 other federal agencies for activities related to the 2017 disasters.[6]

Since the mid-2000s, FEMA has taken some steps to address identified fraud risks in its disaster assistance programs. Specifically, our prior work found that FEMA strengthened its fraud prevention controls and took other actions to address fraud risks in the Individuals and Households Program (IHP)—one component of the Individual Assistance program.[7] As a result, we identified about $39 million (2.7 percent) of IHP assistance provided following Hurricane Sandy in 2012 that was at risk of being improper or fraudulent, compared to between $600 million and $1.4 billion (10 to 22 percent) of similar assistance provided following hurricanes Katrina and Rita in 2005.

However, the 2017 disasters highlighted the challenges FEMA may continue to face with fraud risks. According to FEMA officials, FEMA identified a well-organized and coordinated identity theft fraud scheme that affected Texas, Florida, Puerto Rico, the U.S. Virgin Islands, and California—a scheme it had not identified following prior disasters. Further, officials from one county we visited as part of this review expressed concern about the risk of fraud and the county's ability to handle disaster payment activities given the volume of transactions the county expects. Moreover, we have previously reported that changes within a program—such as changes in the implementation of the Individual Assistance and Public Assistance programs in areas impacted by the 2017 disasters—can affect the extent to which controls continue to be effective or appropriate for addressing fraud risks.[8]

As described below, FEMA took some steps to address identified fraud risks following the 2017 disasters and earlier events. We are continuing to assess the extent to which FEMA's actions to manage fraud risks in the Public Assistance program align with leading practices described in our Fraud Risk Framework.[9]

---

[6] Supplemental Appropriations for Disaster Relief Requirements Act, 2017, Pub. L. No. 115-56, div. B, 131 Stat. 1129, 1136 (2017); Additional Supplemental Appropriations for Disaster Relief Requirements Act, 2017 Pub. L. No. 115-72, div. A, 131 Stat. 1224, 1224 (2017); Further Additional Supplemental Appropriations for Disaster Relief Requirements Act, 2018, Pub. L. No. 115-123, div. B, subdiv. 1, 132 Stat. 64, 65 (2018).

[7] GAO, *Hurricane Sandy: FEMA Has Improved Disaster Aid Verification but Could Act to Further Limit Improper Assistance*, GAO-15-15 (Washington, D.C.: Dec. 12, 2014).

[8] GAO, *A Framework for Managing Fraud Risks in Federal Programs*, GAO-15-593SP (Washington, D.C.: July 28, 2015).

[9] GAO-15-593SP

GAO-18-472 2017 Hurricanes and Wildfires

Commit: Commit to combating fraud by creating an organizational culture and structure conducive to fraud risk management.

The first component of the Fraud Risk Framework calls for agencies to, among other things, designate an entity to design and oversee fraud risk management activities and to involve all levels of the agency in setting an antifraud tone. Multiple entities within FEMA have designated responsibilities related to fraud risk management. Specifically, the Fraud and Internal Investigations Division (FIID), established in response to fraud associated with major hurricanes in the mid-2000s, is responsible for identifying, mitigating, and preventing fraudulent losses of federal funds and assets by, among other things, reviewing FEMA programs to identify potential improvements to internal controls to prevent and detect fraud, waste, and abuse. In addition, the Director of Risk Management and Compliance is responsible for assisting FIID in the development of antifraud controls. FEMA's Fraud Prevention and Investigation Directive, signed by the Administrator of FEMA in 2014, establishes antifraud responsibilities for several other entities within FEMA, including the Administrator, Regional Administrators, and the Chief Financial Officer, among others. Further, the directive requires all FEMA employees, contractors, and other personnel to take all necessary and proper actions to eliminate fraud, waste, and abuse in FEMA programs.

FIID provides detailed fraud awareness and prevention training—a key responsibility of antifraud entities, according to the Fraud Risk Framework— to FEMA staff, including those responsible for processing disaster assistance applications, according to FIID officials. Increasing employees' awareness of potential fraud schemes—by providing training to stakeholders responsible for program implementation—can help create a culture of integrity and help enable employees to better detect potential fraud.

For the 2017 disasters, FIID added fraud alerts and updates to the daily, pre-shift briefings provided to FEMA IHP intake personnel. These briefings communicated information that the Fraud Risk Framework identifies as key to effective antifraud training, including how to report suspicions of fraud, waste, and abuse; procedures registration and intake personnel and processing staff should follow if an application involves possible fraud or a high-risk applicant; and information on emerging fraud risks and trends identified during the 2017 disasters.

Assess: Plan regular fraud risk assessments and assess risks to determine a fraud risk profile.

The second component of the Fraud Risk Framework calls for federal managers to identify and assess risks, examine the suitability of existing fraud controls, document a fraud risk profile, and prioritize and determine responses to remaining risks. FEMA has taken some actions to identify and assess fraud risks related to the 2017 disasters. After identifying the identity theft fraud scheme following the 2017 disasters, FEMA hired a contractor in December 2017 to identify and assess fraud risks to the Individual Assistance program, including identifying FEMA stakeholders' fraud risk tolerance and developing a fraud risk profile. In addition, the tasks listed in the contract include, among other things, using the fraud risk profile to assess FEMA's existing controls, reviewing data from past incidents of fraud to identify any control gaps and deficiencies, and making recommendations on ways to improve or add controls. The estimated completion date for the

        GAO-18-472 2017 Hurricanes and Wildfires

2017 Hurricanes & Wildfires: GAO's Initial Observations (9/2018)

contracted work is August 2018. In addition to the contracted work, FIID is responsible for independently reviewing FEMA programs to identify potential improvements to internal controls to prevent and detect fraud, waste, and abuse. FIID has conducted four reviews of the IHP since 2014 to determine if any indications of fraud are associated with applicants' case files. These reviews did not identify any needed program improvements, according to a FIID official.

FEMA does not have plans to award a contract to identify and assess fraud risks in its Public Assistance program, according to FEMA officials. Instead, according to FEMA's monitoring plan, FEMA incorporates consideration of fraud risk as part of its monitoring approach for Public Assistance grant recipients and conducts a risk assessment of recipients on a rotating, 2-year schedule. Specifically, to determine a grant recipient's risk level, FEMA considers patterns that may reflect recipient issues, such as a history of irregularities in expenditures, a history of disallowed or inappropriate use of funds, and risk of fraud, waste, and abuse. In addition, FEMA considers other factors, such as audit findings, changes in recipient staff, and the dollar value of the grant. According to FEMA officials, FEMA implemented additional controls in Puerto Rico for the Public Assistance grant program based on the results of its risk assessment of Puerto Rico. The additional controls include a manual drawdown process that requires the territorial government of Puerto Rico to fully substantiate all costs claimed for reimbursement before FEMA will authorize the funds for release. In similar risk assessments, FEMA found that grants provided to the U.S. Virgin Islands for recovery from hurricanes Irma and Maria were medium-to-high risk. As a result, FEMA determined it would conduct an onsite monitoring visit for these grants in 2018.

Design and Implement: Design and implement a strategy with specific control activities to mitigate assessed fraud risks and collaborate to help ensure effective implementation.

The third component of the Fraud Risk Framework calls for federal managers to design, implement, and document an antifraud strategy with specific control activities—including reporting mechanisms, data-analytics activities, and fraud-awareness initiatives, among others—to mitigate assessed fraud risks. Further, the Fraud Risk Framework identifies the consideration of the benefits and costs of control activities to address fraud risks as a leading practice, as it can help managers determine if the benefits of a control activity exceed its costs—such as delays for legitimate applicants. During the 2017 disasters, FEMA took steps to design and implement the following antifraud controls, among others:

- **Reporting mechanisms**: Members of the public and FEMA staff have multiple options to report potential fraud, and FEMA publicized these reporting mechanisms following the 2017 disasters in several ways. For example, FEMA's webpages related to Hurricane Harvey in Texas and Hurricane Irma in Florida include examples of fraud schemes, how to report fraud by phone or email to the National Center for Disaster Fraud, and a link to the fraud website for the DHS Office of the Inspector General fraud, waste, and abuse hotline. We also observed disaster fraud hotline posters on display in the Joint Field Office in San Juan, Puerto Rico. The posters—in both English and Spanish—included multiple options for reporting potential fraud, as shown by the example in figure 27. The Fraud Risk Framework identifies establishing reporting mechanisms, including hotlines and other mechanisms for receiving tips, as a leading practice for managing fraud risks. Further, the Fraud Risk Framework notes that it

    GAO-18-472   2017 Hurricanes and Wildfires

2017 Hurricanes & Wildfires: GAO's Initial Observations (9/2018)

is a leading practice for managers to provide multiple options for potential reporters of fraud to communicate and to promote the existence of reporting mechanisms.

Figure 27: Examples of Disaster Fraud Hotline Posters Displayed in the Joint Field Office in San Juan, Puerto Rico

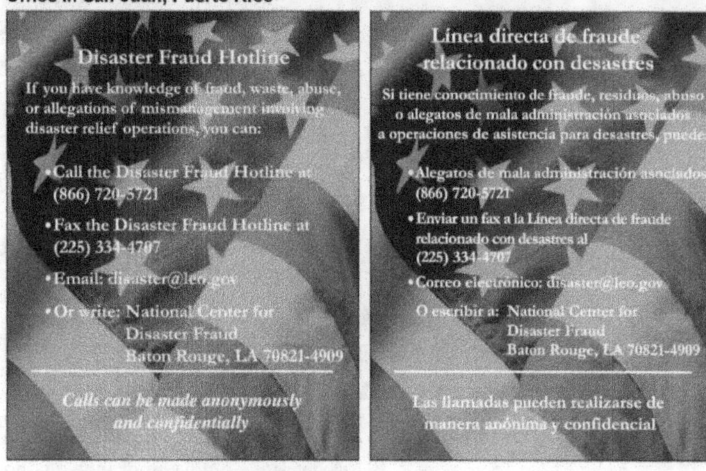

Source: National Center for Disaster Fraud. | GAO-18-472

- **Data-analytics activities:** According to the DHS Fiscal Year 2017 Agency Financial Report, FIID conducts data mining of FEMA's databases to identify IHP applications containing common indicators of fraud. The Fraud Risk Framework identifies the implementation of data-analytics activities, including data mining to identify red flags that may indicate suspicious activity, as a leading practice for detecting potential fraud. According to FIID officials, FIID uses data-mining queries to identify red flags, such as indicators that a damaged dwelling may not be the applicant's primary residence, or instances in which the same Social Security Number was used for different damaged dwellings.

  After FIID officials became aware of the identity theft fraud scheme, FIID ran new queries for the 2017 disasters to flag applications with indicators of this scheme, such as applications with questionable banking information, and subjected these cases to additional validation, according to FEMA officials. About 30 percent of Individual Assistance applications in California were flagged as potentially fraudulent because they matched at least one of these queries, which caused a delay in the distribution of funds to actual survivors, according to FEMA officials. According to a FEMA official, the process appears to have been effective at stopping payment on fraudulent applications, although not all of the identified applications were necessarily fraudulent as they may have met one of the flags for legitimate reasons. FEMA will need to assess the process, including the delay for legitimate applicants, according to the FEMA official. According to the contract to identify and assess fraud risks to the Individual Assistance program, the contractor is to develop an implementation strategy, including a cost-benefit analysis, for recommended improvements to existing controls or development of additional controls.

Further, FEMA has taken steps to improve its antifraud controls to prevent and detect fraud and improper payments in response to our findings and recommendations from prior reports. For example, in 2008 FEMA began requiring, among other things, that an inspector meet with an applicant to verify occupancy and confirm that a property was damaged after we identified instances in which FEMA made IHP payments to applicants who used ineligible or bogus addresses following hurricanes Katrina and Rita in 2005.[10] Also, after we determined that FEMA made nearly $17 million in potentially fraudulent or otherwise improper rental assistance payments to individuals through the IHP after they had moved into FEMA trailers following hurricanes Katrina and Rita, we recommended that FEMA take steps to address the issue.[11] In January 2010, FEMA addressed this recommendation by upgrading its data system to display all housing assistance an applicant had received, improving the ability of FEMA caseworkers to identify potential overlapping assistance.

In addition to designing antifraud control activities, collaboration with stakeholders is essential to help ensure that antifraud controls are implemented effectively, according to the Fraud Risk Framework. Specifically, the framework notes that a leading practice for establishing collaborative relationships is to provide guidance and other support to help external parties, such as state and local officials, effectively carry out fraud risk management activities. According to FEMA officials, FEMA offers technical assistance, such as programmatic eligibility reviews, to help prevent fraud and established the Procurement Disaster Assistance Team in 2014 to help increase grant compliance among recipients and subrecipients. The Procurement Disaster Assistance Team is tasked with proactively developing and providing training and guidance materials. Officials from one county in California receiving Public Assistance grant funds that we interviewed noted that they received training from FEMA on fraud issues, although officials from another county we interviewed indicated that additional training could be helpful.

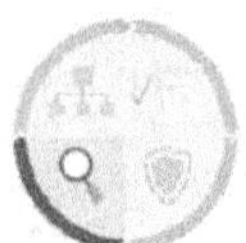

Evaluate and Adapt: Evaluate outcomes using a risk-based approach and adapt activities to improve fraud risk management.

Finally, the Fraud Risk Framework calls for agencies to evaluate outcomes using a risk-based approach and adapt activities to improve fraud risk management. FEMA has taken steps to measure outcomes of its antifraud approach for the IHP. FIID evaluates the success of its antifraud approach for the IHP—which has shifted from a reactive to a preventative model, according to FEMA officials—by comparing the amount of potentially fraudulent funds it has prevented from being disbursed with what is submitted for recoupment. Specifically, according to the DHS Fiscal Year 2017 Agency Financial Report, FIID locks IHP applicant files that contain common indicators of fraud in order to prevent fraudulent funds from being disbursed. As a result, according to the report, FIID prevented $20.6 million from being disbursed in fiscal year 2017 and submitted $3.6 million for recoupment, compared with fiscal year 2014 when it prevented $4.4 million from being disbursed and submitted $7.2 million for recoupment.

---

[10]GAO, *Hurricanes Katrina and Rita: Unprecedented Challenges Exposed the Individuals and Households Program to Fraud and Abuse; Actions Needed to Reduce Such Problems in Future*, GAO-06-1013 (Washington, D.C.: Sept. 27, 2006).

[11]GAO, *Hurricanes Katrina and Rita Disaster Relief: Continued Findings of Fraud, Waste, and Abuse*, GAO-07-300 (Washington, D.C.: Mar. 15, 2007).

In addition, FIID takes steps to adapt its antifraud data analytics for the IHP. According to FEMA officials, after FIID identified the identity theft fraud scheme following the 2017 disasters, FEMA suspended emergency payments for critical needs to over 200,000 suspicious applicants in Texas, Florida, Georgia, Puerto Rico, and the U.S. Virgin Islands, which prevented millions of dollars in potentially fraudulent disaster payments from being disbursed. FIID also evaluates the success of its data-mining queries by calculating the percentage of IHP applicants in the query that were found to be fraudulent. FIID then implements the most effective queries for all disasters, according to FEMA officials. Further, according to FEMA program officials, they evaluate the effectiveness of internal controls through testing to identify improper payments, quality control reviews, and audits.

Prior Relevant GAO Reports on Fraud Risk Management in FEMA's Disaster Assistance Programs

A Framework for Managing Fraud Risks in Federal Programs. GAO-15-593SP. Washington, D.C.: July 28, 2015.

Hurricane Sandy: FEMA Has Improved Disaster Aid Verification but Could Act to Further Limit Improper Assistance. GAO-15-15. Washington, D.C.: December 12, 2014.

Hurricanes Katrina and Rita Disaster Relief: Continued Findings of Fraud, Waste, and Abuse. GAO-07-300. Washington, D.C.: March 15, 2007.

Hurricanes Katrina and Rita: Unprecedented Challenges Exposed the Individuals and Households Program to Fraud and Abuse; Actions Needed to Reduce Such Problems in Future. GAO-06-1013. Washington, D.C.: September 27, 2006.

Contact

View GAO-18-472. For more information, contact Rebecca Shea at (202) 512-6722 or shear@gao.gov.

Appendix VIII: Payment Integrity and Prior Identified Requirements for Disaster Relief Funding

Overview

When disasters occur, the destruction they cause must be addressed immediately, and disaster relief funding must be delivered expeditiously. However, the risk for improper payments increases when billions of dollars are being spent quickly. For many years, GAO and the Inspector General community have identified internal control weaknesses in the federal government related to agencies receiving supplemental funds for disaster assistance.

Standards for Internal Control in the Federal Government sets the standards for an effective internal control system for federal agencies and provides the overall framework for designing, implementing, and operating an effective internal control system.

Mandated Requirements to Ensure Payment Integrity for the 2017 Disasters

With supplemental appropriations totaling at least $120 billion in additional funding for activities related to the 2017 hurricanes and wildfire disasters, Congress provided an oversight framework for these funds related to internal control and improper payments. Congress included the following key payment integrity provisions to help assure that all the funds are being spent as efficiently and effectively as possible:[12]

- Federal agencies are required to submit their plans for ensuring internal control over disaster relief funding to GAO, respective Inspectors General, the Office of Management and Budget (OMB), and Congress.

- OMB is required to issue standard guidance for federal agencies to use in designing internal control plans for disaster relief funding.

Observations from Prior Work on Payment Integrity

We have previously reported deficiencies related to federal agencies' establishment of required internal control plans in response to natural disasters and OMB's guidance for development of those plans. Specifically, in 2013, we reported on deficiencies in the internal control plans related to Hurricane Sandy disaster funding. These concerns may continue to be an issue for agencies after the 2017 disasters and we will monitor their efforts as part of our ongoing work.

Federal Agencies' Internal Control Plans

Agencies prepared Hurricane Sandy disaster relief internal control plans based on OMB guidance but did not consistently apply the guidance in preparing these plans. OMB Memorandum M-13-07, Accountability for Funds Provided by the Disaster Relief Appropriations Act, directed federal agencies to describe incremental risks they identified for Hurricane Sandy disaster relief funding and provide internal control strategies for mitigating these risks. Each of the 19 agencies responsible for the 61 programs receiving funds under the Disaster Appropriations Act 2013 submitted an internal control plan with specific program details using a template that OMB provided. In November 2013, we reported that agencies' plans ranged from providing most of the required information to not providing any information on certain programs. For example, each of the 61 programs was required to discuss its protocol for improper payments; however, we found that 38 programs included this information, 11 included partial information, and 12 included no information.

OMB Guidance for Development of Internal Control Plans

We also reported that OMB's guidance was an important step in the oversight of Hurricane Sandy disaster funding, addressing internal controls, improper payments protocol, and unexpended grant funds. However, we identified several weaknesses in OMB's guidance that limited its

---

[12] See Pub. L. No. 115-123, § 21208, 131 Stat. 64 (2018); Pub. L. No. 115-72, § 305, 131 Stat. 1224, 1227-28 (2017).

effectiveness in providing a comprehensive oversight mechanism for these funds. Specifically, the guidance (1) focused on identifying incremental risks without demonstrating that known risks had been adequately addressed; (2) provided agencies with significant flexibility as it did not require documentation or criteria for claiming exceptions, such as why the OMB requirements were not feasible or practicable; and (3) resulted in certain agencies developing their internal control plans at the same time that funds needed to be quickly distributed. We recommended that OMB develop more robust guidance for agencies to design internal control plans for future disaster relief funding. In commenting on the draft report, OMB staff generally agreed with our recommendation. On July 15, 2016, OMB issued the revised Circular No. A-123, *Management's Responsibility for Enterprise Risk Management and Internal Control*. The circular requires agencies to implement enterprise risk management, which includes developing a risk profile that analyzes the risks faced in achieving strategic objectives and identifies options for addressing them. However, the revised circular did not include specific guidance for identifying risks related to disaster funding; thus, the recommendation remains open. We plan to continue monitoring OMB's progress in implementing this recommendation.

Prior Relevant GAO Reports on Payment Integrity Related to Disaster Relief Fundings

Hurricane Sandy Relief: Improved Guidance on Designing Internal Control Plans Could Enhance Oversight of Disaster Funding. GAO-14-58. Washington, D.C.: November 26, 2013.

Contact

View GAO-18-472. For more information, contact Beryl H. Davis at (202) 512-2623 or davisbh@gao.gov

Appendix IX: FEMA's Public Assistance Grant Program

Overview

FEMA's Public Assistance grant program is administered through a partnership between FEMA and the state grantee, which provides funding to local officials.

In recent years, FEMA has redesigned the PA program to address past challenges and make the program easier for FEMA and grantee officials to manage. These efforts represent FEMA's "new delivery model" for awarding PA program grants. Officials implemented the new model in Texas and Florida after hurricanes Harvey and Irma, and announced the national use of the new model for PA concurrent with this decision.

Public Assistance Program Activities for Disaster Recovery

As of February 2018, FEMA had obligated close to $1.5 billion in PA grants to three states and two territories recovering from hurricanes Harvey, Irma, and Maria, as well as the California wildfires for emergency work projects—such as debris removal. For the longer-term projects—such as rebuilding of public facilities and infrastructure it may take months, and in some cases years, to award grant funds to state and local governments to aid in their disaster recovery—FEMA had obligated close to $2 billion as of February 2018 . See figure 28 for the PA obligations for emergency and permanent projects for the 2017 disasters.

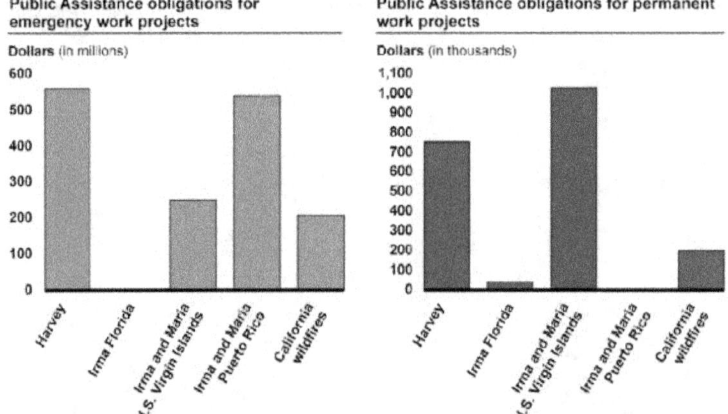

Figure 28: Public Assistance Obligations for Emergency and Permanent Work for Each of the 2017 Disasters, as of February 2018

Source: Federal Emergency Management Agency's Emergency Management Mission Integrated Environment | GAO-18-472

Note: Emergency work projects include debris removal and emergency protective measures, such as flood fighting activities, evacuation and sheltering of disaster survivors, and providing medical care and transport. Permanent work projects include the repair of damaged facilities such as the repair of dirt roads.

FEMA and local officials we interviewed in Texas, Florida, Puerto Rico, and the U.S. Virgin Islands noted early recovery challenges, in part, related to the new approaches to PA grant administration. Specifically, officials identified:

Debris Removal Challenges: Local officials managing the recovery from each disaster raised concerns about challenges with debris removal, for

example, such as the limitations of local officials' pre-positioned contracts that slowed the pace of removal.

PA New Delivery Model: Texas, Florida, and California are using the new PA model. Under the new model, FEMA redesigned processes for developing, reviewing, and approving grant applications. The agency created specialized roles; implemented a centralized and standardized grant processing approach; took steps to increase hazard mitigation; and is developing a new information system to better maintain and share grant documentation. However, all three states have faced challenges with implementation due to lack of experience and expertise.

PA Alternative Procedures: FEMA began the pilot approach after Hurricane Sandy, to provide more flexibility for program administration and incentivize applicants to complete projects in a timely and cost-effective manner. Puerto Rico will use the PA Alternative Procedures; however, the process is under development in Puerto Rico and FEMA has not used it at this scale before.

Experiences with the PA program in the affected states varied across the four 2017 disasters, but early observations from officials indicate that challenges with debris removal, the new PA delivery model, and the PA Alternative Procedures may result in long-term effects on community and infrastructure recovery.

Debris Removal Challenges in Each Disaster

- *Hurricane Harvey (Texas)*: Local officials in Texas noted that debris removal was a challenge, but indicated that they were able to make progress through internal efforts and coordination with FEMA. For example, local officials in one jurisdiction noted problems with the use of pre-positioned contracts. In this case, the officials hired military personnel to help move debris. In another case, local officials noted delays in debris removal due to resource constraints—having only 25 trucks—and receiving slow responses from FEMA, on questions such as how to address debris removal from gated communities. Local officials that did not note concerns with debris removal credited coordination with FEMA officials, expedited funding from FEMA, and daily calls with the state as the basis for their success.

- *Hurricane Irma (Florida)*: Local officials in Florida highlighted debris removal as the greatest challenge they experienced early in the recovery. The Federal Coordinating Officer (FCO)—the lead federal official in charge of response—in Florida reported that there was a shortage of contractors for debris removal because contractors are primarily located in the Gulf Coast area and serve a national market. See figure 29 for a picture of debris that was awaiting pick up by contractors in Big Pine Key, Florida. Also, many debris contractors were still engaged in Texas following Hurricane Harvey. Further, some preexisting contracts were awarded up to 5 years before Hurricane Irma, but the market had changed and newer contracts were offering more money per cubic yard of debris removal. As such, some vendors, despite being under contract in other locations, prioritized work in jurisdictions that offered higher rates according to the FCO in Florida. According to officials in one county, they had to compete for debris removal contractors, after contractors increased their prices, due to the high demand across Texas and other parts of Florida in the aftermath of the hurricanes. Local officials in Florida also faced challenges identifying who was responsible for debris removal from waterways, raising concerns about the environmental impacts.

2017 Hurricanes & Wildfires: GAO's Initial Observations (9/2018)

Source: GAO. | GAO-18-472

- *Hurricane Irma and Hurricane Maria (U.S. Virgin Islands)*: Officials faced unique challenges with staging and debris removal, due to the widespread vegetative damage across the islands. According to a FEMA official, there were challenges supporting the debris removal operation because local officials did not want to burn the vegetative debris.

- *Hurricane Irma and Hurricane Maria (Puerto Rico)*: According to FEMA and local officials in Puerto Rico, debris removal will require coordination among local contractors hired by each municipality, the U.S. Army Corps of Engineers, and other agencies supporting recovery. According to Puerto Rico officials, local officials may experience challenges with reimbursement for debris removal activities. Further, the officials said there were resource constraints, so they had to prioritize debris removal from state-managed roads, before clearing local roads.

- *California Wildfires*: In northern California alone, the wildfires created the largest amount of debris since the 1906 earthquake, and state officials and contractors have almost completed efforts to remove debris as of March 2018, according to state officials. In California, the debris removal contract with the U.S. Army Corps of Engineers created recovery challenges due to the lack of flexibility in contracting requirements, according to local officials. Furthermore, according to California officials, the contract process resulted in a bid protest that would have delayed debris removal, but FEMA and state officials worked together to address these issues and prevent delays.

Local Experiences with the New PA Delivery Model

- *Hurricane Harvey (Texas)*: Local officials' early recovery experiences with the PA program varied. Generally, local officials noted the potential for the new process or information system to improve PA grant delivery. However, local officials also noted a lack of consistency in eligibility determinations and the knowledge and experience of program staff as presenting a potential challenge for their overall recovery. For example,

2017 Hurricanes & Wildfires: GAO's Initial Observations (9/2018)

officials in one county raised concerns about inconsistent eligibility determinations, where there are still open disaster declarations and PA projects from flooding events in 2015 and 2016 that occurred prior to Hurricane Harvey. FEMA had not obligated funds for these projects, due to changing eligibility determinations made by FEMA officials throughout the process, which may subsequently impact obligations for Hurricane Harvey projects, according to county officials. However, FEMA headquarters officials noted that the new delivery model has not changed eligibility criteria or authorities for eligibility determinations and was not being applied retroactively to old disasters. In another county, officials also noted that FEMA staff could not answer questions on the new PA process and this raised concerns that PA staff were not documenting information in the new IT system. In particular, the officials cited challenges with support for developing mitigation proposals, and hired contractors to help develop mitigation project proposals after hazard mitigation specialists were unable to provide assistance. Moreover, the officials stated that they did not receive training on the new model until after Hurricane Harvey. Other local officials also noted similar gaps in FEMA-provided training and said they lacked enough skilled staff to support their projects.

- *Hurricane Irma (Florida)*: According to local officials, problems with FEMA customer service raised concerns about the long-term effect on recovery efforts. Local officials noted that PA staff did not have the knowledge or experience necessary to provide the support they needed throughout the process. For example, in one county PA staff provided assistance learning how to use the new IT system, but had not provided the detailed training on what types of information are required. In contrast, another local county official noted positive experiences with PA staff, and cited the potential for the new delivery model and new IT system to improve the program operations while reducing the administrative costs.

- *California Wildfires*: According to state officials, wildfires cause more damage to individual property owners, and therefore the public infrastructure recovery will be limited and the majority of PA projects will be emergency protective measures and debris removal. According to officials in one county, they had prior experience with the new model and process and received quick support when questions arose on the new IT system. Therefore, there have not been any problems or delays processing projects, according to local officials. The officials added that they have opted not to submit all damages, due to the documentation burden, as it is not worth their time to compile the paperwork for the project based on the amount of the award. In a second, more rural county, officials faced similar challenges but cited a lack of training for their county, inadequate support from FEMA, and untrained PA staff as challenges for their PA recovery process under the new model.

Use of PA Alternative Procedures Pilot Project

In response to the hurricanes, the governor of Puerto Rico requested the use of the PA Alternative Procedures, which FEMA began piloting after Hurricane Sandy. In Puerto Rico, Alternative Procedures are to be used for all large permanent work projects, FEMA, in collaboration with local officials, issued guidance specific to the Hurricane Maria recovery in Puerto Rico in April 2018. According to FEMA officials, using these flexibilities is unlikely to result in a faster recovery, but may offer more opportunities to rebuild with greater resilience from future hurricanes and natural hazards. FEMA officials also noted that capacity limitations—both in the PA workforce and in local officials' experiences with the program—have hampered early recovery efforts. According to FEMA officials, they did not use the new model in Puerto Rico specific to the Hurricane Irma recovery because PA program officials released their new model guidance after Hurricane Irma recovery efforts were already underway, and officials did not want to change the process again after Hurricane Maria.

In all other locations, state and local officials have the option to use the PA Alternative Procedures. For example, in the U. S. Virgin Islands, local officials are using the Alternative Procedures pilot to meet their needs. FEMA officials in the U. S. Virgin Islands noted similar challenges with a lack of PA funding and territorial personnel to develop PA projects, as well as limitations in the skill level for those PA staff assigned to the islands. According to FEMA officials, the U.S. Virgin Islands hired an emergency management contractor to assist in preparation and oversight of PA projects to address the staffing challenges that exist for FEMA and local officials. FEMA officials also said that complex projects, such as a wastewater treatment plan in St. Thomas and two major hospitals, may present fiscal challenges in the long term.

Prior Relevant GAO Reports on FEMA's Public Assistance Program Efforts

Disaster Assistance: *Opportunities to Enhance Implementation of the Redesigned Public Assistance Grant Program.* GAO-18-30, Published: November 8, 2017.

Hurricane Sandy: *An Investment Strategy Could Help the Federal Government Enhance National Resilience for Future Disasters.* GAO-15-515, Published: July 30, 2015

Appendix X: Disaster Resilience and Hazard Mitigation

Overview

The costs of severe weather events, such as those seen in 2017, are likely to continue to rise due to climate change. We have reported that, enhancing disaster resilience and hazard mitigation is essential for controlling federal fiscal exposure to disasters. However, the current funding approach, which emphasizes the post-disaster environment, can create a reactionary and fragmented approach where disasters determine when and where investment occurs. A national strategic approach to prioritizing investments could help ensure that federal funds are directed towards the most effective risk reduction efforts.

The Mitigation Framework Leadership Group—the interagency body responsible for guiding federal hazard mitigation efforts under the National Preparedness System—has released a draft National Mitigation Investment Strategy, which articulates key principles and desired outcomes to help guide a national approach to resilience investments. In addition, FEMA has included new guidance and training as part of its new delivery model for Public Assistance to help ensure that applicants seek opportunities to incorporate hazard mitigation.

Resilience and Hazard Mitigation

Disaster resilience is the ability to prepare and plan for, absorb, recover from, and more successfully adapt to adverse effects. Hazard mitigation actions are undertaken to enhance disaster resilience by reducing or eliminating long-term risk to people and property from natural hazards and their effects.

Figure 30: Resilience – What, Why and How

What is resilience?

Disaster resilience is the ability of individuals, communities, localities, states, regions and the nation to respond and recover from disasters in a manner that minimizes life and property losses and enables rapid return of normal economic and other life activities.

Why is disaster resilience important?

The growing number of major disaster declarations has contributed to increasing federal disaster assistance expenditures. Disaster resilience is one of the primary means the federal government has to help control the federal fiscal exposure to disasters.

How is disaster resilience achieved?

Governments at all levels and the private sector have various responsibilities and a stake in increasing disaster resilience. Because planning to increase resilience starts with understanding disaster risk, some resilience-related activities, like flood mapping and threat and hazard assessment, are designed to increase knowledge. In addition, state and local laws and regulations can heavily influence resilience efforts, for example, by strengthening building codes.

Source: GAO analysis. | GAO-18-472

Federal Pre-Disaster and Post-Disaster Hazard Mitigation Programs

The Federal Emergency Management Agency (FEMA) and other federal agencies have multiple funding mechanisms, including those outlined below, to help states and localities enhance disaster resilience and hazard mitigation—the majority of which are available after a disaster strikes.

FEMA's Pre-Disaster Mitigation Program provides funding to state, local, and tribal governments to help plan for and implement hazard mitigation projects prior to a disaster. The program's goal is to reduce overall risk to the population and structures from future hazard events.

FEMA's Hazard Mitigation Grant Program provides funding to protect states, tribes, and territories after a major disaster is declared. The recipient can then use the funds for eligible projects anywhere in the state, tribe, or territory to reduce the risk of future disaster damage.

FEMA's Public Assistance Program provides funding for hazard mitigation measures to the parts of a facility that were damaged by a disaster. Funding is limited to declared counties and eligible damaged facilities. Mitigation measures can also be applied, in certain circumstances, to non-damaged facilities under the Public Assistance Alternative Procedures—procedures that give jurisdictions more flexibility in determining how, where, and what to rebuild, particularly after incurring significant damage—so long as they are otherwise eligible under the Public Assistance program.

Housing and Urban Development Community Development Block Grant – Disaster Recovery provides funding to address needs not met by other disaster recovery programs post-disaster, which can include disaster resilience-building projects. Funding is provided to affected cities, counties, and states, especially in low-income areas, through congressional supplemental appropriations.

FEMA and local officials noted how previous mitigation projects lessened the damage from the 2017 disasters in some areas and described some challenges incorporating resilience as well as plans to incorporate resilience moving forward.

Examples of Previous Successes and Challenges with Hazard Mitigation

- *Hurricane Harvey (Texas):* FEMA officials said Hurricane Harvey demonstrated how prior hazard mitigation projects prevented greater damages (e.g. elevated homes and equipment sustained less damages as shown in figure 31).

Figure 31: Elevated Air Conditioning Unit in Greater Houston Area, October 2017

Source: GAO. | GAO-18-472

- *Hurricane Irma (Florida):* FEMA officials said Florida strengthened its building codes for resilience as a result of lessons learned from Hurricanes Andrew in 1992 and Mathew in 2016 (e.g. elevating homes). State officials noted that some areas did not lose power during Hurricane Irma due to a previous hazard mitigation effort that reinforced power poles as shown in figure 32.

2017 Hurricanes & Wildfires: GAO's Initial Observations (9/2018)

Source: GAO. | GAO-18-472

- *Hurricane Irma and Hurricane Maria (Puerto Rico):* Puerto Rico's construction codes required buildings to withstand winds of 145 miles per hour, but the force of Hurricane Maria's winds exceeded that speed at 175 miles per hour resulting in damage, according to FEMA officials.

- *Hurricane Irma and Hurricane Maria (U.S. Virgin Islands):* Previous resilience efforts helped in the U.S. Virgin Islands. For example, hurricanes Irma and Maria destroyed 90 percent of the power grid; however, due to a hazard mitigation project undertaken as a result of Hurricane Marilyn in 1995, 30 percent of the power grid was able to be restored quickly, according to FEMA officials.

Examples of Plans to Incorporate Resilience Following the 2017 Disasters

- *Hurricane Harvey (Texas):* State officials noted that localities may be more willing to incorporate resilience post-Harvey due to grants from Rebuild Texas—a state-run program intended to make counties more resilient to future storms and flooding. In addition, FEMA officials said they have staff identifying opportunities for mitigation on infrastructure projects.

- *Hurricane Irma (Florida):* FEMA has held workshops with local residents on hazard mitigation measures such as adding window shutters, strapping down roofs, and installing different types of glass, according to agency officials.

2017 Hurricanes & Wildfires: GAO's Initial Observations (9/2018)

- *Hurricane Irma and Hurricane Maria (Puerto Rico):* Puerto Rico received $18.5 billion from the Housing and Urban Development Community Development Block Grant-Disaster Recovery program. While most will be spent on housing, the governor plans to invest remaining funds in power grids, infrastructure, and other hazard mitigation measures according to Puerto Rico officials.

- *Hurricane Irma and Hurricane Maria (U.S. Virgin Islands):* U.S. Virgin Islands officials are receptive to investing in infrastructure improvements, according to FEMA officials. For example, U.S. Virgin Islands officials formed a task force—including FEMA mitigation and critical infrastructure officials, the Virgin Islands Territorial Emergency Management Agency, the Department of Transportation, and other members of the governors' office—focused on rebuilding power infrastructure and two major hospitals in a resilient way, according to FEMA officials.

- *California Wildfires:* FEMA officials said they have provided wildfire resilience materials at local rebuilding fairs and are working with the state to provide mitigation grant application workshops.

Prior Relevant GAO Reports on Federal Resilience Efforts

Disaster Assistance: Opportunities to Enhance Implementation of the Redesigned Public Assistance Grant Program. GAO-18-30. Washington, D.C.: November 8, 2017.

Climate Change: Information on Potential Economic Effects Could Help Guide Federal Efforts to Reduce Fiscal Exposure. GAO-17-720. Washington, D.C.: September 28, 2017.

Climate Change: Improved Federal Coordination Could Facilitate Use of Forward-Looking Climate Information in Design Standards, Building Codes, and Certifications. GAO-17-3. Washington, D.C.: November 30, 2016.

Hurricane Sandy: An Investment Strategy Could Help the Federal Government Enhance National Resilience for Future Disasters. GAO-15-515. Washington, D.C.: July 30, 2015.

Contact

View GAO-18-472. For more information, contact Chris Currie at (404) 679-1875 or curriec@gao.gov.

Appendix XI: Department of Defense's Support of Civil Authorities during the 2017 Hurricanes and Wildfires

Overview

While DOD's primary mission is to defend the nation, the department is often asked to play a prominent role supporting civil authorities and must be prepared to provide rapid response when called upon during disasters and declared emergencies (natural or man-made). DOD provides such support through its Defense Support of Civil Authorities mission.

Consistent with the *National Response Framework*—a guide to how the federal government, states and localities, and other public and private-sector institutions should respond to disasters and emergencies—DOD primarily provides support through two approaches: (1) when requested (e.g., mission assigned) by a federal agency (e.g. FEMA, the Department of Health and Human Services, or U.S. Department of Agriculture) and approved by the Secretary of Defense, the department provides federal military forces, DOD civilians, DOD contract personnel, and DOD component assets; and (2) the U.S. Army Corps of Engineers serves as the DOD coordinating and primary federal agency for public works and engineering related response efforts.

Separate from DOD's efforts, National Guard units provide support to their governor or other governors through state-to-state emergency management assistance compact agreements. In this capacity, National Guard units and personnel do not operate as a DOD (federal) capability or resource. Instead, they serve under state law and are funded with state resources—a status commonly referred to as State active-duty status. In addition, when approved by the Secretary of Defense with the concurrence of the affected governor, National Guard units also provide support with DOD funding -- commonly referred to as Title 32 status. In both situations, the National Guard is under the control of their governor.

Summary of DOD's Support for 2017 Disasters

The Department of Defense (DOD) provided extensive support during the 2017 hurricanes and wildfires. This support included routine support (e.g. providing food, water, planners, debris removal, temporary roofing, and federal partners access to DOD bases and facilities for staging response personnel and equipment) as well as capabilities that have not been routinely requested (e.g. using U.S. Navy ships as helicopter platforms, procuring and installing large generators, providing medical support for prolonged period of time, and power grid restoration). As shown in table 8, DOD components and organizations at all levels provided support:

Table 8: DOD Components and Personnel that Provided Support

Department of Defense Components[a]
• Office of the Deputy Assistant Secretary of Defense for Homeland Defense Integration and Defense Support of Civil Authorities
• Joint Staff
• U.S. Northern Command
• U.S. Transportation Command
• National Guard Bureau
• Defense Logistics Agency
• U.S. Army Corps of Engineers
• Defense Coordinating Officers and Elements
• U.S. bases (e.g. Joint Base San Antonio, Texas, and Fort Benning, Georgia)
• Military units and personnel

Source: DOD | GAO-18-472

[a] Separate from DOD's Title 10 efforts (and the 164 National Guard members who responded in Title 10 federal status), more than 56,000 Guard members from 49 states, the District of Columbia, the U.S. Virgin Islands, and Puerto Rico provided support in either State Active Duty or Title 32 status for Hurricanes Harvey, Irma, and Maria; and the California Wildfires, according to the National Guard Bureau.

The Federal Emergency Management Agency (FEMA) issued work orders directing DOD to provide support and assistance for the 2017 disasters (mission assigned). As shown in figure 33, the number of mission assignments, cost of mission assignments, and value of contracts issued by DOD varied for each of the 2017 disasters. For example, the estimated cost for a mission assignment that requested Civil Air Patrol assistance was $5,000 while the cost for the U.S. Army Corps of Engineers to restore the Puerto Rico electrical power grid was $577,000,000.

2017 Hurricanes & Wildfires: GAO's Initial Observations (9/2018)

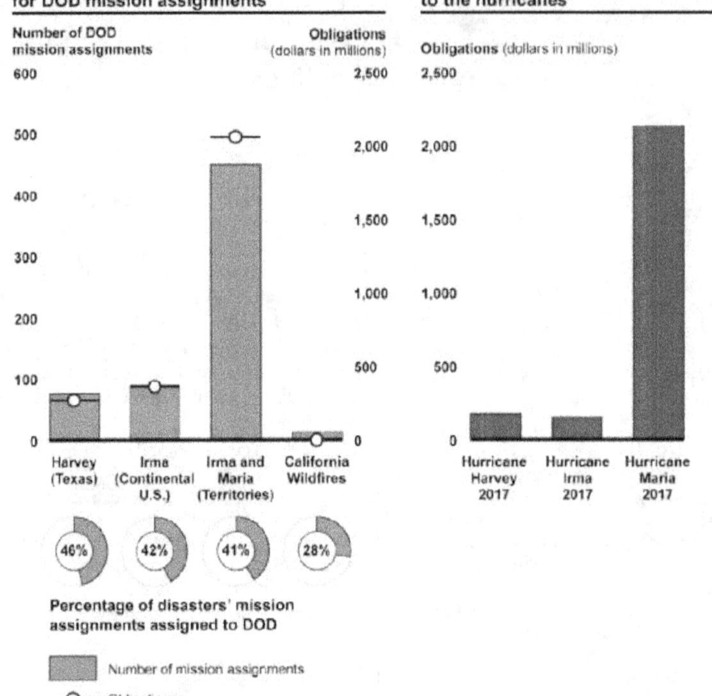

Figure 33: DOD Mission Assignment and Contract Activity for Four 2017 Disasters

Source: GAO analysis of mission assignment data from the Federal Emergency Management Agency's (FEMA) Web-Based Emergency Operations Center (WebEOC), obligations from FEMA's Integrated Financial Management Information System, and contracting data from the Federal Procurement Data System-Next Generation. | GAO-18-472

Note: Mission assignment totals and percentages reflect data entered into FEMA's Web-based Emergency Operations Center system of approved resource requests by response officials, where data are available, as of January 2018. This does not include 1,285 request records (out of 3,338 total) for which data are not available to determine whether FEMA sourced the request through a mission assignment or other source, and 74 records for which data are not available to determine which agency FEMA assigned out of the 1,515 mission assignments reviewed.

DOD was asked to support more mission assignments in the U.S. Virgin Islands and Puerto Rico than in Texas and Florida due to a number of factors. According to DOD, state and local officials in Texas and Florida were more experienced and prepared to respond to the hurricanes that affected their states and were able to rely on National Guard and other resources from unaffected areas of the state. Also, according to DOD officials, due to the circumstances—including power grid destruction and being accessible only by air or sea—DOD was asked to provide support in the U.S. Virgin Islands and Puerto Rico that the department has not typically provided for prior hurricanes.

Observations from Affected States and Territories

Hurricane Harvey (Texas): While DOD provided support prior to Hurricane Harvey's landfall (e.g. pre-positioned generators and fuel), the majority of mission assignments that FEMA requested from DOD occurred after the storm stalled over southeast Texas. Such support included:

- Army units provided high-water vehicles and Marine Corps units provided amphibious vehicles and boats to rescue over 6,000 citizens from flooded

GAO-18-472 2017 Hurricanes and Wildfires

areas in support of Texas and to transport supplies for the American Red Cross and support FEMA logistics efforts, as shown in figure 34.

Figure 34: Army High-Water Vehicle use in Texas

Source: U.S. Army. | GAO-18-472

- Air Force, Navy, and Army aircraft provided search and rescue aircraft saving over 1,000 individuals. Air Force also provided airborne command and control aircraft and imagery that provided improved capability for numerous interagency aircraft supporting search and rescue operations to safely operate in very busy airspace.

- Air Force C-130s sprayed over 2.7 million acres of areas that had troublesome mosquito populations.

- Joint Base San Antonio provided two separate locations (Randolph AFB and Seguin Auxiliary Airfield) as staging areas for thousands of tractor trailers that were used to distribute commodities. Naval Air Station Corpus Christi provided FEMA the use of a nearby training airfield where tents, showers and feeding facilities could be established to house emergency responders so they did not compete with hurricane survivors for local hotel spaces.

Hurricane Irma (Florida): With DOD providing ongoing support for Hurricane Harvey victims and Hurricane Irma having hit the Caribbean a few days earlier, DOD provided support prior and subsequent to the hurricane hitting Florida. DOD support included:

- U.S. Transportation Command provided emergency response planners and used its aircraft to fly FEMA's urban search and rescue teams, Health and Human Services disaster medical assistance teams, and relief supplies and equipment into the state, as shown in figure 35.

Source: U.S. Air Force. | GAO-18-472

- Navy personnel from the USS *New York*, USS *Iwo Jima*, and USS *San Jacinto* provided 6,372 meals, 14,719 gallons of water, and 1 medical evacuation in the vicinity of Key West.

- Special Operations personnel supported FEMA's public affairs efforts.

- DOD provided geo-imagery analysts to FEMA's National Response Coordination Center that assisted FEMA with damage assessment capabilities.

- 10 military installations were used for commodity and equipment staging, FEMA Incident Management Assistance Teams, operations facilities, and Urban Search and Rescue teams' accommodations.

Hurricane Irma and Hurricane Maria (Puerto Rico/U.S. Virgin Islands): DOD was able to reposition U.S. Navy ships that were enroute to support Hurricane Harvey to the U.S. Virgin Islands; these and other DOD capabilities that were providing assistance to the Virgin Islands were able to provide immediate support to Puerto Rico after Hurricane Maria hit the island as shown in figure 36. DOD support included:

- The Marine Corps provided two Doppler radar units, meteorologists, and radar technicians that provided weather forecasts and facilitated aviation safety on the U. S. Virgin Islands and Puerto Rico.

2017 Hurricanes & Wildfires: GAO's Initial Observations (9/2018)

Source: U.S. Navy. | GAO-18-472

- U.S. Army Reserve unit provided mortuary affairs services at multiple locations, including local hospitals.

- DOD supported the State Department in evacuating approximately 6,000 U.S. citizens from the British Virgin Islands to Puerto Rico.

- Army and Air Force set up medical support hospitals and the Navy provided medical services aboard and alongside the USNS *Comfort*. For example, the Army deployed a temporary medical facility to St. Croix that included emergency medical care services, urgent care medical services, temporary patient holding, and ancillary services to triage and medically treat approximately 200 disaster victims per day to stabilize medical care at local hospitals.

- Special operations units provided information support, which included public affairs messaging to the affected population and had a major impact in communicating messages to the affected population when there was little or no radio or TV public broadcasts.

- U.S. Army Corps of Engineers provided temporary emergency power, temporary roofing, debris management, infrastructure assessment, critical public facility restoration and temporary housing. The U.S. Army Corps of Engineers is also repairing the power grid in Puerto Rico.

- Defense Logistics Agency provided, among other things, power poles, pharmaceuticals, handheld radios, generators, water, meals, human remains pouches, and fuel.

2017 California Wildfires: According to DOD officials, National Guard personnel in State Active Duty status primarily provided wildfire fighting capabilities. However, DOD provided commodity support and access to military bases. For example,

- Defense Logistics Agency fulfilled 3,500 orders placed by the U.S. Forest Service for emergency equipment and supplies, including 5 million AA batteries.

- Air Force provided access and use of military bases (including Travis Air Force Base and Beale Air Force Base) to stage ambulances and their

2017 Hurricanes & Wildfires: GAO's Initial Observations (9/2018)

crews, as shown in figure 37, as well as housing support for federal
personnel in various agencies.

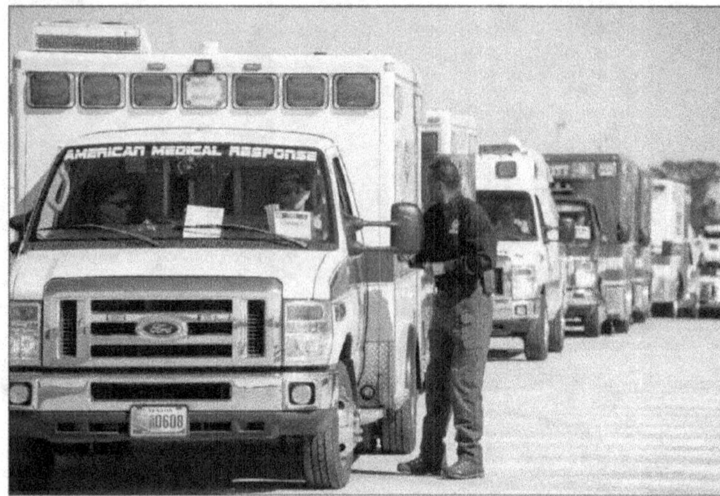

Figure 37: Ambulance and Support Vehicles Staged at Travis Air Force Base,
California

Source: U.S. Air Force. | GAO-18-472

Challenges and Lessons Learned from 2017 Disasters

DOD officials identified a number of challenges that they encountered during
disasters that they recognize need to be addressed by DOD and its federal
partners in the future. Such challenges include:

- *FEMA and Emergency Support Function lead agencies' dependence on
  DOD capabilities.* DOD officials stated that federal agencies have over
  time become too dependent on DOD capabilities during disasters. While
  DOD possesses some unique capabilities, some of the requested
  capabilities could potentially reside in other federal agencies,
  nongovernmental organizations, or the private sector. Similarly,
  according to DOD officials, the department's ability to deploy quickly
  and/or for extended periods of time may make DOD a preferable solution
  for response capabilities and support. The increased reliance may create
  vulnerability, if in the future, DOD capabilities are needed to conduct
  DOD's primary mission—to defend the nation from threats concurrent
  with a domestic disaster response.

- *DOD units and personnel were deploying without authorization.* DOD
  officials, including those from the National Guard Bureau and DOD
  coordinators located in FEMA regions, told us units were activating or
  taking action too early, which results in units self-deploying without
  authorization to disaster areas and potentially adversely impacting
  FEMA-coordinated response efforts in the areas where the units deploy.

- *Potential impact to readiness.* DOD and National Guard efforts to support
  civil authorities in the hurricanes and wildfires in the United States (as
  well as provide humanitarian support to other countries and territories)
  may have affected the readiness of units and commands to conduct
  global military operations from 2018-2020, according to DOD and
  National Guard officials.

2017 Hurricanes & Wildfires: GAO's Initial Observations (9/2018)

- *Unclear mission integration.* DOD officials noted that integrated planning for some Emergency Support Functions, such as public health and medical services, prior to the 2017 disasters had not occurred. Such planning could have identified the status of capabilities across the government, including DOD capabilities (e.g. medical command and control elements and medical response elements). This would have clearly defined how federal departments and agencies, including DOD, should be providing support (e.g. patient evacuation and deployable medical treatment facilities).

Prior RelevantGAO Reports on DOD Support to Civil Authorities

Defense Civil Support: DOD Needs to Address Cyber Incident Training Requirements. GAO-18-47. Washington, D.C.: November 30, 2017.

Defense Civil Support: DOD, HHS, and DHS Should Use Existing Coordination Mechanisms to Improve Their Pandemic Preparedness. GAO-17-150. Washington, D.C.: February 10, 2017.

Defense Civil Support: DOD Needs to Identify National Guard's Cyber Capabilities and Address Challenges in Its Exercises. GAO-16-574. Washington, D.C.: September 6, 2016.

Defense Civil Support: DOD Has Made Progress Incorporating the Homeland Response Force into the Chemical, Biological, Radiological, and Nuclear Response Enterprise. GAO-16-599. Washington, D.C.: June 28, 2016.

Civil Support: DOD Needs to Clarify Its Roles and Responsibilities for Defense Support of Civil Authorities during Cyber Incidents. GAO-16-332. Washington, D.C.: April 4, 2016.

Civil Support: DOD Is Taking Action to Strengthen Support of Civil Authorities. GAO-15-686T. Washington, D.C.: June 10, 2015.

Homeland Defense: DOD Needs to Address Gaps in Homeland Defense and Civil Support Guidance. GAO-13-128. Washington, D.C.: October 24, 2012.

Contact

View GAO-18-472. For more information, contact Joseph W. Kirschbaum at (202) 512-9971 or kirschbaumj@gao.gov or Chris Currie at (404) 679-1875 or curriec@gao.gov.

2017 Hurricanes & Wildfires: GAO's Initial Observations (9/2018)

Appendix XII: Federal Emergency Management Agency (FEMA) Regional Structure

FEMA has 10 Regional offices located across the United States as depicted below in figure 38.

Region I: Connecticut, Maine, Massachusetts, New Hampshire, Rhode Island, Vermont

Region II: (New Jersey, New York, Puerto Rico, and the U.S. Virgin Islands

Region III: (Delaware, District of Columbia, Maryland, Pennsylvania, Virginia and W. Virginia

Region IV: Alabama, Florida, Georgia, Kentucky, Mississippi, N. Carolina, S. Carolina and Tennessee

Region V: Illinois, Indiana, Michigan, Minnesota, Ohio and Wisconsin

Region VI: Arkansas, Louisiana, New Mexico, Oklahoma and Texas

Region VII: Iowa, Kansas, Missouri and Nebraska

Region VIII: Colorado, Montana, N. Dakota, S. Dakota, Utah and Wyoming

Region IX: Arizona, California, Hawaii, Nevada, American Samoa, Guam, Commonwealth of the Northern Mariana Islands, Republic of the Marshall Islands, and Federated States of Micronesia

Region X: Alaska, Idaho, Oregon and Washington

Figure 38: Map of Federal Emergency Management Agency (FEMA) Regions and Their Member States and Territories

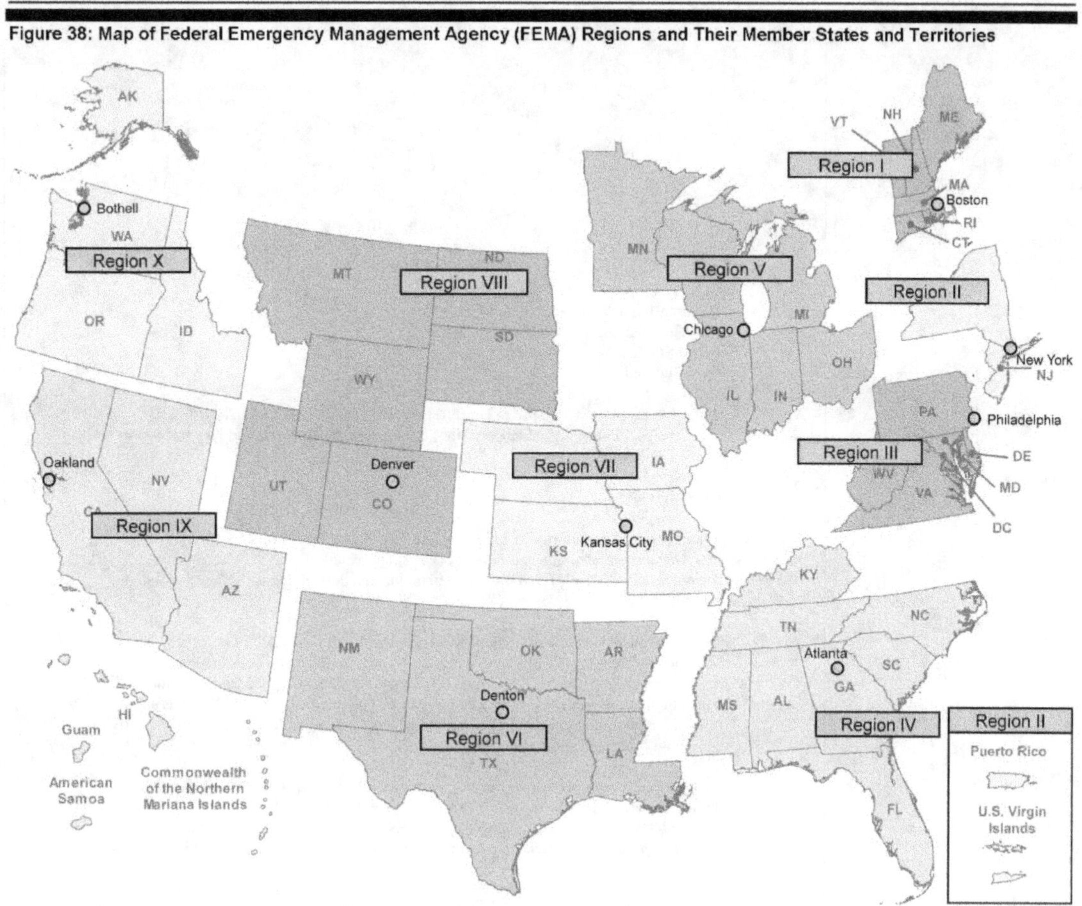

Source: Federal Emergency Management Agency; Map Resources (map). | GAO-18-472

August 28, 2018

Chris P. Currie
Director, Homeland Security and Justice
U.S. Government Accountability Office
441 G Street, NW
Washington, DC 20548

Re: Management Response to Draft Report 18-472, "2017 HURRICANES AND
        WILDFIRES: Initial Observations on the Federal Response and Key Recovery
        Challenges"

Dear Mr. Currie:

Thank you for the opportunity to review and comment on the subject draft report. The
U.S. Department of Homeland Security (DHS) appreciates the U.S. Government
Accountability Office's (GAO) work in planning and conducting its review and issuing
this report.

The Department is pleased to note GAO's recognition of the Federal Emergency
Management Agency (FEMA) and its partners' preparedness and coordination efforts
before, during, and after the 2017 hurricanes and wildfires. Of particular note, the draft
report highlighted many of the challenges that complicated response and recovery
efforts. Overall, the report provides many insights to the emergency management
community that stakeholders and others may not have had otherwise.

Last year's disasters were a devastating experience for millions of Americans, with more
disaster survivors registering for FEMA assistance than the previous 10 years combined.
The Nation responded to three major hurricanes (Harvey, Irma, and Maria) and then
California wildfires in quick succession. These events came at a time when FEMA was
already supporting 692 federally declared disasters and tested the Nation's ability to
respond to and recover from multiple concurrent disasters. FEMA Urban Search and
Rescue Task Forces, comprised of state and local emergency responders, saved or
assisted in saving nearly 9,500 lives across the three hurricanes. These numbers stand in
addition to the thousands of lives saved or assisted by the Department of Defense, the
U.S. Coast Guard, state and local first responders, and neighbors helping neighbors.
Concurrent with response operations, FEMA moved quickly to meet long-term survivor
needs.

In addition to conducting concurrent response operations for Hurricanes Harvey, Irma,
and Maria, FEMA took action on Hurricanes Jose and Nate. The impacts from those
two storms were minimal by comparison, but nevertheless required FEMA's focus and
resources. Hurricane Jose also complicated Hurricane Irma and Hurricane Maria
response efforts in the Caribbean by limiting sea transport of food and water as well as
transit of U.S. Naval response assets to the U.S. Virgin Islands and Puerto Rico.
Hurricane Nate resulted in Major Disaster declarations in two states, Alabama and
Mississippi.

The draft report also highlights the positive driving force of pre-existing relationships
and coordination. During the aftermath of Hurricanes Harvey and Irma in September
2017, Acting Secretary of Homeland Security Elaine Duke activated the Surge Capacity
Force for only the second time in history. This time the program was expanded beyond
DHS to the entirety of the Federal Government. In total, more than 4,000 federal
employees deployed and performed duties in positions within several of FEMA's
incident workforce field programs. Based on this experience, FEMA has taken action to
increase preparedness for the 2018 Hurricane Season by updating hurricane plans,
annexes, and procedures for states, tribal lands, and territories. FEMA has also made
improvements in staffing for incidents, logistics operations, and refining
communications from land mobile radios to satellite communications. Finally, FEMA
has updated high priority national level contracts to be better prepared to cope with
responding to multiple concurrent disasters across the Nation.

FEMA is constantly reviewing its program delivery, decision-making processes, and
response efforts to ensure that it can improve, minimize errors, and better serve
survivors. This approach allows FEMA to build a culture of preparedness, ready the
Nation for catastrophic disasters, and reduce the complexities. FEMA has reflected this
commitment by incorporating objectives in its 2018-2022 Strategic Plan to include
improving the readiness of incident workforce cadres; building staff, equipment, and
contract capacity to achieve and maintain a higher logistics readiness rate; improving
continuity and resilient communications capabilities; and streamlining the disaster
survivor and grantee experience. For example, FEMA has already published alternative
procedures guidance to promote outcome-based recovery in Puerto Rico by simplifying
the funding process, reducing the time to receive federal funding, and providing the
Commonwealth greater flexibility to rebuild its infrastructure. In addition, FEMA has
initiated an update to the National Response Framework based on lessons learned in
2017 and is continuing work on a housing assistance initiative with the goal of
empowering state and local governments to provide scalable disaster housing solutions
tailored to the impacts of disasters and the needs of affected communities.

Disaster can strike at any time and in any place, building slowly, or occurring suddenly
without warning. FEMA is part of a larger team of federal agencies, state, local, tribal,

2

and territorial governments, and non-governmental stakeholders that share responsibility for emergency management and National preparedness. Those closest to impacted areas are the true first responders during any emergency or disaster – individuals, families, neighbors, and local communities. Whatever the scenario, FEMA serves in a coordination and integration role, collaborating with others to ensure we are a more prepared and resilient Nation.

Again, thank you for the opportunity to review and comment on the draft report. Technical comments were provided under separate cover. Please feel free to contact me if you have any questions. We look forward to working with you again in the future.

Sincerely,

JIM H. CRUMPACKER, CIA, CFE
Director
Departmental GAO-OIG Liaison Office

3

2017 Hurricanes & Wildfires: GAO's Initial Observations (9/2018)

Appendix XIV: GAO Contacts and Staff Acknowledgments

GAO Contact:	Chris Currie, (202)512- 8777 or CurrieC@gao.gov
Staff Acknowledgement:	In addition to the contacts above, the following staff members made significant contributions to this report: Aditi S. Archer, Assistant Director, Edith Sohna, Analyst-in-Charge, Thomas E. Baril, Jr. Claudia Becker, Lorraine Ettaro, Suellen Foth, Kathryn Godfrey, Eric Hauswirth, Ellie Klein, Monica Kelly, Caryn Kuebler, Elisha Matvay, Amanda K. Miller, Heidi Nielson, Amanda Parker, Meghan Perez, George Scott, Katherine Trimble, Matthew Valenta, Erin Villas, Adam Vogt, and Su Jin Yon.

Related GAO Products

Federal Coordination Reports

2017 Disaster Contracting: Observations on Federal Contracting for Response and Recovery Efforts. GAO-18-335. Washington, D.C.: February. 28, 2018.

Defense Civil Support: DOD Needs to Address Cyber Incident Training Requirements. GAO-18-47. Washington, D.C.: November 30, 2017.

Defense Civil Support: DOD, HHS, and DHS Should Use Existing Coordination Mechanisms to Improve Their Pandemic Preparedness. GAO-17-150. Washington, D.C.: February 10, 2017.

Defense Civil Support: DOD Needs to Identify National Guard's Cyber Capabilities and Address Challenges in Its Exercises. GAO-16-574. Washington, D.C.: September 6, 2016.

Defense Civil Support: DOD Has Made Progress Incorporating the Homeland Response Force into the Chemical, Biological, Radiological, and Nuclear Response Enterprise. GAO-16-599. Washington, D.C.: June 28, 2016.

Civil Support: DOD Needs to Clarify Its Roles and Responsibilities for Defense Support of Civil Authorities during Cyber Incidents. GAO-16-332. Washington, D.C.: April 4, 2016.

Disaster Response: FEMA Has Made Progress Implementing Key Programs, but Opportunities for Improvement Exist. GAO-16-87. Washington D.C.: February 5, 2016.

Emergency Preparedness: Opportunities Exist to Strengthen Interagency Assessments and Accountability for Closing Capability Gaps. GAO-15-20. Washington, D.C.: December. 4, 2014 and reissued December. 9, 2015.

Disaster Contracting: FEMA Needs to Cohesively Manage Its Workforce and Fully Address Post-Katrina Reforms. GAO-15-783. Washington, D.C.: September 29, 2015.

Federal Emergency Management Agency: Additional Planning and Data Collection Could Help Improve Workforce Management Efforts. GAO-15-437. Washington, D.C.: July 9, 2015.

2017 Hurricanes & Wildfires: GAO's Initial Observations (9/2018)

High-Risk Series: An Update. GAO-15-290. Washington, D.C.: February 11, 2015.

Emergency Preparedness: Opportunities Exist to Strengthen Interagency Assessments and Accountability for Closing Capability Gaps. GAO-15-20. Washington, D.C.: December 4, 2014.

National Preparedness: Actions Taken by FEMA to Implement Select Provisions of the Post-Katrina Emergency Management Reform Act of 2006. GAO-14-99R. Washington, D.C.: November 26, 2013.

FEMA Reservists: Training Could Benefit from Examination of Practices at Other Agencies. GAO-13-250R. Washington, D.C.: March 22, 2013.

Homeland Defense: DOD Needs to Address Gaps in Homeland Defense and Civil Support Guidance. GAO-13-128. Washington, D.C.: October 24, 2012.

Disaster Assistance Workforce: FEMA Could Enhance Human Capital Management and Training. GAO-12-538. Washington, D.C.: May 25, 2012.

Federal Emergency Management Agency: Workforce Planning and Training Could Be Enhanced by Incorporating Strategic Management Principles. GAO-12-487. Washington, D.C.: April 26, 2012.

Disaster Recovery: FEMA's Public Assistance Grant Program Experienced Challenges with Gulf Coast Rebuilding. GAO-09-129. Washington, D.C.: December 18, 2008.

Actions Taken to Implement the Post-Katrina Emergency Management Reform Act of 2006. GAO-09-59R. Washington, D.C.: November 21, 2008.

Federal Coordination Testimonies

Federal Emergency Management Agency: Progress and Continuing Challenges in National Preparedness Efforts. GAO-16-560T. Washington, D.C.: April 12, 2016.

2017 Hurricanes & Wildfires: GAO's Initial Observations (9/2018)

Civil Support: DOD Is Taking Action to Strengthen Support of Civil Authorities. GAO-15-686T. Washington, D.C.: June 10, 2015.

Hurricane Katrina: GAO's Preliminary Observations Regarding Preparedness, Response, and Recovery. GAO-06-442T. Washington, D.C.: March 8, 2006.

Federal Funding Reports

Federal Disaster Assistance: Individual Assistance Requests Often Granted, but FEMA Could Better Document Factors Considered. GAO-18-366. Washington, D.C: May 31, 2018.

Disaster Assistance: Opportunities to Enhance Implementation of the Redesigned Public Assistance Grant Program. GAO-18-30, Washington, D.C.: November 8, 2017.

Federal Disaster Assistance: Federal Departments and Agencies Obligated at Least $277.6 Billion during Fiscal Years 2005 through 2014. GAO-16-797. Washington, D.C.: September 22, 2016.

A Framework for Managing Fraud Risks in Federal Programs. GAO-15-593SP. Washington, D.C.: July 28, 2015.

Federal Emergency Management Agency: Opportunities Exist to Strengthen Oversight of Administrative Costs for Major Disasters. GAO-15-65. Washington, D.C.: December 17, 2014.

Hurricane Sandy: FEMA Has Improved Disaster Aid Verification but Could Act to Further Limit Improper Assistance. GAO-15-15. Washington, D.C.: December 12, 2014.

Hurricane Sandy Relief: Improved Guidance on Designing Internal Control Plans Could Enhance Oversight of Disaster Funding. GAO-14-58.Washington, D.C.: November 26, 2013.

Fiscal Exposures: Improving Cost Recognition in the Federal Budget. GAO-14-28. Washington, D.C.: October 29, 2013.

Federal Disaster Assistance: Improved Criteria Needed to Assess a Jurisdiction's Capability to Respond and Recover on Its Own. GAO-12-838. Washington, D.C.: September 12, 2012.

2017 Hurricanes & Wildfires: GAO's Initial Observations (9/2018)

Disaster Resilience Reports

Disaster Assistance: Opportunities to Enhance Implementation of the Redesigned Public Assistance Grant Program. GAO-18-30. Washington, D.C.: November 8, 2017.

Climate Change: Information on Potential Economic Effects Could Help Guide Federal Efforts to Reduce Fiscal Exposure. GAO-17-720. Washington, D.C.: September 28, 2017.

Climate Change: Improved Federal Coordination Could Facilitate Use of Forward-Looking Climate Information in Design Standards, Building Codes, and Certifications. GAO-17-3. Washington, D.C.: November 30, 2016.

Hurricane Sandy: An Investment Strategy Could Help the Federal Government Enhance National Resilience for Future Disasters. GAO-15-515, Washington, D.C.: July 30, 2015.

2017 Hurricane Season
FEMA After-Action Report

July 12, 2018

Letter from the Administrator to the Emergency Management Community

The 2017 Hurricane Season was a devastating experience for millions of Americans, with more disaster survivors registering for assistance than the previous 10 years combined. While the Nation responded to three major hurricanes in quick succession—Harvey, Irma, and Maria—California simultaneously suffered historic wildfires. FEMA and its partners rose to these challenges and I am incredibly proud of how we performed in extraordinary circumstances. Not surprisingly, the unprecedented scale and rapid succession of these disasters stretched response and recovery capabilities at all levels of government, and is transforming the way emergency managers prepare for and respond to disasters. The challenges we faced required that we innovate and deliver our programs differently. Looking ahead, we will take bold action to improve the Nation's overall readiness and resiliency for future incidents.

FEMA's *2018-2022 Strategic Plan* builds on the lessons from 2017 and an intensive stakeholder engagement process to point the way forward for our Agency and the emergency management community. First, we must build a national culture of preparedness. Second, we must ready the Nation for catastrophic disasters. Third, we must reduce the complexity of FEMA, making the Agency's programs and services easier and more efficient.

Building a Culture of Preparedness

Building a culture of preparedness within our communities and our government will support a national effort to be ready for the worst disasters—at the individual; family; community; state, local, tribal, and territorial (SLTT); and federal levels. Those closest to the impacted areas are the true first responders during any emergency or disaster. In 2017, brave residents joined first responders, along with state and local emergency managers, non-profit organizations, the private sector, and federal staff in working together to serve survivors. Countless Texans and Louisianans took to their boats and rescued fellow residents who were stranded by rising floodwaters. In Puerto Rico, "health brigades" of local volunteers knocked on doors to identify and assist those who could not leave. We must continue to support these types of life-saving activities by private citizens. In addition, we must encourage citizens to buy insurance and be prepared for disasters. Communities must mitigate the effects of possible incidents to be more resilient.

The 2017 Hurricane Season also reminds us of the importance of preparedness of SLTT governments. While FEMA has and will continue to work with all levels of government to get much needed commodities to survivors, the hurricanes also showed that governments need to be better prepared with their own supplies, to have pre-positioned contracts with enforcement mechanisms, and to be ready for the financial implications of a disaster. Establishing "rainy day" or disaster relief funds and increasing awareness of federal procurement standards will help communities prepare for the initial outlay of expenses and ensure their eligibility for federal reimbursement.

Readying the Nation for Catastrophic Disasters

Responding to overwhelming incidents requires emergency managers to adapt, innovate quickly, and engage new partners to address unanticipated impacts and cascading effects. While plans are based on the best information available, no disaster follows the plan. Every response requires adaptation, which is why flexible authorities and programs are important.

July 12, 2018

The response to the hurricanes demonstrated the need for emergency managers at all levels to improve collaboration with the critical infrastructure sectors. These disasters demonstrate that our current organizing structures are insufficient to promote this collaboration. We need to revise the National Response Framework and, as required, the Response Federal Interagency Operational Plan to emphasize stabilization of critical lifelines and coordination across the critical infrastructure sectors. As a Nation, closer partnerships with the private sector are crucial in providing commodities and support to survivors.

No jurisdiction or federal agency has all the staff and resources it will need to respond to a catastrophic incident. During the 2017 hurricanes, state and local governments shared resources through mutual aid protocols, including the Emergency Management Assistance Compact. Efforts to streamline resource sharing, such as National Incident Management System resource typing and the National Qualification System, can create additional capacity for emergency management programs across the country. By building capacity at the state and local levels, federal financial support may not require a federal staff presence in small disasters.

FEMA and our territory and federal partners faced challenges supplying limited temporary power generation capacity, highlighting that governments at all levels and private sector owners of critical infrastructure need to further invest in resilient electrical grids and prepare for outages. Operable communications are critical to effective disaster operations. In the aftermath of Hurricane Maria, 95 percent of cell towers in Puerto Rico were out of service and outages continued in the ensuing months. As a result, local, territorial, and federal agencies faced difficulties knowing what was needed and where in the immediate aftermath of the storm. We must ensure survivable communications capability to enable coordination between government leadership and to maintain connection with the critical infrastructure sectors. We, as a Nation, have more work to do collectively to prepare for and respond to major infrastructure outages.

Reducing the Complexity of FEMA

FEMA will work with all of our partners, including Congress, to better serve survivors before, during, and after disasters. Some of these actions cannot be accomplished within existing authorities or by administrative action. Collectively, we must continue to simplify our processes and leverage new approaches and technology to reduce complexity and increase efficiency, focusing on outcome-based recovery.

The 2017 hurricanes reinforce that there is no easy or one-size-fits-all solution to housing tens of thousands of displaced survivors. FEMA needs to simplify the process of applying for assistance to make our programs easier to navigate. SLTT officials—within and beyond the emergency management community—are better able to shape the future recovery of their communities. Working together, we can build capability to better enable federally supported, state-managed, and locally executed methods to shelter and house survivors.

With this report, FEMA and the emergency management community have an opportunity to learn from the 2017 Hurricane Season and build a more prepared and resilient Nation.

/s/

Brock Long
FEMA Administrator

FEMA 2017 Hurricane Season After-Action Report (7/2018)

Table of Contents

Executive Summary

The 2017 Atlantic Hurricane Season was one of the most active seasons in U.S. history, causing widespread damage to, or destruction of, critical infrastructure, livelihoods, and property. The hurricane season was accompanied by devastating wildfires in California that burned for months. Between April and November there were 17 named storms, of which 10 became hurricanes (Figure 1). This After-Action Report focuses on three of these storms that made landfall as major hurricanes in the United States in quick succession. Specifically, this report focuses on the response and initial recovery from August 25 to November 30, 2017.

- On August 25, **Hurricane Harvey** made landfall in Texas as a Category 4 storm. For several days, the storm hovered near the Houston metropolitan area and set a record for the most rainfall from a U.S. tropical cyclone. Of households impacted by Hurricane Harvey, 80 percent did not have flood insurance.

- On September 6, **Hurricane Irma** became one of the strongest Atlantic hurricanes on record. The storm's center passed just north of the U.S. Virgin Islands and Puerto Rico and destroyed critical infrastructure on St. Thomas and St. John in the U.S. Virgin Islands, as well as Puerto Rico and the Florida Keys. Hurricane Irma was the first major hurricane to make landfall in Florida since 2005. The public followed evacuation orders as the storm approached Florida, resulting in one of the largest sheltering missions in U.S. history. Hurricane Irma also impacted the Seminole Tribe of Florida and the states of Alabama, Georgia, North Carolina, South Carolina, and Tennessee.

Figure 1: The 2017 Hurricane Season was exceptionally active, with 17 named storms (source: National Hurricane Center).

- The center of **Hurricane Maria** passed southeast of St. Croix, U.S. Virgin Islands on September 19 as a Category 5 storm, and made landfall in Puerto Rico as a Category 4 storm the next day. Hurricane Maria severely damaged or destroyed a significant portion of both territories' already fragile critical infrastructure. Maria left Puerto Rico's 3.7 million residents without electricity. The resulting response represents the longest sustained air mission of food and water delivery in Federal Emergency Management Agency (FEMA) history.

In addition to the three major hurricanes making landfall, Hurricane Jose threatened the Caribbean and the East Coast of the United States for nearly two weeks, requiring FEMA resources and interfering with sea transport to the Caribbean. Similarly, Hurricane Nate made landfall near the mouth of the Mississippi River, but its impacts were relatively limited. Nearly simultaneously, FEMA also supported California in responding to some of the most devastating wildfires to ever impact the state. Last year's hurricanes and wildfires came at a time when FEMA was already supporting 692 federally declared disasters and tested the Nation's ability to respond to and recover from multiple concurrent disasters.

Hurricanes Harvey, Irma, and Maria caused a combined $265 billion in damage and resulted in widespread displacement of survivors.

From Hurricane Harvey's landfall in Texas on August 25 to the end of the 2017 Hurricane Season on November 30, the President granted 10 Major Disaster declarations and 10 Emergency declarations for communities impacted by these three storms. As of April 30, 2018, FEMA had obligated $21.2 billion towards the impact of these hurricanes, including disaster assistance to survivors and the affected communities. FEMA coordinated large deployments of federal personnel, both before and after the storms' landfalls, to support response and initial recovery efforts across 270,000 square miles. These deployments included over 17,000 FEMA and federal Surge Capacity Force personnel, and nearly 14,000 staff from various offices of the Department of Defense (DoD) operating under DoD's Defense Support of Civil Authorities process.

FEMA Urban Search and Rescue Task Forces, comprised of state and local emergency responders, saved or assisted nearly 9,500 lives across the three hurricanes. These numbers stand in addition to the thousands of lives saved or assisted by DoD, the U.S. Coast Guard, state and local first responders, and neighbors helping neighbors. Concurrent with response operations, FEMA moved quickly to meet long-term survivor needs.

The unprecedented scale, scope, and impacts of the complex combination of hurricanes Harvey, Irma, and Maria and the California Wildfires tested the capabilities FEMA has developed and improved since hurricanes Katrina and Sandy. The 2017 Hurricane Season involved major operations across multiple incidents that required decision-makers to rapidly observe and react to unfolding events. FEMA surged and redeployed resources for incidents across a wide geographic area to support millions of survivors in their time of need.

By May 2018, nearly 4.8 million households affected by the 2017 hurricanes
and California Wildfires registered for assistance—
more than the previous 10 years combined.

Key Findings

Following the 2017 Hurricane Season, FEMA conducted an After-Action Review of the Agency's preparation for, immediate response to, and initial recovery operations for hurricanes Harvey, Irma, and Maria. The lessons learned from this review are driving targeted improvements within key areas of FEMA's response and initial recovery operations. Findings from the 2017 Hurricane Season are also guiding FEMA's ongoing efforts to help the whole community improve preparedness.

FEMA analyzed an extensive set of data and supporting information from across the Agency and its partners and identified 18 strategic-level key findings across five focus areas:

Focus Area 1: Scaling a Response for Concurrent, Complex Incidents
Key Findings
1. FEMA leaders at all levels made major adaptations to Agency policy and programs to respond to significant operational challenges during the hurricane season.
2. FEMA's plans guided response operations, but enhancements to the planning process and format are needed to improve usability during operations.
3. FEMA could have better leveraged open-source information and preparedness data, such as capability assessments and exercise findings, for Puerto Rico and the U.S. Virgin Islands.

FEMA 2017 Hurricane Season After-Action Report (7/2018)

Focus Area 1: Scaling a Response for Concurrent, Complex Incidents

Recommendations Summary

- Revise the National Response Framework and, as required, the Response Federal Interagency Operational Plan to emphasize stabilization of critical lifelines and coordination across critical infrastructure sectors
- Leverage the new FEMA Integration Teams and technical assistance to help states build capacity
- Work with whole community partners to improve risk management and strengthen capabilities
- Create preparedness and planning products that are easily accessible, modular, inclusive, and readily executable
- Drive outcome-based recovery through expanded use of Stafford Act Section 428 Authorities for Public Assistance Alternative Procedures

Focus Area 2: Staffing for Concurrent, Complex Incidents

Key Findings

4. FEMA entered the hurricane season with a force strength less than its target, resulting in staffing shortages across the incidents.
5. The Agency has made progress on disaster workforce certification, but had not achieved its targets. Field leaders reported some resultant inefficiency in program delivery.
6. FEMA strategically consolidated ongoing disaster operations facilities across the country to reallocate personnel to the hurricane-affected field operations, which increased capacity to deliver FEMA programs.
7. FEMA augmented its disaster workforce through a combination of initiatives it has used before, as well as innovative and newly expanded methods—these initiatives met their stated intent, but can be matured.

Recommendations Summary

- Revise the National Response Framework and, as required, the Response Federal Interagency Operational Plan to emphasize stabilization of critical lifelines and coordination across critical infrastructure sectors
- Support states in building a greater capacity to respond to and recover from disasters by maintaining financial support while right-sizing the federal deployment footprint
- Build and maintain a national incident workforce that includes emergency managers from state, local, tribal, and territorial governments
- Use the Urban Search and Rescue Task Force model to further build Incident Management Assistance Teams' capability
- Complete a disaster workforce review within the Agency, to include incident management, incident support, and mission essential functions
- Streamline and increase certifications across FEMA's incident workforce

FEMA 2017 Hurricane Season After-Action Report (7/2018)

Focus Area 3: Sustained Whole Community Logistics Operations

Key Findings

8. FEMA assumed a more active role in coordinating whole community logistics operations for Puerto Rico and the U.S. Virgin Islands due to these territories' preparedness challenges, geographic distance, and pre-existing, on-the-ground conditions.

9. While FEMA mobilized billions of dollars in commodities, the Agency experienced challenges in comprehensively tracking resources moving across multiple modes of transportation to Puerto Rico and the U.S. Virgin Islands due to staffing shortages and business process shortfalls.

10. FEMA provided logistical coordination to move and distribute commodities from staging areas to survivors in Puerto Rico, supplementing a role that should largely be managed and coordinated at the state or territory level.

11. In a three-month period, FEMA issued more contract actions than in an entire previous fiscal year to meet disaster requirements, which strained the Agency's contracting personnel.

Recommendations Summary

- Revise the National Response Framework and, as required, the Response Federal Interagency Operational Plan to emphasize stabilization of critical lifelines and coordination across critical infrastructure sectors
- Promote federally supported, state-managed, locally executed logistics operations
- Increase FEMA readiness stocks outside the continental United States
- Increase transportation planning, management, and contract support capacities
- Broaden FEMA's capability to quickly get teams on the ground to stage and deliver key commodities to disaster survivors, even in the most remote locations
- Streamline storage and movement across multiple modes of transportation that facilitate and speed delivery
- Develop a more comprehensive understanding of local, regional, and national supply chains, as well as stronger relationships with critical private sector partners to support rapid restoration in response to catastrophic incidents
- Support state, local, tribal, and territorial governments in improving capability for disaster cost recovery, pre-event contracting and contract enforcement and vendor-managed inventory

Focus Area 4: Responding During Long-Term Infrastructure Outages

Key Findings

12. To overcome limited situational awareness created by the loss of communications in Puerto Rico, FEMA executed creative solutions to assess the situation and prioritize response activities, including emergency repairs to infrastructure.

13. Challenged by an inoperable telecommunications environment in Puerto Rico, FEMA had to adapt field communications, program delivery, and command and control activities.

14. FEMA and its federal partners installed a record number of generators to provide temporary power to critical infrastructure while facing significant challenges in identifying generator requirements and shortfalls in available generators.

FEMA 2017 Hurricane Season After-Action Report (7/2018)

Focus Area 4: Responding During Long-Term Infrastructure Outages

Recommendations Summary

- Revise the National Response Framework and, as required, the Response Federal Interagency Operational Plan to emphasize stabilization of critical lifelines and coordination across critical infrastructure sectors
- Establish a standing Power Task Force as a collaborative, steady-state partnership and transition it to a crisis action planning cell under Emergency Support Function #12 partners during disaster operations
- Encourage investment in redundant assets to maintain communications and supply temporary power
- Encourage critical infrastructure owners and operators, and state and local governments, to invest in more resilient infrastructure
- Include continuity and resilient all-hazards communications capabilities in plans and guidance

Focus Area 5: Mass Care to Initial Housing Operations

Key Findings

15. FEMA supported American Red Cross and Emergency Support Function #6 partners to provide more than one million shelter nights within the first 60 days, while facing challenges transitioning survivors out of congregate sheltering.
16. In Texas and Florida, FEMA helped survivors quickly transition from congregate shelters to other options such as hotels. However, across all operations, FEMA faced challenges implementing non-congregate sheltering programs.
17. FEMA created new, streamlined housing inspection procedures to reduce inspection delays.
18. FEMA applied lessons learned from recent housing operations and exercises to expand temporary and permanent housing solutions, including supporting a state-managed housing mission.

Recommendations Summary

- Revise the National Response Framework and, as required, the Response Federal Interagency Operational Plan to emphasize stabilization of critical lifelines and coordination across critical infrastructure sectors
- Build capability and empower the implementation of federally supported, state-managed, locally executed sheltering and housing solutions
- Improve the delivery and effectiveness of housing options, including exploring grant-making authority
- Clarify federal roles and responsibilities for housing programs, including approaches to long-term housing
- Evaluate and implement appropriate housing solutions, including the use of Recreation Vehicles, Direct Repair, and Direct Lease options
- Promote all-hazard insurance so that individuals can reduce their losses and speed their recovery

Next Steps

While the 2017 Hurricane Season has concluded, recovering from these devastating hurricanes will take years. FEMA is committed to supporting the long-term recovery of affected governments and survivors. In addition, FEMA has already begun acting on these recommendations to improve future disaster operations.

Introduction

In the three weeks between August 25 and September 20, hurricanes Harvey, Irma, and Maria made landfall in the United States in rapid succession. These hurricanes were followed by devastating wildfires in California. The hurricanes and wildfires collectively affected more than 47 million people—nearly 15 percent of the Nation's population. Hurricanes Harvey, Irma, and Maria caused a collective $265 billion in damages (Figure 2) and were each individually among the top five costliest hurricanes on record (Figure 3). The fact that these historic storms occurred concurrently and were followed by the California Wildfires presented an unprecedented scale of operations, extremely complex logistics, and numerous novel challenges across the Nation. Leaders had to determine how to allocate and subsequently redistribute limited resources across disasters. This report focuses on FEMA's response and initial recovery efforts from August 25 to November 30, 2017.

According to the National Oceanic and Atmospheric Administration (NOAA), Hurricane Harvey resulted in 103 direct and indirect fatalities in the United States and Hurricane Irma resulted in 96 direct and indirect fatalities. The fatality count from Hurricane Maria in Puerto Rico was being reviewed by the government of Puerto Rico at the time of this report.

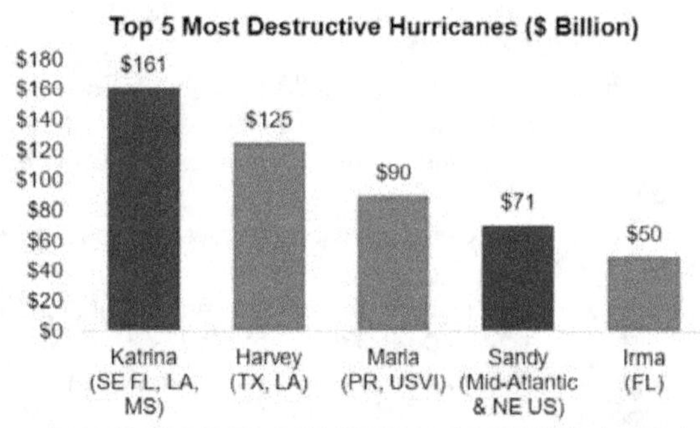

Figure 2: The 2017 Hurricane Season is estimated to have caused $265 billion in damages and losses (source: NOAA National Centers for Environmental Information).

Hurricanes Harvey and Irma marked the first instance of two Atlantic hurricanes making landfall as Category 4 storms in the continental United States in the same season. Hurricane Harvey dropped more than 60 inches of rain east of Houston—the most rain ever recorded during a single storm in the United States. Overall, Texas experienced significant flooding that forced 780,000 survivors from their homes, of whom more than 42,000 were temporarily housed in 270 shelters in the days following landfall.

Hurricane Irma impacted the U.S. Virgin Islands and Puerto Rico, with the storm's center passing just north of the territories as a Category 5 hurricane on September 6. The storm caused high storm surge, flooding, extensive damage to buildings and infrastructure, and widespread power outages.

Hurricane Irma continued north and made landfall in the Florida Keys as a Category 4 hurricane on September 10 and then made a second landfall on the Florida peninsula as a Category 3 hurricane later that day. Storm surge and powerful winds caused heavy damage to infrastructure across the State. Florida jurisdictions issued evacuation orders for a record-breaking 6.8 million people, contributing to one of the largest sheltering missions in U.S. history. Florida housed a peak of 191,764 people in nearly 700 shelters across the State. In addition to Florida,

Figure 3: When adjusted for inflation, the 2017 hurricanes are among the top five costliest on record dating back to 1980 (source: NOAA National Centers for Environmental Information).

Irma also impacted the Seminole Tribe of Florida, and the states of Alabama, Georgia, North Carolina, South Carolina, and Tennessee.

On September 19, the center of Hurricane Maria passed just south of the U.S. Virgin Islands as a Category 5 hurricane and made landfall on Puerto Rico as a Category 4 hurricane the next day. Hurricane Maria was the first Category 4 storm to make landfall on Puerto Rico in 85 years. Following the storm, every airport and seaport in Puerto Rico was closed and even after reopening had limited capacity for approximately seven days post-landfall due to restrictions. Less than 12 percent of the territory's population had access to cell phone service in the immediate aftermath of the storm. The majority of the main island's power grid was down until November 17, with outages continuing through May 2018. Additionally, the storm disrupted critical supply routes from Puerto Rico to the U.S. Virgin Islands. In sum, the three storms affected diverse geographic areas of varying size and population density (Figure 4).

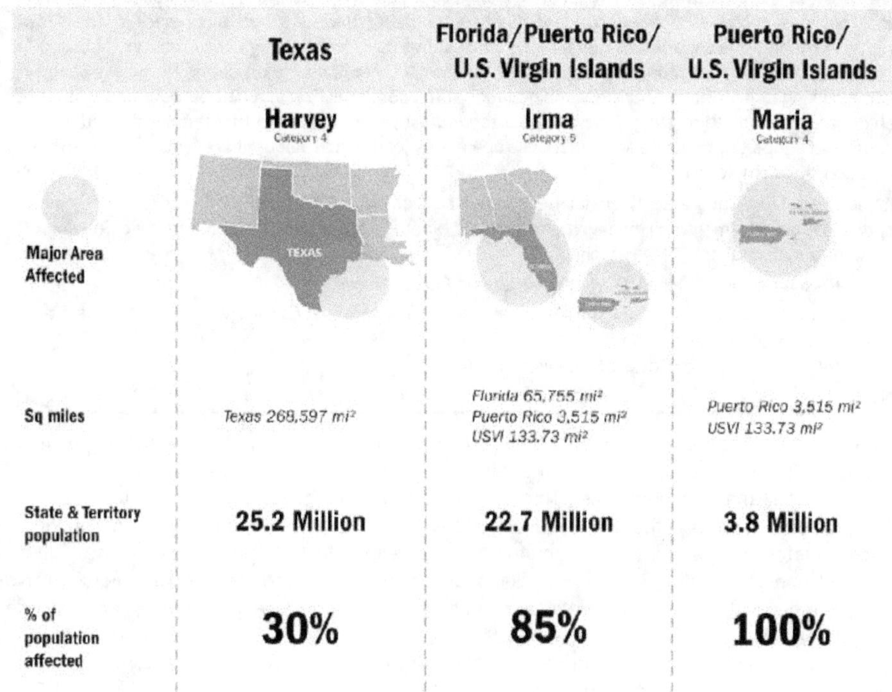

Figure 4: Hurricanes Harvey, Irma, and Maria affected more than 28 million people in Texas, Florida, U.S. Virgin Islands, and Puerto Rico.

Throughout the 2017 Hurricane Season, FEMA managed concurrent, complex incidents across geographically dispersed areas over a long duration of time. The Agency also coordinated with federal and state, local, tribal, territorial (SLTT), and whole community partners to accelerate the large-scale distribution of resources to survivors.

FEMA 2017 Hurricane Season After-Action Report (7/2018)

FEMA provided over $2 billion worth of commodities to affected states and territories.

As part of the Federal Government's response to three near-simultaneous incidents, FEMA deployed more than 17,000 personnel, including 4,063 non-FEMA and non-Department of Defense (DoD) federal employees through the federal Surge Capacity Force (SCF) and other methods. By comparison, FEMA deployed 9,971 staff for Hurricane Sandy response operations in 2012. In addition, DoD deployed nearly 14,000 personnel to affected areas across three different FEMA regions.

Activation of National and Regional Response Coordination Centers during the 2017 Hurricane Season

On August 25, FEMA activated the National Response Coordination Center (NRCC), the multi-agency center that provides overall federal support coordination for major disasters and emergencies. The NRCC remained operational for a record-breaking 76 consecutive days coordinating concurrent operations, and operating at the highest federal response level for over 3 times longer than during Hurricane Sandy in 2012. During its activation, the NRCC maintained 24/7 operations, transitioned between day and night shifts, and rotated teams every 7 days. This extended activation confirmed that the center's staff were capable of supporting cross-Regional response operations for multiple, sequential events that vary in type, duration, and complexity.

In addition, FEMA activated Regional Response Coordination Centers (RRCCs) in FEMA Regions to coordinate overall emergency management activities with the impacted states and territories (Appendix C includes a map of all 10 FEMA Regions):

- Region II supported the U.S. Virgin Islands and Puerto Rico;
- Region IV supported Florida, the Seminole Tribe of Florida, Alabama, Georgia, North Carolina, South Carolina, and Tennessee; and
- Region VI supported Texas and Louisiana.

Between August 25 and October 16, the President issued a total of 20 disaster or emergency declarations for the three storms: Hurricane Harvey (3 declarations), Hurricane Irma (13 declarations), and Hurricane Maria (4 declarations). Through its Incident Management Assistance Teams (IMATs), FEMA provided a forward federal presence of senior-level emergency managers to support the impacted states and territories in preparing for and responding to the storms. At the height of concurrent operations, all 28 of FEMA's National Urban Search and Rescue Task Forces rapidly deployed to support life-saving operations, searching more than 30,900 structures, and saving or assisting nearly 9,500 people. By the end of the hurricane season on November 30, more than 4.7 million households affected by hurricanes Harvey, Irma, and Maria had registered for federal assistance with FEMA, more than all who registered for hurricanes Katrina, Rita, Wilma, and Sandy combined.

In addition to conducting concurrent response operations for hurricanes Harvey, Irma, and Maria, FEMA also had to take action on hurricanes Jose and Nate. The impacts from those two storms were minimal by comparison, but nevertheless required FEMA's focus and resources. While Hurricane Jose never made landfall, FEMA deployed IMATs to three states and bolstered staging areas with additional commodities. Hurricane Jose also complicated Hurricane Irma and Hurricane Maria response efforts in the Caribbean by limiting sea transport of food and water as well as transit of U.S. Naval response assets to the U.S. Virgin Islands and Puerto Rico. Hurricane Nate made landfall as a Category 1 storm on October 7, striking Mississippi and Alabama in the Gulf Coast and resulting in Major Disaster declarations in each state.

Nearly simultaneously, the response to the historic wildfires across the Western United States, including 5 of the 20 most destructive wildfires in modern California history, required the deployment of additional FEMA personnel, commodities, and equipment. As of November 30, the fires had claimed 44 lives and damaged or destroyed nearly 10,000 structures. The response to the California Wildfires required a greater amount of DoD contracts and mission assignments than the hurricane response in support of Texas and Florida combined.

As shown in Figure 5, FEMA supported 59 Major Disaster declarations and 16 Emergency declarations in 2017.

Calendar Year 2017 Major and Emergency Disaster Declarations by County

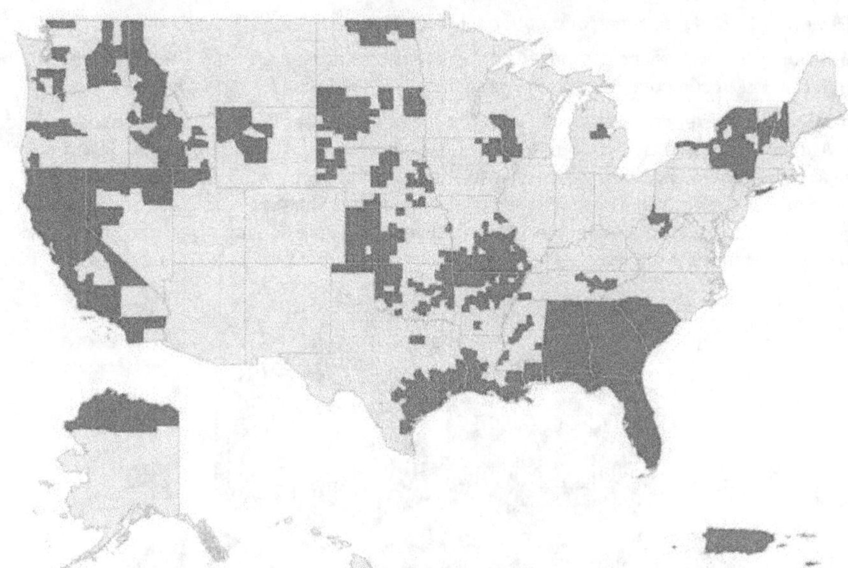

Figure 5: During the course of an exceptionally active year of disasters, FEMA supported 75 Major and Emergency Disaster declarations.

Report Scope, Methodology, and Organization

This report reviews the Agency's preparations for, immediate response to, and initial recovery from hurricanes Harvey, Irma, and Maria, focusing on the timeframe of August 25, 2017 through November 30, 2017. While hurricanes Jose and Nate and the California Wildfires affected resources that FEMA had available during the hurricane season, this report primarily focuses on FEMA's support to the states and territories most impacted by hurricanes Harvey, Irma, and Maria: Texas, Florida, Puerto Rico, and the U.S. Virgin Islands. While FEMA coordinates disaster response and recovery efforts across the Federal Government and works closely with non-federal whole community partners, this report focuses on lessons learned for several key areas of internal FEMA response and initial recovery operations. FEMA will continue to review ongoing recovery operations and is using the findings in this report as well as future reports to drive improvements across the Agency's resilience, response, and recovery programs.

The *2017 Hurricane Season After-Action Report* reflects a wide variety of input from FEMA and its whole community partners. To collect data for this report, FEMA:

- Sent teams to observe and document response and recovery operations and decision-making in Texas, Florida, Puerto Rico, RRCCs, and the NRCC;[a]

- Interviewed hundreds of personnel, including Agency leadership and staff in headquarters, regional, and field offices;

- Developed a hurricane season chronology with more than 4,000 unique data points on key FEMA and selected non-FEMA federal decisions and actions for hurricanes Harvey, Irma, and Maria;

- Analyzed 17 different quantitative datasets to indicate how FEMA's response efforts evolved over time;

- Reviewed 12 state, regional, and national-level plans; and

- Convened working groups comprised of subject-matter experts and stakeholders representing 13 different FEMA components, who provided data and validation for report findings.

The balance of this report is organized into five focus areas that FEMA selected based on priorities from Agency leadership at headquarters, regional, and field offices (Figure 6). FEMA developed strategic-level key findings by synthesizing the data collected from the sources listed above with a focus on operational impact. These findings directly informed FEMA's *2018-2022 Strategic Plan*. Each section also includes Agency recommendations aligned to Strategic Plan objectives. Finally, Appendix A provides disaster data that has been updated from the original timeframe of the report through May 2018.

Figure 6: The After-Action Report covers key findings in five focus areas that span FEMA's response and early recovery efforts for the 2017 Hurricane Season.

---

[a] FEMA did not deploy Continuous Improvement Program staff to the U.S. Virgin Islands during the timeframe covered by this report. Data collection on FEMA's operations in the U.S. Virgin Islands was conducted remotely. Teams in Florida also observed operations for the Seminole Tribe of Florida.

 July 12, 2018

Scaling a Response for Concurrent, Complex Incidents

The unprecedented combination of multiple, large, and complex disasters—such as hurricanes Harvey, Irma, and Maria—required FEMA to adapt to evolving disaster response and recovery needs. FEMA could not isolate one incident from the other, but rather apportioned and allocated resources based on emergency management experience in a dynamic environment. FEMA had to employ all available capacity in the most effective manner possible and re-allocate resources for newly emerging requirements (i.e., from Harvey to Irma, and then to Maria, and finally the California Wildfires). In such instances, FEMA often modified or quickly reinterpreted policies, programs, and authorities. The 2017 Hurricane Season revealed areas where the Agency was both well prepared to handle these challenges and areas where it can improve.

Key Finding #1: FEMA leaders at all levels made major adaptations to Agency policy and programs to respond to significant operational challenges during the hurricane season.

FEMA's decision-making process during the 2017 Hurricane Season is informing the Agency's approach to future concurrent, complex incidents. To address the challenges of this hurricane season, FEMA leaders adapted agency policy and programs to provide support to the impacted states, tribes, and territories. The Agency continues to assess outcomes from these decisions. This finding describes policy adaptations in five areas: (1) relocating regional staff to FEMA Headquarters; (2) state-managed survivor housing mission; (3) updated Public Assistance delivery model; (4) Public Assistance alternative procedures, and (5) addressing deferred maintenance.

Figure 7: FEMA Region II personnel convene to review hurricane operations.

Relocating Regional Staff to FEMA Headquarters

Shortly after Hurricane Maria made landfall in Puerto Rico, FEMA leadership decided to transition incident support responsibilities to FEMA Headquarters, as provided for by Agency policy. The RRCC and NRCC are the centralized locations for the Federal Government and other partners to coordinate disaster support. Typically, FEMA Regions support field operations from the RRCC; however, FEMA's transition policy allows for impacted Regions to transfer those responsibilities to the NRCC during large-scale incidents. FEMA's transition and devolution policy does not require the temporary relocation of regional staff from the RRCC to the NRCC, but findings from recent exercises had recommended it. Thus, when primary incident support and coordination transitioned to the NRCC for Puerto Rico and the U.S. Virgin Islands, a number of Region II staff from each incident support section moved from Region II to the NRCC to improve coordination by co-locating expertise and field contacts of Region II staff. Although the storm did not impact the Region II RRCC operations in New York, the transition and subsequent relocation of regional staff allowed for consolidated operations at the NRCC.

State-Managed Survivor Housing Mission

Given the magnitude of housing challenges facing Texas, FEMA recognized that it needed more ways to provide housing assistance and adapted programs to better meet the State's needs. FEMA has historically led the coordination of direct housing assistance (e.g., manufactured housing units, recreation vehicles) through its Individuals and Households Program (IHP). To address the historic

6

scale of housing needs following Hurricane Harvey, FEMA and the State of Texas negotiated a formal agreement to establish a state-managed housing mission, authorizing the state to provide housing services on behalf of FEMA. This agreement, created due to an absence of a grant-making authority, was intended to provide Texas with greater flexibility to use its own authorities to secure housing solutions that met State and disaster-specific objectives, as well as develop a more streamlined approach to long-term recovery. This state-managed housing mission is further discussed under Key Finding #18.

Updated Public Assistance Delivery Model

FEMA expedited implementation of an updated delivery model for the Public Assistance (PA) Grant Program. After an internal analysis in 2014 revealed PA delivery model shortfalls, FEMA began developing a revised delivery approach that could more easily adapt to the size, complexity, and cost of recovery operations. FEMA initiated pilots of this updated PA delivery model in 2016, and had planned for it to replace the legacy model in early 2018. To streamline internal operations and improve the overall experience for local communities as they worked to rebuild public infrastructure damaged during the hurricane season, FEMA leadership expedited the launch of the updated PA delivery model on September 12, 2017, amid the early responses to hurricanes Harvey and Irma. However, FEMA later determined that neither Puerto Rico nor the U.S. Virgin Islands had the capacity or the experience to effectively implement this approach.

> **Public Assistance Grant Program**
>
> Public Assistance is FEMA's largest grant program and accounts for, on average, 51 percent of FEMA grant funding. The program provides emergency assistance to save lives and protect property, and assists communities with repairing public infrastructure affected by federally declared incidents.

Public Assistance Alternative Procedures

On October 30, 2017, the Commonwealth of Puerto Rico elected to use alternative procedures for all Public Assistance funding for permanent work, an approach which allows for the consolidation of projects and streamlines funding by relying on fixed estimates instead of documented, actual costs. Previous pilot programs of these alternative PA procedures were optional for communities on a project-by-project basis. Under normal PA procedures, processing all project reimbursements based on documented, actual costs can take up to several years. Using alternative procedures, after FEMA and the grantee agree on a total cost estimate, funding that corresponds with that estimate can be made available before starting permanent work. The alternative procedures were intended to move FEMA and the Commonwealth toward outcome-based recovery by simplifying the funding process, reducing the time to receive federal funding, and providing greater flexibility for Puerto Rico to rebuild its infrastructure to be more effective, efficient, and resilient.

> **Public Assistance Alternative Procedures Authorities**
>
> In 2013, the *Sandy Recovery Improvement Act of 2013* authorized alternative procedures for Public Assistance. Alternative procedures allow FEMA to issue one consolidated grant based on a cost estimate rather than issuing individual grants for each community project.

Addressing Deferred Maintenance Challenges

In responding to the challenges posed by the impact of Hurricane Maria, FEMA recognized that it needed additional authorities to provide support for infrastructure repair in Puerto Rico and the U.S. Virgin Islands. Due to poor pre-disaster infrastructure conditions in both locations, FEMA could not determine whether some or all of post-hurricane recorded damages were attributable to the disasters. Additionally, FEMA could not make necessary repairs to damaged system components that remained connected or serviced by undamaged, outdated elements. In February 2018, Congress passed the

Bipartisan Budget Act of 2018. The law gives FEMA additional authorities under Section 428 of the *Robert T. Stafford Disaster Relief and Emergency Assistance Act of 1988, as amended* (Stafford Act). Under this law, FEMA can provide assistance for critical services to replace or restore components of the facility or system that are not damaged by the disaster when those repairs are necessary to fully effectuate the replacement or restoration of disaster-damaged components to restore the function of the facility or system to industry standards. These provisions will improve the resilience of electric, communications, and other critical facilities in the territories.

Key Finding #2: FEMA's plans guided response operations, but enhancements to the planning process and format are needed to improve usability during operations.

FEMA planners collaborate with SLTT partners to develop plans before disasters. FEMA and its partners draw on a range of available data, including the Threat and Hazard Identification and Risk Assessment (THIRA) and State Preparedness Report (SPR), to inform these plans (See Key Finding #3). The plans describe how FEMA and the jurisdiction will respond to and recover from incidents, and include planning assumptions. Plans aim to align operations with their needs among interagency Emergency Support Functions (ESFs) and whole community partners. Plans provide responders with an understanding of the concept of operations, critical considerations for crisis action planning, options for adapting to unmet needs, and sufficient detail to help expedite ordering resources and moving commodities and people.

Prior to the hurricane season, FEMA had plans in place with each of the affected states and territories, and had either recently updated the plan or had committed to performing an update of all such plans.

Table 1: FEMA consulted various plans to inform disaster operations during the 2017 Hurricane Season.

	Applicable Plans Consulted to Inform Operations	
National	Federal Interagency Operational Plans, Response & Recovery	Developed 2016
	Power Outage Incident Annex	Developed 2016
	Catastrophic Housing Annex	Developed 2012, Update underway
Hurricane Harvey	Region VI All Hazards Plan	Developed 2013, Update begins in 2018
	Texas Hurricane Plan	Developed 2017, Update yearly
Hurricane Irma (Florida)	Region IV All Hazards Plan	Developed 2012, Update begins in 2018
	Florida Tropical Storm Incident Annex	Developed 2015
	Region IV Hurricane Incident Annex	Developed 2016
Hurricane Irma/Maria (Caribbean)	Region II All Hazards Plan	Developed 2012, Update begins in 2019
	Outside Continental United States Hurricane Response Plan	Developed 2014, Update underway
Hurricane Irma (U.S. Virgin Islands)	U.S. Virgin Islands Earthquake and Tsunami Operational Plan	Developed 2012
Hurricane Maria (Puerto Rico)	Puerto Rico Earthquake and Tsunami Operational Plan	Developed 2012

FEMA plans are developed based on a FEMA Operational Planning Manual that provides a standard methodology and structure, while allowing flexibility for the FEMA Regions to meet the specific needs and preferences of the supported state or territory. As a result, the plans across the three Regions had varying levels of detail on the tasks to be executed and ways to address potential challenges. The extent to which plans integrated response and recovery operational tasks also varied.

The goal of the planning process and written plan is to facilitate effective unity of effort, organization, communication, and action to manage dynamic situations. In Texas, hurricane response plans reflected inter-state agreements for the disaster support Texas would receive and helped FEMA estimate how much federal support would be required to respond to Hurricane Harvey. The plans included information updated as recently as June 2016 on evacuation procedures, resource distribution networks, and logistics facilities.

In Florida, plans developed by FEMA and the State in 2015 and 2016 provided accurate estimates of disaster impacts before on-the-ground assessments were possible. The plans anticipated significant short-term sheltering needs following Hurricane Irma, and informed mass care operations to help provide basic needs for the 191,764 survivors in congregate shelters. Further, the plans accurately anticipated the loss of power to six million customers, and accounted for the state's ability to restore most communications and power within approximately one week.

Table 2: Comparison of key planning assumptions and field reports in Texas and Florida.

Disaster Impact	Planning Assumption	2017 Field Report
Texas		
Points of Distribution (POD)	Projected a need to support up to 80 PODs	41 PODs were required
State-to-State Mutual Aid Support	Anticipated states would activate mutual aid agreements to provide support	34 states and 1 territory provided mutual aid support
Florida		
Power Outages	Projected 31.3% of residents would lose power	31.8% of residents lost power
Short-term Sheltering	Projected a need to shelter 349,799 survivors	191,764 survivors sought temporary shelter
Hospitals Impacted	Projected 15% of hospitals would be impacted	16% of hospitals were impacted

The fact that the planning assumptions for the Texas and Florida hurricane plans were similar to the ultimate incidents (Table 2) illustrates how planning can help to expedite and inform decision making to quickly manage a crisis situation.

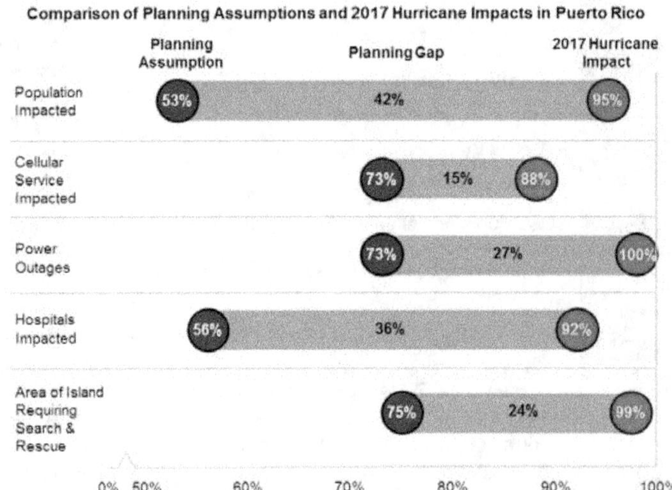

Figure 8: Planning assumptions underestimated impacts of 2017 hurricanes in Puerto Rico.

FEMA 2017 Hurricane Season After-Action Report (7/2018)

The planning assumptions for a hurricane, earthquake, or tsunami striking Puerto Rico and the U.S. Virgin Islands under-estimated the actual requirements in 2017 (Figure 8), which necessitated FEMA depend on crisis action planning (see description below) during the incident to address the shortfalls in the planning assumptions.

For example, the plans did not address insufficiently maintained infrastructure (e.g., the electrical grid), which explained some of the differences between the expected and actual impacts (see Key Finding #3). In addition, they did not address financial liquidity challenges facing the Territorial government.

Planning During Operations

As multiple, complex incidents occurred in quick succession in 2017, FEMA employed a number of planning strategies to adapt to previously unforeseen situations during the hurricane season. These strategies can inform future improvements to the planning process.

Crisis Action Planning to Address New Challenges

The Agency employed a crisis action planning process across its programs and with its interagency partners to address challenges not accounted for in the plans. For example, amid operations for Hurricane Harvey, planners looked ahead to begin estimating requirements to respond to a potential Hurricane Irma landfall on U.S. Virgin Islands, and then on Florida, and again for hurricanes Jose, Nate, and Maria.

Requirements for concurrent, complex incidents contributed to the need for crisis action planning. Existing plans were developed for the occurrence of a single incident, rather than concurrent incidents. In Puerto Rico and the U.S. Virgin Islands, the plans assumed that at least one incident support base—a commodity distribution staging area—in either Puerto Rico or the U.S. Virgin Islands would survive the impact of a major hurricane and that all commodities destined for one impacted territory would flow through the other. Hurricanes Irma and Maria affected both territories' incident support bases, forcing FEMA to find alternative ways to manage commodities during initial response operations.

> **Crisis Action Planning Teams**
>
> Throughout the hurricane season, FEMA stood-up multiple Crisis Action Planning (CAP) teams—cross-programmatic groups of Agency experts—to analyze and deliver recommendations to FEMA leadership on a range of complex issues. Five CAP teams supported work in the following critical areas:
>
> - Private sector and supply chain management;
> - Power restoration;
> - Responder lodging;
> - Petroleum fuel;
> - Survivor sheltering and housing; and
> - Surge disaster staffing.

Plans also did not sufficiently anticipate situations in which state or territory government officials would be unable to meet their responsibilities to manage operational or resource requirements due to a lack of communications or other capability shortfalls.

When hurricanes Irma and Maria followed Hurricane Harvey in quick succession across multiple states and FEMA Regions, the Agency responded by adapting its functions. For instance, the lack of available lodging for responders necessitated the quick identification of berthing ships to account for the lack of hotels and space for soft-sided shelters. Massive competing requirements for fuel and for transferring fuel from storage to fuel trucks necessitated the formulation of fuel truck routing, prioritizations, and sourcing additional vehicles and drivers. Private sector partners assisted FEMA in planning for an unprecedented movement of personnel and material.

Planning to Manage Time and Distance Challenges to Logistics

To better inform deployment and logistical support decision making, FEMA planners have increasingly employed the practice of pre-disaster resource phasing planning. While FEMA had committed to updating the Region II Caribbean Response Plan just before the 2017 Hurricane Season, operators

FEMA 2017 Hurricane Season After-Action Report (7/2018)

did not have an existing Resource Phasing Plan (RPP) during the response. Instead, based on lessons from other past RPP efforts, FEMA planners developed an RPP during response operations for the flow of resources into Puerto Rico and U.S. Virgin Islands following the passage of hurricanes Irma and Maria based on the maximum resources that can be shipped via air or sea. The RPP was developed in conjunction with the ESFs, used to inform the priority movements of resources through air and sea modes of transportation, and updated daily to accommodate changes in movement capability.

Understanding and Accommodating Infrastructure Interdependencies

The cascading impacts experienced across the infrastructure sectors, exacerbated by deferred maintenance issues, severely complicated the private sector's ability to return to normal operations. The interdependencies amongst the sectors also added a multitude of non-traditional operational support requirements upon federal supporting agencies. For instance, FEMA's plans did not anticipate the massive requirements to directly assist electricity, telecommunications, and fuel sector utilities with air and sea movement. Further, plans did not anticipate the need to move critical pharmaceutical supplies off Puerto Rico to meet national demands. The current federal operational planning process has begun to take into account private sector partnerships; however, the federal concepts of operations, including the National Response Framework, remain limited to federal assets in support of the states or territories. Crisis action planning and coordination with the infrastructure sectors during the incident assisted with identifying these requirements and helping to prioritize limited resources.

Key Finding #3: FEMA could have better leveraged open-source information and preparedness data, such as capability assessments and exercise findings, for Puerto Rico and the U.S. Virgin Islands.

FEMA leadership acknowledged that the Agency could have better anticipated that the severity of hurricanes Irma and Maria would cause long-term, significant damage to the territories' infrastructure. Leadership also recognized that emergency managers at all levels could have better leveraged existing information to proactively plan for and address such challenges, both before and immediately after the hurricanes.

Fiscal and Deferred Maintenance Challenges Facing Puerto Rico and the U.S. Virgin Islands

All jurisdictions face challenges in preparing for and managing large-scale incidents. In Puerto Rico, fiscal pressures limited investments and maintenance in critical infrastructure, including the electrical system, and decreased funding for emergency management. When hurricanes Irma and Maria struck Puerto Rico, the territory was $74 billion in debt and its economy had contracted nearly 15 percent during the preceding 10 years. Likewise, the U.S. Virgin Islands reported a $30 million budget shortfall in 2014. As both territories faced fiscal challenges, spending for emergency management declined or stagnated at relatively low levels between 2013 and 2017.

> **Emergency Management Assistance Compact**
>
> Emergency Management Assistance Compact (EMAC) is an all-hazards, all-discipline mutual aid compact that allows states to send personnel, equipment, and commodities to assist with response and recovery efforts in other states. EMAC was most effective this hurricane season where FEMA and states had previously included use of the compact in pre-disaster planning and preparedness activities, such as in Texas and Florida. There were some concerns regarding Puerto Rico's ability to reimburse states that provided assistance under EMAC, but EMAC Liaison Team leaders noted that some states are inclined to respond to EMAC requests without consideration of reimbursement.

Challenges with Existing Preparedness Information

FEMA collected information on jurisdictions' preparedness for responding to disasters in a variety of ways, including through exercise after-action reports, THIRA and SPR data, grant expenditure data, and other preparedness measures. FEMA routinely analyzes this information, in part, to determine how the Agency can help build and supplement the emergency preparedness capabilities of its state and territorial partners and to inform steady-state plans (see Key Finding #2).

FEMA has used this information to inform response activities. Response planners used results from the THIRA and SPR to inform planning for hurricanes Harvey, Irma, and Maria. While some data were more helpful than others, FEMA staff at multiple levels indicated that existing preparedness data would need to be more specific to aid the Agency in adjusting its response operations and supporting actionable operational decisions. FEMA recognized this limitation before the 2017 Hurricane Season and had begun developing new THIRA and SPR methodologies to provide more actionable information, but those new methods were not in effect in 2017.

> **Threat and Hazard Identification and Risk Assessment and State Preparedness Report Data**
>
> Each year, states, territories, major urban areas, and tribes conduct a risk assessment, called the THIRA, to better understand their risks and set targets for their preparedness capabilities. States and territories also conduct an annual capability assessment, called the SPR, to evaluate their current preparedness capabilities against the targets set in the THIRA. Jurisdictions use the capability gaps identified in the THIRA and SPR processes to inform planning, grant investments strategies, and other decision making.

Exercises are another useful tool for jurisdictions to identify emergency preparedness capability strengths and shortfalls, which can then be used to inform future preparedness efforts and response operations. For example, by the time Hurricane Irma hit in 2017, pre-disaster training and exercises proved to be critical in Florida's ability to efficiently execute mutual aid agreements. In other instances, FEMA and its partners could have better leveraged exercise data. FEMA faced challenges in the Caribbean during the hurricane season, as discussed further in Key Finding #10, which it could have anticipated based on findings from exercises. A 2011 exercise after-action report for Puerto Rico anticipated that the territory would require extensive federal support in moving commodities, including from the mainland to the territory and to distribution points throughout the territory. An after-action report from the 2014 Alaska Shield National Level Exercise noted that resource delivery timelines were longer than expected when working outside the continental United States and that a lack of staff at resource staging areas contributed to challenges in tracking and managing commodity deliveries.

Recommendations

To enhance the Nation's capability to respond to and recover from incidents, FEMA must implement a cross-sector approach to the Agency's planning, organizing, response, and recovery operations. Complex catastrophes threaten the cross-cutting lifelines society relies on to function, such as water and power. While these lifelines span jurisdictions and public and private sector divisions, government response efforts continue to be organized along self-imposed divides that fragment the physical and social landscape of affected areas. This new approach should account for the capabilities of the private sector both before and during incidents. The critical infrastructure sectors, which the

> **Recommendations Summary**
>
> - Revise the National Response Framework and, as required, the Response Federal Interagency Operational Plan to emphasize stabilization of critical lifelines and coordination across critical infrastructure sectors
> - Leverage the new FEMA Integration Teams and technical assistance to help states build capacity
> - Work with whole community partners to improve risk management and strengthen capabilities
> - Create preparedness and planning products that are easily accessible, modular, inclusive, and readily executable
> - Drive outcome-based recovery through expanded use of Stafford Act Section 428 Authorities for Public Assistance Alternative Procedures

Department of Homeland Security (DHS) National Protection and Programs Directorate support, and National, Regional, and State Business Emergency Operations Centers provide an operational and informational architecture, but the emergency management community collectively lacks a doctrinal foundation to organize and unify national efforts.

To codify the way forward, FEMA should work with its partners and the White House to revise the current **National Response Framework and, as required, the Response Federal Interagency Operational Plan to emphasize stabilization of critical lifelines and create a cross-sector coordination emergency support function and coordinating structures** (e.g., business emergency operation centers). The National Response Framework sets the strategy and doctrine for how the whole community builds, sustains and delivers capabilities across the Response mission area. The accompanying Response Federal Interagency Operational Plan describes how the Federal Government aligns resources and delivers capabilities. The new Framework and Federal Interagency Operational Plan should prescribe unity of effort through rapid stabilization around lifelines such as power, communications, health and medical, food and water, wastewater, and transportation. The rapid stabilization of the lifelines would be the organizing principle of the doctrine.

Since these lifelines span ESFs, Sector-Specific Agencies (SSAs), and core capabilities, FEMA and its public and private sector partners should revise the current National Response Framework to create a cross-sector coordination emergency support function (ESF #14, which was formerly Long-Term Community Recovery, could be repurposed to this new mission). The revision would cement in doctrine and practice the public-private sector partnership that is essential to stabilization and unity of effort, and bring new capacity to whole community response operations.

FEMA is placing its personnel in state emergency management offices to jointly plan with states and territories to build their capabilities. FEMA is **leveraging these new FEMA Integration Teams and technical assistance to help states build their capacity.** These teams, called for in the Agency's *2018-2022 Strategic Plan*, are working with their counterparts to increase state planning, logistics, and mitigation capabilities. By increasing direct engagement, FEMA can build a more in-depth collective understanding of capabilities, gaps, and risks; better understand the readiness of our partners and their needs during a disaster; and focus planning processes on the most consequential risks. These teams will contribute to achieving national unity of effort and the "federally supported, state-managed, and locally executed" relationship that is the backbone of our Nation's emergency management system.

In addition, FEMA is **working with whole community partners to improve risk management and strengthen capabilities** to adopt a new assessment methodology that requires all states, territories, tribes, and major urban areas to use standard, outcome based language to set objectives and assess their current capabilities against those objectives. These standardized targets reflect critical and measurable elements of managing risk, and respondents can use them to inform planning, exercises, evaluation, and continuous improvement, leading to stronger community-based capabilities. Further, before an incident, FEMA and its key public and private sector partners should improve their collective capacity to capture and organize data on critical lifelines. With more accurate data that increased collaboration will provide, FEMA should focus on **making preparedness and planning products easily accessible, modular, inclusive, and readily executable**. Finally, FEMA should review the effectiveness of the **use of Section 428 of the Stafford Act authorities to achieve outcome-based recovery**. FEMA should continue to use these authorities to better guide efficient recovery operations.

FEMA Strategic Plan Alignment

- *Objective 1.4, Better Learn from Past Disasters, Improve Continuously, and Innovate,* highlights the importance of self-evaluation and continuous improvement.
- *Objective 2.2, Enhance Intergovernmental Coordination through FEMA Integration Teams,* looks to improve how FEMA directly engages with its partners by enhancing presence with emergency management colleagues at the state.

Staffing for Concurrent, Complex Incidents

When Hurricane Harvey made landfall in Texas, FEMA already had 692[b] open disasters. Of that total, it had staff deployed to 32 disasters across 19 field offices. The President approved an additional 30 declarations between August and November (Figure 9).[c] The severity of three concurrent major hurricanes required FEMA to deploy a high number of staff to each affected area. FEMA leadership recognized early that the unprecedented demands for staff to support wide-scale response efforts, in addition to existing response and recovery

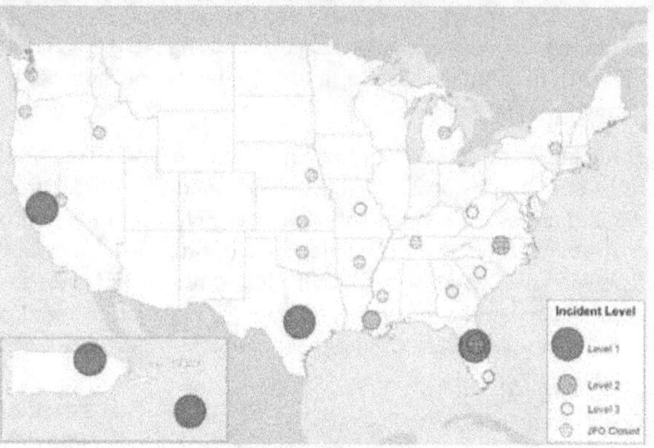

Figure 9: Open FEMA field offices between August 25 and November 30.

operations to other disasters, would exceed the Agency's organic capabilities. To overcome these staffing challenges, FEMA implemented innovative methods to augment the disaster workforce. FEMA can formalize and improve many of the innovative solutions that were implemented effectively to meet this historic demand.

By November 30, FEMA had deployed more than 17,000 people, in total, to the disasters, which included FEMA's workforce (i.e., force strength, later defined in Key Finding #4) and staff augmenting FEMA's workforce. Deployments ranged from days to months. The total number of overall staff deployed on a single day peaked at 11,775 across the concurrently affected states; the number of FEMA staff deployed peaked at 5,887. The fact that FEMA deployed thousands of non-Agency staff illustrates the measures FEMA took to supplement its capabilities (see Figure 10).

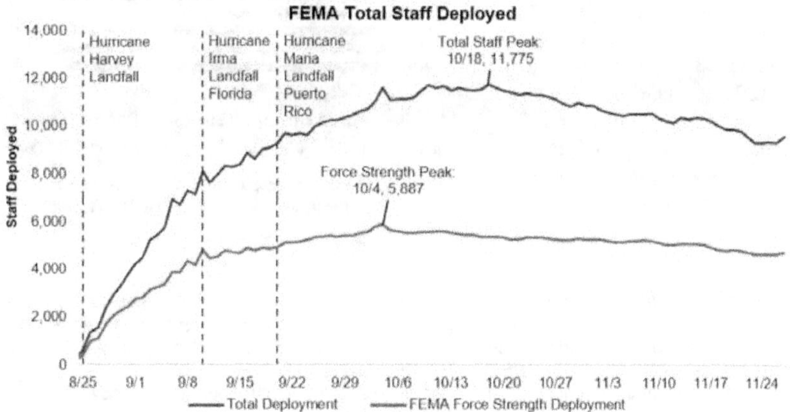

Figure 10: Total FEMA staff deployments between August 25 and November 30.

[b] This total includes emergency, major, and fire management assistance declarations.
[c] FEMA field offices active between August 25 and November 30. FEMA closed offices to rebalance staff to support response operations for Hurricanes Harvey, Irma, and Maria and other closures were previously planned.

July 12, 2018

Key Finding #4: FEMA entered the hurricane season with a force strength less than its target, resulting in staffing shortages across the incidents.

The Agency uses the metrics of force strength and force structure to: (1) estimate the staffing needed to respond to incidents given certain planning factors; (2) determine the Agency's ability to respond to current and future disasters; and (3) analyze the number of disaster response personnel available against that target.

Force structure establishes the estimated incident personnel staffing requirements for FEMA. FEMA's force structure as of 2017, which was based on a 2015 analysis, estimated that the Agency required 16,305 disaster management personnel. FEMA determined that figure based on a planning assumption that would allow the Agency to respond to two Level 1 incidents, four Level 2 incidents, and three Level 3 incidents.[d] Based on historical requirements, FEMA estimated that 6,630 staff were required to support one Level 1 incident, a number greater than the peak staff at any of the 2017 hurricanes. While only 10 Level 1 incidents had taken place between 1997 and 2014, FEMA responded to five Level 1 incidents in 2017.

Force strength is the actual number of personnel in FEMA's incident workforce cadres[e] who have completed the administrative requirements for deployment. Force strength does not include FEMA employees who do not have a primary incident management position, FEMA employees who supported response operations from their home office, or the methods of staff augmentation covered in Key Finding #7.

FEMA has made progress in increasing its force strength, but was short of its target during the 2017 Hurricane Season. As of August 2017, FEMA's force strength was 10,683—which was 86 percent of its target for Fiscal Year (FY) 17 (see Figure 11 for a breakdown per cadre).[f,g]

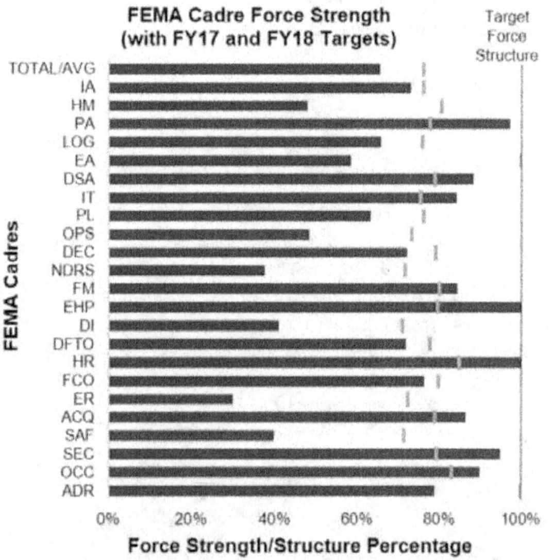

Figure 11: Cadre force strength compared to FY 17 goal. (See footnote below for cadre definitions.)

---

[d] Level 1: Incident requires extraordinary coordination among federal and SLTT entities due to massive levels and breadth of damage, severe impact or multi-state scope. Level 2: Incident requires a high amount of direct federal assistance for response and recovery efforts and elevated coordination among federal and SLTT entities. Level 3: Incident requires coordination among involved federal and SLTT entities.

[e] Incident workforce cadres are functional organizations responsible for response and recovery operations.

[f] Cadres are arranged in the graphic from largest to smallest based on force structure. The largest cadre's (IA) force structure is 2,932 and the smallest cadre's (ADR) force structure is 57.

[g] ACQ- Acquisitions, ADR- Alternative Dispute Resolution, DEC- Disaster Emergency Communications, DFTO- Disaster Field Training Officer, DI- Disability Integration, DSA- Disaster Survivor Assistance, EA- External Affairs, EHP- Environmental and Historic Preservation, ER- Equal Rights, FCO- Federal Coordinating Officer, FM- Financial Management, HM- Hazard Mitigation, HR- Human Resources, IA- Individual Assistance, IT- Information

Between August 25 and November 30, FEMA deployed 73 percent of its force strength to support disaster operations. The responses to hurricanes Harvey, Irma, and Maria, in combination with the California Wildfires and other ongoing disasters, imposed an unprecedented strain on FEMA's disaster workforce. Figure 12[h] shows FEMA's force strength deployments to hurricanes Harvey, Irma, and Maria.

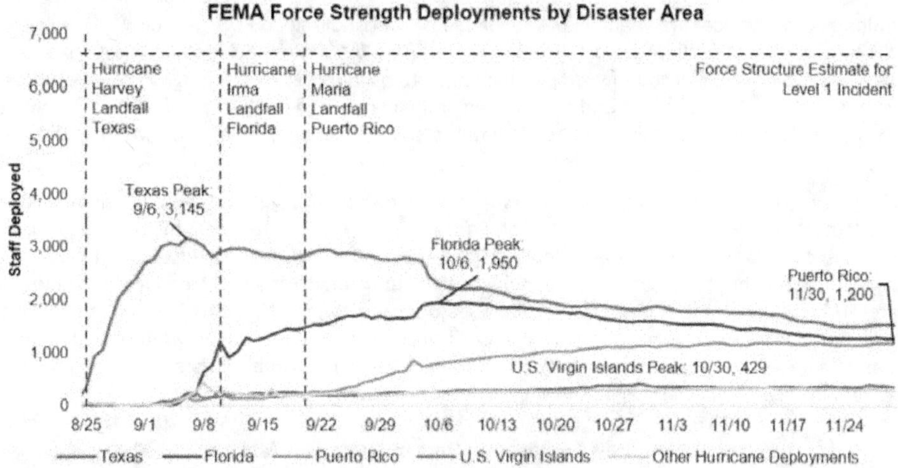

Figure 12: Peak FEMA force strength deployments between August 25 and November 30.

FEMA Cadre Staffing

The Agency expressed concern about cadre staffing levels throughout the 2017 Hurricane Season because staffing shortfalls posed potential risks to response and recovery operations. From August 25 to November 11:

- 13 of FEMA's 23 cadres were operating at 25 percent or lower staffing levels for 45 days or more
- Eight of these cadres were at less than 25 percent for approximately 70 days, including: DI, DSA, EHP, ER, HM, IA, IT, LOG, SAF, and SEC

In addition to staffing shortfalls, FEMA nearly exhausted staff for two forms of specialized response teams, the Mobile Emergency Response Support (MERS) teams and IMATs. Table 3 shows the days which had the lowest percentage of available IMAT and MERS resources. FEMA maintains three Type 1 and 13 Type 2 IMATs. FEMA deployed 12 IMATs to the hurricane-affected localities and deployed the four remaining teams to other incidents across the country. Given the number of near-simultaneous incidents, FEMA senior leadership expressed concerns regarding the shortage of available IMATs. To address the shortfall, FEMA redeployed IMATs and assembled additional personnel into ad hoc teams to fill necessary gaps.

Table 3: Percent of specialized team deployments and availability.

Team	Number of Deployed and Available Teams
Type 1 IMATs as of September 20	Deployed: 3 Available: 0 (0%)
Type 2 IMATs as of September 20	Deployed: 13 Available: 0 (0%)
MERS as of September 23	Deployed: 34 Available: 2 (5.5%)

Technology, LOG-Logistics, NDRS- National Disaster Recovery System, OCC-Office of Chief Council, OPS-Operations, PA- Public Assistance, PL-Planning, SAF- Safety, SEC- Security.
[h] FEMA force strength staffing in Puerto Rico peaked at 1,221 on December 6, 2017.

Key Finding #5: The Agency has made progress on disaster workforce certification, but had not yet achieved its targets. Field leaders reported some resultant inefficiency in program delivery.

Shortly before Hurricane Sandy in 2012, the Agency implemented the performance-based FEMA Qualification System (FQS) to track and measure the knowledge and skills of its incident management workforce. Over the past five years, FEMA has implemented and refined FQS, including: (1) realigning tasks that staff must perform for certification; (2) reducing the time to achieve certification; and (3) expanding FQS functionality during complex incidents. To become certified through FQS, an employee must meet training, experience, and job skill requirements for a given FQS position. FEMA uses its Deployment Tracking System to record deployments, certification status, and field requests for personnel.

The Agency has a workforce certification target of 80 percent. On August 27, 56 percent of incident management employees were considered certified, according to all current FQS requirements. Figure 13 shows that the workforce initially deployed to Texas had a high number of certified personnel, although that number fell as the disaster stabilized and hurricanes Irma and Maria struck the United States. However, incident management employees deployed to Florida, the U.S. Virgin Islands, and Puerto Rico had lower certification rates initially due to competing demands for certified staff. Despite initial differences, the average certification rate in each incident location differed from one another and from the agency-wide average by less than seven percentage points.

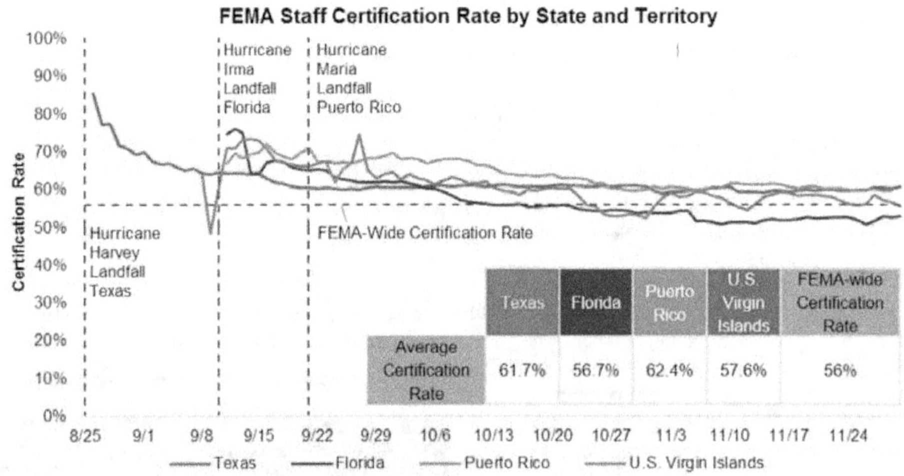

	Texas	Florida	Puerto Rico	U.S. Virgin Islands	FEMA-wide Certification Rate
Average Certification Rate	61.7%	56.7%	62.4%	57.6%	56%

Figure 13: Certification rate of FEMA personnel assigned by Hurricane from August 26 to November 30.

As seen in Figure 14,[ ] 19 of the 23 workforce cadres did not meet their target certification rate for FY 17. Due to this shortage, FEMA was unable to fill crucial positions in field offices with certified staff. Historically, FEMA staff have reported that relatively low certification rates may negatively impact program delivery. For example, tasks could take longer to perform, and supervisors with limited training could be overstretched.

The Public Assistance (PA) cadre overhauled its qualifications in 2017, which causes their qualification rate to appear artificially low.
Cadres are arranged in the graphic from largest to smallest based on force structure. The largest cadre's (IA) force structure is 2,932 and the smallest cadre's (ADR) force structure is 57.

   July 12, 2018

FEMA 2017 Hurricane Season After-Action Report (7/2018)

In the face of these certification shortages, the Agency adapted to meet mission needs. For example, FEMA awarded some employees field promotions to fill leadership gaps. Many of these field leaders proved valuable additions to the disaster workforce and many have retained their certifications based on demonstrated performance. Field promotions, however, placed staff in positions beyond their experience and, in some instances, beyond their capabilities.

The current certification process also does not consistently reflect employees' proficiencies in performing field tasks. Field interviews indicated that numerous less-experienced and less-trained staff could perform their duties at the certified level during the hurricane season even though they were not FQS-certified. The Agency temporarily changed certification procedures during the hurricane season to more rapidly certify employees who had demonstrated their skills outside the traditional process. FEMA instituted interim changes, including certifying staff who were successfully serving in positions, waiving certain training requirements, and training personnel at the field offices.

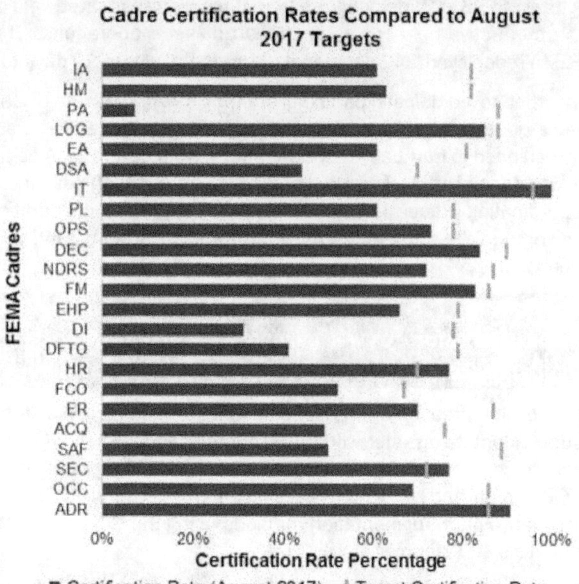

Figure 14: FEMA cadre certification rates (in blue) compared to target (in gray), as of August 21.

<h3>Key Finding #6: FEMA strategically consolidated ongoing disaster operations facilities across the country to reallocate personnel to the hurricane-affected field operations, which increased capacity to deliver FEMA programs.</h3>

In anticipation of concurrent impacts from Hurricane Irma, FEMA leadership transitioned staff in existing field offices to hurricane-affected areas. On September 4, FEMA began to transition 9 active field offices[k] supporting 13 disasters to its regional offices prior to their anticipated closure date. All field offices that FEMA temporarily transitioned were performing recovery operations. While regional Agency leadership had the option to resume field office operations following the hurricane response, none did. The respective FEMA regional offices assumed responsibility for supporting these operations once the field offices transitioned.

Table 4: FEMA redeployed staff to hurricane-affected field offices.

	Within 15 Days	Within 30 days	Within 60 Days	Within 90 days
Number of Staff Redeployed to Harvey, Irma, or Maria	182	223	234	242
Cumulative Percentage of Redeployed Staff	61%	75%	79%	81%

---

[k] A temporary coordination center established locally to manage response and recovery efforts.

A total of 298 staff demobilized from the nine transitioned field offices. Some staff remained deployed to other active field offices to support disaster operations. Of the 298 staff that were demobilized, FEMA redeployed 242 personnel (81 percent) within 90 days to support the hurricanes (Table 4).

In order to adjudicate particular staffing needs with field leadership, FEMA made every effort to redistribute these personnel equitably across the active disaster areas. Of the 242 responders transitioned to hurricane response efforts from other FEMA operations, roughly half (49 percent) were in management-level positions in existing field offices, including a highly experienced Federal Coordinating Officer. This effort allowed FEMA to provide additional management staff to support life-saving and life-sustaining efforts in the hurricane-affected areas that otherwise would have been unavailable.

Key Finding #7: FEMA augmented its disaster workforce through a combination of initiatives it has used before, as well as innovative and newly expanded methods—these initiatives met their stated intent, but can be matured.

Faced with three major hurricanes and insufficient organic staff to respond, FEMA acted decisively to supplement its disaster workforce. FEMA used a variety of conventional mechanisms to augment its workforce throughout the hurricane season, including local hires, contract staff, mission assignments, FEMA Corps, and National Processing Service Center (NPSC) surge staff. The Agency also implemented innovative staff augmentation methods using the SCF, and State Supplemental Staffing to add to its organic staff resources.

FEMA took numerous steps to counteract staffing shortfalls, including canceling Pre-Approved Non-Availability[i] for reservist employees, extending the deployments of full-time employees (who do not traditionally work in the field for extended periods), extending SCF deployments, centralizing deployment operations from field and regional offices to headquarters, and deploying new personnel directly from an abbreviated onboarding program. Figure 15 illustrates the sequence of the various staff augmentation mechanisms and policies FEMA used by date.

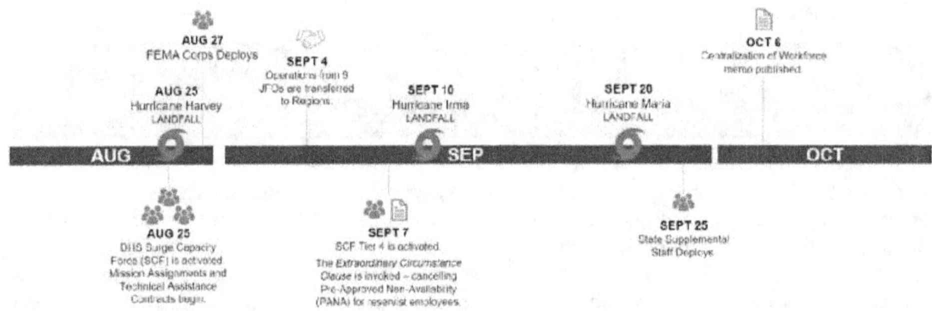

Figure 15: FEMA implemented initiatives to augment its disaster workforce during the hurricane response.

---

[i] A special form of unpaid time during which a Reservist is unavailable. This designation is only available to Reservists when they are not activated for deployment.

By augmenting staff, FEMA mitigated staffing shortages. Figure 16[m] shows all staff deployed by FEMA field office, including the following types of augmentation staff: FEMA Corps, Local Hires, and SCF.[n] In addition to the staff transferred from transitioned field offices listed in Key Finding #6, FEMA redeployed 2,961 responders to an incident area to support ongoing response operations from August 21 to November 30.

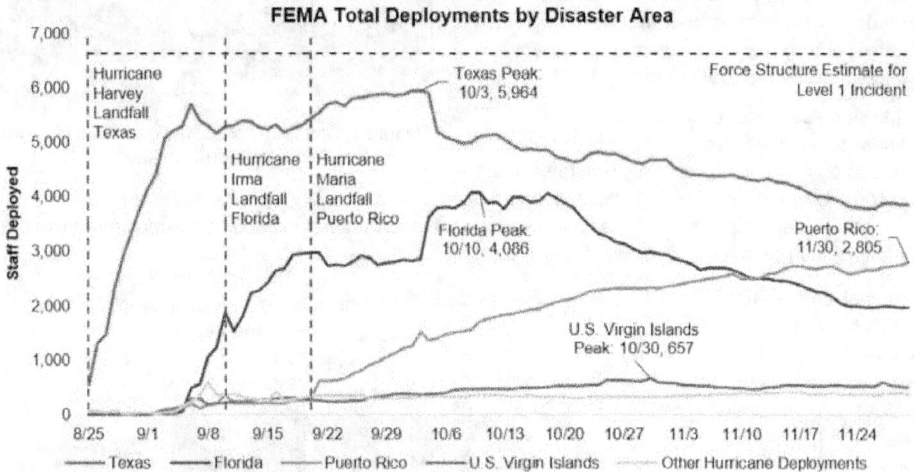

Figure 16: FEMA total deployments by disaster area between August 25 and November 30.

Conventional Augmentation Methods

FEMA relied on established workforce programs to augment its disaster workforce, and used Personnel Mobilization Centers (PMC) in Denton, Texas, and Anniston, Alabama, to equip and train staff.

> **Personnel Mobilization Centers**
>
> FEMA opened a PMC in Denton, Texas for Hurricane Harvey and in Anniston, Alabama, for hurricanes Irma and Maria. FEMA uses PMCs to receive, equip, and deploy emergency responders. Over 1,700 staff mobilized through the Denton PMC, and more than 5,000 mobilized through the Anniston PMC— the most ever.

FEMA deployed 63 **FEMA Corps** teams consisting of roughly 430 members to support operations in Texas, Florida, and Puerto Rico. FEMA Corps is an emergency management service program within the Corporation for National and Community Service that deploys young adults aged 18-24 over a 10-month service term. FEMA deployed FEMA Corps teams early in Hurricane Harvey, with 41 teams arriving within 15 days of the disaster declaration starting on August 27. In addition, FEMA used four ad hoc FEMA Corps teams with Spanish-speaking members to supplement staff in Puerto Rico.

---

[m] The graph covers only FEMA-deployed personnel. Puerto Rico had a proportionately higher number of DoD and National Guard Bureau personnel (10,602 on November 9, according to FEMA field reports) than other disasters, which supplemented FEMA staff.

[n] On January 26, staffing in Puerto Rico peaked at 2,997; the number of staff decreased after that date.

Local Hires are residents from the affected area who FEMA hires to assist in response operations from 120 days up to one year. FEMA expedited the local hiring process in response to hurricanes Harvey, Irma, and Maria, hiring 4,095 local hires from August to November. Because of the training and experience local hires receive, they represent a future emergency management capability in affected states and territories.

Figure 17: First round of FEMA Local Hires in Puerto Rico after Hurricane Maria.

A **Mission Assignment** (MA) is an order that FEMA issues to another federal agency directing the completion of a specific task. During the hurricane season, FEMA not only used MAs to support response and recovery operations through capabilities from other federal agencies, but also mission assigned other federal agencies for supplementary staff, including interpreters and external affairs experts.

National Processing Service Center (NPSC) call center specialists accept calls from survivors seeking federal disaster assistance. FEMA used **NPSC Surge** to augment its call-taking force from 590 to a peak of 7,377 through FEMA staff, selected federal agencies, contractors, and local hires. Figure 18 shows the peak staffing amount of each type of NPSC Surge during this hurricane season.

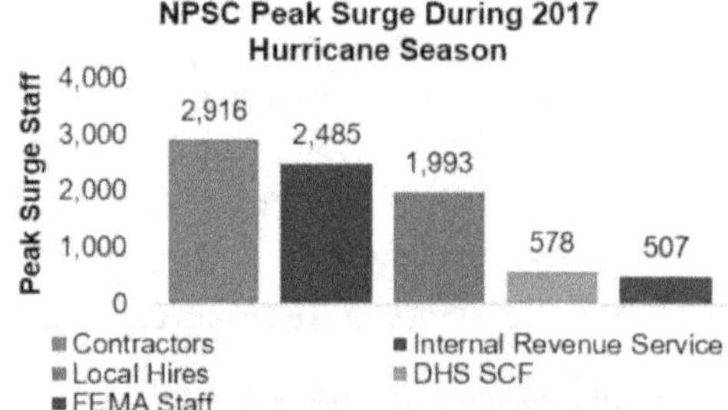

Figure 18: FEMA deployed multiple NPSC surge employee types to support disaster survivor calls.

FEMA uses **Technical Assistance Contracts** to supplement and support FEMA staff and to provide technical expertise, particularly in Public Assistance (PA) and Individual Assistance (IA) program execution. FEMA faced challenges with the contracting process due to the number of newly hired contractors, inflexible job descriptions, and high turnover rates during longer deployments. Further, FEMA struggled to process the high volume of contractor security requests.

Innovative Force Augmentation Methods

In addition to conventional mechanisms to augment its workforce, FEMA implemented innovative solutions to meet the increased staffing needs during the hurricane season.

The **Surge Capacity Force** program deploys non-FEMA federal employees in the aftermath of a disaster to support response and recovery efforts. FEMA had used the SCF only once before in response to Hurricane Sandy, with a total of 1,194 members from DHS supporting operations for that storm. Across hurricanes Harvey, Irma, and Maria, FEMA deployed 2,740 individuals from eight DHS components, with 701 responders deploying for more than 45 days. FEMA also expanded SCF to agencies outside DHS for the first time, including 34 federal departments and agencies in the program, increasing SCF personnel by 1,323 employees.

In total, 4,063 non-FEMA federal employees, more than three times the amount FEMA surged for Hurricane Sandy, deployed to the hurricane-affected areas. FEMA rostered an additional 6,334 volunteers from various federal agencies through November 30 to support future disaster operations. Figure 19 shows the total SCF deployments by location from August 25 to November 30.

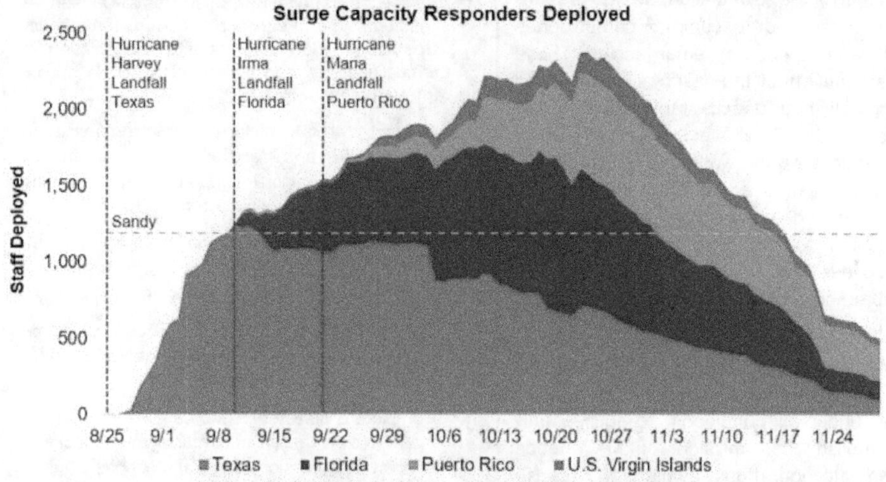

Figure 19: SCF deployments for the 2017 Hurricane Season.

While the SCF met its intent of injecting staff into operations to perform work that required little training, reports from field offices and headquarters indicated that opportunities exist for FEMA to identify needed specialized skills from surge staff and match them with field needs. Further, field interviews indicated that surge staff who have management positions in their home offices could have been better used to supplement leadership shortages.

State Supplemental Staffing augmented the FEMA incident management workforce with experienced state and local emergency management personnel from non-impacted states. FEMA deployed 30 personnel from four states (Figure 20) who were contracted for 60 days (with the option to renew for up to 120 days). The majority of the state supplemental staff deployed to Puerto Rico, with remaining staff deployed to Texas, Florida, and the NPSCs—providing much needed skills and experience to respond in challenging conditions. State supplemental staff were able to fill management roles that other types of surge employees could not. However, coordinating contracts with state and local agencies, processing security clearances, and staff recruitment procedures caused some delays and limited the number of participants. FEMA used this as a pilot program for the establishment of a National Qualification System.

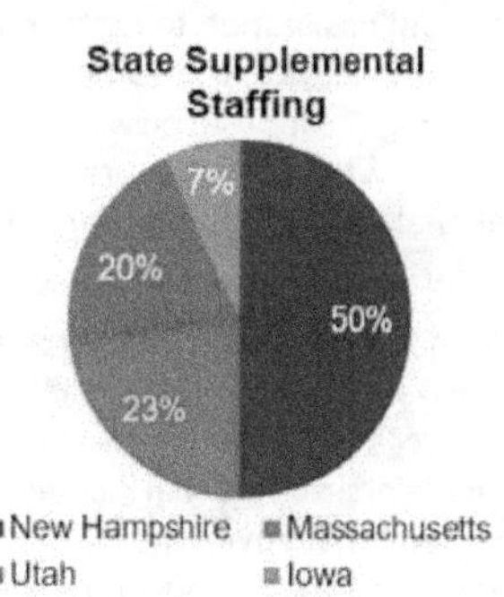

Figure 20: Representatives from four states supplemented FEMA staffing.

"This program is a game changer. It is always that the states depend on FEMA, and now this time FEMA needed the states. This opens up a whole new way to look at how we can help each other." – State of Utah supplemental staffing participant

FEMA 2017 Hurricane Season After-Action Report (7/2018)

Recommendations

FEMA's incident workforce is historically over-committed to smaller disasters, leaving a fraction of the Agency's capacity to prepare for and respond to complex catastrophes and national security emergencies. These constraints affect the Agency's readiness to respond without unacceptable delays. FEMA began the 2017 disaster season with nearly 30 percent of its workforce deployed on smaller disasters across the country, which then required extraordinary and disruptive measures to reallocate and redistribute employees to meet the evolving requirements for hurricanes Harvey, Irma, Maria, and the California Wildfires.

FEMA's responsibilities require it to have the capacity to respond in the shortest possible time, under all conditions, to successfully accomplish its mission. FEMA needs immediate operational availability because complex, no-notice catastrophes do not provide time to maximize readiness by amassing a workforce and extracting response resources from multiple smaller-scale commitments. To be better positioned for future challenges, FEMA should **support states in building a greater capacity to respond to and recover from small-scale disasters by providing necessary financial assistance to state-managed disasters while right-sizing the federal deployment footprint.** State and territorial governments should be able to respond to small-scale disasters either organically or through collaboration with neighboring states and territories. Strengthened states and territories, in turn, allow the Nation to preserve sufficient capacity to promptly respond to complex catastrophes and national security emergencies.

> **Recommendations Summary**
>
> - Revise the National Response Framework and, as required, the Response Federal Interagency Operational Plan to emphasize stabilization of critical lifelines and coordination across critical infrastructure sectors
>
> - Support states in building a greater capacity to respond to and recover from disasters by maintaining financial support while right-sizing the federal deployment footprint
>
> - Build and maintain a national incident workforce that includes emergency managers from state, local, tribal, and territorial governments
>
> - Use the Urban Search and Rescue Task Force model to further build the Incident Management Assistance Teams' capability
>
> - Complete a disaster workforce review within the Agency, to include incident management, incident support, and mission essential functions
>
> - Streamline and increase certifications across FEMA's incident workforce

During the 2017 Hurricane Season, FEMA augmented its workforce in innovative ways and newly expanded initiatives. The expansion of SCF to draw on the entirety of the federal workforce was decisive in augmenting FEMA's incident workforce. To streamline and standardize national staffing resources for future incidents, FEMA is developing the National Qualification System (NQS) to **build and maintain a national incident workforce that includes emergency managers from state, local, tribal, and territorial governments.** This will provide the ability to quickly amass and deploy qualified state, local, and tribal teams and personnel throughout the United States on short-notice. Enhanced state organic capacity, NQS, and the SCF will provide the means to manage the host of smaller-scale disasters that occur annually, while allowing FEMA to retain sufficient immediate operational readiness for complex catastrophes and national security emergencies.

To ensure the readiness of its organic staff, FEMA is **conducting a Coordinated Workforce Review of its force structure for incident management, incident support, and mission essential functions.** Further, the Agency is examining the FEMA Qualification System to **streamline and increase certifications across the Agency's workforce.**

To improve the capabilities of its key specialized teams, FEMA should **use the Urban Search and Rescue Task Force model to further build Incident Management Assistance Teams' capability.** This transformation will streamline their structure and deployment process, and focus field leader training on critical thinking and situational leadership.

Finally, **revising the National Response Framework and, as required, the Response Federal Interagency Operational Plan to emphasize stabilization of critical lifelines and cross-sector coordination** would provide the means to effectively and efficiently allocate the national incident workforce to the most decisive place, time, and purpose.

> **FEMA Strategic Plan Alignment**
> - *Objective 2.1, Organize the "BEST" (Build, Empower, Sustain, and Train) Scalable and Capable Workforce,* aims to strengthen the disaster workforce by renewing the focus on developing a standardized and qualified national incident workforce and maximizing the existing workforce. FEMA must build on its inherent capabilities and strengthen our partners to support the nationwide incident workforce to form a more complete, interoperable incident workforce capability.

FEMA 2017 Hurricane Season After-Action Report (7/2018)

Sustained Whole Community Logistics Operations

FEMA coordinated logistics missions for the complex combination of hurricanes Harvey, Irma, and Maria. These missions involved more than $2 billion dollars' worth of commodities moving across multiple states and territories (Figure 21). FEMA collaborated with private industry, non-governmental organizations (NGOs), and federal agency partners to manage these disaster logistics operations.

Hurricanes Harvey and Irma impacted Texas and Florida earlier in the season and partners provided commodities via ground transportation. However, the responses to Puerto Rico and U.S. Virgin Islands introduced the complexity of supporting a logistics supply chain that stretched outside the continental United States, enduring for multiple weeks and to multiple islands. Hurricane Maria caused widespread damage to island seaports, airports, and roads. These closures increased transit times and limited the territories' capacity to receive commodity shipments. Thus, FEMA's logistics effort featured notable and persistent coordination challenges in resource prioritization, resource movement and tracking, commodity distribution efforts, and contracting processes.

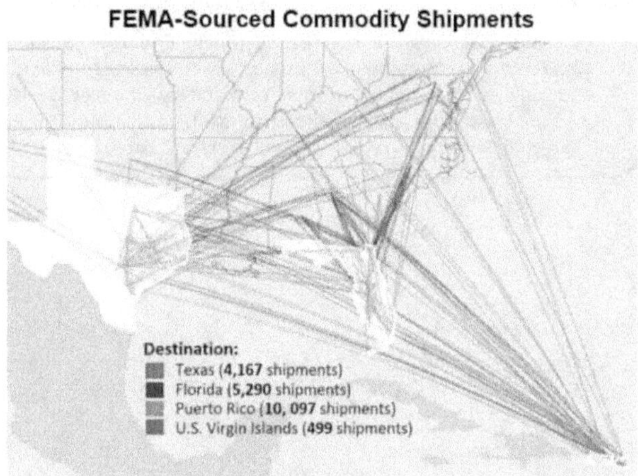

Figure 21: Commodity shipments from August 25 - November 30, 2017 directly to Texas, Florida, Puerto Rico, and U.S. Virgin Islands by air, sea, and ground transportation routes.

> **Key Finding #8: FEMA assumed a more active role in coordinating whole community logistics operations for Puerto Rico and the U.S. Virgin Islands due to these territories' preparedness challenges, geographic distance, and pre-existing, on-the-ground conditions.**

The characteristics and impacts of each of the hurricanes posed challenges for all logistics operations, some more severe than others. For example, FEMA's logistical support of the movement of commodities differed in Florida and Texas, compared to the Caribbean islands, because of the ability to conduct land-based delivery of resources in Florida and Texas versus air and sea delivery to the islands. In Florida and Texas, FEMA provided a support function to the states whereas in Puerto Rico, FEMA took on an active role of coordinating logistics operations. The need for FEMA logistical support is also determined by SLTT preparedness (see Key Finding #10 for more details on how FEMA augmented support for Puerto Rico).

Hurricane Harvey stalled over parts of southeastern Texas, resulting in flooding and weather conditions that temporarily closed ports, airports, and roads, and prevented access to the disaster area. Hurricane Irma tracked northward along the western coast of Florida and then moved through central and western Florida. The timeline of this statewide impact prevented FEMA from immediately moving resources south to heavily damaged areas, such as the Florida Keys.

Despite these challenges, FEMA conducted logistics operations in both states without major resource coordination or movement constraints for two main reasons. First, the proximity to FEMA's two largest distribution center warehouses in Fort Worth, Texas and Atlanta, Georgia, combined with pre-positioned commodities in Texas, Florida, and neighboring states, allowed the Agency to quickly meet resource needs. Second, because Texas and Florida are on the U.S. mainland, FEMA and its partners could move resources by relying primarily on ground transportation. In Texas and Florida, almost all interstate routes and state highways were open within a few days, enabling the private sector supply chain, as well as FEMA and whole community partners, to quickly move resources to, from, and within the states. For example, almost immediately after landfall, FEMA moved a large volume of commodities into both states. The combination of these factors enabled FEMA to coordinate logistics operations in Texas and Florida following established plans, albeit on a larger scale.

In Puerto Rico and the U.S. Virgin Islands, however, FEMA encountered significant challenges in coordinating and moving additional resources due to these territories' geographic distances from the U.S. mainland and challenging on-the-ground conditions.

FEMA maintained a stockpile of commodities at the Caribbean Distribution Center warehouse in Puerto Rico to facilitate a quick response to incidents in both Puerto Rico and the U.S. Virgin Islands. For

Table 5: FEMA's on-hand inventory of selected commodities at the Caribbean Distribution Center warehouse before (9/1) and after (9/15) Hurricane Irma, showed depletion of commodities prior to Hurricane Maria.

Commodity	Date: 9/1	Date: 9/15	% Change
Water (liters)	718,370	69,300 ▼	90%
Meals	250,572	97,632 ▼	61%
Cots	4,422	0 ▼	100%
Medical Kits	8	6 ▼	25%
Tarps	13,272	0 ▼	100%
Blue Roof Sheeting	15,344	180 ▼	99%
Total	**1,001,988**	**167,118** ▼	**83%**

example, in response to Hurricane Irma, FEMA moved containers of commodities from the Caribbean Distribution Center to the Port of St. Thomas. However, distribution activities following Hurricane Irma created an immediate deficit of commodities at the warehouse (Table 5), requiring additional items to be transported in the days immediately prior to and following Hurricane Maria's landfall.

In response to Hurricane Irma impacts, FEMA distributed more than 80 percent of its inventory for selected commodities from the Caribbean Distribution Center warehouse. Hurricane Maria struck before supplies were replenished.

The Agency worked extensively with private sector entities, NGOs, and other federal agencies to procure additional commodities and then coordinated the use of air and maritime transportation assets to move them. FEMA worked closely with DoD on airlifts; contracted with commercial air carriers; and expanded its existing maritime shipping contract to transport resources from the mainland to the territories. Instances of these efforts immediately following Hurricane Maria landfall on September 20 included the following:

- **September 23:** A barge arrived at the Port of San Juan in Puerto Rico, after the port reopened, and offloaded 924,000 liters of water, 6,000 cots, and 31 generators.

- **September 23:** The first aircraft delivering commodities arrived at San Juan International Airport.

- **September 24:** A Maritime Administration ship arrived at port in St. Thomas and offloaded shipments which included 1.1 million meals, 27 General Services Administration vehicles, and 9,496 hygiene kits.

- **September 23 - October 19:** FEMA-coordinated daily flights delivering commodities to Puerto Rico.

FEMA 2017 Hurricane Season After-Action Report (7/2018)

The average transit time for resources moved by barge to the Caribbean is six to seven days, with additional time on either end for loading and offloading shipments at port. Figure 22 shows FEMA's commodity delivery data; however, due to data tracking issues (see Key Finding #9) not all early deliveries mentioned above were captured.

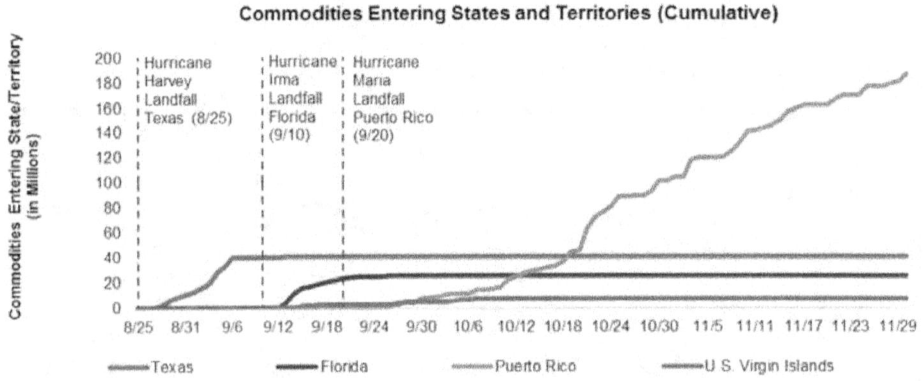

Commodities Entering States and Territories (Cumulative)

Figure 22: Cumulative commodities that entered each of the four states and territories to support the corresponding storm, i.e. Hurricane Harvey in Texas, Hurricane Irma in Florida, Hurricanes Irma and Maria in Puerto Rico and the U.S. Virgin Islands.

Operating in such a transportation-constrained environment necessitated that FEMA take the lead in coordinating the entire logistics supply chain for both Puerto Rico and the U.S. Virgin Islands, including prioritizing how and when resources moved. For example, FEMA coordinated with National Voluntary Organizations Active in Disaster partners to prioritize mass care commodities for transport to the islands since these partners could not move their own resources during the first weeks of response operations. At the request of the Governor of Puerto Rico, FEMA established and managed a warehouse in Jacksonville, Florida to receive donated items, with the intent of transporting them to Puerto Rico. FEMA also coordinated with other federal agencies and the private sector to move equipment necessary to support response operations, such as utility poles, generators, water pumps, aviation equipment, water treatment units and bucket trucks.

> **FEMA Moves Resources to Ensure Continuity of Medical Supply Chain**
>
> Puerto Rico typically receives its medical gases from two manufacturers on the main island, both of which lost power after Hurricane Maria. This threatened the supply of gases for healthcare and created the potential for a serious risk to public health. The Department of Health and Human Services, working with FEMA, convened a task force to identify solutions to the gas supply disruption. The solution was coordinating shipments of large containers of liquid oxygen and liquid nitrogen to Puerto Rico from the continental U.S.

Key Finding #9: While FEMA mobilized billions of dollars in commodities, the Agency experienced challenges in comprehensively tracking resources moving across multiple modes of transportation to Puerto Rico and the U.S. Virgin Islands due to staffing shortages and business process shortfalls.

FEMA's Logistics Supply Chain Management System (LSCMS) tracked the movement of millions of commodities into Texas, Florida, Puerto Rico, and the U.S. Virgin Islands. LSCMS worked well as the primary tracking system for commodities moved using ground transportation in Texas and Florida. However, LSCMS reporting was not current for commodities that required multiple modes of transportation when shipped to Puerto Rico and the U.S. Virgin Islands (e.g., moving commodities by a combination of airplane, barge, and truck). For example, LSCMS records of meals and water delivered to Puerto Rico lagged behind the real-time shipment data tracked and reported by support staff at headquarters. This was partially due to a lack of trained personnel on the ground to record the repackaging and changes in transportation mode for shipped commodities.

The lack of reliable telecommunications connectivity in the U.S. Virgin Islands and Puerto Rico, combined with the lack of available logistics staff and business processes that should have been adjusted for the scope and scale of the incident, exacerbated these data discrepancies. However, adequate information was still available to make inbound supply chain and shipping decisions. In addition, FEMA struggled to quickly redirect and deploy trained LSCMS staff by the time Hurricane Maria made landfall; 81 percent of the total number of LSCMS-trained staff were already committed to Texas or Florida operations (Figure 23).

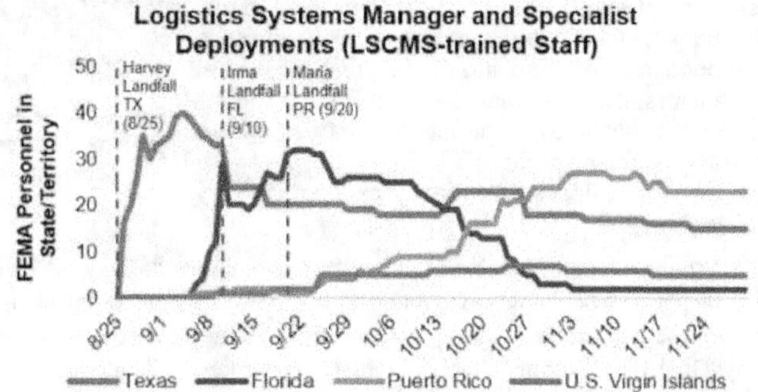

Figure 23: LSCMS-trained staff deployments in states and territories affected by hurricanes Harvey, Irma, and Maria.

FEMA's logistics business processes also complicated the Agency's ability to track commodities sourced through external partners. Though LSCMS has the capability to track resources from federal partners such as the Defense Logistics Agency, private sector partners, and other outside organizations, FEMA did not contractually require these partners to use the LSCMS vendor portal to upload shipment information. As a result, FEMA lacked real-time visibility into the supplies moved by partners and relied on other information-sharing processes to obtain accurate tracking information. Shipping containers often arrived in Puerto Rico labeled simply as "disaster supplies," requiring FEMA staff to unload and open containers to determine their contents.

Key Finding #10: FEMA provided logistical coordination to move and distribute commodities from staging areas to survivors in Puerto Rico, supplementing a role that should largely be managed and coordinated at the state or territory level.

FEMA's planning efforts typically account for the delivery of commodities from centralized FEMA warehouses to staging areas located in or near affected jurisdictions. State or territorial governments then receive the commodities from these staging areas and manage the actual distribution to survivors. FEMA strategic doctrine calls on the Agency to assume the responsibilities of SLTT governments, the private sector, and NGOs when the effects of a major incident incapacitate those organizations' ability to perform their functions effectively and efficiently until they can resume operations. However, FEMA's operational plans did not include these planning assumptions and thus did not account for continuing commodity distribution beyond the handoff to the state or territory.

Following Hurricane Harvey, the Texas National Guard managed commodity distribution. FEMA maintained visibility into distribution efforts by accessing Texas' crisis management software platform to view distribution point locations, inventory, and overall commodity burn rates. The response following Hurricane Irma in Florida was similar, although Florida's emergency operations plans and distribution operations place greater emphasis on the State of Florida to handle the distribution process.

Puerto Rico did not have the same level of preparedness to manage a commodity distribution mission. As a result, FEMA took on a more direct role in coordinating the final mile of commodity delivery. In addition to taking on this role, FEMA faced challenges moving commodities from ports to other locations. Major modes of transportation were closed and debris blocked extensive road networks across the territories, which required an in-depth assessment and clearance effort to reopen roads. Additionally, the limited number of FEMA logistics personnel on the island and the fact that most local contractors also were disaster survivors meant the Agency was not able to contract enough truck drivers to transport commodities. This issue, coupled with damaged or impassable roads, caused delivery delays.

Figure 24: Regional staging area trucks are loaded with meals to be transported to municipalities for distribution to survivors in Puerto Rico.

FEMA found alternative methods to facilitate commodity delivery, which included working extensively with federal partners on the island to move food and water from federal incident support bases to Puerto Rico's regional staging areas. At these locations, FEMA turned over commodities to the Puerto Rico National and State Guard for distribution to the 78 Puerto Rico municipalities. The municipalities, in turn, organized their own survivor distribution efforts aided by local organizations and NGOs. In some instances, FEMA delivered directly to municipalities. FEMA also partnered with DoD to airdrop commodities directly to isolated communities as early as three days after Maria's landfall.

To facilitate commodity distribution in communities, FEMA leased box trucks with drivers for each of the regional staging areas, conducted direct deliveries to municipalities, and used federal staff and NGOs to distribute food and water directly to survivors. This expanded logistics network moved commodities to more survivor-accessible locations. However, the increase and fluctuating number of delivery points and remote locations required significantly more transportation assets, personnel, and coordination than FEMA had initially anticipated. Furthermore, the large number of partners conducting distributions and the lack of a unified tracking system created difficulties in FEMA's efforts to monitor commodity consumption rates and accordingly adjust operations. While FEMA adapted and performed a more direct logistics coordination role, its normal logistics business processes were not suited to this role.

Key Finding #11: In a three-month period, FEMA issued more contract actions than in an entire previous fiscal year to meet disaster requirements, which strained the Agency's contracting personnel.

For the three fiscal years prior to FY 17, all of FEMA's annual contract obligations, both disaster and non-disaster, averaged approximately $1.3 billion. By comparison, between August 25, 2017 and November 30, 2017, FEMA obligated more than $3 billion across 1,464 contract actions solely for hurricanes Harvey, Irma, and Maria disaster operations. By end of May 2018, this number increased to 2,872 contract actions with FEMA obligations totaling over $3.9 billion.

Before incidents, FEMA establishes pre-negotiated contracts for commodities and services typically required during disaster response. These contracts facilitate the rapid movement of resources and commodities to areas most in need. Additionally, pre-negotiated contracts are meant to lessen the burden on ad hoc contract needs in the midst of disaster response. Immediately prior to Hurricane Harvey, FEMA had 59 of these pre-negotiated contracts in place (Table 6). Due to the amount of contract actions FEMA executed during the hurricane season, the Agency is considering increasing this number for future disasters.

Table 6: FEMA's pre-negotiated contracts by type.

Contract Type	Quantity
Commodities (e.g., Tarps, Water, Blankets, Meals etc.)	15
Services (e.g., Housing Inspections, Ambulances, Sheltering, Transportation, etc.)	44
Total	**59**

Given the unprecedented resource needs of consecutive response operations, FEMA not only exhausted commodities on hand but also exhausted pre-negotiated contracts to provide meals, tarps, water, and other resources during the responses to hurricanes Harvey and Irma. Therefore, the concurrent response for Hurricane Maria required FEMA to rapidly solicit vendors outside its pre-negotiated contracts to satisfy resource and program needs. As the Agency continued to receive requirements for meals, tarps, and water for quantities in the millions—often for delivery within days or hours—FEMA contracted with entities that were assessed as technically acceptable and committed to meeting the requirements, in accordance with the provisions of the Federal Acquisition Regulation. To protect the rights of the Government, FEMA creates contracts that clearly define the terms and conditions required for successful performance under the contract, particularly with respect to delivery schedule and quantities. Overall, FEMA executed a successful acquisitions process, with the Agency canceling just three contracts. These cancellations did not hinder FEMA's ability to deliver on its mission.

These increased contracting demands from the hurricane season severely taxed FEMA's acquisitions process and contracting personnel—both contracting officers and contracting officer's representatives. Over several months of concurrent disaster operations, FEMA staff modified and monitored existing contracts, issued new contracts, and cancelled underperforming contracts, while also scoping requirements for emerging needs. This workload—coupled with coordinating the additional oversight and review requirements for many high-value contracts (over $500K), and executing contracting actions for other federal agency partners—challenged FEMA's procurement personnel. Several FEMA staff cited the need to leverage more contracting personnel across the Agency to build additional capacity.

As part of its disaster contracting efforts, FEMA relied upon its authorities under the *Defense Production Act* to award an unprecedented number of contracts with "priority" ratings. This rating legally obligates vendors to deliver resources by a specific date with the government contracts taking priority over all other contracts. From August 25 through November 30, FEMA issued 515 priority-rated contracts and task orders across hurricanes Harvey, Irma, and Maria operations. By comparison, Hurricane Katrina and Hurricane Sandy each resulted in one priority-rated contract award. Notably for the first time, the Department of Health and Human Services granted FEMA authority to priority-rate contracts for consumable medical supplies and durable medical equipment. The Department of Transportation granted the authority to prioritize the lease of a berthing ship for responder housing in Puerto Rico.

In addition, FEMA took action to address previously known challenges in how SLTT government and eligible non-profit organizations procure resources under FEMA grants. FEMA can reimburse SLTT governments and certain non-profit organizations for eligible contract costs. Recipients and subrecipients are required to follow federal procurement standards. Historical data, primarily documented in DHS Office of Inspector General audits issued from Fiscal Years 2009 through 2014, concluded that procurement under grants at the state and local level is subject to a number of challenges, especially within the area of ineffective contracting practices. Deficiencies in this area include: non-compliant use of competitive procedures, inadequate contract cost and price analysis, ineffective or inappropriate use of contract types (or both), and failure to take all the necessary steps under socioeconomic contracting.

In response to these and other procurement challenges, FEMA implemented a number of measures during the 2017 Hurricane Season. FEMA provided compliance training to FEMA, state, and local government officials to achieve greater compliance with procurement under grants. FEMA also deployed personnel to Texas, Florida, Puerto Rico, and the U.S. Virgin Islands, to provide real-time procurement support. In Texas, for example, FEMA staff deployed for more than 70 days and helped establish and train the Texas State Attorney Workgroup, the first of its kind, to assist local governments with procurement issues. In Puerto Rico, Florida, and the U.S. Virgin Islands, FEMA set up processes and developed templates and tools to address contract review and technical assistance requests from recipients and subrecipients, significantly increasing the Agency's capacity to provide pre-award and post-award procurement support. Since September 2017, FEMA has provided 470 hours of procurement training to FEMA personnel, recipients, and subrecipients.

Recommendations

The unparalleled scope and scale of the 2017 Hurricane Season underscored the need for, and identified several limitations in, implementing timely national response capabilities that are fully integrated with and supportive of private sector supply chain restoration. In 2017, public and private sector response and recovery efforts were too "stove-piped" to share timely information, too slow to consult, and as a result, often too late to synchronize stabilization efforts. The public and private sector are inextricably linked and must have shared situational awareness and the ability to synchronize their respective efforts to be successful. FEMA should work with its key partners to **develop a more comprehensive understanding of local, regional, and national supply chains, as well as stronger relationships with critical private sector partners to support rapid restoration in response to catastrophic incidents.** As a result, the Agency is adopting new response principles to closely align public and private sector efforts in a unified effort focused on rapid stabilization of key lifelines.

While FEMA works to build a public and private sector coalition around the principle of rapid stabilization, the agency should also accelerate ongoing efforts to: **increase FEMA readiness stocks outside the continental** United States; increase transportation planning, **management and contract support capacities;** broaden FEMA's capabilities to quickly get teams on

Recommendations Summary

- Revise the National Response Framework and, as required, the Response Federal Interagency Operational Plan to emphasize stabilization of critical lifelines and coordination across critical infrastructure sectors

- Promote federally supported, state-managed, and locally executed logistics operations

- Increase FEMA readiness stocks outside the continental United States

- Increase transportation planning, management, and contract support capacities

- Broaden FEMA's capability to quickly get teams on the ground to stage and deliver key commodities to disaster survivors, even in the most remote locations

- Streamline storage and movement across multiple modes of transportation that facilitate and speed delivery

- Develop a more comprehensive understanding of local, regional, and national supply chains, as well as stronger relationships with critical private sector partners to support rapid restoration in response to catastrophic incidents

- Support state, local, tribal, and territorial governments in improving capability for disaster cost recovery, pre-event contracting and contract enforcement, and vendor-managed inventory

FEMA 2017 Hurricane Season After-Action Report (7/2018)

the ground to stage and deliver key commodities to disaster survivors even in the remotest locations; and streamline storage and movement across multiple modes of transportation that facilitate and speed delivery. FEMA has reviewed and adjusted planning factors for the Caribbean as a result of lessons learned from the 2017 Hurricane Season and has significantly increased disaster commodity stock targets on the islands. FEMA is adding 300 new emergency generators to its inventory with a new contract that simplifies generator maintenance and support. FEMA is repairing and expanding its Caribbean logistics distribution center to accommodate additional commodities. Additionally, FEMA has updated the National Evacuation and Caribbean Transportation contracts in advance of the 2018 Hurricane Season.

FEMA's existing logistics capabilities must be integrated with expanded regional and state, local, tribal, and territorial logistics capabilities to **promote federally supported, state-managed, and locally executed logistics operations**. FEMA Integration Teams are important contributors to assisting states in increasing organic logistical capabilities. The Agency should **support state, local, tribal, and territorial governments in improving capability for disaster cost recovery, pre-event contracting and contract enforcement, and vendor-managed inventory.** FEMA should continue to develop a pre-event toolkit to enhance the ability of state and local leaders to direct and manage disaster resources. The toolkit will consist of: recommendations for pre-positioned contracts; emergency acquisition guidance from a regulatory, legislative, and policy perspective; commodity specific solicitation templates; guidance on staffing models to support procurement; and disaster case management capability. FEMA is also developing disaster financial management planning guidance specific to: FEMA Public Assistance and Hazard Mitigation grants, Department of Housing and Urban Development Community Development Block Grants – Disaster Recovery, and agriculture post-disaster grants; disaster finance accounting systems and management practices necessary to track, calculate and justify the costs of an emergency; and local reimbursement reconciliation.

These efforts should be fully integrated into an updated national response architecture and new "cross-sector" Emergency Support Function. **Revisions to the National Response Framework and, as required, the Response Federal Interagency Operational Plan** should emphasize the seamless integration of public, private sector, and volunteer organization actions to stabilize critical lifelines and establish the coordinating structures, communications, information exchanges and decision making that optimize getting the right capability to the right place at the right time for the disaster survivor.

FEMA Strategic Plan Alignment

- *Objective 2.3, Posture FEMA and the Whole Community to Provide Life-Saving and Life-Sustaining Commodities, Equipment, and Personnel from All Available Sources*, notes the importance of involving the whole community to quickly and fully meet all the needs of a catastrophic disaster.

FEMA 2017 Hurricane Season After-Action Report (7/2018)

Responding During Long-Term Infrastructure Outages

The Federal Government assists jurisdictions with the response to and recovery from significant power outages when utilities are unable to restore power quickly. Federal assistance may include provision of emergency funding, critical services, and equipment, including the installation of generators. In Texas and Florida, long-term infrastructure outages were isolated within the areas impacted by hurricanes Harvey and Irma. Functioning power and communications infrastructure facilitated FEMA's standard response operations. Approximately 10 days after Hurricane Harvey's landfall, 55,000 customers in Texas were without power, down from a peak of approximately 300,000 customers. In Florida, 75,000 customers were without power 10 days after Hurricane Irma made landfall, down from a peak of more than six million customers.

Figure 25: Staging area for utility truck and construction crews assisting in restoration of power to damaged areas caused by Hurricane Irma.

In contrast, the long-term and extensive infrastructure outages following Hurricane Maria in Puerto Rico required FEMA staff to think creatively and adapt operations for a longer time period. Due to the exceptional circumstances in Puerto Rico and large-scale impacts of power and communications outages, this section focuses solely on operations in Puerto Rico.

Key Finding #12: To overcome limited situational awareness created by the loss of communications in Puerto Rico, FEMA executed creative solutions to assess the situation and prioritize response activities, including emergency repairs to infrastructure.

FEMA and its partners generally rely on states, tribes, and territories to provide prioritized lists of infrastructure facilities for assessment and restoration based on local needs. Due to the severe and widespread impacts of Hurricane Maria and the limited situational awareness in Puerto Rico, FEMA assumed a more active role in assisting the territorial government with prioritizing infrastructure restoration.

FEMA and supporting federal agencies struggled to gain situational awareness and assess the status of critical infrastructure, in part due to communications outages across Puerto Rico. On September 21, one day after Hurricane Maria made landfall, FEMA (along with other federal, territorial, and local partner agencies) had little information about the status of infrastructure, including hospitals, roads, and water facilities. This diminished situational awareness continued through the first 72 hours after landfall. On September 23, a FEMA briefing noted that FEMA and the territory had not begun water and wastewater assessments, and that communications challenges inhibited reporting of road outage assessments. By September 27, one week after landfall, FEMA knew more, but still lacked key information about critical infrastructure. For example, Agency partners did not have information on the status of 24 of 52 wastewater treatment plants or 37 of 69 hospitals.

> **Situational Awareness**
>
> Situational awareness is the ability to identify, process, and comprehend critical information about an incident. Gaining and maintaining situational awareness requires extensive information collection and on-going monitoring of information.

Because FEMA and its partners lacked situational awareness early in the response, the Agency initially could not be certain that FEMA and interagency partner efforts were sufficient to stabilize the incident in Puerto Rico. To address this challenge, FEMA and territorial field leadership established priorities focused on immediate needs and critical lifelines, including temporary power, water and wastewater, and healthcare. Field teams used data analysis tools to track and visualize data on these priorities, which provided situational awareness to field staff and FEMA's federal and territorial partners.

FEMA and its partner agencies, working in coordination with the Puerto Rican government, used the following methods to improve situational awareness:

- **Field Assessments**: Debris and damaged roads initially impeded access to impacted areas. To overcome these obstacles, some teams used a limited number of helicopters to visit critical infrastructure. However, they sometimes struggled to immediately report findings due to communications challenges, requiring teams to fly back with updates, and therefore delaying action.

- **Air Reconnaissance**: On September 22, two days after Hurricane Maria made landfall, FEMA conducted an air reconnaissance mission on the northeastern and southeastern portions of Puerto Rico to collect data and take photos of critical infrastructure elements. Although enough air assets were available, there were persistent challenges in communicating collected data to enhance situational awareness for decision-makers in the field.

- **Satellite Phones**: FEMA provided satellite phones to hospitals and mayors; however, the phones were not always an effective method for two-way communication due to weather impacts and user inexperience. Additionally, activating these phones often required user instructions, a line-of-sight with satellites, and implementation of a routine process.

- **Mayor Engagement**: FEMA worked with DHS and other federal agencies to provide Spanish speaking staff to the 78 Puerto Rico mayors to address communication challenges. These staff engaged mayors face-to-face several times per week to gather information from local officials on critical unmet needs and to gain situational awareness.

- **Crowdsourcing Information**: FEMA used crowdsourcing to a greater degree than it had previously to gain situational awareness on critical infrastructure. After Hurricane Maria, crowdsourcing efforts helped the Agency better understand the extent of the damage as digital volunteers collected and analyzed images of damage in Puerto Rico. Crowdsourcing volunteer networks brought together over 5,400 digital volunteers to collect information on critical information requirements such as hospital status, road and bridge closures, and food and fuel availability in Puerto Rico. Crowdsourcing was a useful strategic decision support tool, but required ground-truthing.

FEMA field leadership centralized response efforts around seven major population areas in Puerto Rico to accelerate stabilization. By the end of November, FEMA reported progress in restoring the priority infrastructure areas. For example, FEMA's daily field briefing for November 29 reported that 92 percent of customers had water service.

Key Finding #13: Challenged by an inoperable telecommunications environment in Puerto Rico, FEMA had to adapt field communications, program delivery, and command and control activities.

Hurricane Maria severely damaged Puerto Rico's communications infrastructure, which limited the ability of FEMA field personnel to leverage traditional commercial cellular and broadband communications services to coordinate response operations. Following landfall, 95 percent of cell towers were out of service, and outages continued in the ensuing months (Figure 26). The outages impeded field personnel access to key operating and management systems, including FEMA's crisis management system and the FEMA National Emergency Management Information System (NEMIS), which FEMA uses to process disaster survivor registrations. Both systems are not optimized for use over contingency communications systems (e.g., satellite). Field personnel also often lacked training on how to prioritize use so as not to overload those contingency systems.

FEMA struggled to overcome its reliance on commercial cellular and broadband communications to execute program delivery and conduct command and control activities. For example, limited cellular service impacted the ability of disaster survivors to register for FEMA assistance. FEMA deployed Disaster Survivor Assistance teams across Puerto Rico to assist survivors, but the limited cellular service likewise hindered their efforts to register survivors for disaster assistance and

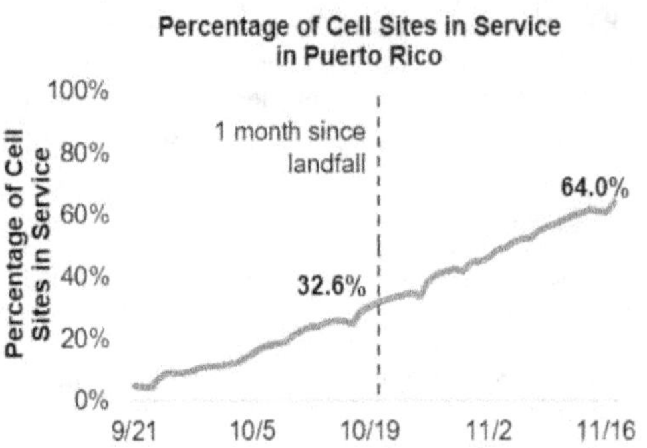

Figure 26: Cell service slowly came back online in Puerto Rico after Hurricane Maria.

conduct case inquiries and updates. These teams typically use tablets with cellular and wireless broadband access to register survivors. In the absence of mobile communications, the teams used paper registrations and forms on offline laptops and tablets. These new, non-standard processes caused inaccuracies and omissions, delaying the provision of benefits to survivors. Limited commercial communications and user unfamiliarity with contingency communications options also impacted command and control activities, including resource requests. FEMA staff used handwritten resource requests and subsequently had to review, prioritize, sign, scan, and manually enter more than 2,000 requests into FEMA's crisis management system, further contributing to delays. FEMA also experienced shortfalls incorporating the Integrated Public Alert and Warning System into the response, and could have better prioritized the transportation and use of contingency communications equipment, and trained personnel.

To overcome communications challenges in Puerto Rico, FEMA deployed its MERS resources with mobile satellite, mobile radio, and logistics support services to provide command and control communications, situational awareness, and program delivery (Figure 27). FEMA initially deployed MERS assets to Puerto Rico following Hurricane Irma and sent additional assets after Hurricane Maria. FEMA also deployed satellite phones, procured and leased satellite devices, and worked with other federal agencies, such as DoD and the U.S. Secret Service, to obtain additional resources. Still, FEMA faced challenges. Some FEMA satellite phones

Figure 27: Emergency communications vehicles in transit to support communications in Puerto Rico.

could not correctly operate in the Caribbean. Many staff who received satellite phones did not know how to properly use them. The demand for satellite phones and other contingency devices exceeded FEMA's pre-staged supplies both in the territory and on the U.S. mainland. Procurement and logistics challenges delayed the acquisition and shipment of additional devices to Puerto Rico.

Key Finding #14: FEMA and its federal partners installed a record number of generators to provide temporary power to critical infrastructure while facing significant challenges in identifying generator requirements and shortfalls in available generators.

The extent and duration of outages in Puerto Rico were significantly greater than FEMA faces in most disasters. Typically, FEMA and its partners provide temporary emergency power to critical infrastructure facilities, such as emergency operations centers, fire and police stations, hospitals, and water facilities, with SLTT jurisdictions determining the prioritization of temporary emergency power. For example, following hurricanes Katrina and Sandy, the Federal Government provided temporary emergency power to a few hundred facilities by installing generators for usually 60 days or less.

After Hurricane Maria caused a large-scale power outage in Puerto Rico by severely damaging an already weakened power grid, many critical infrastructure facilities across the territory struggled to gain temporary power. These facilities either lacked back-up generators or had generators that failed or were non-operational. While regulations require hospitals to maintain emergency generators, the storm's impact either damaged these generators or they were otherwise inadequate to fulfill the hospitals' needs.

By the end of May 2018, FEMA and its partners completed 2,338 generator installations in Puerto Rico.

To meet the overwhelming demand for temporary power, FEMA, at the territory's request, assigned the U.S. Army Corps of Engineers (USACE) to install generators at many critical infrastructure facilities. By October, FEMA and its partners had set a record for generator installations, surpassing the previous record of 310 generators installed during Hurricane Katrina (Figure 28). By the end of November, more than two months after landfall, USACE had completed 693 generator installations; this number had increased to 2,338 by the end of May 2018. FEMA also expanded traditional approaches for providing temporary power by supporting repairs and upkeep for non-federal generators already installed at critical infrastructure facilities. FEMA and USACE provided one-time repairs and refueling of private generators. By repairing private generators, FEMA and USACE reduced the need for federally provided generators, freeing up inventory for other critical facilities.

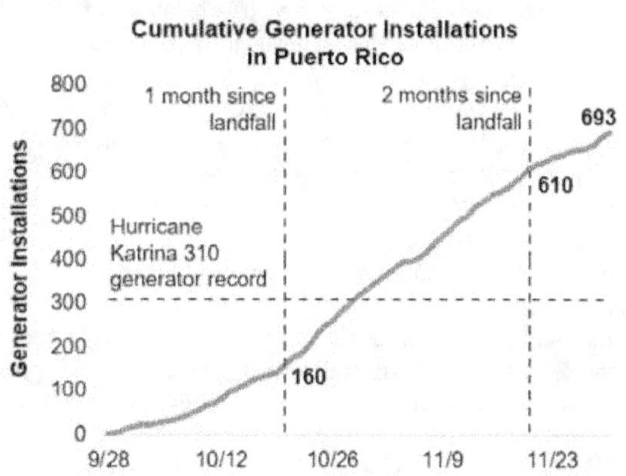

Figure 28: FEMA and its partners completed nearly 700 generator installations from late September to the end of November.

Despite the record number of generator installations and expanded efforts to provide temporary power, the number of generator requests received from the Puerto Rican government challenged FEMA and its partners. Even as the power grid came back online in some areas, FEMA and its partners were unable to provide generators to all requested critical infrastructure sites due to limited generator availability, failures due to prolonged use, lapse in servicing, and fueling issues. Additionally, extensive

FEMA 2017 Hurricane Season After-Action Report (7/2018)

storm damage and pre-existing safety conditions at some facilities created challenges for generator installation.

From late September until the end of November, FEMA received generator requests from roughly 1,400 facilities; by May 2018, the total number of requests had increased to 2,273. FEMA and its partners assessed the initial requests and determined that only a subset of several hundred facilities required generators. To meet this still high demand, FEMA augmented its inventory with generators from the Defense Logistics Agency and USACE.

Figure 29: Power generators and fuel tankers arrive to the port of San Juan, Puerto Rico.

When Hurricane Maria hit, FEMA had 695 generators in stock, ranging in size from 50 kilowatts to 800 kilowatts, including 73 already in Puerto Rico and 31 en route to the island in response to Hurricane Irma. These large-capacity generators often supported water pumping stations. While the available generators varied in size, FEMA did not have enough generators of all sizes to meet the needs in Puerto Rico, and, in particular, lacked enough small generators. To address this challenge and meet generator requirements, FEMA sometimes used generators that were larger than necessary, further contributing to overall inventory shortfalls.

Faced with unprecedented demand, FEMA and its partners conducted extraordinary prioritization of generator installations for critical infrastructure, focusing mainly on hospitals and water facilities. Still, FEMA could not fulfill every request from the priority list of facilities. For example, after providing generators to 30 critical medical facilities, including 14 hospitals and 16 diagnostic and treatment centers, FEMA had difficulty prioritizing requests from lower-level medical facilities serving disaster survivors. Ultimately, the Puerto Rico Aqueducts and Sewers Authority, which owns and operates the majority of the island's public water and wastewater systems, was the largest recipient of FEMA-provided generators. By the end of November, FEMA continued the generator mission as partners worked to bring Puerto Rico's power grid back online.

Temporary Emergency Power to National Public Warning System Station Generators

FEMA successfully maintained the National Public Warning System radio broadcast station generators in cooperation with local support, for over two months, to ensure continuous broadcasting of critical response and recovery information to residents in Puerto Rico and the U.S. Virgin Islands.

Recommendations

The private sector, states, and Federal Government all play crucial roles in the reliability, resilience, and security of critical infrastructure. To better prepare to respond during long-term infrastructure outages, FEMA should work with key partners to **revise the National Response Framework and, as required, the Response Federal Interagency Operational Plan to emphasize addressing the interdependencies and cascading impacts among critical lifelines and cross-sector coordination.** FEMA should also work with key partners to establish criteria for stabilization of communities, and **encourage investment in redundant assets to maintain communication and supply temporary power.** Power is the backbone of America's economic sectors, generating the energy that empowers its people and businesses. The lifelines of communications, health and medical, food and water, wastewater, and transportation all represent critical downstream dependencies of power. Further, power is a key interdependency and vulnerability among all sectors. The restoration of power is so consequential to

FEMA 2017 Hurricane Season After-Action Report (7/2018)

an effective response that a coordinated effort among utilities, local and state governments, the Department of Energy, USACE, and DHS is imperative. To ensure a unified national restoration effort, FEMA and these key partners are **establishing a standing Interagency Power Task Force as a collaborative partnership among key departments, agencies and non-governmental partners**. The task force will serve during steady state as a standing coordinating element and during incidents transition to a crisis planning component of ESF #12. The process for restoring power generation, transmission, and distribution systems is complex and includes immediate post-storm temporary power restoration, initial restoration of the supporting power grid, as well as solutions that can strengthen reliability and resilience over the long-term. The task force will serve as the integrating mechanism during steady state for analysis, assessments, situational awareness, and routinized coordination. During complex catastrophes, it will conduct analysis, planning, and synchronization of assistance to support execution of the Power Outage Incident Annex, using coordinating structures such as the Electricity Information Sharing and Analysis Center.

> **Recommendations Summary**
>
> - Revise the National Response Framework and, as required, the Response Federal Interagency Operational Plan to emphasize stabilization of critical lifelines and coordination across critical infrastructure sectors
> - Establish a standing Power Task Force as a collaborative, steady-state partnership and transition it to a crisis action planning cell under ESF #12, Energy, during disaster operations
> - Encourage investment in redundant assets to maintain communications and supply temporary power
> - Encourage critical infrastructure owners and operators, and state and local governments, to invest in more resilient infrastructure
> - Include continuity and resilient all-hazards communications capabilities in plans and guidance

As the 2017 hurricanes demonstrated, the impacts of long-term infrastructure outages jeopardize the ability and speed of communities and individuals to recover, and can have dire economic and social consequences. In addition to addressing lessons and best practices for operating during extended infrastructure outages, FEMA should work with and **encourage critical infrastructure owners and operators, and state and local governments, to invest in more resilient infrastructure**. These investments, including pre-disaster mitigation, will not only reduce disaster costs but also can have life-saving impacts during incidents. For example, FEMA and its partners need to capture collective investments in mitigation and their impact on risk reduction, and should encourage adoption and enforcement of modern building codes.

Resiliency is particularly important for lifelines such as communications. Every day, individuals, organizations, and government institutions provide critical services that depend on reliable access to communications systems. **Continuity planning and resilient all-hazards communications capabilities must be built into FEMA and its partners' plans and guidance for catastrophic disasters**. FEMA should assist states and local municipalities to prepare for major outages and their disruptive effects by providing expertise in continuity of government.

> **FEMA Strategic Plan Alignment**
>
> - *Objective 1.1, Incentivize Investments that Reduce Risk, Including Pre-Disaster Mitigation, and Reduce Disaster Costs at all Levels,* promotes the effectiveness of pre-disaster mitigation measures.
> - *Objective 2.4, Improve Continuity and Resilient Communications Capabilities,* reinforces the importance of investing in resilient and redundant all-hazards communications capabilities as an indispensable element of an emergency management organization and highlights the fact that they must be built into catastrophic preparedness efforts. Additionally, this objective concludes that continued integration of continuity subject matter expertise and coordination into response and recovery operations is required.

Mass Care to Initial Housing Operations

Hurricanes Harvey, Irma, and Maria led to unprecedented demands on FEMA to support feeding, sheltering, and housing activities across multiple, concurrent, and geographically dispersed operations. ESF #6 (Mass Care, Emergency Assistance, Temporary Housing, and Human Services), co-led by FEMA and the American Red Cross, coordinated with federal, SLTT, and non-governmental partners to provide more than one million shelter nights and the longest feeding mission in FEMA's history in Puerto Rico and the U.S. Virgin Islands.

Impacted states, tribes, and territories (specifically Texas, Florida, Puerto Rico, and the U.S. Virgin Islands) conducted extended congregate sheltering operations as a result of widespread damage to residences and critical infrastructure. FEMA and its partners faced challenges facilitating the transition of survivors from emergency congregate sheltering to temporary and permanent housing solutions. While FEMA programs supported Texas' and Florida's efforts to move most survivors out of congregate shelters within 60 days, shelter operations in Puerto Rico and the U.S. Virgin Islands extended past 90 days. (Figure 30 provides an overview of the three classifications for sheltering and housing solutions managed under ESF #6.)

Congregate Shelters
Facilities that provide safe, sanitary, and secure places to temporarily shelter groups of people

Direct Housing Solutions
FEMA-led housing programs that provide long-term housing solutions to FEMA applicants

Non-Congregate Shelters
Facilities that provide temporary shelter for people in non-group settings, like hotels or ships

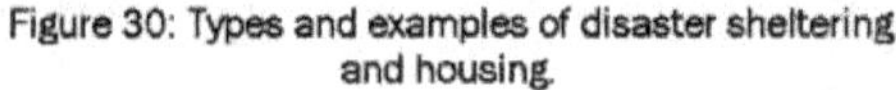

Figure 30: Types and examples of disaster sheltering and housing.

By October 9, FEMA had received more Individual Assistance registrations than for hurricanes Katrina, Rita, Wilma, and Sandy combined. By November 30, FEMA registered more than 4.7 million households, administered $2.6 billion to applicants through the Individuals and Households Program (IHP), and provided almost 60,000 households with Transitional Sheltering Assistance (TSA) (e.g., hotel rooms). Through November 30, FEMA had provided more than 2.7 million hotel nights through TSA; this number had increased to nearly 5.3 million hotel nights by May 1, 2018. However, as a result of the concurrent incidents, the volume of applicants requiring inspections, financial assistance, and help transitioning to temporary or permanent housing necessitated innovations in FEMA's processes to expedite delivery of financial and direct housing assistance. To adapt, FEMA streamlined pre-existing processes and implemented new direct housing solutions, including piloting the first state-managed housing mission since 2000.

The aftermath of Hurricane Harvey alone left nearly 80,000 homes with at least 18 inches of floodwater, and 23,000 of those homes with more than five feet of floodwater. Almost 780,000 Texans evacuated their homes. Of the total households impacted by Hurricane Harvey, 80 percent did not have flood insurance. Initial projections showed a potential of 32,500 households needing direct housing assistance, including in the greater Houston metropolitan area. Although FEMA traditionally provides direct housing assistance in the form of manufactured housing units, the challenging circumstances that Harvey left in Texas followed by additional needs for subsequent disasters, required that FEMA implement multiple, creative solutions.

Key Finding #15: FEMA supported American Red Cross and Emergency Support Function #6 partners to provide more than one million shelter nights within the first 60 days, while facing challenges transitioning survivors out of congregate sheltering.

ESF #6 partners provided more than one million shelter nights to displaced survivors this hurricane season. Figure 31 shows congregate shelter populations in Texas, Florida, Puerto Rico, and the U.S. Virgin Islands from August 25 to October 1. Following Hurricane Irma, in Florida, 191,764 survivors transitioned from congregate shelters within 15 days.[o] Relatively low levels of damage to survivor residences, available non-congregate accommodations, and a high degree of state and local preparedness mitigated the need to extend congregate sheltering operations. In Florida, all congregate shelters closed as of October 21.

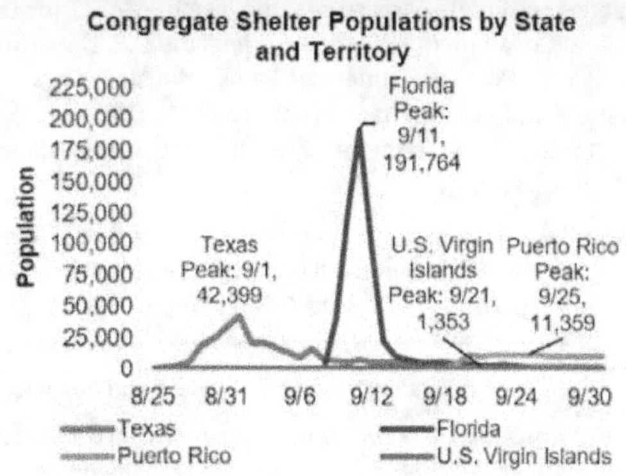

Figure 31: Peak congregate shelter populations in Texas, Florida, Puerto Rico, and the U.S. Virgin Islands.

At its peak, whole community partners in Texas sheltered 42,399 survivors in congregate shelters, with approximately 1,403 survivors remaining in shelters 30 days after Hurricane Harvey made landfall. The last shelter in Texas closed 63 days after Hurricane Harvey made landfall. In Texas, survivors remained in congregate shelters for many reasons including: unprecedented and widespread flooding, limited access to non-congregate options, and continued displacement from inaccessible or uninhabitable homes. The need to support extended sheltering operations strained whole community partners' ability to find and maintain qualified shelter staff. Recognizing that Hurricane Harvey made landfall before the peak of the hurricane season, the American Red Cross reserved staff in anticipation of additional disaster needs. Instead, the American Red Cross leveraged private sector partnerships to support congregate sheltering operations and FEMA activated staffing contracts to support a mega shelter in Dallas.

Dallas Mega Shelter

The City of Dallas opened a mega shelter three days after Hurricane Harvey made landfall and remained open for 26 days. At its peak, the shelter provided for 3,500 survivors.

Unlike congregate sheltering operations in Florida and Texas, congregate shelter operations in Puerto Rico and the U.S. Virgin Islands extended well beyond 90 days (Table 7). While FEMA registration data suggests that most survivors in both territories chose to remain in their damaged homes, those who relied on congregate facilities for an extended period were unable to access or repair their residences because of the severity of damages.

Table 7: Shelter populations over time.

State	30 Days	60 Days	90 Days
Texas	1,403	186	0
Florida	177	0	0
Puerto Rico	4,154	1,497	466
U.S. Virgin Islands	309	69	26

---

[o] Figures do not include sheltering operations for the Seminole Tribe of Florida.

To facilitate survivor recovery and assist survivors transitioning out of congregate shelters across all disaster-affected areas, FEMA established Multi-Agency Shelter Transition Taskforces (MASTT). MASTT staff helped survivors move into non-congregate sheltering options, such as TSA, or access local, state, and NGO resources. Taskforce composition and participation, however, varied by operation. As a best practice, in Puerto Rico representatives of MASTT included disaster case management and state and Federal Government entities, including the U.S. Department of Housing and Urban Development (HUD), the Puerto Rico Department of Family Housing, Community Services and Indigenous Affairs, and the Puerto Rico Department of Health. The MASTT in Puerto Rico took on additional roles coordinating with Puerto Rico's Department of Housing to better determine survivor needs and to identify rental properties for survivors.

Overall, whole community partners supported unprecedented mass care operations and assisted in the transition of survivors out of congregate shelters. However, partners met notable challenges in the territories because of impacts from multiple hurricanes.

Feeding Mission: Successes and Areas for Improvement in the Caribbean

As of November 30, FEMA's sustained air mission of food and water delivery was the longest in its history. This also marked the first time FEMA used non-perishable grocery and snack boxes in a feeding mission. Grocery boxes were 25-30 pounds and supplied approximately 12 meals; snack boxes weighed about 5 pounds and contained light meals including granola bars, candy, chips, fruit cups, desserts, and canned food. During the mission, FEMA distributed commodities using air drops and other innovative methods but also encountered challenges, such as:

- Puerto Rico's originally designed mass-feeding plan accounted for distributing 500,000 meals outside of congregate shelters or points of distribution, but not to the entire territory. The plan was modified to prioritize the 22 hardest hit municipalities; and
- Commodities procured through Logistics or Mass Care differed in their content requirements; more integration between the Agency's Logistics, Mass Care, and Procurement teams was necessary to coordinate feeding operations.

Key Finding #16: In Texas and Florida, FEMA helped survivors quickly transition from congregate shelters to other options such as hotels. However, across all operations, FEMA faced challenges implementing non-congregate sheltering programs.

FEMA employed a variety of non-congregate sheltering solutions to meet survivor needs, including the TSA program, a host-state agreement, the Sheltering and Temporary Emergency Power (STEP) pilot program, and the Volunteer Agencies Leading and Organizing Repair (VALOR) initiative.

Transitional Sheltering Assistance

TSA provides short-term, non-congregate sheltering through the provision of hotel and motel rooms to applicants who are unable to return to their primary residence following a disaster. The program allows hotels throughout the country to participate. In Texas, the State requested and FEMA approved the TSA program on August 27, two days after landfall. In Florida, the State requested TSA on September 10, when the storm made landfall; FEMA approved the request two days later. In Puerto Rico, the Territory requested that FEMA activate the TSA program on October 25, more than a month after landfall. FEMA approved the request three days later. The U.S. Virgin Islands did not request TSA because there was only one operating hotel on the islands. In total, approximately 2.2 million applicants were eligible for the program, and FEMA provided more than 2.7 million hotel nights to those survivors through November 30.

FEMA 2017 Hurricane Season After-Action Report (7/2018)

FEMA's use of TSA provided an option for applicants to quickly leave congregate shelters, but participation in the program varied across disasters. In addition, hotels and motels near the heavily damaged areas either were unavailable or declined to participate in TSA, requiring applicants to relocate or stay elsewhere in non-participating hotels.

Although TSA provided a non-congregate sheltering option, recovery resource providers, such as MASTT and disaster case workers, could more easily conduct outreach to survivors who remained in the congregate shelters. Additionally, applicants who moved into TSA-participating hotels away from their primary residence had difficulty accessing wrap-around services (e.g., feeding) or arranging to travel back to their residence to be present for a housing inspection (see Key Finding #17 for more information on housing inspections). As of November 30, 21,401 households remained checked into hotel rooms through TSA as a result of hurricane impacts. While TSA provides a safe sheltering option, for many survivors staying in a hotel may become more long-term than intended.

Host-State Agreement

From September to November, approximately 179,000 individuals, including hurricane survivors, left Puerto Rico for the continental United States. On October 5, FEMA entered into a host-state agreement with Florida to support Puerto Rico's evacuees. At the time, Florida whole community partners were engaged in disaster recovery operations from Hurricane Irma, which allowed state partners to readily assist evacuees from Puerto Rico. However, both Floridians and Puerto Ricans faced challenges accessing recovery resources. Survivors in Florida experienced a decreasing supply of non-congregate sheltering solutions.

> **FEMA Host-State Agreements**
>
> Under a host-state agreement, a state or territory provides transportation and/or sheltering support to evacuees from another state or territory that has received a Presidential emergency or Major Disaster declaration. The state may also seek reimbursement for eligible sheltering and evacuation costs through existing mutual aid agreements with FEMA.

> **Multi-Agency Resource Centers**
>
> States in several FEMA Regions stood up Multi-Agency Resource Centers under their own authority to assist Puerto Rican evacuees.
>
> | FEMA Region | Families Assisted |
> | --- | --- |
> | I | 3,705 |
> | II | 2,854 |
> | III | 1,816 |
> | IV | 9,141 |
> | V | 982 |

FEMA also supported Puerto Rican evacuees by activating the Immediate Disaster Case Management (IDCM) program. IDCM provides recovery service access and case managers to displaced survivors through a mission assignment with the Department of Health and Human Services. While FEMA traditionally only allows IDCM programs to operate in the disaster-affected area, the IDCM program for the hurricane season provided services to survivors in Puerto Rico, as well as to those that evacuated from Puerto Rico to Florida and other states.

Sheltering and Temporary Essential Power

FEMA supports the ability for survivors to shelter at home through STEP, which provides interim repairs of necessary utilities, such as electricity, heat, and hot water. State and local governments implement STEP and therefore determine the program's administrative structure, which necessitates customization and can impact implementation timelines. Though FEMA created STEP during Hurricane Sandy and has used it in several large disasters since, the Agency has not established standard national policies or training for the program. In Puerto Rico, unreliable power and access to water caused additional delays to STEP implementation. The time between STEP policy approval and the date of the first STEP construction repairs is shown in Table 8.

Table 8: STEP policy approval and first STEP construction dates.

State/Territory	Sheltering and Temporary Essential Power (STEP) Policy Approval Date	First STEP Construction Date
Texas	September 15	December 23, 2017
Florida	September 24	December 16, 2017
Puerto Rico	October 19	January 22, 2018
U.S. Virgin Islands	October 14	March 3, 2018

Voluntary Agencies Leading and Organizing Repair

FEMA established a Crisis Action Planning (CAP) Team to address Puerto Rico's sheltering needs through innovative methods. The CAP Team developed the VALOR initiative, a novel approach to use voluntary agencies to execute STEP functions. The VALOR initiative provided rebuilding materials to voluntary agencies active in Puerto Rico, who then provided basic repair services to survivors' homes, making them safe and habitable. The first VALOR repairs started in January 2018.

FEMA employed a variety of sheltering, temporary, and permanent housing solutions during this hurricane season. While transitional housing programs were effective in both Texas and Florida, response operations in Puerto Rico and U.S. Virgin Islands continued to require modifications to effectively move survivors from congregate shelters to temporary or permanent housing solutions.

Key Finding #17: FEMA created new, streamlined housing inspection procedures to reduce inspection delays.

From August 25 through November 30, FEMA registered 4.7 million households for disaster assistance, more than hurricanes Katrina, Rita, Wilma, and Sandy combined. As of November 30, FEMA had informed approximately 50 percent of these applicants that a home inspection would be necessary. FEMA requires inspections to assess damages and estimate the value of property loss. The volume of inspections needed overwhelmed the Agency's capacity to complete traditional on-site inspections in a timely manner.

On October 1, FEMA advised applicants in Texas that inspection wait times could be as long as 45 days. By November 13, FEMA extended the notice of inspection delays to applicants in Florida, Puerto Rico, and the U.S. Virgin Islands as well. The concurrent disasters and the high demand for inspections created longer average wait times than those during Hurricane Sandy, although they were comparable to those for hurricanes Katrina and Rita (Table 9). Wait times for inspections can delay the delivery of financial or direct housing assistance to survivors. To meet the historically high need for inspections across all disaster affected regions, FEMA contracted additional inspectors to supplement existing inspection staff. Additionally, to reduce the time survivors had to wait for inspections, FEMA introduced new and alternate methods that streamlined and expedited the process (Table 10).

Table 9: Historical average wait time for site inspections (as of November 30, 2017).

Disaster	Number of Inspections	Avg. Wait Time (Days)
Katrina	1,385,329	35
Rita	623,635	27
Wilma	439,081	14
Sandy	343,003	7
Harvey	584,056	24
Irma	967,163	27
Maria	260,989	39

Table 10: New and alternate inspection processes implemented during the hurricane season.

New or Alternate Site Inspection Process	Description of New and Alternate Inspection Process	State or Territory Implemented
Applicant Self-Assessment Automated Outreach	FEMA delivered automated outreach via text message, phone, and email. This allowed applicants to self-report a general degree of damage for their home, which afforded FEMA the ability to triage resources to disaster survivors with the greatest needs first.	TX, FL, GA
Desktop Inspections	FEMA performed an interview with applicants to determine the extent of disaster-caused damage. The applicant's answers to the questions determined the applicable level of damage per descriptions provided. Each level of damage reflected a set amount of financial assistance for real and/or personal property disaster damage.	FL, GA
Flood Rapid Damage Assessment	FEMA developed the Flood Rapid Damage Assessment by compiling historical NEMIS data from FEMA information and data analysis reports and conducting a statistical analysis of various types of homes, foundation types, and water levels to create factors for individual inspection line items. This method was only used for rapidly assessing flood damage, but not for wind-related damage.	TX
Reduced Inspection Processes	FEMA implemented a method to alleviate the burden of inspection assignment for applicants who would not benefit from an on-site inspection. One month of Rental Assistance was expedited without an inspection for applicants that reported either inaccessibility or utility outage, without disaster-caused damage to their home or property. Initial Rental Assistance was expedited to homeowners with flood insurance and only reported flood damage, because flood insurance does not provide temporary housing assistance and applicants would be pending results from their flood insurance adjuster.	FL, GA, PR, USVI
Remote Sensing Imagery	FEMA used remote sensing imagery, in coordination with open-source housing and occupancy data, to identify applicants residing in areas damaged or destroyed by the disaster. FEMA used GIS data to identify flood depths in areas within a flooding incident. While effective in Texas and Florida, remote sensing imagery was not efficient in Puerto Rico and the U.S. Virgin Islands due to challenges related to map availability, topography, and inconsistent address conventions.	TX, FL, PR, USVI
Award Packages (Banded Inspections)	FEMA developed award packages, which provided financial assistance grants by levels of disaster-caused damage to real property and personal property, as determined by the results of an on-site or desktop inspection.	FL, GA
Inspections Triage	FEMA prioritized inspections based on responses to the Applicant Self-Assessment Automated Outreach.	FL, TX, GA
LexisNexis	FEMA leveraged LexisNexis database for identity, occupancy, and ownership verification to increase overall inspection efficiency by eliminating the need for site inspectors to verify registrant ownership.	FL, TX, GA

These alternate inspection processes, which FEMA used in different combinations across the disaster-affected areas, reduced the number of field inspections needed by approximately 146,000, saving nearly $38 million. FEMA is evaluating the impact and effectiveness of these new and alternate inspection processes in expediting financial assistance.

FEMA 2017 Hurricane Season After-Action Report (7/2018)

Key Finding #18: FEMA applied lessons learned from recent housing operations and exercises to expand temporary and permanent housing solutions, including supporting a state-managed housing mission.

In April 2017, the Acting Administrator of FEMA issued a memorandum stating that FEMA must build "capability within the first 100 days of a disaster to register at least one million survivors for individual and other needs assistance [and] provide temporary housing to at least 20,000 displaced families." The memo prompted the creation of the intra-FEMA 'Housing Assistance Initiative', which established 13 working groups to address disaster-housing challenges. Three of these working groups focused on a Recreation Vehicle (RV) study, exploring how FEMA could provide direct repairs to damaged homes, and building capacity of states to provide disaster housing. FEMA staff likewise incorporated lessons learned from the 2016 Louisiana severe storms and flooding disaster and the Agency's response in support of North Carolina for the 2016 Hurricane Matthew to improve the agency's processes for delivering safe and durable housing for displaced survivors. FEMA will continue to assess these programs throughout the recovery phase of these disasters.

> **Using Public Assistance (PA) and Individual Assistance (IA) to Provide Sheltering and Housing Programs**
>
> PA may fund the repair, restoration, reconstruction, or replacement of public facilities or infrastructure damaged or destroyed by a disaster. Unlike IA, FEMA requires that the disaster-affected state and local governments share up to 25 percent of the overall PA program costs. PA sheltering programs include VALOR, STEP, and Host State agreements.
>
> IA provided direct assistance to individuals and families through numerous housing programs such as Direct Lease, Permanent Housing Construction-Repair, and Manufactured Housing Units.

Direct Lease Program

Due to the shortage of available housing resources to accommodate the large number of survivors requiring housing assistance, FEMA developed a new Direct Lease program. This program facilitated survivor access to property not typically used for temporary housing, such as corporate lodging or vacation rentals. In addition, Direct Lease can be a potentially safer option for displaced families with access and functional needs compared to a manufactured housing unit.

FEMA approved the maximum amount of funds under the Direct Lease program to meet survivor needs in different locations. Due to a shortage of affordable rental properties, FEMA raised the amount of money approved for acquiring properties under the Direct Lease to 300 percent above HUD's fair market rent (FMR) rate in the Florida Keys, and to 200 percent of FMR in other Florida counties. In Puerto Rico and U.S. Virgin Islands, FEMA raised its Direct Lease cap to 200 percent of the HUD FMR, given the lack of available rental properties due to continued utility outages. Raising the Direct Lease cap increases the number of potential housing units available for disaster survivors.

Recreation Vehicles

FEMA also recognized the need to re-incorporate RVs into the menu of temporary housing options for the first time since hurricanes Katrina and Rita. FEMA-supplied RVs are certified to meet Recreation Vehicle Industry Association and California Air Resource Board standards, or are certified compliant with the *Toxic Substances Control Act Title VI* for formaldehyde emissions from composite wood products found in RVs. FEMA Housing Assistance Initiative, specifically the RV Study Group's extensive research, influenced the decision to include RVs among the Agency's temporary

Figure 32: FEMA staging area for MHUs, Travel Trailers, and non-motorized RVs.

FEMA 2017 Hurricane Season After-Action Report (7/2018)

housing options. A Housing Tabletop Exercise sponsored by FEMA earlier in 2017 also identified potential target populations and delivery processes for future RV use. FEMA used RVs in specific locations in both Texas and Florida because of their ability to be placed on smaller parcels of land where Manufactured Housing Units were not feasible.

Direct Repair

The Stafford Act authorizes FEMA to provide Permanent Housing Construction to disaster damaged homes in insular areas[p] and locations where no alternative housing resources are available, and where temporary housing assistance is unavailable, not feasible, or not cost-effective. Direct repairs and new construction provided under Permanent Housing Construction are limited to real property components eligible under FEMA Housing Assistance such as heating, ventilating, air conditioning, walls, floors, and ceilings. Recognizing that areas in Texas impacted by Hurricane Harvey met the criteria for direct repairs, FEMA authorized this option for the first time in a non-remote location on the continental United States. The decision was intended to expedite delivery of direct housing assistance to applicants and provide equitable, cost-saving housing solutions to impacted populations.

State-Managed Housing Mission

Given the breadth of damage and diverse geography in the area of impact, FEMA recognized that it needed more ways to provide housing assistance in Texas. Both FEMA and Texas officials identified that state-managed, locally executed direct repair and lease initiatives could provide housing solutions while supporting the State of Texas, communities, and survivors. Initially, FEMA investigated the option of providing a grant to Texas to deliver direct housing. A grant for direct housing would allow Texas to manage both FEMA-granted dollars for direct housing as well as HUD-granted Community Development Block Grant Disaster Recovery (CDBG-DR) dollars in a continuum. HUD CDBG-DR grants are applied for and received by the state, and are typically received after FEMA direct housing assistance. FEMA found that under the Stafford Act, it can only provide financial assistance, or direct assistance for housing, not grant dollars. Under Section 306 of the Stafford Act, however, FEMA could enter into an Intergovernmental Service Agreement (IGSA) with the State of Texas to implement a direct housing mission. An IGSA is an agreement between a federal agency and a state to provide a given service.

Inter-Governmental Service Agreement Development Timeline

- **August 25**: President declares major disaster for Hurricane Harvey
- **September 10**: FEMA approves State of Texas request for direct housing assistance. FEMA conditioned the approval based on entering an IGSA with terms and conditions the state and FEMA agree to for implementing direct housing assistance
- **September 13**: First draft of IGSA including general contract terms and conditions and programmatic terms
- **September 14 – September 21**: Discussions within FEMA, with other federal agencies (DHS, the White House Office of Management and Budget, and HUD), and with Texas General Land Office (GLO) regarding duplication of benefits within FEMA programs and with other federal agency programs, eligibility determinations, and direct housing options offered through the IGSA
- **September 22**: FEMA and GLO sign IGSA
- **September 28**: Direct housing operations begin
- **October 7**: The first applicant moves into a travel trailer

The Texas General Land Office (GLO) implemented its first state-managed disaster housing mission by executing an IGSA with FEMA on September 22. The IGSA enabled the state to provide direct housing

---

[p] According to the National Response Framework, insular areas include Guam, the Commonwealth of the Northern Mariana Islands, American Samoa, and the U.S. Virgin Islands.

                                                                                       July 12, 2018

assistance services on behalf of FEMA and was intended to allow greater flexibility in securing housing solutions as well as a streamlined approach to long-term recovery. However, FEMA and the Texas GLO required some time to execute contracting requirements per the IGSA and the Federal Acquisitions Regulations, as well as set up initial coordination and staffing structures (see the Inter-Governmental Service Agreement Development Timeline call-out box). Activities were designed to enhance state and local capacity to manage the immediate operation, and build capacity for future incidents as states have more familiarity with the needs of their residents, local laws and ordinances, and are better situated to design and administer solutions for the survivors. Although FEMA implemented a new and creative solution, the solution required time for FEMA and the Texas GLO to determine implementation methods while households remained displaced. With improved pre-event planning and coordination with partners, and more flexible authorities, FEMA and its federal partners could better support states, communities, and survivors in implementing housing assistance.

FEMA implemented innovative solutions aimed at overcoming shortages of available rental resources, expediting the delivery of direct housing assistance to qualified survivors, and supporting a unique state-led housing mission. The impact of these solutions will be assessed further in the recovery phase of the disasters.

Recommendations

Lessons from the 2017 Hurricane Season highlight the need for an in-depth and critical look at the Nation's post-disaster housing strategies. In April 2017, FEMA formed a Housing Assistance Initiative to work with its partners, industry, and academia on a new strategic vision for housing. FEMA should continue to build on that initiative and recent lessons learned to **revise the National Response Framework and, as required, the Response Federal Interagency Operational Plan to emphasize stabilization of critical lifelines and coordination across the critical infrastructure sectors**. Restoration of critical lifelines can accelerate survivors' return to habitable dwellings.

Currently, short-term sheltering programs last longer than their designed duration. For example, as of November 30, over 13,000 survivors remained sheltered in TSA in Texas, highlighting the need for a shift in the provision of post-disaster housing.

Through the State Preparedness Report, states and territories have communicated that they believe addressing housing gaps to be a responsibility of the Federal Government.

Recommendations Summary

- Revise the National Response Framework and, as required, the Response Federal Interagency Operational Plan to emphasize stabilization of critical lifelines and coordination across critical infrastructure sectors

- Build capability and empower the implementation of federally supported, state-managed, locally executed sheltering and housing solutions

- Improve the delivery and effectiveness of housing options, including exploring grant-making authority

- Clarify federal roles and responsibilities for housing, including long-term housing solutions

- Evaluate and implement appropriate housing solutions, including the use of Recreation Vehicles, Direct Repair, and Direct Lease options

- Promote all-hazard insurance so that individuals can reduce their losses and speed their recovery

However, state and local governments are best positioned to determine housing options for their citizens, with support from the Federal Government. While 2017 saw improvements—such as the first-ever Intergovernmental Service Agreement with Texas to have its General Land Office serve as overall housing program administrator—these efforts still experienced state staffing shortfalls and information sharing challenges among partners. FEMA should work with its partners to **build capability and**

FEMA 2017 Hurricane Season After-Action Report (7/2018)

empower the implementation of federally supported, state-managed, locally executed sheltering and housing solutions. FEMA could leverage technical assistance or the FEMA Integration Teams to help build this capacity to manage disaster housing programs.

FEMA and its federal, state, local, tribal, territorial, industry, and academic partners must re-examine housing and the inspection process, in a way that is unconstrained by current policy, regulatory and legislative restrictions. FEMA and its partners should pursue changes to reduce duplication and to streamline the process for inspections. Federal housing assistance can be adapted to build SLTT capacity to manage disaster housing programs on behalf of their citizens. FEMA and its partners should work with federal partners and Congress to improve the delivery and effectiveness of housing options, including exploring grant-making authority.

Additionally, FEMA should work with the Department of Housing and Urban Development and the other federal agencies engaged in the Housing Recovery Support Function to further clarify federal roles and responsibilities for disaster housing, including approaches to long-term housing. Changes should offer state, local, tribal, and territorial partners the flexibility to provide housing options that work for their citizens, complement local housing markets conditions, and are timely, cost-effective, and incentivize innovation. The goal will include an expeditious and smooth transition for survivors from immediate to mid- to long-term housing solutions. In parallel, FEMA should evaluate and implement appropriate housing solutions, including the use of Recreation Vehicles, Direct Repair, and Direct Lease options.

The 2017 Hurricane Season again reinforced that individuals with adequate insurance coverage recover faster and more fully after a disaster. In addition to closing the insurance gap through the National Flood Insurance Program, FEMA should promote all-hazard insurance so that individuals can reduce their losses and speed their recovery. This can help people understand how much insurance coverage they need so that individuals can reduce their losses and speed their recovery. Financial preparedness, including having an insurance policy on personal and public properties, is critical to rebuilding a home, replacing belongings, and restoring order to a family and community.

FEMA Strategic Plan Alignment

- *Objective 1.2, Close the Insurance Gap,* drives FEMA to be a catalyst to increase the public's knowledge of risk and to encourage adequate insurance coverage.

- *Objective 1.3, Help People Prepare for Disasters,* focuses FEMA on identifying ways to weave preparedness into people's everyday lives.

- *Objective 3.1, Streamline the Disaster Survivor and Grantee Experience,* challenges FEMA to create innovative and efficient solutions to provide the most effective survivor support and also increase the ability of SLTT governments to drive their own recovery.

- *Objective 3.2, Mature the National Disaster Recovery Framework,* provides coordinating structure for collaborating among stakeholders to help communities rebuild strong, reduce future risk, and decrease disaster costs.

Conclusion

The Nation faced an unprecedented 2017 Hurricane Season. The scale and rapid succession of these disasters stretched response capabilities at all levels of government, and called upon emergency managers to respond in new and innovative ways to support survivors and the affected communities.

FEMA is constantly reviewing its program delivery, decision-making processes, and responses to ensure that we can improve, minimize errors, and better serve survivors. This After-Action Report highlights a number of areas where FEMA can learn from this historic disaster season and better position the Agency for incidents to come. FEMA asks that the emergency management community as a whole to work together to create better outcomes for survivors after a disaster. FEMA calls on its federal, whole community, and SLTT partners to work to transform emergency management so that, together, we can innovate and implement new approaches and technology, reduce complexity, increase efficiency and improve outcomes for survivors and affected communities after a disaster.

Strengthening the Agency

FEMA has taken action to prepare for the 2018 Hurricane Season based on a number of the findings in this After-Action Report. FEMA has updated hurricane plans, annexes, and procedures for the states and territories. The Agency has made improvements in staffing for incidents including the creation of a standard operating procedure for a Personnel Mobilization Center, a central location for equipping and training staff prior to disaster deployments. FEMA improved its logistics operations ahead of the 2018 Hurricane Season, including increasing meal and water supplies in the Caribbean by more than six fold. FEMA has also added 300 new emergency generators to the inventory and updated high priority national level contracts, to include the National Evacuation Contract, Caribbean Transportation Contract, and National Ambulance Contract. FEMA is refining communications from land mobile radios to satellite communications. FEMA is also modernizing the housing inspections process to improve the survivor experience and lessen the inspection burden for the disaster survivor.

In addition to taking immediate action, FEMA has incorporated many of the findings from this report into FEMA's *2018-2022 Strategic Plan*. The strategic plan not only provides direction on immediate actions, but will guide implementation of long-term goals, such as building a culture of preparedness, increasing state capacity, enhancing intergovernmental coordination through our FEMA Integration Teams, improving the readiness of our incident workforce by organizing a scalable and capable workforce, and posturing FEMA and the whole community to provide life-saving and life-sustaining commodities, equipment, and personnel from all available sources. While the Strategic Plan outlines the way forward for FEMA and catalyzes change for the community, improving outcomes of disaster survivors and affected communities requires a commitment from the entire federal family, from whole community partners, and from SLTT governments.

A Call to Action for Emergency Managers and Partners

Based on findings identified in this report, FEMA calls on its federal and private sector partners to adopt a critical lifelines approach to stabilizing an incident. This approach includes revising the National Response Framework and, as required, the Response Federal Interagency Operational Plan as well as creating a cross-sector emergency support function and coordinating structures. The new Framework and Federal Interagency Operational Plan should prescribe unity of effort through rapid stabilization around lifelines such as power, communications, health and medical, food and water, wastewater, and transportation. The rapid stabilization of the lifelines should be the organizing principle of the doctrine.

As power is the foundation of America's economic sectors, FEMA charges its private sector partners in collaboration with federal partners to establish a standing Interagency Power Task Force to serve

FEMA 2017 Hurricane Season After-Action Report (7/2018)

during steady state as a standing coordinating element and transition to a crisis action planning cell under ESF #12 during incidents.

FEMA's mission is bounded by laws and regulations but, for a disaster survivor, recovery is a continuum. As partners, we need to transform the way we facilitate recovery for the Nation's citizens in the face of increasing severe weather events.

FEMA challenges its federal partners to think beyond current policy, regulatory, and legislative restrictions to determine how best to deliver post-disaster housing to the Nation's affected citizens after any given disaster. In addition, FEMA, other federal agencies, Congress, and the larger community of partners should collaborate on changes required to improve housing delivery and enable more efficient delivery of other disaster assistance.

The work of emergency management does not belong just to FEMA. It is the responsibility of the whole community, federal, SLTT, private sector partners, and private citizens to build collective capacity and prepare for the disasters that we will inevitably face. Jointly, we must continue to move forward by leveraging innovative approaches, engaging with new technology, reducing complexity, and strengthening our partnerships to improve outcomes for the Nation's affected communities and provide support for survivors.

Ultimately, the lessons learned from the 2017 Hurricane Season will contribute to FEMA's efforts to work with our partners to help people before, during, and after disasters.

Acronym List

ACQ	Acquisitions
ADR	Alternative Dispute Resolution
AAR	After-Action Report
CAP	Crisis Action Planning
CDBG-DR	Community Development Block Grant – Disaster Recovery
DC	Distribution Center
DEC	Disaster Emergency Communications
DFTO	Disaster Field Training Officer
DI	Disability Integration
DoD	Department of Defense
DRC	Disaster Recovery Center
DRF	Disaster Relief Fund
EA	External Affairs
EHP	Environmental and Historic Preservation
EMAC	Emergency Management Assistance Compact
ER	Equal Rights
FEMA	Federal Emergency Management Agency
FM	Financial Management
FMR	Fair Market Rent
FQS	FEMA Qualification System
FY	Fiscal Year
GIS	Geographic Information Systems
GLO	General Land Office
HM	Hazard Mitigation
HR	Human Resources
HUD	Department of Housing and Urban Development
IA	Individual Assistance
IDCM	Immediate Disaster Case Management
IGSA	Inter-Governmental Service Agreement
IHP	Individuals and Households Program
IMAT	Incident Management Assistance Team
IT	Information Technology
LOG	Logistics
LSCMS	Logistics Supply Chain Management System
MASTT	Multi-Agency Shelter Transition Taskforce
MERS	Mobile Emergency Response Support
NDRS	National Disaster Recovery System
NEMIS	National Emergency Management Information System
NGO	Non-governmental organizations
NLE	National Level Exercise
NPSC	National Processing Service Center
NRCC	National Response Coordination Center
OCC	Office of Chief Council
OPS	Operations
PA	Public Assistance
PL	Planning
PMC	Personnel Mobilization Centers
RRCC	Regional Response Coordination Center

FEMA 2017 Hurricane Season After-Action Report (7/2018)

RV	Recreational Vehicle
SAF	Safety
SCF	Surge Capacity Force
SEC	Security
SLTT	State, Local, Tribal, and Territorial
SPR	State Preparedness Report
STEP	Sheltering and Temporary Emergency Power
THIRA	Threat and Hazard Identification and Risk Assessment
TSA	Transitional Sheltering Assistance
USACE	U.S. Army Corps of Engineers
VALOR	Volunteer Agencies Leading and Organizing Recovery

Appendix A: Updated Disaster Data

The *2017 Hurricane Season After-Action Report* (AAR) reviews FEMA's preparations for, immediate response to, and initial recovery from hurricanes Harvey, Irma, and Maria, covering the timeframe of August 25, 2017 through November 30, 2017. This appendix provides current disaster data as of May 2018.

COMMONLY APPEARING INFORMATION			
Key Finding	Information in AAR	As of Nov 30, 2017	As of May 2018
N/A	Number of Individual Assistance registrations for Harvey, Irma, and Maria	4,700,000	4,769,000
N/A	Number of Individual Assistance registrations for Harvey, Irma, Maria, and the California Wildfires	4,736,660	4,797,906
N/A	Number of FEMA personnel deployed to Harvey, Irma, and Maria	17,000	20,300

STAFFING FOR CONCURRENT, COMPLEX INCIDENTS			
Key Finding	Information in AAR	As of Nov 30, 2017	As of May 2018
#4	Number of FEMA's force strength	10,683	11,476
#4	Peak number of FEMA force strength deployments to Puerto Rico	1,200	1,221
#5	Percent of FEMA incident management employees who are certified	56%	62%
#7	Peak number of FEMA personnel deployed to Puerto Rico	2,805	2,997
#7	Number of local hires hired for Harvey, Irma, and Maria	4,095	5,329

SUSTAINING WHOLE COMMUNITY LOGISTICS OPERATIONS			
Key Finding	Information in AAR	As of Nov 30, 2017	As of May 2018
#11	Value of obligations to FEMA contract actions for Harvey, Irma, and Maria	$3,002,921,782	$3,921,324,543
#11	Number of contract actions for Harvey, Irma, and Maria	1,464	2,872
#11	Number of priority-rated contracts issued by FEMA	515	574

RESPONDING DURING LONG-TERM INFRASTRUCTURE OUTAGES			
Key Finding	Information in AAR	As of Nov 30, 2017	As of May 2018
#12	Percent of customers with water service in Puerto Rico	92%	99%

RESPONDING DURING LONG-TERM INFRASTRUCTURE OUTAGES			
Key Finding	Information in AAR	As of Nov 30, 2017	As of May 2018
#13	Percent of cell sites in service in Puerto Rico	64%	96%
#14	Number of generator installations completed in Puerto Rico	693	2,338
#14	Number of generator installation requests for facilities in Puerto Rico	1,400	2,273

MASS CARE TO INITIAL HOUSING OPERATIONS			
Key Finding	Information in AAR	As of Nov 30, 2017	As of May 2018
#15	Total amount of IHP dollars disbursed for Harvey, Irma, and Maria	$2,600,000,000	$3,860,000,000
#16	Number of households provided with TSA for Harvey, Irma, and Maria	60,000	89,000
#16	Number of households eligible for TSA for Harvey, Irma, and Maria	2,200,000	2,300,000
#16	Number hotel nights provided to households for Harvey, Irma, and Maria	2,800,000	5,300,000
#17	Number of housing inspections for Harvey	584,056	608,516
#17	Number of housing inspections for Irma	967,163	1,059,212
#17	Number of housing inspections Maria	260,989	803,704

FEMA 2017 Hurricane Season After-Action Report (7/2018)

Appendix B: Progress in National Preparedness

Years of preparedness investments, incorporation of lessons from major disasters, and legislative changes to FEMA's statutory authorities have contributed to a more prepared and more resilient Nation. FEMA has adapted and improved its capabilities since Hurricane Katrina in 2005, and supported efforts to increase preparedness across the whole community—including state, local, tribal, and territorial (SLTT) governments, non-governmental organizations, and the private sector.

In response to congressional legislation, FEMA, in coordination with federal and whole community partners, implemented changes that reflect important lessons learned from major incidents (Figure 33). After September 11, 2001, Congress passed the *Homeland Security Act of 2002*, which created the Department of Homeland Security (DHS) by combining 22 different departments and agencies, including FEMA. FEMA continued to operate under the authorities of the *Robert T. Stafford Disaster Relief and Emergency Assistance Act of 1988, as amended* and maintained its focus on reducing the loss of life and property and protecting the Nation from all hazards.

Hurricane Katrina revealed national shortcomings in preparing for and responding to a major disaster, including inadequate coordination with state and local partners. The *Post-Katrina Emergency Management Reform Act of 2006* addressed these gaps by clarifying FEMA's responsibilities, enhancing its regional offices, providing the Agency with new preparedness functions, and strengthening federal incident response teams. This act also clarified FEMA's authority to pre-stage initial resources in preparation for response operations prior to a disaster declaration.

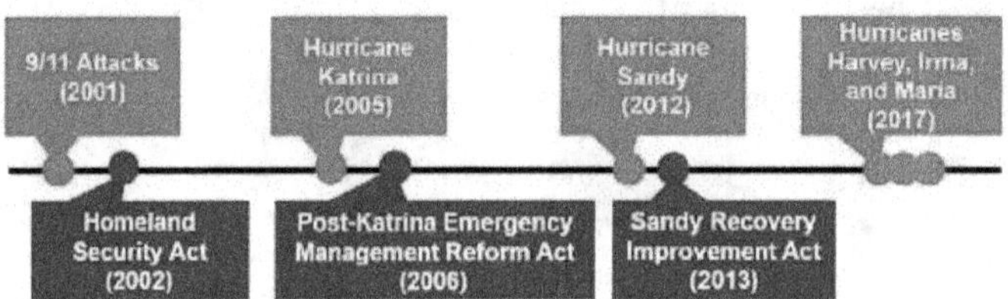

Figure 33: FEMA authorities and capabilities have evolved and improved after each major incident since September 11, 2001.

Lessons learned from Hurricane Katrina informed the development of the National Preparedness Goal and the National Preparedness System in 2011. Both the Goal and the System emphasize an all-of-Nation approach to preparing for threats and hazards that pose a significant risk to the country. This flexible and scalable structure was tested during Hurricane Sandy. FEMA pre-positioned assets and the President signed Emergency declarations before the storm made landfall in October 2012. In January 2013, only a few months after Hurricane Sandy devastated large areas of the Northeast, Congress passed the *Sandy Recovery Improvement Act of 2013*. This Act provided FEMA greater flexibility in administering assistance programs, improving the Nation's ability to efficiently respond to and recover from disasters such as hurricanes Harvey, Irma, and Maria.

This After-Action Report, as well as other efforts across the Federal Government and whole community, are important tools for identifying critical lessons learned, implementing best practices, and driving continuous improvement. Over the past several years, FEMA has worked closely with its SLTT partners across the country to develop catastrophic, worst-case scenario plans that are flexible and scalable to incidents of all magnitudes. FEMA also provides grant funding, training and exercise support, and technical assistance to help SLTT governments build and sustain their capabilities for a range of hazards, including hurricanes. Through these efforts, the Federal Government and its SLTT partners can identify areas for improvement and enhance their capabilities before the next major disaster.

Appendix C: FEMA Regions

FEMA has 10 Regional Offices located across the continental United States. Regional staff collaborate with state, local, tribal, and territorial governments; Members of Congress; other federal agencies; non-profit groups; the private sector; and other key stakeholders to administer all FEMA-related programs to protect against, respond to, recover from, and mitigate all hazards in the Region.

- **Region I:** Connecticut, Maine, Massachusetts, New Hampshire, Rhode Island, Vermont
- **Region II:** New Jersey, New York, Puerto Rico, Virgin Islands
- **Region III:** District of Columbia, Delaware, Maryland, Pennsylvania, Virginia, West Virginia
- **Region IV:** Alabama, Florida, Georgia, Kentucky, Mississippi, North Carolina, South Carolina, Tennessee
- **Region V:** Illinois, Indiana, Michigan, Minnesota, Ohio, Wisconsin
- **Region VI:** Arkansas, Louisiana, New Mexico, Oklahoma, Texas
- **Region VII:** Iowa, Kansas, Missouri, Nebraska
- **Region VIII:** Colorado, Montana, North Dakota, South Dakota, Utah, Wyoming
- **Region IX:** Arizona, California, Hawaii, Nevada, Pacific Islands
- **Region X:** Alaska, Idaho, Oregon, Washington

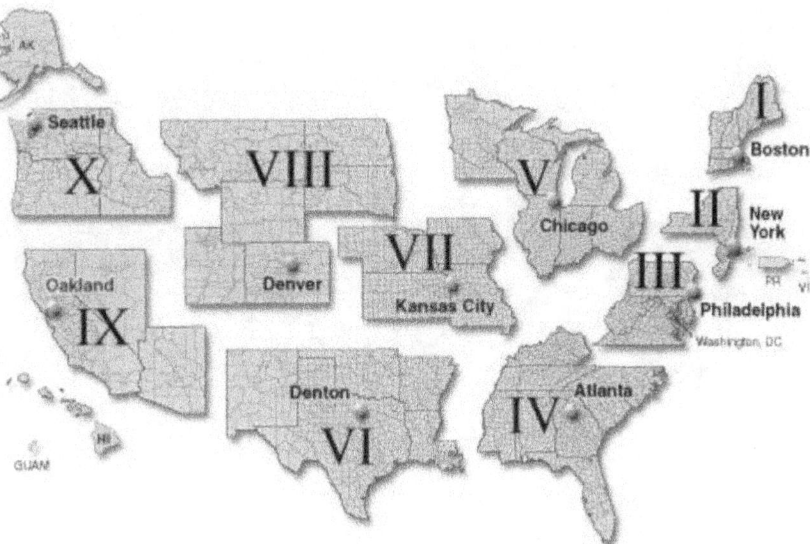

Figure 34: Map of FEMA Regions and Regional Offices.

2017 National Preparedness Report

Homeland Security

The *National Preparedness Report* summarizes the progress that the Nation has made in becoming more secure and resilient across five mission areas: Prevention, Protection, Mitigation, Response, and Recovery. The report identifies cross-cutting findings that apply across the mission areas, as well as key findings for each individual mission area. The report offers all levels of government, the private and nonprofit sectors, and the public practical insights into preparedness to support decisions about program priorities, resource allocation, and community actions.

What is the *National Preparedness Report*?

The *National Preparedness Report* is an annual requirement of *The Post-Katrina Emergency Management Reform Act of 2006* and a key element of the National Preparedness System. The report evaluates and measures gains that individuals and communities, private and nonprofit sectors, faith-based organizations, and all levels of government have made in preparedness. It also identifies where challenges and opportunities for improvement remain. The 2017 *National Preparedness Report* focuses primarily on preparedness activities undertaken or reported during calendar year 2016 and summarizes progress in building, sustaining, and delivering the 32 core capabilities outlined in the *National Preparedness Goal*.

CROSS-CUTTING FINDINGS

The *National Preparedness Report* identifies four cross-cutting findings that stretch across the different mission areas. Analysts identified these findings through the evaluation of preparedness indicators—such as training participation and exercise frequency—that apply to all 32 core capabilities; assessments submitted by states and territories; and analysis provided by Federal agencies.

Environmental Response/ Health and Safety, Intelligence and Information Sharing, Operational Communications, Operational Coordination, and Planning are five core capabilities in which the Nation has developed proficiency, but in which it likely faces a future capability gap.	Cybersecurity, Economic Recovery, Housing, Infrastructure Systems, Natural and Cultural Resources, and Supply Chain Integrity and Security remain national areas for improvement. One additional core capability— Risk Management for Protection Programs and Activities—emerged as a new area for improvement in 2016.	States and territories reported similar levels of capability compared to 2015, highlighting that larger-scale preparedness investments are necessary to drive major improvements on an annual basis; since 2012, states and territories reported proficiency increases in the Mitigation mission area, but proficiency decreases in the Prevention, Protection, and Recovery mission areas.	Exercises conducted under the National Exercise Program tested all 32 core capabilities, and especially highlighted improvements and lessons learned for Intelligence and Information Sharing, Public Information and Warning, and Operational Coordination, as well as core capabilities in the Recovery mission area.

KEY FINDINGS

The 2017 *National Preparedness Report* offers 30 key findings that highlight successes and challenges across the five mission areas. The key findings are based on the analysis of qualitative and quantitative data from all levels of government and the private and nonprofit sectors. Several criteria contribute to the identification of findings—including quantitative data that show trends over time, demonstrated progress in establishing or implementing national-level strategies and policies, and significant shifts in resources to support preparedness. The sections below highlight selected key findings that address areas that may be of high public interest.

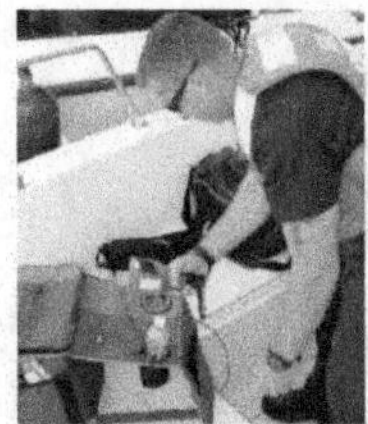

Prevention

The Prevention mission area prepares the Nation to avoid, prevent, or stop an imminent terrorist attack within the United States. In 2016, events such as the June attack at the Pulse nightclub in Orlando, Florida, and the September bombings in New York City and New Jersey highlighted the importance of Prevention capabilities. A key finding in this mission area is:

- *In 2016, the U.S. Department of Homeland Security's Office of Intelligence and Analysis, in collaboration with Federal, state, and local partners, implemented an enhanced process for assessing fusion center performance.*

Protection

The Protection mission area secures the homeland against acts of terrorism and human-induced or natural disasters. Throughout 2016, malicious cyber activities, such as ransomware attacks on critical services, highlighted the need for strengthened Protection capabilities. Selected key findings in this mission area include:

- *Lessons learned from the 2015 Office of Personnel Management data breaches continue to prompt actions to better safeguard sensitive data on government employees and contractors, and to update procedures for background investigations and security clearances.*
- *Among the different measures adopted to address the Zika epidemic, state, territorial, and local governments, as well as Federal agencies, effectively distributed preventative supplies and communicated protection measures.*

Mitigation

The Mitigation mission area reduces loss of life and property by lessening the impact of disasters. Record flooding in areas of Louisiana, Texas, and West Virginia, along with a sixth consecutive year of drought in California, underscored the value of risk-mitigation activities. Selected key findings in this mission area include:

- *Federal departments, the private sector, and industry groups have launched new efforts to improve understanding of the value of stronger building codes and to increase their adoption.*
- *As the costs of wildfire suppression rise, public and private initiatives to fund wildfire risk reduction projects are emerging.*

Response

The Response mission area focuses on saving lives, protecting property and the environment, and meeting basic human needs after an incident. Throughout 2016, a number of events demonstrated the importance of building these capabilities, including Hurricane Matthew—a major hurricane that led to flooding as it traveled up the Southeast coast. Selected key findings in this mission area include:

- *Federal agencies demonstrated agility by anticipating and reacting to evolving response needs during Hurricane Matthew.*
- *Public- and private-sector partners are collaborating to advance diagnostics, case monitoring, and case management in response to the Zika virus outbreak.*

Recovery

The Recovery mission area focuses on maintaining and restoring important community assets after an incident, such as housing, infrastructure, businesses, and health and social services, as well as ensures consideration for natural and cultural resources. In 2016, the Flint Michigan Water Contamination was one of several examples that showed how Recovery capabilities help communities coordinate and tackle challenges. Selected key findings in this mission area include:

- *Re-establishing child care services is an important element in helping families to recover, but most child care centers face severe challenges after a disaster.*
- *Recent flooding events highlight ongoing gaps in delivering housing solutions efficiently and effectively after disasters.*

ONGOING CHALLENGES

While the 2017 *National Preparedness Report* highlights numerous achievements toward implementing the *National Preparedness Goal*, it also points to areas where progress has been slow to occur. As identified in this and previous *National Preparedness Reports*, the Nation still faces a number of persistent and emerging challenges. These include:

- *Detecting and preventing attacks by homegrown violent extremists*
- *Balancing competing demands between increasing security and minimizing disruptions to travel and commerce*
- *Inspiring individuals to prepare for emergencies*
- *Improving responder capacity and coordination in catastrophic events*
- *Comprehensively addressing the housing needs of disaster survivors*

These challenges require sustained effort and innovative approaches to overcome. Future reports will continue to monitor and assess our Nation's progress in addressing these and emerging preparedness challenges.

TABLE OF CONTENTS

2017 National Preparedness Report

Homeland Security 2017 National Preparedness Report

National preparedness actions help to prevent, protect against, mitigate, respond to, and recover from the threats and hazards posing the greatest risk to the Nation's security. Each year, the *National Preparedness Report* presents a Federal assessment of the Nation's progress toward achieving the *National Preparedness Goal* (see below) of a secure and resilient Nation.[1] Because preparedness is a shared responsibility across the entire Nation, the report aims to guide decisions of all preparedness stakeholders—including individuals, families, and communities; private and nonprofit sectors; faith-based organizations; and all levels of government—regarding program priorities, resource allocations, and community actions.[2] The 2017 edition of the *National Preparedness Report* primarily focuses on events that occurred or were reported on in 2016, but also covers a small number of events that occurred in early 2017.

Overview of the National Preparedness Goal & System

The *National Preparedness Goal* ("the Goal") describes what it means for the United States to be prepared for all types of disasters and emergencies, whether these are natural hazards (e.g., earthquakes, hurricanes, infectious diseases), accidental hazards (e.g., chemical spills), or human-induced threats (e.g., terrorism, cyberattacks). The Goal defines a vision for preparedness nationwide, namely:

> A secure and resilient Nation with the capabilities required across the whole community to prevent, protect against, mitigate, respond to, and recover from the threats and hazards that pose the greatest risk.

To achieve this vision, preparedness stakeholders collectively need to effectively build, sustain, and deliver 32 "core capabilities" identified in the Goal (see Table 1). The core capabilities are distinct, critical elements needed to achieve the goal of a secure and resilient Nation. They are not exclusive to any single level of government or organization. The core capabilities provide consistent, standard, national-level definitions applicable for use by the whole community. Preparedness stakeholders—including private and nonprofit sectors, faith-based organizations, and all levels of government—can and do use the core capabilities to align their planning, training, exercise, and resourcing efforts.

Within the Goal, the core capabilities are grouped into five mission areas:

- ***Prevention:*** *Preventing, avoiding, or stopping an imminent, threatened, or actual act of terrorism or extremist violence*
- ***Protection:*** *Protecting citizens, residents, visitors, and assets against the greatest threats and hazards in a manner that allows interests, aspirations, and way of life to thrive*
- ***Mitigation:*** *Mitigating the loss of life and property by lessening the impact of future disasters*
- ***Response:*** *Responding quickly to save lives, protect property and the environment, and meet basic human needs in the aftermath of an incident*
- ***Recovery:*** *Recovering through a focus on the timely restoration, strengthening, and revitalization of infrastructure, housing, and a sustainable economy, as well as the health, social, cultural, historic, and environmental fabric of communities affected by an incident*

---

[1] The *National Preparedness Report* addresses several reporting requirements from *The Post-Katrina Emergency Management Reform Act of 2006*, including the Federal Preparedness Report, State Preparedness Report, and Catastrophic Resource Report.
[2] The reader recognizes that the Federal Government may identify products it uses or that have been implemented to support its emergency management efforts. This data is provided for informational purposes only, and the Federal Government does not endorse any non-Federal events, entities, organizations, services, or products.

1

MISSION AREAS AND CORE CAPABILITIES

Table 1. The Goal outlines 32 core capabilities needed for a secure and resilient Nation. Each core capability is associated with one or more of the five mission areas.

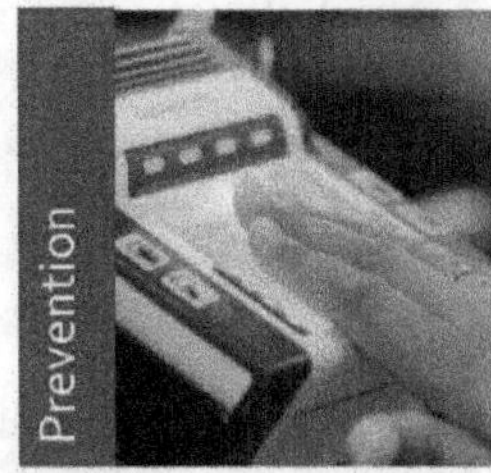

Core Capabilities	Prevention	Protection	Mitigation	Response	Recovery
Planning	●	●	●	●	●
Public Information and Warning	●	●	●	●	●
Operational Coordination	●	●	●	●	●
Intelligence and Information Sharing	●	●			
Interdiction and Disruption	●	●			
Screening, Search, and Detection	●	●			
Forensics and Attribution	●				
Access Control and Identity Verification		●			
Cybersecurity		●			
Physical Protective Measures		●			
Risk Management for Protection Programs and Activities		●			
Supply Chain Integrity and Security		●			
Community Resilience			●		
Long-term Vulnerability Reduction			●		
Risk and Disaster Resilience Assessment			●		
Threats and Hazards Identification			●		
Critical Transportation				●	
Environmental Response/Health and Safety				●	
Fatality Management Services				●	
Fire Management and Suppression				●	
Logistics and Supply Chain Management				●	
Mass Care Services				●	
Mass Search and Rescue Operations				●	
On-scene Security, Protection, and Law Enforcement				●	
Operational Communications				●	
Public Health, Healthcare, and Emergency Medical Services				●	
Situational Assessment				●	
Infrastructure Systems				●	●
Economic Recovery					●
Health and Social Services					●
Housing					●
Natural and Cultural Resources					●

The 2017 *National Preparedness Report* uses the five mission areas to organize its findings and to aid readers in identifying the sections most relevant to them. While the 32 core capabilities provide a basic nomenclature for describing the Nation's security and resilience posture, the mission areas provide a higher-level structure that is more reflective of the way organizations and individuals view their role in preparedness.

To complement this organizing structure, the National Preparedness System ensures a consistent process for moving forward with achieving the Goal. The National Preparedness System includes six components (see Figure 1):

- *Identifying and Assessing Risk: Collecting information on existing, potential, and perceived threats and hazards to assess risks*
- *Estimating Capability Requirements: Identifying the specific capabilities and activities needed to best address risks*
- *Building and Sustaining Capabilities: Determining the best ways to use limited resources to build and maintain capabilities informed by risk assessments*
- *Planning to Deliver Capabilities: Coordinating preparedness efforts with all relevant preparedness stakeholders, including individuals, businesses, nonprofits, community and faith-based groups, and all levels of government*
- *Validating Capabilities: Using exercises and assessments to identify gaps in existing plans/capabilities, and implementing corrective actions to ensure continuous improvement in meeting preparedness goals*
- *Reviewing and Updating: Performing regular reviews to keep preparedness efforts up-to-date with evolving risks and resources*

Encircling these six components are three concepts critical to successfully implementing the process. **Core Capabilities** identify the distinct critical elements to build, sustain, and deliver through the process. A **Whole Community** focus ensures the National Preparedness System addresses preparedness activities from a broad range of stakeholders, including all levels of government, private and nonprofit sectors, faith-based organizations, communities, and individuals. Finally, the **National Incident Management System (NIMS)** provides whole community partners with shared vocabulary, systems, and processes to help successfully deliver the core capabilities.

As shown in Figure 1, the six components, while forming a cyclic process, are also highly interconnected and interdependent. The *National Preparedness Report* addresses each part of the National Preparedness System, but plays a particularly important role in "Validating Capabilities," where it serves as the principal analysis and reporting product to monitor the Nation's progress in building, sustaining, and delivering the 32 core capabilities.

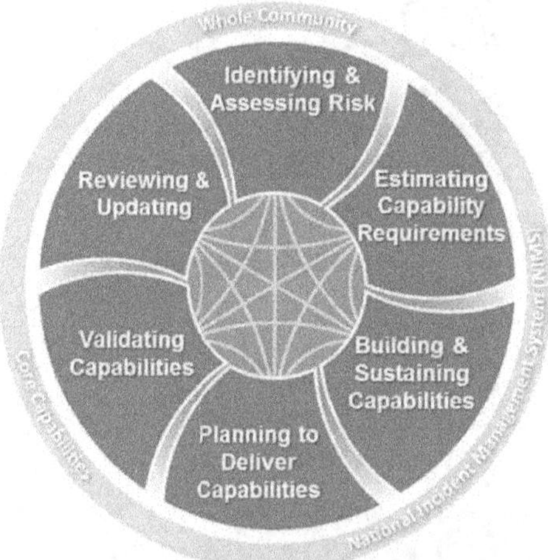

Figure 1. The National Preparedness System includes six interconnected components. It outlines an organized process for the whole community to move forward in building and sustaining the core capabilities outlined in the Goal, and helps ensure their successful delivery through the shared use of the vocabulary, systems, and processes identified in NIMS.

Homeland Security 2017 National Preparedness Report

REPORT ORGANIZATION

Following the **Introduction**, the 2017 *National Preparedness Report* continues with the **2016 Year in Review**, which highlights real-world incidents that attracted national headlines in 2016 and serve as the basis for several of the report's key findings. Next, the **Cross-Cutting Findings** section presents four findings that use various preparedness datasets to compare performance among all 32 core capabilities.

The main body of the report is divided into five sections, each based on one of the Goal's five mission areas—Prevention, Protection, Mitigation, Response, and Recovery. Each section begins with a **Mission Area Overview** that contains the following components:

- *Core Capabilities in Practice: Discusses the core capabilities and how they function, including examples that highlight the connections among core capabilities*
- *Summary of Progress: Provides a status update on preparedness efforts for core capabilities in the mission area*
- *By the Numbers: Measures achievements in current programs and initiatives*
- *Mission Area Snapshots: Provides short accounts of preparedness accomplishments and best practices from across the country*
- *Preparedness Indicators: Presents measures that demonstrate agency or program performance in the mission areas, for tracking in this and future National Preparedness Reports*

Subsequent to the overviews are the mission area **Key Findings**, each of which is an assessment of a specific area of national preparedness within that mission area. In total, the report includes 30 key findings across the five mission areas.

The report concludes with a section on **Ongoing Challenges**, which identifies persistent or emerging issues that the new Administration will likely face in each of the mission areas.

In addition, the 2017 *National Preparedness Report* includes five appendices:

- *Appendix A: Acronym List defines the acronyms appearing in the report*
- *Appendix B: Research Approach describes the steps taken to ensure a comprehensive report and the criteria used to help identify the report's key findings*
- *Appendix C: 9/11 Retrospective highlights ways in which the Nation has restructured and retooled its preparedness efforts since the 9/11 tragedy*
- *Appendix D: Capabilities to Sustain Selection Methodology describes the two-part analysis used to identify which of the 32 core capabilities are capabilities to sustain*
- *Appendix E: Areas for Improvement Selection Methodology describes how national areas for improvement were selected from the 32 core capabilities*

Homeland Security 2017 National Preparedness Report

2016 YEAR IN REVIEW

2017 National Preparedness Report

Each year, jurisdictions face threats that test their capabilities and reveal where strengths in delivering these capabilities exist and gaps remain. In particular, major disasters and emergencies that stress the Nation's collective abilities and resources play an important role in assessing progress toward achieving the Goal.

This year was no exception. In 2016, the following notable incidents informed several of the report's key findings.

January 16

The City of Flint, Michigan, continues to recover from a public health crisis resulting from contamination of its drinking water supply. Dangerously high levels of lead leached into the public water system after the city switched its primary water supply in April 2014. On January 16, 2016, the State of Michigan received an emergency declaration under the *Robert T. Stafford Disaster Relief and Emergency Assistance Act* (Stafford Act), which authorizes Federal aid to supplement state and local response efforts under certain conditions. Specifically, the emergency declaration authorized the Federal Emergency Management Agency (FEMA) to provide water, water filters, water testing kits, and related items to Flint residents. In addition, the U.S. Department of Health and Human Services (HHS)—the designated lead agency for coordinating Federal support for response and recovery efforts in Flint—and other Federal agencies have provided assistance under their existing authorities. Their efforts have been addressing not only the ability to access safe water (covered by the emergency declaration), but also a broader suite of response and recovery activities. For additional analyses on these efforts, see page B3.

January 22

A blizzard struck the Mid-Atlantic and southern New England from January 22 to 24, resulting in historic amounts of snowfall and crippling winter storm conditions. The blizzard covered 434,000 square miles and affected approximately 102.8 million people, with almost 24 million people inhabiting areas that received more than 20 inches of snowfall. Governors in 10 states declared states of emergency, and major cities such as New York and Baltimore set all-time snowfall records (27.5 inches and 29.2 inches, respectively). The blizzard highlighted recent improvements in weather forecasting, with forecasters able to predict the weather system responsible for the blizzard a week in advance. In reaction, the Washington Metropolitan Area Transit Authority made the rare decision to shut down bus and rail service in the DC region ahead of the storm. In New York City, the mayor imposed a travel ban, which included shutting down trains and large segments of the subway system. Even so, the storm resulted in more than 30 fatalities, caused heavy flooding along the East Coast, stranded thousands of air travelers, and left thousands without electricity.

April 18

From March to June 2016, Texas experienced several severe storms, resulting in three presidential disaster declarations covering 39 counties. Intense rains on April 18 in the Greater Houston region led the National Weather Service to issue the largest flash-flood warning in at least a decade and required more than 1,200 high-water rescues. Following the city's worst flooding event in 15 years, the Mayor of Houston established a "flood czar" to oversee future flood-prevention efforts.

May 9

In 2016, California experienced its sixth consecutive year of drought, prompting the Governor of California to issue an Executive Order on May 9 to further institutionalize California's recent water-conservation efforts (see page 55 for additional details). The dry conditions contributed to wildfires. Through November 26, more than 7,000 wildfires burned nearly 560,815 acres. In addition, California faces an expanding epidemic of trees killed by drought and bark beetles (estimated at more than 102 million trees since 2010), increasing public safety risks such as wildfires. To mitigate these risks, the California Department of Forestry and Fire Protection has been working with Federal, local, and utility partners to remove dead and dying trees; as of November 18, 2016, they have removed more than 423,000 trees that pose the greatest risk. For an analysis of additional wildfire risk-reduction projects, see page 55.

June 12

An armed gunman attacked the Pulse nightclub in Orlando, Florida, resulting in the deadliest mass shooting in U.S. history, with 49 fatalities and 53 injured. Response efforts to the attack provide an example of the change in police tactics toward immediately engaging the shooter and quickly accessing the injured. For example, officers began evacuating victims from the scene, even though the shooter was still barricaded elsewhere in the nightclub. For additional analysis of how recent events are providing new insights into active shooter tactics and needs, see page 75.

June 22

In June, extreme heat struck the southwestern United States. On June 22, the peak of one heatwave, approximately 124 million individuals were under extreme heat warnings. In July, several southern U.S. cities broke monthly temperature records. Extreme heat kills hundreds of individuals in the United States each year and causes many more to become seriously ill. Scientists expect heatwaves to increase in severity, frequency, and duration. To help address this growing hazard, HHS's Centers for Disease Control and Prevention (CDC), the National Oceanic and Atmospheric Administration (NOAA), and other domestic and international partners released the National Integrated Heat Health Information System in May 2016. The system helps build understanding and facilitate communication and collaboration efforts to reduce extreme heat–related fatalities and illnesses. In addition, for the first time, America's PrepareAthon!—which supports grassroots efforts to increase community preparedness and resilience—designated an Extreme Heat Week (from May 23 to 27). During that week, Federal departments and agencies took part in various actions (e.g., webinars, presentations) to raise public awareness and prepare the Nation for extreme heat.

June 23

A band of severe thunderstorms struck West Virginia, resulting in a 1,000-year rainfall event (i.e., a rainfall event that has a 0.1 percent chance of occurring in any given year) that produced one-quarter of the state's annual rainfall in a single day and left thousands stranded, 100 homes badly damaged or destroyed, and 22 dead. The U.S. Small Business Administration (SBA) approved more than $47 million in low-interest disaster loans for affected residents and businesses. Nearly another $40 million of housing and other needs assistance has gone to eligible survivors through FEMA's Individuals and Households Program.

July 29

Zika, a viral infection primarily spread by certain mosquitoes, poses serious health risks to infants born from women infected with the virus during pregnancy. On December 31, 2015, the United States experienced the first of many locally transmitted cases of the Zika virus in the U.S. territory of Puerto Rico. Seven months later, on July 29, 2016, the Florida Department of Health reported the mosquito-borne spread of Zika in a neighborhood of Miami, Florida, marking the first occurrence of locally transmitted Zika in the continental United States. As of December 28, 2016, CDC reported more than 39,700 cases of Zika virus infections in U.S. states and territories, with the highest number of cases reported in Puerto Rico, Florida, and New York. Most cases in the continental United States are travel-related. However, in addition to Puerto Rico and Florida, health officials have reported local Zika transmission in Texas, the U.S. Virgin Islands, and American Samoa. On February 23, 2016, in the absence of supplemental emergency funds, HHS reprogrammed more than $500 million to immediately prepare for and respond to the Zika virus. In September 2016, Congress approved $1.1 billion in Zika emergency funding to control the spread of Zika-carrying mosquitoes, continue development of vaccines and surveillance systems, and improve diagnostic tests. For example, given the major risks of Zika to pregnant women, CDC quickly established pregnancy registries to capture information about pregnant women and their infants with laboratory evidence of Zika. These registries have provided estimates of the risks of Zika and have informed clinical guidance for the evaluation and testing of pregnant women and infants. For additional analysis on U.S. response efforts to address the Zika virus outbreak, see page 64 and 66.

August 11

From August 11 to 13, Louisiana faced its second major flooding event of the year. Portions of the state experienced a 1,000-year rainfall event, causing river levels to exceed record heights and flooding in several areas for the first time. The August Louisiana floods were the worst U.S. natural disaster since Hurricane Sandy, damaging more than 109,000 homes and causing an estimated $8.7 billion in damages. Flood insurance policyholders in Louisiana filed 26,128 claims and received more than $2.26 billion (as of January 31, 2017). More broadly, flood insurance claims nationwide in 2016 exceeded 82,000 claims. In 2016, the National Flood Insurance Program (NFIP) experienced its third most severe loss of record, with losses exceeding $4 billion (due in large part to the August Louisiana floods). For additional analyses of response and recovery efforts for these floods, as well as remaining challenges highlighted by these events, see pages 70, 84, and 87.

September 9

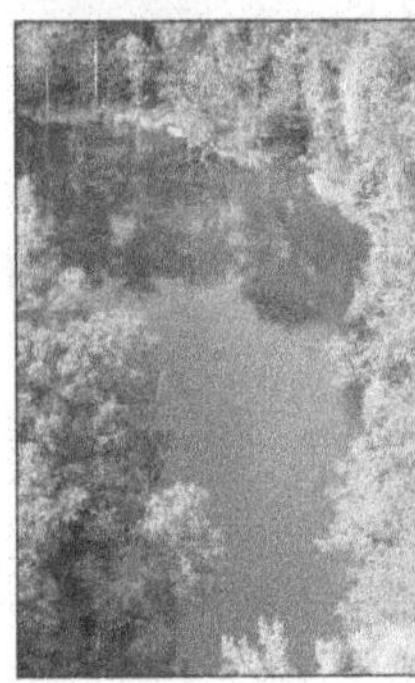

From September 9 to 21, the Colonial Pipeline Company shut down its East Coast gasoline supply pipeline following the discovery of a leak in the pipeline near Helena, Alabama. This pipeline system supplies 2.5 million barrels per day of transportation fuels to locations in the Southeast and along the eastern seaboard (as far north as New York Harbor), and is a critical supply of fuel in many southeastern states. In the weeks following the shutdown, the reduction in gasoline volumes led to shortages in the Southeast, with retail price spikes of more than 20 cents per gallon reported in some markets. A subsequent explosion and fire on October 31 near the site of the original leak forced an additional closure of the pipeline. Federal agencies—including the U.S. Department of Homeland Security (DHS), the U.S. Department of Energy (DOE), and the U.S. Department of Transportation (DOT)—monitored both incidents, with DOE working closely with industry and affected states to conduct modeling and analysis of the regional fuel supply situation and manage information sharing among key stakeholders.

September 17

Two improvised explosive devices (IEDs) detonated (one in New York City and the other in Seaside Park, New Jersey), with one explosion injuring more than 30 people and causing millions of dollars of property damage. Similar to the San Bernardino and Pulse nightclub attacks, the individual involved in these attacks appeared to have been inspired by foreign terrorist ideologies. Moreover, these attacks reiterate the challenges of uncovering plots by lone (or small numbers of) attackers and the need to secure high-risk chemicals that can be used to make IEDs. Federal Bureau of Investigation (FBI) agents had investigated the man accused of planting the New York and New Jersey bombs more than two years earlier, finding no ties to terrorism. Fortunately, increasing awareness of IED threats and the importance of reporting suspicious activity by the public assisted investigators and contributed to finding other unexploded IEDs.

September 20

KrebsonSecurity.com—a popular blog focusing on online crime investigations, cyber threats and cybersecurity, data breaches, and cyber justice—was the target of a distributed denial-of-service (DDoS) attack. DDoS attacks prevent legitimate users from accessing information or services. A botnet allegedly comprising more than 380,000 hacked "Internet of Things" devices—such as routers, network-enabled cameras, and digital video recorders—was responsible for the attack, which was among the largest DDoS attacks on record. For additional information on the growing challenge that the Internet of Things presents to information security and cybersecurity, see page 94.

September 22

After investigating a criminal attempt at selling Yahoo! user account information, Yahoo! researchers uncovered a data breach that had gone undetected for two years and compromised more than 500 million user accounts. The Chief Information Security Officer of Yahoo! announced the existence of the breach on September 22. Nearly three months later, Yahoo! disclosed that a separate attack in 2013 compromised more than 1 billion accounts. Even as the Federal Government continues to implement lessons learned from the 2015 U.S. Office of Personnel Management (OPM) breaches (see page 38), these new discoveries and other incidents in 2016 involving critical systems—such as attempted attacks on voter registration systems (see page 37) and holding hospital systems hostage for ransom (see page 37)—continue to raise cybersecurity concerns.

September 30

In an above-normal hurricane season, five named storms made landfall in the United States during 2016, the most since 2008. The strongest and longest-lived of these was Hurricane Matthew, which reached maximum sustained winds of 160 miles per hour and was a major hurricane from September 30 to October 7. Forecasted as passing very near or over the east coast of Florida with potentially disastrous impacts, Hurricane Matthew eventually made landfall in South Carolina on October 8 as a category 1 hurricane. The hurricane's path up the Southeast coast of the United States resulted in storm surge and beach erosion from Florida through North Carolina and caused extensive inland flooding in the Carolinas. Pre-disaster emergency declarations issued October 6 for Florida, Georgia, South Carolina, and North Carolina authorized FEMA to mobilize equipment and resources to anticipated affected areas. For additional analysis of how Federal agencies anticipated and reacted to developing needs during Hurricane Matthew, see page 68.

Homeland Security 2017 National Preparedness Report

October 21

Dyn, a major provider of Domain Name System resolution (i.e., the computers that translate website names into Internet protocol addresses), was subject to two large-scale DDoS attacks. As a result, major websites such as Twitter, Netflix, Spotify, Airbnb, and The New York Times were temporarily inaccessible to users. Similar to the September 20 attack on the KrebsonSecurity.com blog website, a significant portion of the attack stemmed from botnets consisting of "Internet of Things" devices, highlighting the cybersecurity vulnerabilities of these devices. Moreover, by targeting critical cyber infrastructure, attackers can cause more harm than attacks on individual sites or organizations.

October 27

In late October, fake 911 calls inundated several U.S. public safety answering points (PSAPs). A teenage hacker—arrested on October 27 in Maricopa County, Arizona—had created malware to exploit an iPhone vulnerability, forcing iPhones to place fraudulent 911 calls. The malware, promulgated using Twitter, spread and instigated a significant DDoS attack that affected PSAPs in 12 states, including Washington, California, and Arizona.

November 28

Severe drought left the Southeast vulnerable to numerous wildfires in late 2016. At the peak of the drought, more than 16.5 percent of the total area of Kentucky, Tennessee, North Carolina, Georgia, Alabama, and Mississippi was under conditions of exceptional drought (i.e., the most intense level of drought), affecting nearly 6.9 million people. The drought contributed to hundreds of wildfires. For example, a wildfire that ignited near Gatlinburg, Tennessee, in late November grew to become the largest fire in the state in 100 years, resulting in 14 fatalities, at least 180 injured, and more than 2,400 structures damaged or destroyed. Authorities evacuated more than 14,000 people from the city. Tennessee Highway Patrol troopers conducted door-to-door canvassing to assist with notifications and evacuations in addition to the National Guard, which used HHS emPOWER Initiative data to rapidly identify at-risk individuals with access and functional needs.

SUPPORTING DISASTER SURVIVORS AND CAPABILITY DEVELOPMENT

MAJOR DISASTER DECLARATIONS

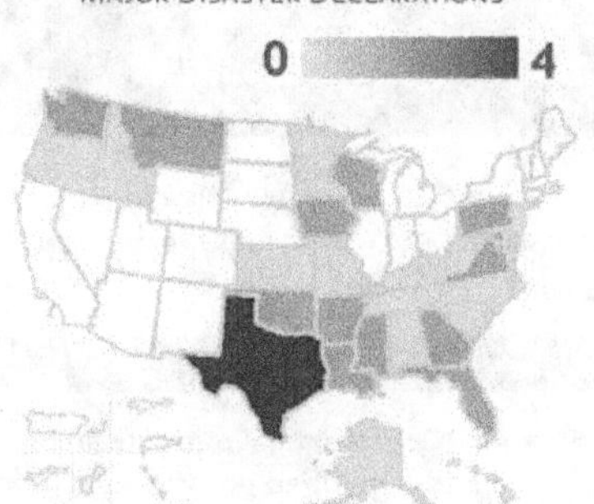

In 2016, Federal agencies assisted in 46 major disaster declarations across 30 states, territories, and tribes.

FIRE MANAGEMENT ASSISTANCE DECLARATIONS

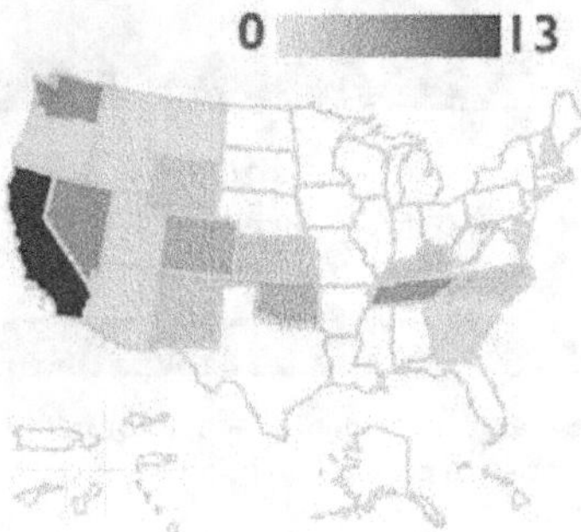

In 2016, Federal agencies assisted with 50 instances of fire management across 19 states.

DROUGHT DESIGNATIONS

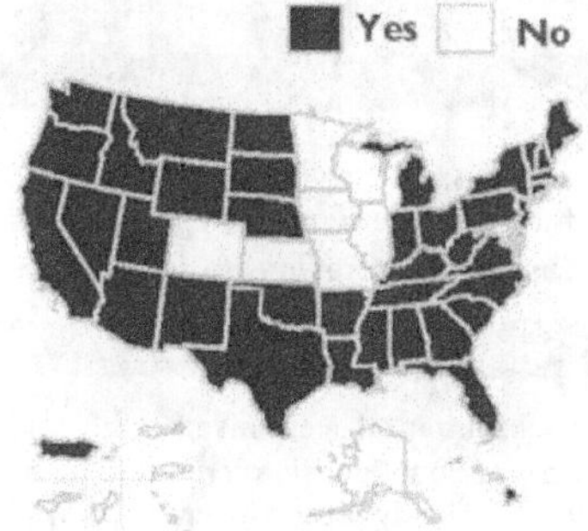

In 2016, Federal agencies assisted with USDA-designated drought disasters for 1,025 counties across 42 states and territories.

DISTRIBUTION OF FEMA PREPAREDNESS (NON-DISASTER) GRANTS BY CORE CAPABILITY, FISCAL YEAR 2015

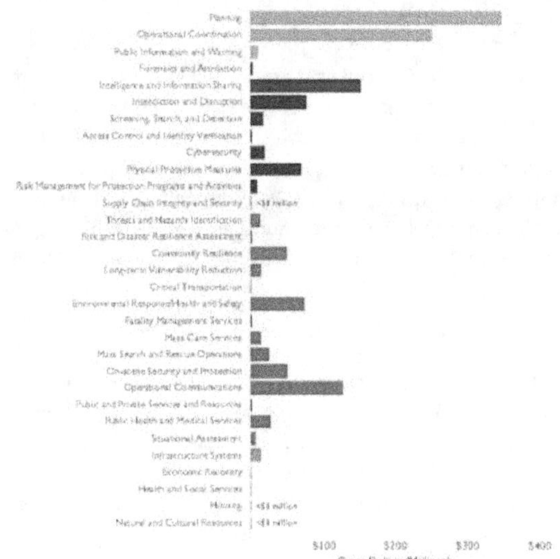

Grant recipients use the Biannual Strategy Implementation Report (BSIR) to track planned and actual grant expenditures, and categorize expenses into five POETE elements. The BSIR is a snapshot of obligated funding for the given reporting period and do not necessarily reflect grant expenditures.

In fiscal year 2016, FEMA provided more than $2.3 billion in preparedness grants.

In addition, HHS provided more than $900 million in public health and healthcare system preparedness grants to states and localities.

In fiscal year 2016, FEMA training programs achieved approximately 2.7 million course completions across all core capabilities.

The 2017 *National Preparedness Report* identifies four cross-cutting findings—stretching across the five mission areas—through the evaluation of preparedness indicators (e.g., training participation, exercise frequency) that apply to all 32 core capabilities; assessments submitted by states and territories; and analysis provided by Federal agencies.

Cross-Cutting Finding:

Environmental Response/Health and Safety, Intelligence and Information Sharing, Operational Communications, Operational Coordination, and Planning are five core capabilities in which the Nation has developed proficiency, but in which it likely faces a future capability gap.

Each *National Preparedness Report* identifies a subset of the core capabilities as "capabilities to sustain." To be a capability to sustain, a core capability must satisfy two conditions. First, the Nation must show proficiency in executing that core capability. Second, there must be indications of a potentially growing gap between the demand for and the performance of that core capability in the future.

Consistent with previous reports and with the methodology outlined in Appendix D, the 2017 *National Preparedness Report* identifies the following five core capabilities as capabilities to sustain.

Environmental Response/Health and Safety

This core capability focuses on ensuring the health and safety of the public and workers, as well as the environment, from hazards encountered during response efforts. Extensive amounts of training and exercises occur in this core capability relative to others. Moreover, a broad range of Federal, state, and local assets exist, which support responses to thousands of hazardous materials incidents each year. This national competency is reflected in the 2016 State Preparedness Report results, in which states and territories rated Environmental Response/Health and Safety among the top ten core capabilities in proficiency. Greater demands, however, may occur for this core capability in the future, since more than half of Federal agencies playing key roles in supporting response efforts have identified this core capability as a priority in their latest strategic plans.

Intelligence and Information Sharing

Intelligence and Information Sharing is the capacity for all levels of government and the community to communicate and receive timely and actionable information. More than half of state and territory responses to the 2016 State Preparedness Report indicated proficiency in this capability. In addition, the Nation has developed a number of assets to support this capability, including FBI-led Joint Terrorism Task Forces (JTTFs), state and major urban area fusion centers, and various information-sharing systems (e.g., Homeland Security Information Network [HSIN], TRIPwire). Technological developments, however, require the careful balancing of intelligence collection and privacy protections (see page 39). The emergence and growth of threats also places added demands on public- and private-sector stakeholders to share and exchange information (see page 37). Intelligence and Information Sharing remains critical to states and territories—80 percent of which regard it as a high priority—and the capability is of growing emphasis among Federal agencies in the Prevention and Protection mission areas.

Operational Communications

This Response core capability addresses the ability of emergency responders to communicate during an incident. Fifty-five percent of state and territory responses to the 2016 State Preparedness Report indicate proficiency in carrying out Operational Communications, placing it in the top ten among all core capabilities. Ensuring that responders from multiple jurisdictions and agencies can communicate on interoperable systems, however, requires sustained attention through exercises, planning, and technological acquisitions. For example, Operational Communications is among the top five most commonly assessed core capabilities in FEMA's National Exercise Program (NEP). Moreover, First Responder Network Authority (FirstNet) is engaged in a complex, long-term project to provide a single interoperable broadband network for responders nationwide (see page 72).

Operational Coordination

Operational Coordination spans all mission areas and addresses those actions necessary to establish and maintain a unified and coordinated structure for operations, as well as processes to integrate all appropriate stakeholders. In 2016, response and recovery efforts during real-world incidents (e.g., the Zika virus outbreak) highlighted progress among Federal agencies in improving their coordination for incidents that do not receive a presidential disaster declaration (see page 66). Moreover, states and territories have consistently rated themselves as among the most proficient in carrying out Operational Coordination. While this remained true in 2016, comparisons between 2015 and 2016 State Preparedness Report results show a decline in proficiency by more than five percentage points, signaling an increasing gap in preparedness. Nearly 18 percent of states and territories also selected Operational Coordination as a core capability in greatest danger of future decline (the seventh-highest result for all core capabilities).

Planning

Common to all mission areas, the Planning core capability addresses the need for a systematic process that engages all relevant stakeholders in the development of strategic, operational, and tactical approaches to effectively deliver core capabilities. State and territory self-assessments continue to place Planning among the top ten ranked core capabilities every year, with 58 percent of ratings in the 2016 State Preparedness Report indicating proficiency in Planning. Similar to Operational Coordination, stakeholders nationwide continue to pay significant attention to Planning, as evidenced by relatively high training and exercise participation, as well as Federal preparedness grant investments. In their 2016 State Preparedness Report responses, more states and territories identified Planning as one of their most improved core capabilities than any other. Planning requires ongoing attention as threats remain dynamic. Terrorists continue to refine ways to radicalize individuals (see page 39), new infectious disease outbreaks can require adapting and supplementing existing approaches (see pages 64 and 66), and technology provides new threat vectors and capabilities for adversaries (see page 93).

Cross-Cutting Finding:

Cybersecurity, Economic Recovery, Housing, Infrastructure Systems, Natural and Cultural Resources, and Supply Chain Integrity and Security remain national areas for improvement. One additional core capability—Risk Management for Protection Programs and Activities—emerged as a new area for improvement in 2016.

The *National Preparedness Report* identifies a subset of core capabilities each year as national areas for improvement.

12

Selection criteria for areas for improvement include the report's key findings on preparedness; State Preparedness Report results; data on the frequency of exercises; funding support; and future trends and drivers affecting preparedness. Appendix E details the approach used for selecting this year's areas for improvement.

The 2017 *National Preparedness Report* identifies seven core capabilities as national areas for improvement. One of these appears as an area for improvement for the first time in the *National Preparedness Report*: Risk Management for Protection Programs and Activities. The remaining six—Cybersecurity, Economic Recovery, Housing, Infrastructure Systems, Natural and Cultural Resources, and Supply Chain Integrity and Security—have appeared in previous *National Preparedness Reports*. For Cybersecurity, Infrastructure Systems, and Housing, this represents their sixth consecutive year as areas for improvement.

Cybersecurity

The Cybersecurity core capability addresses protecting and restoring electronic communications systems (e.g., critical communications infrastructure), information, and services from damage, unauthorized use, and exploitation. Throughout 2016, public- and private-sector organizations suffered malicious cyber activity. Critical services in particular—such as healthcare and law enforcement—saw increases in ransomware attacks, and voter registration systems have come under threat as well. The Federal Government has sought to address cyber threats through policies that improve the coordination of its response and through the application of lessons learned from previous incidents, such as the 2015 OPM breach. The increasing use of the collaboratively developed Cybersecurity Framework (see page 15 for additional details) for managing cybersecurity risks in critical infrastructure, as well as more broadly throughout the economy and

society (including by some states and localities), has been a positive development. While states and territories continue to indicate that Cybersecurity is a high priority, more rate themselves as lacking proficiency in it than any other core capability. See pages 37 and 38 for additional information on these issues.

Economic Recovery

This core capability focuses on returning economic and business activities to a healthy state and on developing new business and employment opportunities that result in economically viable communities. States and territories identified Economic Recovery as the second lowest-rated core capability for the second year in a row, and jurisdictions also reported the largest proficiency decreases in Economic Recovery, which dropped by 10 percent from 2012–2016.

Housing

This core capability focuses on implementing affordable and accessible housing solutions that effectively support the needs of the whole community and contribute to its sustainability and resilience. Flooding events in 2016, such as historic summer flooding that occurred in Louisiana, underscored the longstanding challenges the Nation has faced in meeting the housing needs of survivors, including survivors with disabilities and others with access and functional needs. Assistance to renters continues to be a challenge, as does the availability and rapid deployment of manufactured housing units, and the time and additional resources that may be required to build back housing more resiliently to better prepare for the next storm. Federal agencies have taken actions to strengthen the Housing core capability, such as the creation of updated housing doctrine and a toolkit to help recovery stakeholders support people who may be disproportionately affected by disasters (e.g., people with disabilities and individuals and families at risk of homelessness), but difficulties persist. Few training opportunities and exercises address housing, and in 2016, Housing remained among the lowest-rated core capabilities—as states and territories reported the third-lowest levels of proficiency. See pages 87, 89, and 97 for additional information on these issues.

Infrastructure Systems

The focus of Infrastructure Systems is on stabilizing critical infrastructure functions, minimizing health and safety threats, and efficiently restoring and revitalizing systems and services to support a viable, resilient community. While Federal departments and agencies took steps to address challenges to this core capability, as detailed on page 89, limited evidence exists demonstrating that the Nation has made significant progress in this area. Aging infrastructure in many sectors presents growing risks, as well as decreases resilience. For example, the Flint Michigan Water Contamination highlights the growing threat to national public health from deteriorating water-line infrastructure. States and territories identified this core capability as exhibiting below-average levels of proficiency in 2016.

Natural and Cultural Resources

Natural and Cultural Resources focuses on protecting natural and cultural resources and historic properties through appropriate actions that preserve, conserve, rehabilitate, and restore them consistent with post-disaster community priorities and best practices. While governmental and nongovernmental organizations sponsored forums and training events to bring greater attention to this capability, states and territories collectively rated it as the lowest priority across all capabilities. They also reported the fourth-lowest levels of proficiency, ahead of only Housing, Economic Recovery, and Cybersecurity. In addition, state and local jurisdictions continue to infrequently exercise this capability. Despite the current NEP cycle's emphasis on Recovery core capabilities (see page 18), only seven NEP exercises (out of 167) addressed this core capability (see Figure 2).

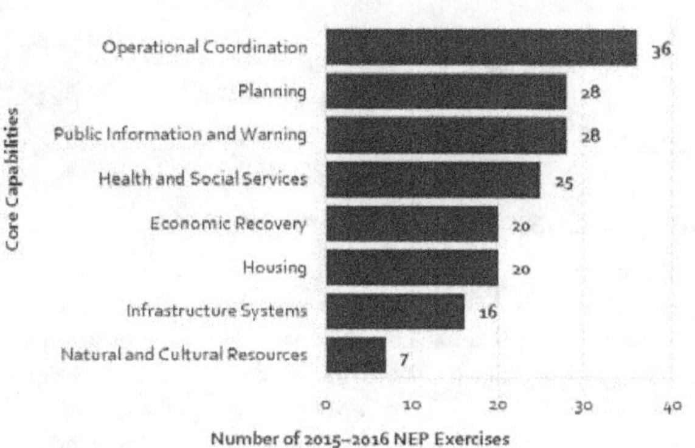

Figure 2. In the 2015–2016 NEP exercise cycle, 69 NEP exercises addressed one or more Recovery core capabilities. (Note: Counts for Operational Coordination, Planning, and Public Information and Warning are specific to the Recovery mission area)

Risk Management for Protection Programs and Activities

This core capability covers the identification, assessment, and prioritization of risks to inform protection activities, which include continuity planning. Its first appearance as an area for improvement in the *National Preparedness Report* is driven by state and territorial self-assessments of proficiency. The percentage of non-proficient ratings for this capability was the fifth-highest across all core capabilities. Risk Management for Protection Programs and Activities also fell in the bottom 25 percent of capabilities that state and local jurisdictions reported exercising in the past five years, and few NEP events tested the capability in 2016. Moreover, there was little evidence that the Nation has made progress toward validating and evaluating progress in this capability over the past year. One exception is the growing use of the Cybersecurity Framework.

CROSS-CUTTING CASE STUDY: CYBERSECURITY RISK MANAGEMENT

Since its publication in February 2014, the Cybersecurity Framework has become the leading management tool in the United States for assessing cyber risks and prioritizing appropriate policies and actions. The Framework—developed out of a year-long collaborative process led by the National Institute of Standards and Technology (NIST), with the active involvement of thousands of experts from the private sector, DHS, and many others—identifies existing cybersecurity standards, guidelines, frameworks, and best practices that increase cybersecurity across all sectors and industry types. It provides a flexible, repeatable, and cost-effective risk-based approach to implementing security practices. According to Gartner (an information technology [IT] research company), 30 percent of U.S. organizations have used the Cybersecurity Framework in the first two years since its release, with that number projected to increase to 50 percent by 2020.

Supply Chain Integrity and Security

This core capability deals with strengthening the security and resilience of the supply chain. States and territories reported relatively low levels of proficiency for this capability, with more than a third of all State Preparedness Report ratings indicating that respondents are not able, or minimally able, to meet their performance targets. In addition, the capability fell in the bottom 25 percent of capabilities that were included in 2016 NEP exercises. State and local jurisdictions also completed relatively few FEMA-sponsored in-person training courses focused on Supply Chain Integrity and Security. Use of larger, more-complex networks of global suppliers, as well as growing dependence on IT systems, places some supply chains at increasing physical (e.g., counterfeit parts) and cyber (e.g., malware) risk.

Cross-Cutting Finding:

States and territories reported similar levels of capability compared to 2015, highlighting that larger-scale preparedness investments are necessary to drive major improvements on an annual basis; since 2012, states and territories reported proficiency increases in the Mitigation mission area, but proficiency decreases in the Prevention, Protection, and Recovery mission areas.

Each year, through the State Preparedness Report, states and territories self-assess their ability to achieve targets they establish for each core capability through an annual risk assessment process. In the State Preparedness Report, they use a 5-point rating scale—with a 5 being the highest—to assess each of these core capabilities in five areas: Planning, Organization, Equipment, Training, and Exercises. Capabilities change slowly over time; therefore, year-over-year changes in capability ratings are typically small. In 2016, states and territories reported their strongest proficiency ratings (indicated by the percentage of 4 and 5 ratings) in the cross-cutting core capabilities (i.e., Planning, Operational Coordination, and Public Information and Warning) and Response mission area and their lowest proficiency ratings

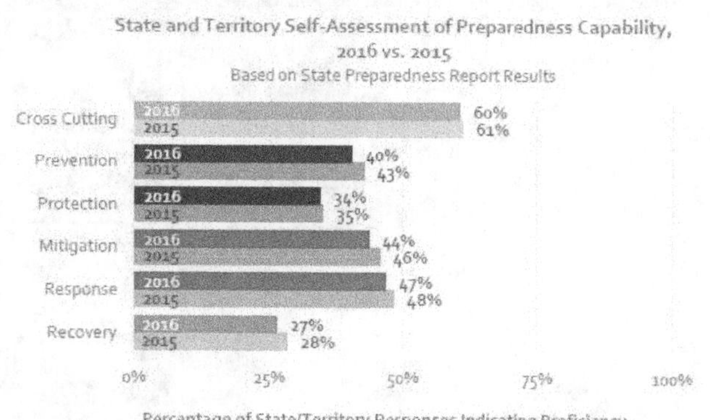

Figure 3. States and territories reported the highest capability ratings in the cross-cutting core capabilities and those within the Response mission area.

in the Recovery and Protection mission areas. State and territory capability levels for each mission area remained consistent with prior years, including with 2015 results (see Figure 3).

Figure 4 shows the breakdown of proficiency scores by core capability. Jurisdictions generally identified the same core capabilities as strengths and weaknesses as they did last year. Modest changes from 2015 include:

- *Capability Strengths:* Fire Management and Suppression replaced Threats and Hazards Identification in the top ten capabilities with the highest proficiency ratings.
- *Capability Weaknesses:* Infrastructure Systems and Forensics and Attribution replaced Supply Chain Integrity and Security and Physical Protective Measures in the bottom ten capabilities with the lowest proficiency ratings.

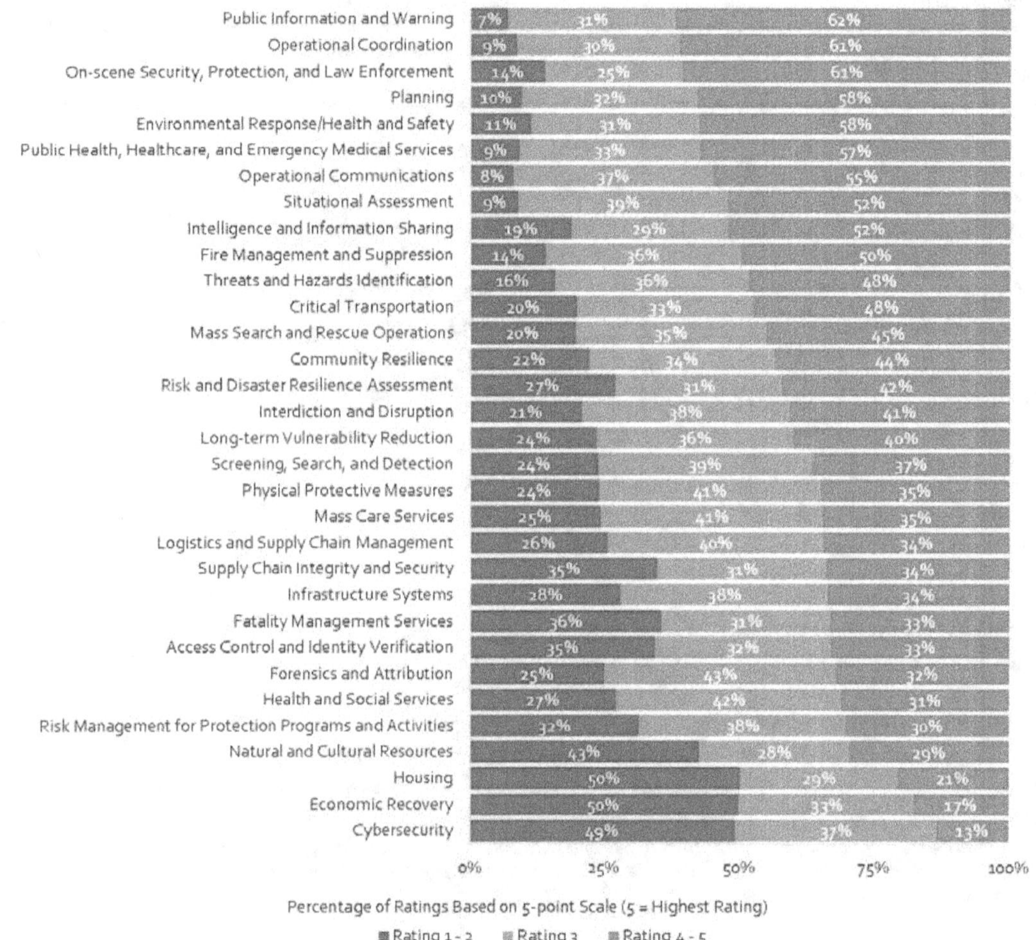

Figure 4. States and territories reported the highest capability ratings in Public Information and Warning and the lowest capability ratings in Cybersecurity and Economic Recovery.

Since 2012, states and territories have reported proficiency increases in the cross-cutting capabilities and the Mitigation mission area. They have reported proficiency decreases in the Protection, Prevention, and Recovery mission areas. The Response mission area ratings have remained essentially unchanged. At the core capability level (see Figure 5), jurisdictions have reported the largest proficiency increases in Public Information and Warning (11 percent since 2012) and Environmental Response/Health and Safety (eight percent since 2012). Jurisdictions reported the largest proficiency decreases during this period in Economic Recovery, which dropped by 10 percent, and Forensics and Attribution, which dropped by eight percent.

Changes in State and Territory Proficiency Levels,
2012-2016
Based on State Preparedness Report Results

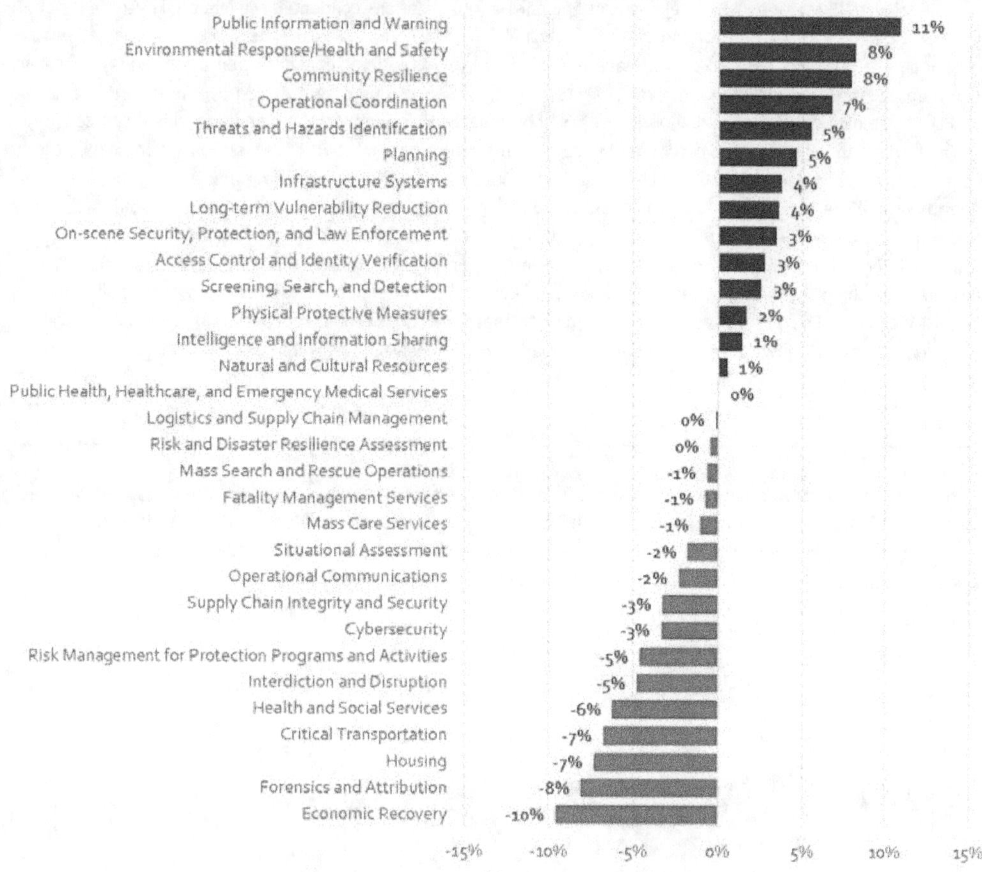

Figure 5. Since 2012, states and territories have reported rating increases in 15 core capabilities and rating decreases in 16 core capabilities.

Cross-Cutting Finding:

Exercises conducted under NEP tested all 32 core capabilities, and especially highlighted improvements and lessons learned for Intelligence and Information Sharing, Public Information and Warning, and Operational Coordination, as well as core capabilities in the Recovery mission area.

FEMA's NEP serves as the Nation's principal mechanism for testing national preparedness through exercises. Operating in two-year cycles, the program features a progressive series of exercises that culminates in a full-scale, national-level, capstone exercise. Each cycle focuses on testing a particular set of strategic priorities, providing a consistent method to validate the capabilities of Federal and non-Federal partners, and gauge progress toward reaching the Goal.

National Exercise Program Capstone Exercise 2016

From April 25 to May 17, 2016, Federal agencies and partner organizations conducted the National Exercise Program Capstone Exercise 2016 ("Capstone 2016"), the culminating exercise for the 2015–2016 NEP cycle. Capstone 2016 examined the ability of senior Federal leaders and key partners to share and act upon information to achieve common and accurate situational awareness, inform crisis action planning, and establish priorities for life-saving and life-sustaining operations in response to a credible threat. Federal departments and agencies organized large-scale activities to defend the homeland and save lives in the face of a weapon-of-mass-destruction (WMD) threat to the Nation's capital, but confronted challenges in situational awareness, public communications, and operational coordination. Federal agencies as a whole lacked consistent situational awareness. At times, the full intelligence and threat picture needed for adequate interagency coordination was known only by a limited number of executive branch leadership and staff. As the Federal Government coordinated its strategic, operational, and tactical activities to respond to the WMD threat, a lack of pre-designated authorities hindered communications with the public and the Federal workforce. Overall, Capstone 2016 reinforced the need to build mechanisms for shared situational awareness in a complex threat environment and for continued comprehensive government-wide planning to strengthen interagency operational coordination.

While the Response mission area remained the most frequently exercised mission area, the other mission areas received increased attention in the 2015–2016 exercise cycle. For example, 41 percent of NEP exercises addressed one or more core capabilities in the Recovery mission area, compared to 27 percent in the 2013–2014 cycle. In 2016, NEP conducted 98 exercises across the country (see Figure 6), which in total tested all 32 core capabilities.

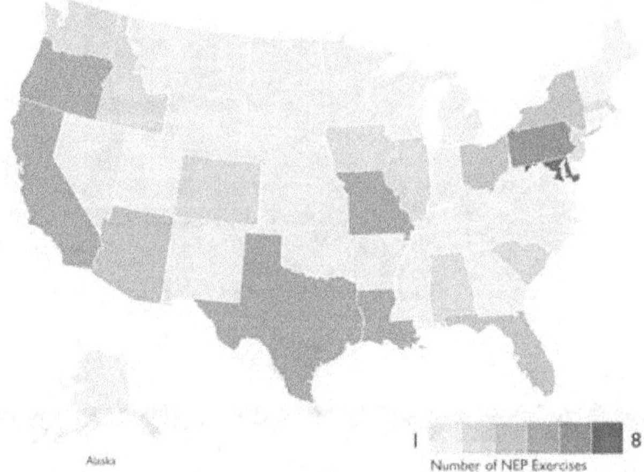

Figure 6. In 2016, NEP exercises across the country tested all 32 core capabilities and addressed a variety of threats and hazards, including active shooter situations, cyber-attacks, and natural disasters.

Based on 2016 exercises, NEP identified 12 findings associated with the current cycle's strategic priorities, each of which aligns to one or more core capabilities (see Table 2).

Table 2. Based on 98 exercises conducted in 2016, NEP identified 12 findings that align to the current cycle's strategic priorities.

Relevant Core Capabilities	Findings
Priority 1: Exchange intelligence, information, data, or knowledge to enable timely and informed decision-making prior to and during an incident that threatens the security of the Nation.	
Intelligence and Information Sharing	• Increased understanding of information sharing protocols and procedures across jurisdictions and with whole community stakeholders remains an outstanding need, particularly for classified or sensitive information. • Pre-existing relationships and networks effectively strengthened prevention and mitigation efforts during an incident.
Priority 2: Identify threats and hazards and share prompt, reliable, and actionable risk information with the public, including actions to be taken and assistance made available during the onset of any hazard that threatens the security of the Nation.	
Public Information and Warning	• Bringing together a broad range of stakeholders prior to an incident to discuss public messaging methods helps ensure the development of more accessible and actionable messages to the whole community, such as messages that are linguistically and culturally appropriate. • By designating a single agency as responsible for developing and disseminating coordinated messaging, law enforcement and emergency response agencies were able to disseminate consistent and regular messaging to dispel public fear.
Priority 3: Establish and maintain a unified and coordinated operational structure and process, capable of identifying, prioritizing, and delivering resources across all hazards and lead-Federal agency authorities, including catastrophic incidents where a Stafford Act declaration is not likely and domestic response to foreign nations overwhelmed by a disaster.	
Operational Coordination	• Insufficient understanding exists among state and local governments, tribal nations, and Federal agencies regarding roles and responsibilities during non-Stafford Act incidents. • Responders have difficulty establishing unified command and coordinating an effective interagency response. • Responders and incident commanders need further training in using the Incident Command System. • State and local responders are not adequately trained to operate key situational awareness systems and software platforms during incident response. • Threat- and hazard-specific response plans are beneficial, and emergency managers and responders should familiarize themselves with these plans. • An effective incident response is tied to effective operational communications.
Priority 4: Establish and maintain plans, authorities, responsibilities, and coordination capabilities that support the recovery of local communities affected by catastrophic disasters.	
Recovery Core Capabilities	• NEP exercises reinforced the value of engaging and integrating whole community stakeholders in pre-incident planning. • Increased representation of faith-based, nonprofit, and private sector partners in preparedness activities (e.g., pre-incident planning efforts, training, exercises) is desirable, as emergency managers rely heavily on these partners to supplement government efforts to engage with individuals with disabilities and others with access and functional needs, and ensure support reaches all affected survivors.

Focused on ensuring the Nation is optimally prepared to avoid, prevent, or stop an imminent terrorist attack within the United States

CORE CAPABILITIES IN PRACTICE

The Prevention mission area focuses on ensuring the Nation is prepared to avoid, prevent, or stop an imminent terrorist attack within the United States. The *National Prevention Framework* ("Prevention Framework") describes seven Prevention core capabilities, including how they interact during an imminent threat.

Being prepared to prevent a terrorist attack in the United States begins with **Intelligence and Information Sharing**, which is the ability to develop situational awareness on the actor(s), method(s), means, weapon(s), or target(s) related to an imminent terrorist threat within the United States. Once an imminent threat has been identified, local, state, tribal, territorial, and Federal partners conduct **Planning** activities to develop appropriate courses of action to prevent the attack. Actions include **Screening, Search, and Detection** operations to effectively identify and locate terrorists and their means, methods, and weapons, as well as subsequent **Interdiction and Disruption** operations to help thwart emerging or developing terrorist plots and neutralize terrorist cells, operatives, and operations. While executing these operations, law enforcement officials use **Operational Coordination** to establish and maintain a unified and coordinated operational structure and process that integrates all relevant stakeholders. Law enforcement officials also conduct their activities in a manner that preserves evidence and the Federal Government's ability to prosecute those who violate the law. **Forensics and Attribution** activities are essential to identify terrorist actors, co-conspirators, and sponsors, and prevent initial or follow-on attacks. Throughout the entire sequence of activities, officials provide **Public Information and Warnings** to share prompt and actionable information with the public and other stakeholders, as appropriate.

CORE CAPABILITIES IN THE PREVENTION MISSION AREA

- Forensics and Attribution
- Intelligence and Information Sharing
- Interdiction and Disruption
- Operational Coordination
- Planning
- Public Information and Warning
- Screening, Search, and Detection

While much of the work in the Prevention mission area is classified in nature, the following examples highlight publicly shareable actions taken in 2016 to improve preparedness that demonstrate the relationship among select core capabilities in the Prevention Framework:

☐ **Forensics and Attribution**

The DHS Science and Technology Directorate, in collaboration with the Massachusetts Institute of Technology, developed video forensic tools that enhance the ability of law enforcement and security personnel to rapidly analyze video feeds to conduct unique and specific security assessments for threat indicators and other suspicious behaviors. Amtrak and the Washington Metropolitan Transit Authority are currently testing the tools. The DHS Science and Technology Directorate plans to provide the suite of tools as part of a layered and integrated capability to detect and mitigate threats to surface transportation from explosives.

To improve forensics and attribution capabilities of first responders in cyber-related cases, the FBI's Cyber Division, in collaboration with the International Association of Chiefs of Police and Carnegie Mellon University, developed the Cyber Investigator Certificate Program. Since its inception in October 2015, thousands of law enforcement personnel have received training under this program, which includes modules on recognizing potential sources of digital

21

evidence, securing digital devices, and documenting digital evidence.

☐ **Planning and Operational Coordination**

In 2016, the Federal Experts Security Advisory Panel (FESAP) comprehensively reviewed biosafety and biosecurity practices for federally funded activities and provided specific recommendations to strengthen these practices. In parallel, the National Science and Technology Council established a committee to seek input from stakeholders into how Select Agent Regulations have affected science, technology, and national security in the United States. Based on stakeholder feedback, the committee developed recommendations on ways to improve the regulatory process and address perceived gaps in the regulations. The Federal Government is currently implementing both sets of recommendations, which address the accounting, security, and physical protection of biological materials. The recommendations include actions, regulatory changes, and guidance to improve biosafety and biosecurity, as well as measures to increase material accountability and oversight, to strengthen security-awareness education and the culture of responsibility, and to optimize inspection processes and incident reporting.

☐ **Interdiction and Disruption and Screening, Search, and Detection**

In fiscal year 2016, DHS's National Counter-IED Capabilities Assessment Database program assessed the capabilities of 415 teams—including bomb squads and Special Weapons and Tactics (SWAT) teams—on their ability to counter IEDs. The program facilitates state and local planning, coordination, and risk assessment efforts and focuses on preparing for IED incidents. In addition, the DHS National Protection and Programs Directorate Office of Infrastructure Protection (IP) delivered 385 courses on counter-IED principles, policies, and programs to more than 8,105 participants in fiscal year 2016. The DHS Office for Bombing Prevention (OBP) also developed three new bomb-threat resources: (1) an instructional video, created with the University of Central Florida, which addresses actions to take when facing a bomb threat; (2) updated planning guidance from DHS and FBI for facilities prone to bomb threats; and (3) a website, "What to Do - Bomb Threat," on DHS.gov that makes bomb threat information and resources more accessible.

☐ **Planning and Operational Coordination**

DOE's National Nuclear Security Administration, in collaboration with FBI, led and conducted the "Atomic Thunder" exercise on December 14, 2016, at the Rhode Island Nuclear Science Center. During the exercise, Federal, state, and local government partners developed plans in response to a hypothetical terrorist threat involving the theft and use of radioactive materials. Throughout the exercise, participants developed methods to communicate and coordinate operational roles when responding to such situations.

☐ **Screening, Search, and Detection and Intelligence and Information Sharing**

The DHS BioWatch Program, which detects and provides early warning of bioterrorism incidents, continues to support preparedness activities (e.g., pre-event planning and exercises) and screening and detection operations at a number of large-scale events—including Super Bowl 50, and the Republican and Democratic National Conventions. In 2016, the BioWatch Program established a formalized process for quickly notifying its network of Federal, state, and local partners when detection of a biological agent occurs. The process supports greater collaboration and situational awareness across the network of partners and was successfully used in a detection incident in May 2016. More broadly, Biowatch is only one of multiple biosurveillance efforts that help protect the population from emerging infectious diseases.

SUMMARY OF PROGRESS

The Nation continues to demonstrate varying levels of capability in and attention to the core capabilities in the Prevention mission area. Key findings in this section describe incremental progress in **Forensics and Attribution**, **Interdiction and Disruption**, and **Screening, Search, and Detection**. This progress is balanced by 2016 State Preparedness Report results, which showed that states and territories rated themselves as less proficient in every Prevention core capability except **Screening, Search, and Detection** compared to 2015.

Prevention core capabilities with higher priority ratings had higher proficiency ratings. Only 32 percent of state and territorial responses to the 2016 State Preparedness Report identified their performance in **Forensics and Attribution** as proficient, placing this core capability in the bottom 10 among all core capabilities (see Figure 7). Moreover, only 34 percent of states and territories rated it as a high priority; states and territories selected nearly all other core capabilities as high priority with greater frequency. In contrast, 52 percent of state and territorial responses reported proficient performance

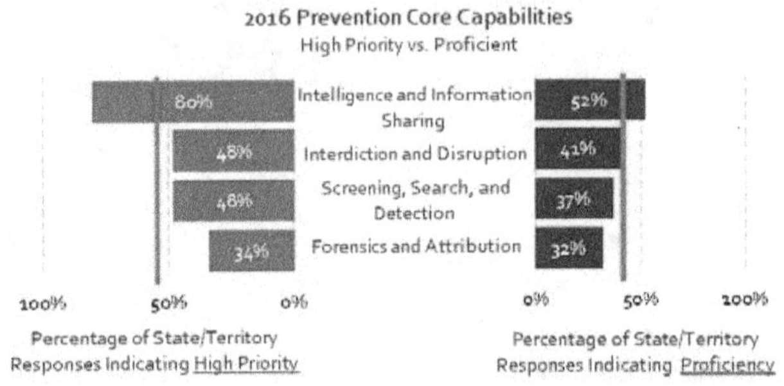

Notes: Vertical red lines (|) indicate the average ratings for all core capabilities. The chart and statements do not include contributions from the three cross-cutting core capabilities—Planning, Operational Coordination, and Public Information and Warning

Figure 7. In their 2016 State Preparedness Report responses, states and territories provided information on their high priority core capabilities, as well as ratings on core capability proficiency.

in **Intelligence and Information Sharing** capabilities. While a slight decrease from 2015, this is the only core capability not specific to the Response mission area that was among the top ten core capabilities by proficiency. Approximately 80 percent of states and territories also identified it as a high priority (fourth highest). In addition to state and territorial efforts, Federal agencies took modest steps to strengthen **Screening, Search, and Detection** capabilities for radiological materials (see page 28).

Table 3 lists the most frequently identified "functional area" gap for each Prevention core capability, as selected by states and territories in their 2016 State Preparedness Report responses. Functional areas break down core capabilities into more granular-level functions, which were identified from an analysis of the Goal, the Prevention Framework, and other national-level preparedness doctrine. **Forensics and Attribution** and **Interdiction and Disruption** were two of the five core capabilities for which states and territories most frequently indicated it was primarily the responsibility of the Federal Government to address gaps.

Table 3. In their 2016 State Preparedness Report responses, states and territories identified remaining gaps in their ability to accomplish various functions associated with each Prevention core capability.

Most Frequently Identified Functional Area Gap in Each Prevention Capability	
Core Capability*	Gap
Forensics and Attribution	Assessing terrorist capabilities
Intelligence and Information Sharing	Gathering intelligence
Interdiction and Disruption	Anti-terrorism operations
Operational Coordination**	Command, control, and coordination
	Establishing a common operating picture
Planning	Whole community involvement and cooperation
Public Information and Warning	New communication tools and technologies
Screening, Search, and Detection	Screening

* For core capabilities that cut across two or more mission areas, the 2016 State Preparedness Report did not include separate data requests that were specific to each mission area. Gaps identified for these core capabilities are identical for the different mission areas.
** The top-two functional area gaps for Operational Coordination were equal in frequency of selection.

The 2017 *National Preparedness Report* identifies **Intelligence and Information Sharing** as a capability to sustain (see page 11). While several indicators (e.g., exercise frequency and State Preparedness Report results) identify this capability as an area of strength, recent declines in proficiency and Federal preparedness grant funding for this capability increase the potential for future gaps to arise. The 2017 *National Preparedness Report* does not identify any Prevention-specific core capabilities as areas for improvement.

23

BY THE NUMBERS

NEW YORK STATE CARRIED OUT OVER 600 COUNTERTERRORISM EXERCISES

New York State's Division of Homeland Security and Emergency Services—along with New York State Police, the Joint Terrorism Task Force, and local law enforcement—conducted over 600 counterterrorism exercises in 2016 at businesses and organizations across the state to test their suspicious activity reporting programs and counterterrorism plans. In total, nearly 100 law enforcement agencies and 300 personnel supported these unannounced exercises.

THE SECRET SERVICE TRAINED 1,640 INDIVIDUALS

The U.S. Secret Service provided 54 presentations on terrorism trends and tactics to 1,640 total participants—including law enforcement, military, civilian security personnel, first responders, legal officials, and U.S. Secret Service personnel across the country—to better prepare them to prevent and respond to evolving terrorist threats.

THE DHS DOMESTIC NUCLEAR DETECTION OFFICE CONDUCTED 110 DEPLOYMENTS

To support state and local security and terrorism prevention capabilities during National Security Special Events (e.g., the Democratic and Republican National Conventions), the DHS Domestic Nuclear Detection Office (DNDO) deployed its six Mobile Detection Deployment Units 110 times in 2016 (compared to 81 times in 2015). These units, which contain radiation detection equipment and staff trained to use it, supplement the radiological and nuclear detection capabilities of local first responders and enhance preparedness against radiological and nuclear threats.

PREVENTION SNAPSHOTS

BOMB-MAKING MATERIALS AWARENESS PROGRAM

In 2016, the OBP began transitioning implementation of its Bomb-Making Materials Awareness Program to a state-led model. This program helps interdict plots involving bombs at the point-of-sale of explosive precursors. OBP's move to decentralize the program increases training capacity and gives states greater ownership of the training content, enabling them to tailor it to meet their specific needs. OBP has already transitioned control of the program in Texas and Arizona, and a number of states—including Georgia, Tennessee, Florida, North Carolina, and Minnesota—will complete their training for transitioning by July 2017. As each state completes the training, OBP identifies lessons learned to share with other states.

LOUISVILLE, KENTUCKY

The Louisville Metropolitan Police Department established a one-hour training session that seeks to improve officer awareness about IEDs and outlines actions for officers to take following the discovery of such a device. The department requires all police officers to attend the session as a part of recurring mandatory training.

Moreover, the city is extending the requirement to all of its emergency services.

COLUMBIA, SOUTH CAROLINA

On August 1, the South Carolina Department of Public Safety hosted a free anti-terrorism training seminar entitled "Recognizing and Mitigating Suicide Bomber Threats" for Federal, state, and local law enforcement. The seminar included a session on tools for early identification of a suicide bomber suspect and offered best practices based on field experience to enable effective incident response.

Homeland Security 2017 National Preparedness Report

PREPAREDNESS INDICATORS

Number of terrorism disruptions by the U.S. Department of Justice (DOJ), primarily by FBI

Preventing and disrupting imminent terrorist attacks is the primary focus of the Prevention mission area. FBI defines a "disruption" as inhibiting or interrupting a threat actor from engaging in criminal or national security-related activity. In fiscal year 2015, DOJ achieved 440 terrorism "disruptions," an increase from 214 disruptions in fiscal year 2014. The fiscal year target values (shown in the figure) represent projections that DOJ determines based on estimated future threats.

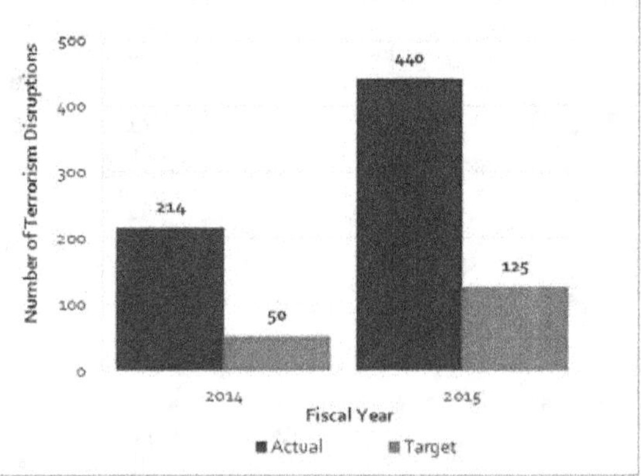

Percentage of intelligence reports rated "satisfactory" or higher in customer feedback that enable customers to understand the threat

Timely intelligence and information is necessary to keep the homeland safe in a constantly changing threat environment. This measure gauges the extent to which DHS intelligence programs have satisfied their Federal, state, and local customers by producing reports that improve awareness and understanding of potential threats. Specifically, the measure aggregates customer ratings of the relevance, timeliness, and usefulness of these reports. Since fiscal year 2012, DHS has consistently exceeded its targets for this measure.

PREVENTION
Key Findings

Federal departments improved their ability to detect insider threats by employing new records-management systems and requiring cleared contractors to maintain formal programs to detect insider threats.

In 2016, DHS and the U.S. Department of Defense (DoD) employed new records-management systems for insider threats to comply with Executive Order (E.O.) 13587, "Structural Reforms to Improve the Security of Classified Networks and the Responsible Sharing and Safeguarding of Classified Information" (October 2011). The E.O. directs Federal departments and agencies to establish, implement, monitor, and report on their insider threat-detection and -prevention programs.

DHS began using a database in March 2016 to better manage and investigate the unauthorized disclosure of classified information. In fiscal year 2016, DHS recorded 53 insider threat notifications. The system also helps DHS track its notifications of suspected insider threats to external partners. DoD began using a similar database in October 2016. In addition to meeting E.O. 13587 requirements, the system addresses DoD's need for a "centralized hub" for insider threat data. DoD uses the system to analyze, monitor, and audit information that insider threats may pose to DoD and to other resources.

DoD also changed national industrial security standards to strengthen detection capabilities for insider threats among cleared contractors working for the Executive Branch. Specifically, DoD requires these contractors to maintain an insider threat program consistent with E.O. 13587. This change applies to the approximately 13,000 contractor facilities that are cleared for access to classified information. Cleared contractors must brief all cleared staff on the program before granting them access to classified information. Further, cleared contractors must report information on an insider threat to a designated agency (such as DHS, DoD, or DOE). To help industry comply with this change, agencies have provided Federal and industry representatives with their procedures to help cleared contractors implement compliant insider threat programs.

PREVENTION CASE STUDY: TRANSPORTATION SECURITY ADMINISTRATION (TSA) ACTIONS TO IMPROVE ITS INSIDER THREAT DETECTION CAPABILITIES

The ability of airport workers to circumvent perimeter and access control security measures and smuggle weapons into restricted areas of airports and onto passenger planes presents a vulnerability for potential terrorist exploitation. DHS, TSA, and FBI consider insider threat to be one of aviation security's most pressing concerns. To address this and other airport perimeter and access control concerns, TSA has enhanced its employee screening practices and capabilities. TSA reported in January 2017 that it increased airport employee screenings, which include physical searches and security background checks, by 43 percent— from 16.9 million in 2015 to 24.2 million in 2016. In addition, TSA conducted a pilot incorporating risk-based scheduling and deployments of security personnel when screening airport employees. The pilot methodology incorporates key requirements defined in the *Federal Aviation Administration (FAA) Extension, Safety, and Security Act of 2016*, including random and unpredictable deployments using game theory and scientific algorithms. TSA also conducted a 90-day pilot test of FBI's Rap Back service (which provides continuous criminal history monitoring) for TSA workers at two major U.S. airports and employees of one commercial airline company. This pilot involved 5,600 individuals covered by the Rap Back service and resulted in 56 notifications of criminal activity and two revoked secure-area access badges. TSA is coordinating with airports and aircraft operators to incorporate the service into their operations. TSA plans to expand the Rap Back service to all U.S. airports by the end of fiscal year 2017. According to TSA, these and other actions taken over the past few years have reinforced layers of security already in place to stop a potential terrorist attack.

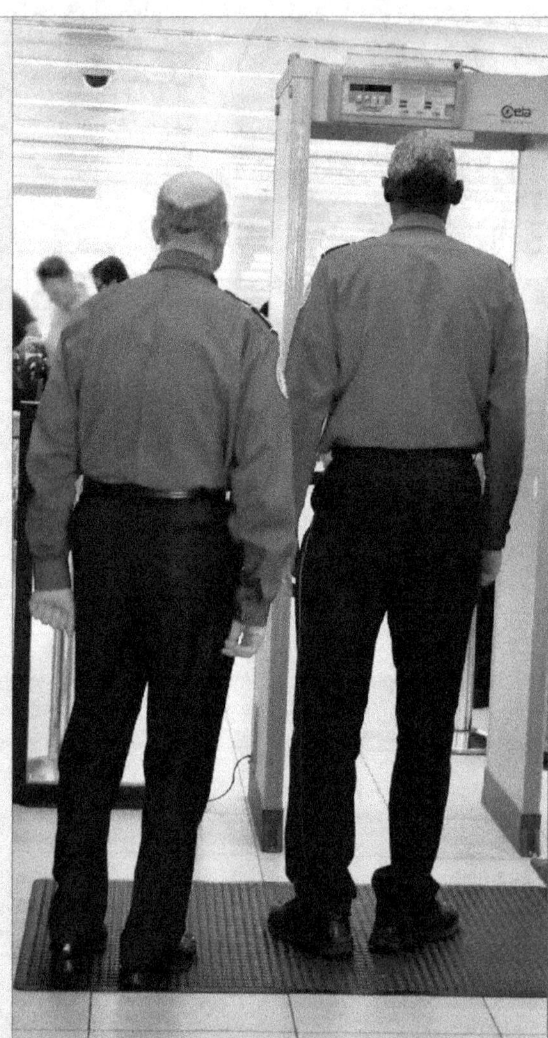

Key Finding:

In 2016, DHS's Office of Intelligence and Analysis (I&A), in collaboration with Federal, state, and local partners, implemented an enhanced process for assessing fusion center performance.

The National Network of Fusion Centers reached maturity in 2015, achieving the full capability to integrate resources among and between individual fusion centers and share intelligence across all levels of government. To further assess the network's performance and help fusion centers mitigate capability gaps, DHS I&A piloted an enhanced assessment process in 2016 that includes 18 performance measures. Specifically, these measures characterize how fusion centers in the network improve Federal, state, local, tribal, and territorial understanding of threat information, and the impact of the network's analytical products and support activities on law enforcement and counterterrorism operations. The enhanced assessment will facilitate improvements in fusion center performance by identifying potential areas in which additional resources should be dedicated.

In 2016, the enhanced assessment measured fusion center outputs in several areas. For example, fusion centers vetted 76,743 tips and leads by fusion centers. Of those, fusion centers provided 39,472 to other Federal, state, local, tribal, and territorial agencies for follow up action. In addition, DHS found that the fusion centers played a direct role in responding to 52 public safety incidents in 2016.

The 77 fusion centers that participated in the pilot assessment (out of 78 total in the network) also demonstrated strong performance in the following areas:

- ***Alignment with Intelligence Community (IC) Needs:*** *Fusion centers made improvements in meeting the demand for intelligence products that address specific IC needs as a result of increased collocation and collaboration within the network. The percentage of Intelligence Information Reports (IIRs) published by DHS I&A that originated from fusion center information and met the specific needs of the IC increased from 90 percent in 2015 to 100 percent in 2016. In addition, 53 percent of fusion distributable center analytic products addressed a specific IC need.*

- ***Usability of Intelligence Products:*** *In addition to increasingly meeting intelligence product demands, the percentage of Federal IIRs originating from fusion center information that the IC used in performing its mission—such as addressing critical intelligence gaps, corroborating existing information, or helping to define an issue or target—increased from 86 percent in 2015 to 98 percent in 2016.*

PREVENTION CASE STUDY: HSIN EXCHANGE

DHS in collaboration with the Terrorist Screening Center (TSC), implemented HSIN Exchange in September 2016 to strengthen information sharing capabilities within and across the National Network of Fusion Centers, and with the TSC. HSIN Exchange builds off of HSIN, an information platform fusion center partners use to share sensitive but unclassified information. HSIN Exchange enhances information and intelligence sharing capabilities within the network by providing two main advantages:

- *HSIN Exchange increases the speed and efficiency of sharing information between fusion centers, as well as with the TSC, because it is a centralized information request management system that replaces multiple, often duplicative individual management systems.*

- *HSIN Exchange uses a standardized process that allows requests for information to be easily tracked from initiation through closeout. These requests for information, which are an essential part of the information sharing and collaboration support among fusion centers and their partners, involve providing analytical assistance or information that could help identify emerging criminal or terrorist activity, and support emergency management operations.*

Key Finding:

The Federal Government has taken steps to improve the security of radioactive materials and enhance its detection capabilities for radiological and nuclear materials.

Radioactive materials serve beneficial purposes, but can pose serious threats in the wrong hands, such as a terrorist seeking to construct a dirty bomb. U.S. Government Accountability Office (GAO) evaluations have previously revealed radioactive

Homeland Security 2017 National Preparedness Report

material security vulnerabilities, such as weaknesses in Nuclear Regulatory Commission (NRC) and "Agreement State"[3] procedures for issuing licenses to possess radioactive materials. To improve the security of radioactive materials, NRC has taken several steps. For example:

- *NRC and state working groups are implementing modifications to guidance that NRC provides to states for evaluating license applicants and verifying licenses.*
- *NRC has conducted training on licensing processes and guidance for NRC and Agreement State officials and will continue to provide new and updated training to ensure adequate implementation of licensing practices. As part of this training, NRC has emphasized, among other things, the need for greater scrutiny when conducting site visits of applicants' facilities.*
- *NRC currently requires on-site security reviews for higher-level quantities of radioactive materials, and is considering extending such on-site reviews to cover smaller sources as well.*

The NRC has also formed an NRC-Agreement State working group to evaluate whether existing regulations and processes governing source protection and accountability for lower-level quantities of radioactive material (namely, Category 3 quantities[4]) continue to ensure adequate protection of public health and safety. The working group will consider numerous items, including potential changes to methods for license verification and source tracking for lower-level quantities of radioactive material based on consideration of the vulnerability of such materials, the risk posed by the materials, and the current threat environment. The working group's recommendations will be provided to the Commission for consideration in August 2017. These are a sample of the initiatives NRC has undertaken and continues to undertake to ensure the safety and security of radioactive materials used for beneficial commercial, academic, and medical applications in the United States. Other notable initiatives include:

- *The NRC leads the Radiation Source Protection and Security Task Force, which was established by the Energy Policy Act of 2005. The task force evaluates the security of radiation sources in the United States from potential terrorist threats, including acts of sabotage, theft, or use of a radiation source in a radiological dispersal device or a radiological exposure device. The task force comprises independent experts from 14 Federal agencies and one state organization, and is chaired by NRC. The task force meets routinely to discuss matters pertaining to radioactive materials security and provides reports on its efforts to the U.S. President and Congress every four years, with the next report planned for completion in 2018.*
- *The NRC completed an evaluation of the regulation for the security of risk-significant radioactive material, 10 CFR Part 37, "Physical Protection of Category 1 and Category 2 Quantities of Radioactive Material," in 2016. As a result of the review, NRC concluded that the rule is effective in protecting risk-significant radioactive material from theft or diversion. The results of the review were reported to Congress in December 2016, and recommendations developed during the review are being used to enhance licensee implementation of security measures for the protection of risk-significant radioactive material currently in use in the United States.*

DoD, through its Defense Advanced Research Projects Agency (DARPA), has taken steps to enhance detection capabilities for nuclear and radiological materials. In 2016, working with the University of Maryland's National Consortium for the Study of Terrorism and Responses to Terrorism, DARPA sponsored two tests of its SIGMA program. SIGMA was launched to develop and test low-cost, high-efficiency radiation sensors networked via smartphones to provide Federal, state, and local

---

[3] The Atomic Energy Act authorizes the NRC to enter into agreements with states in which it relinquishes its regulatory authority over specified radioactive materials. These Agreement States can grant licenses to possess and use radioactive materials and sealed sources and are responsible for conducting regular inspections of licensees.

[4] Thresholds for radioactive material quantities (e.g., Category 1, 2, 3) are included both in the International Atomic Energy Agency Code of Conduct on the Safety and Security of Radioactive Sources and in 10 CFR Part 37. "Risk-significant" quantities of radioactive material are defined as those meeting the thresholds for Category 1 and Category 2.

officials with real-time awareness of potential nuclear and radiological threats. A 1,000-sensor deployment in Washington, D.C. in October demonstrated the program's ability to provide minute-to-minute information concerning radiological and nuclear threats. DARPA plans to continue testing SIGMA on city and regional scales; achieve the ability to continuously monitor large geographic areas in 2017; and transition the system to Federal, state, and local entities in 2018.

PREVENTION CASE STUDY: 2016 NUCLEAR SECURITY SUMMIT OUTCOMES

For decades, the Federal Government has devoted attention to the security of other countries' fissile materials to prevent their use by hostile actors, either abroad or within the United States. The Nuclear Security Summit, first held in 2010, is a world summit aimed at securing nuclear materials and preventing nuclear terrorism. In April, following the March 2016 Nuclear Security Summit, the Federal Government announced measures that the United States will take to support these efforts. These include strengthening other countries' nuclear forensics capabilities and hosting exercises, workshops, and other activities to build partner nations' nuclear security capabilities.

Focused on actions to safeguard the Nation's people, critical assets, and networks against acts of terrorism and manmade or natural disasters in a manner that allows American interests, aspirations, and way of life to thrive

CORE CAPABILITIES IN PRACTICE

The Protection mission area aims to secure the homeland against acts of terrorism and human-induced or natural disasters. The *National Protection Framework* ("Protection Framework") describes 11 Protection core capabilities, including how they operate together to safeguard the Nation against all hazards.

Protecting the Nation requires understanding the threat environment. This understanding is accomplished through **Intelligence and Information Sharing** (i.e., the collection and distribution of timely, accurate, and actionable data), including sharing intelligence and information between the public and private sectors. Through a process of **Risk Management for Protection Programs and Activities**, officials evaluate the likelihood of, vulnerability to, and consequences of different threats against an asset, individual, or event. Once a possible threat vector is identified and its risk is understood, emergency managers disseminate **Public Information and Warning**, as needed. Steady-state protection operations—those conducted regardless of knowledge of an imminent attack, including **Screening, Search, and Detection**, and **Interdiction and Disruption** activities—are routinely informed by the intelligence and risk-management cycles. These operations are conducted using **Operational Coordination** structures to integrate all relevant stakeholders.

Public and private stakeholders apply the remaining steady-state core capability measures, as appropriate. **Access Control and Identity Verification**, for example, controls admittance to critical locations and systems, and is essential for both **Cybersecurity** and **Physical Protective Measures**. **Supply Chain Integrity and Security** helps strengthen the resilience of the Nation's critical supply chains from intentional disruptions or natural hazards. Government officials and private and nonprofit organizations implement all the above capabilities aligned with procedures identified during the **Planning** process, which are then tested and refined during relevant exercises.

CORE CAPABILITIES IN THE PROTECTION MISSION AREA

- Access Control and Identity Verification
- Cybersecurity
- Intelligence and Information Sharing
- Interdiction and Disruption
- Operational Coordination
- Physical Protective Measures
- Planning
- Public Information and Warning
- Risk Management for Protection Programs and Activities
- Screening, Search, and Detection
- Supply Chain Integrity and Security

The following are examples of actions taken in 2016 to improve preparedness that highlight the relationship among select core capabilities in the Protection Framework:

☐ Planning and Risk Management for Protection Programs and Activities

Through the Hometown Security Initiative, IP conducts outreach with businesses and faith-based organizations and provides expert advice and recommendations about measures they can implement to protect facilities, public-gathering sites, and special-event venues. As of January 2017, DHS Protective Security Advisors have shared information and provided technical assistance in more than 2,800 engagements. For example, DHS encourages businesses to take four steps—connect, plan, train, and report—in advance of an incident to better prepare their employees to think about their role in ensuring the safety and security of their businesses and communities. DHS

31

has also established a "Hometown Security" website to make it easier for the public to find community tools and resources about protective measures. Similarly, the DHS Center for Faith-based & Neighborhood Partnerships worked with FEMA to establish a website, "Resources to Protect Your House of Worship," to make it easier for faith-based organizations to find tools, resources, and partners to help them meet their unique needs.

◻ Screening, Search, and Detection

In 2016, U.S. Customs and Border Protection (CBP) began implementing new biometric screening technologies at major U.S. airports to enhance the collection and verification of entry and exit data. Among other benefits, this data helps officials determine whether individuals suspected of terrorism involvement have left the United States. For example, CBP deployed facial comparison technology at select U.S. airports. This technology takes photos of passengers and compares them to the image in the ePassport that they present. CBP discards photos taken of American citizens upon verification. CBP also began using mobile fingerprint collection devices to collect biometric data for outbound operations at 10 international airports and plans to expand these efforts. At the Hartsfield-Jackson Atlanta International Airport, CBP tested and implemented a new departure information system to identify improved, cost-effective real-time photo-matching capabilities that can be deployed at exit points nationwide.

CBP also tested new biometric data collection technology at a land-based departure point. In May 2016, CBP completed the first test on facial and iris identification technology at a U.S. land border crossing—Otay Mesa, California. The results of this test will help CBP determine whether the technology improves identification of visa overstays and persons of law enforcement or national security interest.

SUMMARY OF PROGRESS

Despite evidence of progress in this year's key findings, the Nation remains less proficient in delivering some capabilities in the Protection mission area. Key findings and 2016 State Preparedness Report results identify progress in **Access Control and Identity Verification** and **Screening, Search, and Detection**. Of the 10 capabilities that states and territories rated themselves as having low proficiency in, however, four are in Protection. The 2017 *National Preparedness Report* identifies **Supply Chain Integrity and Security, Risk Management for Protection Programs and Activities,** and **Cybersecurity** as national areas for improvement (see page 12). One Protection capability—**Intelligence and Information Sharing**—is a capability to sustain in this year's report (see page 11).

Real-world incidents in 2016 underscore the mixture of progress and remaining challenges occurring across the Protection mission area. For example, even as **Access Control and Identity Verification** continues to improve following the 2015 OPM breaches (see page 38), the Nation continues to face numerous **Cybersecurity** challenges. These challenges include increased malicious cyber activity directed at public and private services (see page 37), voter registration systems (see page 37), and cyber infrastructure (see page 9). Despite a high degree of interest in **Cybersecurity**—82 percent of states and territories selected it as a high priority (third among all core capabilities)—the capability remained both the lowest rated core capability in proficiency and the capability in greatest danger of decline.

More broadly, State Preparedness Report data reflects both positive and negative changes in capability across the Protection space.[5] Between 2015 and 2016, states and territories reported proficiency gains of approximately three percent in **Supply Chain Integrity and Security** and **Access Control and Identity Verification**—representing the third and fourth largest increases among all core capabilities. Both, however, remain below average among all core capabilities as ranked by proficiency (see Figure 8). In contrast, **Risk Management for Protection Programs and Activities** declined in proficiency by four percent and **Intelligence and Information Sharing** declined by five percent. Nevertheless, **Intelligence and Information Sharing** remained the only Protection capability for which more than half of states and territories rated themselves as proficient. When looking towards the future, states and territories only expressed increasing concern for **Access Control and Identity Verification** as a Protection core capability in greatest danger of decline.

In addition to proficiency, states and territories also exhibited variable views on the importance they placed on various Protection core capabilities. **Cybersecurity** and **Intelligence and Information Sharing** ranked in the top five in terms of

---

[5] Unless otherwise noted, figures and statements do not include contributions from the three core capabilities common to all mission areas—i.e., Planning, Operational Coordination, and Public Information and Warning.

2016 Protection Core Capabilities
High Priority vs. Proficient

Notes: Vertical red lines (|) indicate the average ratings for all core capabilities. The chart and statements do not include contributions from the three cross-cutting core capabilities—Planning, Operational Coordination, and Public Information and Warning

Figure 8. In their 2016 State Preparedness Report responses, states and territories provided information on their high priority core capabilities, as well as ratings on core capability proficiency.

priority, whereas **Risk Management for Protection Programs and Activities** ranked in the bottom five. Proficiency rankings often aligned to priority rankings, with **Cybersecurity** the most notable exception. In more recent years, fewer states and territories have identified Protection core capabilities as high priority. Between 2015 and 2016, the average number of states and territories identifying each Protection core capability as high priority decreased by an average of five states and territories. Moreover, with the exception of **Cybersecurity, Intelligence and Information Sharing,** and **Interdiction and Disruption,** Protection core capabilities have experienced consecutive years of decreasing priority anywhere from two to four years.

Table 4 lists the most frequently identified "functional area" gap for each Protection core capability, as selected by states and territories in their 2016 State Preparedness Report responses. Functional areas break down core capabilities into more granular-level functions, which were identified from an analysis of the Goal, the Protection Framework, and other national-level preparedness doctrine.

Table 4. In their 2016 State Preparedness Report responses, states and territories identified remaining gaps in their ability to accomplish various functions associated with each Protection core capability.

Most Frequently Identified Functional Area Gap in Each Protection Capability	
Core Capability[*]	Gap
Access Control and Identity Verification	Verifying identity
Cybersecurity	Continuity of operations for information technology systems and networks
Intelligence and Information Sharing	Gathering intelligence
Interdiction and Disruption	Anti-terrorism operations
Operational Coordination[**]	Command, control, and coordination
	Establishing a common operating picture
Physical Protective Measures	Site-specific and process-specific risk assessments
Planning	Whole community involvement and cooperation
Public Information and Warning	New communication tools and technologies
Risk Management for Protection Programs and Activities	Risk assessment
Screening, Search, and Detection	Screening
Supply Chain Integrity and Security	Analysis of supply chain dependencies

[*] For core capabilities that cut across two or more mission areas, the 2016 State Preparedness Report did not include separate data requests that were specific to each mission area. Gaps identified for these core capabilities are identical for the different mission areas.
[**] The top-two functional area gaps for Operational Coordination were tied in terms of how frequently they were selected.

BY THE NUMBERS

DOE HAS PROVIDED CYBERSECURITY CAPABILITY MATURITY MODEL (C2M2) TOOLKITS TO 921 RECIPIENTS

In 2016, DOE worked with energy sector partners to expand participation in its C2M2 program, as well as update and enhance C2M2 tools to better account for evolving cyber threats. The program offers several tools to help electricity, oil, and natural gas utilities evaluate the maturity of their cybersecurity programs, and identify and prioritize ways to enhance their cybersecurity posture. Since the program's launch in June 2012, 921 organizations have requested and received the C2M2 toolkit (as of the end of 2016).

DHS IDENTIFIED EIGHT COORDINATING ACTIVITIES FOR THE PROTECTION CORE CAPABILITIES

In August 2016, DHS published the first edition of the *Protection Federal Interagency Operational Plan* (Protection FIOP). The Protection FIOP describes eight coordinating activities (e.g., Border Security, Critical Infrastructure Security and Resilience) that are the primary, but not exclusive, Federal coordinating mechanisms for building, sustaining, and delivering the Protection core capabilities.

THE DHS OFFICE OF CYBERSECURITY AND COMMUNICATIONS ISSUED 12,187 CYBER HYGIENE REPORTS

In fiscal year 2016, the DHS Office of Cybersecurity and Communications National Cybersecurity Assessments and Technical Services team conducted vulnerability scans of public, Internet-connected information systems for hundreds of Federal, state, local, tribal, and territorial government stakeholders, producing 12,187 Cyber Hygiene Reports. These reports include recommendations for addressing identified vulnerabilities, enhancing the ability of stakeholders to protect against potential exploitation by malicious actors.

PROTECTION SNAPSHOTS

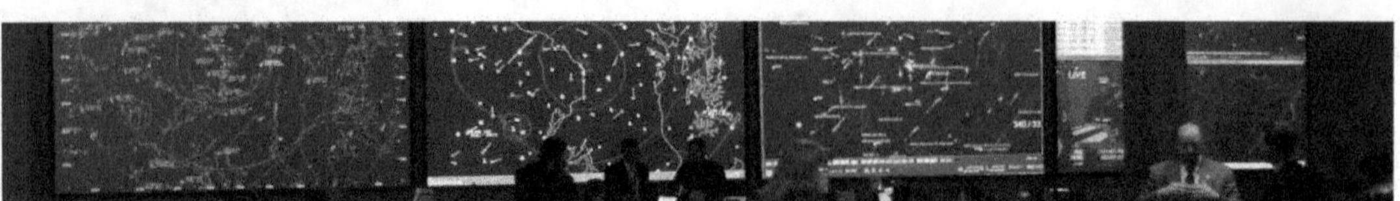

CITY OF LOS ANGELES SUPPLY CHAIN

In 2016, The Los Angeles Emergency Management Department, in partnership with FEMA's National Integration Center, conducted an assessment of the resilience of the city's supply chains to a major earthquake scenario. The assessment found areas for improvement in logistics planning for six critical supply lines: water, food, pharmaceuticals, medical goods, fuel, and transportation. One notable finding is the lack of redundancies among pharmaceutical distributors. Only three companies circulate up to 90 percent of pharmaceuticals in the city.

PHOTODNA

In May 2016, Microsoft announced it would provide support to computer scientists at Dartmouth College to use its PhotoDNA program to track terrorist content on social media. The software develops a digital fingerprint for images that can be tracked across the Internet, enabling social media platforms to quickly detect and remove previously flagged content. In December 2016, Facebook, Microsoft, Twitter, and YouTube announced a collaborative effort to better share the fingerprints of terrorist media, such as those generated by PhotoDNA, in order to counter the proliferation of violent extremist content on their sites.

TSA AIRPORT OPERATIONS CENTER (AOC)

In spring 2016, TSA established the AOC, a public-private partnership with the airline industry to address the increase in passengers for the 2016 summer travel season. The AOC tracks daily screening operations and reassigns officers, canines, and other resources to meet demand in advance of predicted passenger volume. These efforts improved TSA's ability to deploy resources to screen the record number of passengers during the summer months.

PREPAREDNESS INDICATORS

Percentage of international air passengers vetted against the terrorist watchlist through Secure Flight

Screening travelers reduces the likelihood of terrorists entering the country. Secure Flight is a risk-based passenger prescreening program that TSA uses to identify low- and high-risk passengers before they arrive at the airport by matching their names against trusted traveler lists and a watchlist. Specifically, this measure tracks the percentage of air passengers traveling in and out of the United States who are screened against the Terrorist Screening Database, the U.S. Government's consolidated database of individuals who are known or reasonably suspected of being involved in terrorist activities. Over the past six years, TSA has met its target goal of screening 100 percent of these international travelers.

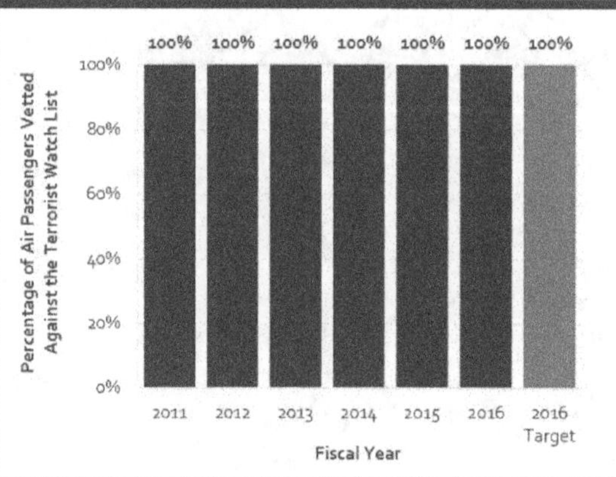

Cybersecurity: Percentage of organizations that have implemented at least one cybersecurity enhancement after receiving a cybersecurity vulnerability assessment or survey

Physical Security: Percentage of facilities that are likely to integrate vulnerability assessment or survey information into security and resilience enhancements

Vulnerability assessments enable critical infrastructure owners and operators to tailor protective measures to their needs. The first measure tracks the extent to which organizations have changed their cybersecurity policies and procedures after DHS cyber assessments. The second measure tracks the percentage of facilities that are likely to inform their security and resilience enhancements using information from DHS vulnerability assessments focusing on physical security. Results suggest that these assessments are prompting critical infrastructure owners and operators to take additional protective actions. In fiscal year 2015, the percentage of organizations incorporating an enhancement based on cyber assessments was 100 percent. The percentage of facilities likely to incorporate an enhancement based on a physical security-oriented assessment was 90 percent.

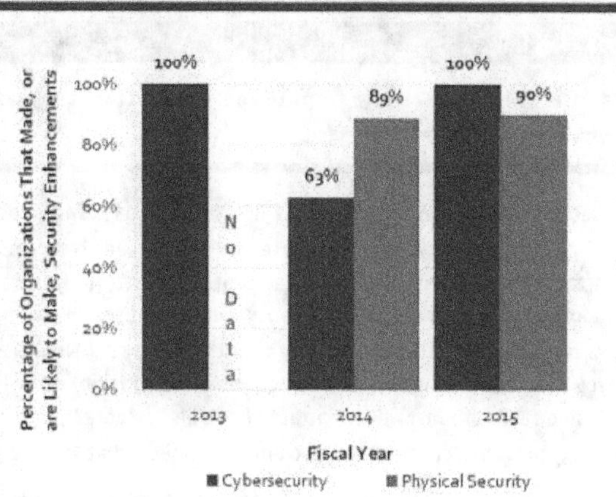

A rise in ransomware (a form of malware) attacks threatens the delivery and continuity of critical services, such as healthcare services.

Ransomware attacks, which lock users out of data files, rose in 2016, threatening critical services such as healthcare and law enforcement. Attacks increased by 300 percent over the first several months of 2016, from an average of 1,000 to 4,000 attacks daily. Victims in the United States paid more than $209 million in ransom payments during the first quarter of 2016, compared to $25 million in all of 2015. One report found that up to three-quarters of healthcare entities may have been victims of ransomware attacks over a 12-month period (starting in 2015). An April 2016 survey of 61 healthcare technology officers found that more than half had reported their facility as being a victim of ransomware attacks in the previous 12 months. Rising rates of ransomware attacks have also affected government networks and services, including law enforcement. Since 2013, ransomware attacks have affected police in at least seven states.

Throughout 2016, Federal departments and agencies took actions to address the challenges of ransomware. For example, the Federal Government published guidance and best practices to private industry and state and local partners to discourage victims from making ransomware payments. The FBI issued two alerts and one notification, which included information on indications of compromised systems and aimed to raise awareness of the threat. HHS alerted healthcare executives to the threat, presented at webinars and industry conferences, published technical assistance resources, and is supporting a task force that is developing recommendations for Congress on steps to improve cybersecurity within the healthcare industry. HHS also published guidance on best practices in the prevention of and response to ransomware attacks. Non-Federal partners supplemented these efforts. For example, the Center for Internet Security—in partnership with FBI, the U.S. Secret Service, and relevant industry information-sharing organizations—conducted a 14-city awareness campaign in 2016 to educate over 4,000 corporate executives on ransomware threats.

Malicious cyber activities targeting voter registration systems prompted local, state, and Federal government agencies to increase collaboration in order to secure election systems.

Attacks on voter registration systems in 2016 contributed to concerns about the vulnerability of election results to cyberattacks. Arizona and Illinois confirmed attempted attacks on voter registration systems in the summer, and FBI reported that other states were likely targeted by malicious actors. However, while voter registration systems faced threats, several factors make other types of voting systems resilient to cyberattacks. For example, machines used to cast votes are not connected to the Internet. Attempts to alter voting systems to affect election outcomes would require large-scale, coordinated physical and cyber manipulation of thousands of individual ballot boxes. Moreover, elections are decentralized across thousands of local jurisdictions using a range of software and hardware, reducing the number of common vulnerabilities nationwide. Variation across voting systems, however, means that the Federal Government faces challenges in issuing standardized assistance to state and local jurisdictions.

To better understand these challenges, DHS collaborated with the National Association of Secretaries of State in August to

37

establish the Election Infrastructure Cybersecurity Working Group. The group collected data on election-related cyber threats and disseminated best practices. DHS also encouraged state and local election agencies to leverage the department's risk and vulnerability assessments. To further promote best practices in the lead-up to the election, the U.S. Election Assistance Commission circulated a checklist and resources on securing voters' data. Prior to the election, 49 state and local election agencies sought cybersecurity assistance from DHS. Such assistance included scanning systems connected to the Internet and conducting risk and vulnerability assessments for important networks, such as those responsible for online voter registration and reporting votes on election night.

In January 2017, DHS designated election infrastructure as a subsector of Government Facilities—one of 16 critical infrastructure[6] sectors. The new designation enables DHS to more easily prioritize cybersecurity assistance to state and local election officials. State and local governments maintain control over the administration of elections in their jurisdictions, though they may request additional aid from the Federal Government to help strengthen, secure, and maintain voting or polling systems.

PROTECTION CASE STUDY: VOTER REGISTRATION SYSTEM BREACHES

Malicious actors target voter registration systems either to extract personal details for identity theft or to disrupt election processes. In the one public case where voter registration data was accessed (Illinois), state election officials reported that malicious actors viewed as many as 90,000 records, exposing information such as names, dates of birth, and driver's license numbers. However, no evidence exists that these actors attempted to modify voter data. In all cases, including those in which details are not available to the public, the IC found no evidence that attacks inhibited voters' ability to cast ballots in the election or targeted vote counting systems.

Key Finding:

Lessons learned from the 2015 OPM data breaches continue to prompt actions to better safeguard sensitive data on government employees and contractors, and to update procedures for background investigations and security clearances.

Protecting personal information housed by the Federal Government against malicious cyber activity remains a longstanding challenge. Attacks on these systems can jeopardize preparedness, exposing data on individuals with background investigations and security clearances and slowing the clearance process. In response to the 2015 OPM breaches, the Federal Chief Information Officer issued guidance in January 2016 to enhance the security and effectiveness of background investigations, including phasing out vulnerable systems. Additionally, the Federal Government created the National Background Investigations Bureau (NBIB) to process the one million annual requests for investigations from Federal agencies in an effort to provide renewed oversight and guidance. NBIB's leadership includes a dedicated senior official for privacy to further ensure the safety of personal data. To better safeguard sensitive data on government employees and contractors, DoD is working with OPM to improve the security of their network.

The Federal Government has also adopted procedural changes to how it safeguards the issuance, maintenance, and protection of background investigations and security clearances. OPM has also increased the frequency with which its

---

[6] The *Critical Infrastructure Protection Act of 2001* defines "critical infrastructure" as "systems and assets, whether physical or virtual, so vital to the United States that the incapacity or destruction of such systems and assets would have a debilitating impact on security, national economic security, national public health or safety, or any combination of those matters."

networks are scanned for evidence of tampering or intrusion to better detect vulnerabilities on Federal systems related to background investigations. Additionally, the White House and OPM continued to pursue a wider series of changes to the background investigation process enacted after the 2015 breaches. OPM is launching programs to ensure that employees' needs for security clearances are continuously reassessed in relation to their duties and that all clearance holders undergo more frequent reinvestigations.

The White House is focusing continued attention on ensuring that users on government systems are who they say they are, which will carry cybersecurity benefits across Federal networks and operations. This is also true of Federal systems accessed by constituents. NIST is in the process of a major update to Special Publication 800-63, "Digital Identity Guidelines," to modernize the types of authenticators acceptable to government and better allow agencies to adopt market innovations. Additionally, the document updates approaches to identity proofing and provides guidelines for agencies to accept commercially provided credentials for access to government services.

Key Finding:

The IC and Federal oversight groups have enhanced privacy protections for intelligence-related information collection.

The Federal departments and agencies that compose the IC took steps to improve U.S. citizen and lawful permanent resident privacy protections and the transparency of intelligence collection and information sharing. These steps are consistent with legal requirements to protect these individuals' privacy rights, while accomplishing important national security missions. The National Security Agency (NSA) found that the IC continued to strengthen privacy protections of personal information through various means, such as training and internal policies. The agency's *Intelligence Reform 2016 Progress Report* noted that the IC continued to enhance and institutionalize transparency through public engagement. In addition, a May 2016 DHS Office of the Inspector General report, *Office of Intelligence and Analysis Can Improve Transparency and Privacy*, found that DHS I&A has made progress in protecting privacy by centralizing oversight of privacy and civil liberties and by working to meet the requirements of legislation, regulations, directives, and guidance. DHS I&A also conducted specialized training for employees on privacy and civil liberties safeguards.

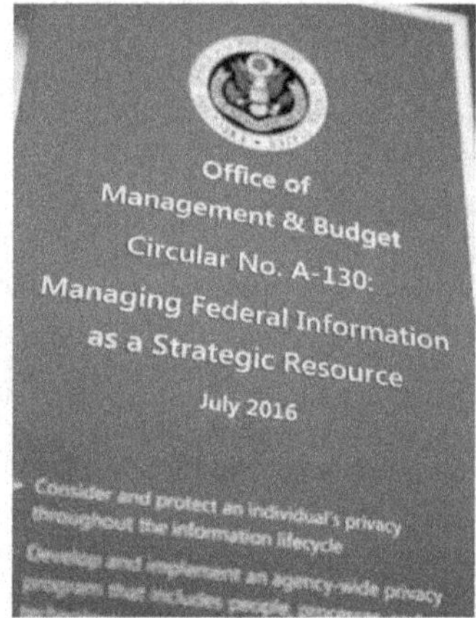

In July, the Office of Management and Budget updated the Federal Government's governing document for establishing how departments and agencies should manage their information resources to account for the dramatic changes in IT, data governance, and security that have occurred since 2000, when the document was last updated. The updated document establishes minimum requirements for Federal privacy programs for the first time, replaces outdated privacy and information-security requirements with new ones, and outlines practices that agencies should incorporate when managing information resources that involve personally identifiable information (PII). In addition, E.O. 13719 (issued in February 2016) established the Federal Privacy Council as the principal interagency forum for improving the privacy practices of Federal agencies and entities acting on their behalf. Over 350 privacy professionals from across the Federal Government participated in the council's Federal Privacy Summit in November, which addressed privacy issues such as encryption, privacy risk assessment, and health privacy.

Key Finding:

Government, academic, and private-sector partners continue to take steps to counter violent extremism through domestic education and other initiatives, including countering terrorist use of social media.

In 2016, the Federal Government continued to build both infrastructure and capacity for countering violent extremism (CVE) activities. In January, DHS and DOJ announced the Countering Violent Extremism Task Force to manage the synchronization and integration of CVE initiatives across the Federal Government. The task force regularly convenes partners to coordinate and share U.S. Government–funded CVE research and analysis. The National Counterterrorism Center (NCTC) also holds quarterly interagency CVE roundtables, which provide the only classified forum for analysts and policymakers to discuss recent IC products and policy developments. DOJ increased its CVE staff from one attorney with collateral responsibilities to four full-time staff members. Additionally, in October, the White House released an updated *Strategic Implementation Plan for Empowering Local Partners to Prevent Violent Extremism in the United States* that calls for strengthening collaboration with the private sector and academia to pursue CVE-relevant communications tools and capabilities. Also in October, DHS released *Department of Homeland Security Strategy for Countering Violent Extremism*, which outlines its approach to CVE and aligns with the White House's strategic implementation plan.

The Federal Government has also continued to pursue community engagement to support CVE efforts. In 2016, FBI and its partners broadened outreach campaigns to counter violent extremism among young people, whom violent extremist groups target for recruitment through the Internet and social media. The FBI published a guide for preventing radicalization to violence in high schools to help these institutions better understand the topic of violent radicalization and identify warning signs. The FBI also launched an interactive website, "Don't Be a Puppet," which combines videos and interactive activities to deliver narratives counter to messages that target teenagers and promote radicalization to violence. In the first eight months since its launch, the website received over 280,000 page views. Among other efforts, the DHS Office for Civil Rights and Civil Liberties delivered Community Awareness Briefings to community stakeholders and law enforcement officers nationwide. Community Awareness Briefings share unclassified information with communities regarding the threat of radicalization to violence. In addition, Federal agencies have sought to expand their outreach through train-the-presenter efforts. The NCTC has trained dozens of local partners to present Community Awareness Briefings and the DHS Office of Civil Rights and Civil Liberties is developing a program to train local law enforcement officials to deliver awareness briefings to their fellow officers.

Students from around the country, with support from Federal and non-Federal partners, also developed their own outreach initiatives. In 2015, DHS worked with DoD, NCTC, and the Department of State to develop the Peer to Peer Challenging Extremism contest. The contest, which challenges educational institutions to develop innovative social media campaigns for countering violent extremism, has expanded from 23 universities to more than 130 around the world in 2016. Under the program, students compete to design, implement, and measure the success of a product or tool that counters violent extremist messages. In June 2016, a team of students from the Rochester Institute of Technology won first place for their "It's Time: ExOut Extremism" social media campaign. The campaign seeks to counter violent extremist narratives by informing Internet users about their possible exposure to violent extremist content when surfing the web or using social media platforms. It also identifies ways in which users can protect themselves by avoiding violent extremist messaging on the Internet and contribute to positive narratives against online violent extremist messaging.

Private technology companies have also contributed to CVE efforts. For example, Google's technology incubator company, Jigsaw, developed a pilot project with other companies to redirect online users susceptible to ISIS's message to YouTube videos that debunk ISIS recruiting themes and strategies. During the tool's pilot test, which lasted eight weeks, 320,000 individuals watched over half-a-million minutes of 116 videos discrediting ISIS recruitment themes. Twitter has also sought to counter terrorists' use of social media to radicalize and recruit followers. As of August 2016, daily suspensions on Twitter of terrorist-linked accounts were up over 80 percent from the previous year. Since mid-2015, the company has suspended at least 360,000 accounts connected to terrorist groups.

Among the different measures adopted to address the Zika epidemic, states, territorial, and local governments, as well as Federal agencies, effectively distributed preventative supplies and communicated protection measures.

Zika emerged in the Americas in late 2015 and has spread throughout the Western Hemisphere. While infected adults can experience no to mild, flu-like symptoms, Zika infection during pregnancy can cause serious birth defects. Protecting infants from congenital Zika syndrome defects is the driving motivation for U.S. Government efforts.

Zika virus disease primarily spreads through infected mosquitoes, but can also be transmitted through sexual contact and transfusion of infected blood products. A pregnant woman can pass the Zika virus to her fetus during pregnancy or around the time of birth. An analysis presented in the April 7, 2017, edition of the CDC's *Morbidity and Mortality Weekly Report* found that 10 percent of pregnancies with laboratory-confirmed Zika virus infection resulted in Zika virus–associated birth defects. Because a Zika vaccine has yet to be fully tested and licensed, the best way to protect oneself from the Zika virus is by taking steps to prevent mosquito bites and the spread of the virus through sexual intercourse. The CDC has developed resources to help all levels of government communicate personal protective measures for preventing Zika virus infection. To help communities promote public awareness of personal protective measures, CDC issued guidance documents in 2016 to inform all levels of government on best practices for Zika virus outreach:

- *The Zika CDC Interim Response Plan outlines communication and community education activities to prepare state and local jurisdictions where local mosquito-borne transmission is possible.*
- *The Zika Communication Planning Guide for States provides states with the resources to develop their own tailored communication strategies and includes sample public outreach products, as well as clinical communication products and deliverables.*
- *The Zika Community Action Response Toolkit (Z-CART) provides a template for state, local, and tribal agencies to develop strategies in the event of a local mosquito-borne transmission of the virus.*
- *Interim Recommendations for Zika Vector Control in the Continental U.S. provides guidance for states to update mosquito-control programs that have focused on West Nile virus transmission.*

Zika Virus Vaccine Development

Vaccines for the Zika virus are under development and some are in clinical trials to test whether they are safe and effective. A licensed Zika vaccine will likely not be available for several years. As part of an overall strategy to support the response to Zika in 2016, the Biomedical Advanced Research and Development Authority (BARDA; which exists within the Office of the Assistant Secretary for Preparedness and Response [ASPR] in HHS), HHS's National Institute of Allergy and Infectious Diseases, and DoD's Walter Reed Army Institute of Research are supporting a diverse portfolio of Zika vaccine candidates, investing in multiple technological platforms to improve the chances of having a successful vaccine. As of December 2016, early phase clinical trials were underway to assess vaccine candidates for their safety, tolerability, and ability to provoke a beneficial immune response. Zika vaccine development represents a crucial step toward protecting infants from Zika virus disease and is one component of an overall Zika medical countermeasure response, which also includes the development of diagnostic tools and blood screening and pathogen reduction technologies.

State and territorial governments, along with non-Federal partners, also developed and implemented their own Zika-prevention programs, focusing on risk communication and outreach to communities. For example, Maryland's state government organized a "Zika Virus Awareness Week" in April 2016 to encourage residents to take actions to reduce their risk of infection. Similarly, the New York City Department of Health and Mental Hygiene sponsored a "Zika Day of Action" in June 2016, deploying outreach teams to subway stations to hand out educational materials on mosquito prevention and testing. In Puerto Rico, where the virus has infected more than 33,000 people (as of December 15, 2016) since the first case was reported on the island in December 2015, the Puerto Rico Department of Health worked with CDC and private-sector partners to carry out public awareness and education campaigns. In June 2016, The Home Depot and the Puerto Rico Department of Health initiated the campaign by hosting more than 800 community members at an event that included a health fair and workshops on Zika prevention. In May 2016, the National Association of Chain Drug Stores Foundation launched a Zika-education initiative in Puerto Rico to encourage pregnant women to consult their pharmacists and doctors on protecting themselves and their unborn children from the Zika virus. The foundation also partnered with CDC to create outreach materials for store displays. HHS's Administration for Children and Families (ACF), with support from CDC, developed and distributed fact sheets in both Spanish and English on Zika for Head Start and child care providers, and parents. ACF programs also provided Puerto Rico with technical assistance on how it could use ACF program waivers and flexibilities to support Zika prevention efforts. Partnership programs across levels of government also provided support in communicating Zika protection measures. From January to October 2016, volunteer health professionals of the Medical Reserve Corps of Puerto Rico—a program supported by HHS's ASPR and administered by the Puerto Rico Department of Health—conducted educational workshops for community members on Zika. During this period, 144 volunteers educated more than 16,000 residents in Puerto Rico on the Zika virus and prevention measures.

Federal, state, local, tribal, and territorial partners have implemented mechanisms to control mosquito populations and distributed protective supplies to prevent the spread of the virus. ASPR led an interagency working group to identify and respond to potential supply shortages for mosquito control products in coordination with manufacturers and distributors. The CDC provided states and territories that have confirmed outbreaks of Zika with immediate services to control mosquito populations, as well as Zika Prevention Kits. In addition, the Strategic National Stockpile (SNS) supported the establishment and implementation of mosquito population-control contracts, which provide access to spraying and other mosquito-control support, for 10 state and local governments (as of December 12, 2016). Building on its experience from Ebola response efforts, CDC used partnerships with its nonprofit foundation and private companies to receive, assemble, and distribute more than 30,000 Zika Prevention Kits through the SNS. The CDC also collaborated with the National Association of Chain Drug Stores, which created Zika prevention messaging, set up store displays about Zika, and began distributing Zika prevention items (e.g. insect repellent) for purchase through local pharmacies and drug stores. However, these efforts may have begun too late in Puerto Rico; by July 7, 2016, the Zika virus was widespread in Puerto Rico, and Zika-infected patients resided in 99 percent of municipalities in the territory.

PROTECTION CASE STUDY: TEXAS A&M DEVELOPS APP TO TRACK MOSQUITO POPULATIONS

To facilitate mosquito control efforts, researchers at Texas A&M University developed a mobile application that tracks sites with standing water that might serve as places where the primary carrier and transmitter of the Zika virus, the *Aedes* mosquito species, lays eggs. *Aedes aegypti* and *Aedes albopictus* mosquitoes often lay eggs in containers of standing water, such as old tires, buckets, and bird baths. Through the app, users can document containers that could potentially be places for mosquito eggs and larvae, along with their locations. The app makes mapped data available to local health officials to use when prioritizing mosquito-control measures.

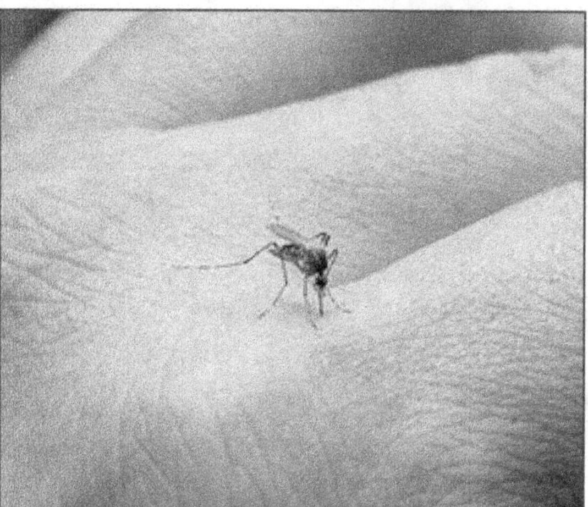

CBP CARGO AND PORT SECURITY PROGRAMS

The Container Security Initiative **operates in**

58
Ports

and **pre-screens**

80%
inbound cargo
prescreened

coming to the United States **from five continents**

Through the Container Security Initiative (CSI), CBP works collaboratively with foreign governments to prescreen cargo bound for the United States by ship. This initiative helps prevent terrorists from using cargo shipments to smuggle individuals or dangerous materials to the United States, securing the Nation's borders and addressing possible threats away from U.S. soil.

The Freight Security Initiative adds an additional layer of security at select ports by scanning 100 percent of all U.S. bound cargo containers for radiation.

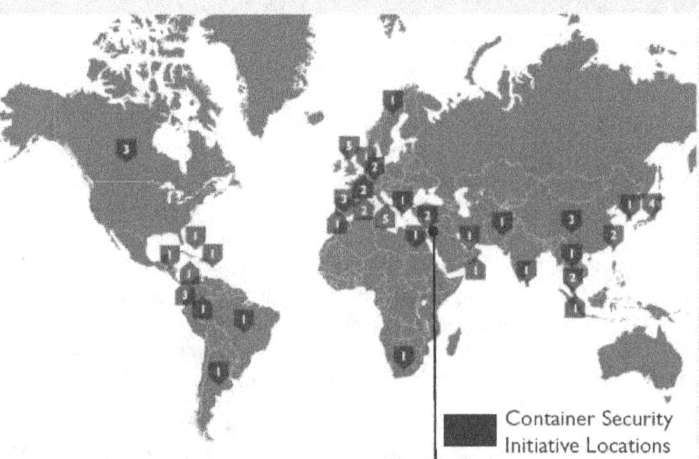

In 2016, CBP added the Port of Aqaba, Jordan, to the list of ports conducting radiation scanning under the Freight Security Initiative.

Increasing Screening Efficiency

For shipments arriving at U.S. points of entry from abroad, CBP uses Radiation Portal Monitors to scan the cargo. This program provides another layer of defense against potential attempts to smuggle radioactive materials into the United States that could be used for weapons such as dirty bombs.

One major problem is **FALSE ALARMS**. From 2002 to May 2016, CBP scanned more than 1.2 billion conveyances for radiological contraband. This resulted in **millions of false alarms** that the agency had to investigate, **drawing resources away from other high priority law enforcement duties**. Efforts by CBP and DNDO to modify the setting these monitors operate at have resulted in major improvements, reducing false alarms by 78 percent at sea ports and 44 percent at land crossings.

Improvements have reduced false alarms by **200,000** each year

43

Focused on reducing loss of life and property by lessening the impact of disasters through increasing risk awareness and leveraging mitigation products, services, and assets

CORE CAPABILITIES IN PRACTICE

The National Mitigation Framework ("Mitigation Framework") describes seven core capabilities, including how they interact to reduce loss of life and property and increase community resilience.

To effectively mitigate risks, a community begins with **Threats and Hazards Identification,** which includes understanding their frequency and magnitude. Next, **Risk and Disaster Resilience Assessments** help communities understand the consequences that these threats and hazards would have if they occurred. Based on this knowledge, community officials can begin **Planning** efforts to manage the risk, as well as provide **Public Information and Warnings** to residents. Once implemented, these plans enable **Long-term Vulnerability Reduction** to disasters through one or more of the following strategies:

CORE CAPABILITIES IN THE MITIGATION MISSION AREA

* Community Resilience
* Long-term Vulnerability Reduction
* Operational Coordination
* Planning
* Public Information and Warning
* Risk and Disaster Resilience Assessment
* Threats and Hazards Identification

* Risk avoidance – *Preventing exposure to an event (e.g., using zoning rules to prevent home construction in high-risk areas)*
* Risk reduction – *Minimizing vulnerabilities (e.g., retrofitting buildings to be more resistant to earthquakes)*
* Risk transfer – *Eliminating or limiting liability for harm, without reducing vulnerability (e.g., purchasing insurance)*

Since a community can rarely avoid risks completely, the Mitigation Framework encourages leadership, collaboration, partnership building, education, and skill building before an event through **Community Resilience,** with the goal of supporting other capabilities and building resilience. The Mitigation Framework also encourages communities to build and sustain capability in **Operational Coordination** in order to integrate critical stakeholders to support efforts during and after an incident.

The following are examples of actions taken in 2016 to improve preparedness that highlight the relationship among select core capabilities in the Mitigation Framework.

◻ Community Resilience and Long-term Vulnerability Reduction

More than 1,100 community members from three towns in Massachusetts and two in New Hampshire started a project to restore native sand dunes. Sand dunes are a natural barrier to coastal winds, flooding, and erosion. Another benefit of this project, spearheaded by the University of New Hampshire, has been the establishment of a beachgrass community garden in Hampton, New Hampshire. The garden provides coastal homeowners in Hampton with free plants that they can transplant to their properties to protect against coastal storms.

◻ Risk and Disaster Resilience Assessment and Community Resilience

The Rhode Island Division of Planning partnered with the Environmental Protection Agency (EPA) to create a framework to help communities assess their economic vulnerability to extreme weather events and improve their economic resilience. The framework is flexible and easy to use. Communities of varying size and resources can use

44

it to identify threats from extreme weather events and assess the economic impacts. The framework also helps the business community develop creative solutions to enhance their resilience. One community in Rhode Island, North Kingstown, has already pilot-tested and provided refinements to the framework.

◻ **Planning and Long-term Vulnerability Reduction**
St. Tammany Parish, Louisiana, adopted an ordinance to address risks from storm surges. Floodwaters from heavy rains frequently trap residents and prevent emergency vehicle access. To address this vulnerability, parish officials approved an ordinance requiring roads constructed in new developments to be a minimum of six feet above sea level. Officials based the higher elevation on historical surge data and carefully weighed the benefits and costs to the environment and businesses. They determined that adopting the higher elevation requirement will reduce long-term maintenance costs in new coastal subdivisions and improve emergency response capabilities.

◻ **Risk and Disaster Resilience Assessment and Threats and Hazards Identification**
NOAA, the U.S. Geological Survey (USGS), and other Federal partners supported a project in California's Sonoma and Mendocino Counties to develop a flood mapping and information tool, "Our Coast, Our Future." The tool enables local decision-makers to identify, understand, and visualize anticipated vulnerabilities resulting from sea level rise and coastal storms (such as increased flooding, shoreline erosion, and degraded salmon habitats). The interactive map feature allows users to view wave heights and flood potentials in their geographic area.

SUMMARY OF PROGRESS

The Mitigation mission area continues to show progress in meeting the challenges posed by increasingly severe natural hazards. Scientific research and data collection, enhanced by advancements in technology, have improved the Nation's ability to understand natural hazards and to avoid, reduce, and transfer the risks they pose. In 2016, states and territories reported the second-highest overall proficiency ratings for capabilities in the Mitigation mission area, and since 2012, they have reported a greater increase in proficiency for Mitigation core capabilities than those in any other mission area. However, 2016 is the first year that states and territories reported lower State Preparedness Report proficiency ratings in Mitigation than the previous year.

The key findings in this section explain how the Nation is building upon its Mitigation capabilities to address specific hazards. The persistence of drought conditions in the West, the rise of human-induced earthquakes in the central United States, and the nationwide threat of flooding have tested the **Threats and Hazards Identification** and **Risk and Disaster Resilience Assessment** core capabilities. Innovations in both of these capabilities, such as development of water forecast tools and flood maps, have helped refine estimates of the risks these natural hazards pose, as well as enhance early warning systems and inform mitigation efforts. However, the number of states and territories that consider themselves proficient in **Threats and Hazards Identification** has decreased more than any other core capability since 2015. **Risk and Disaster Resilience Assessment** is the only Mitigation core capability in which states and territories reported increased proficiency ratings since 2015.

Of the Mitigation core capabilities, **Community Resilience** has shown the most improvement since 2012, with the number of states and territories rating themselves proficient increasing by eight percent. Tribal communities and localities have taken **Community Resilience** into their own hands by either initiating their own risk-reduction projects or, in the case of some tribal communities, avoiding risks altogether by physically relocating. In addition, 81 percent of states and territories consider addressing **Community Resilience** capability gaps their own responsibility rather than the Federal Government's. This is the fourth-highest percentage of any core capability.

The Federal Government's efforts to encourage the adoption of more resilient building codes and to improve the efficacy of the NFIP, in addition to the formation of public-private partnerships to supplement funding for wildfire mitigation projects, have all contributed to **Long-term Vulnerability Reduction**. Despite these efforts, **Long-term Vulnerability Reduction** is the only Mitigation core capability with a lower than average proficiency rating (see Figure 9).

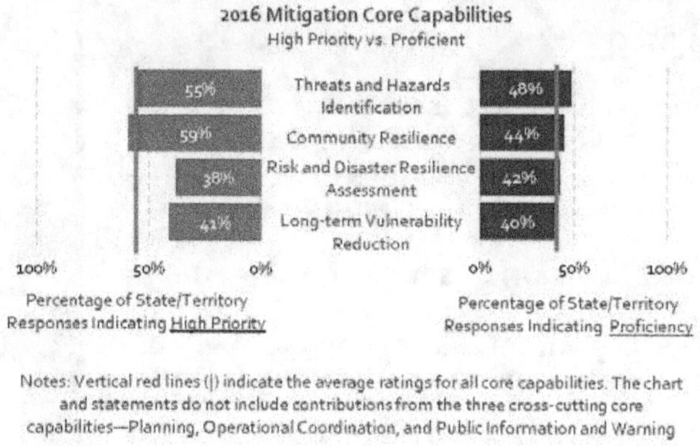

2016 Mitigation Core Capabilities
High Priority vs. Proficient

Notes: Vertical red lines (|) indicate the average ratings for all core capabilities. The chart and statements do not include contributions from the three cross-cutting core capabilities—Planning, Operational Coordination, and Public Information and Warning

Figure 9. In their 2016 State Preparedness Report responses, states and territories provided information on their high priority core capabilities, as well as ratings on core capability proficiency.

Table 5 lists the most frequently identified "functional area" gap for each Mitigation core capability, as selected by states and territories in their 2016 State Preparedness Report responses. Functional areas break down core capabilities into more granular-level functions, which were identified from an analysis of the Goal, the Mitigation Framework, and other national-level preparedness doctrine.

Table 5. In their 2016 State Preparedness Report responses, states and territories identified remaining gaps in their ability to accomplish various functions associated with each Mitigation core capability.

Most Frequently Identified Functional Area Gap in Each Mitigation Capability	
Core Capability*	Gap
Community Resilience	Communication and outreach
Long-term Vulnerability Reduction	Incorporating mitigation measures into construction and development
Operational Coordination**	Command, control, and coordination
	Establishing a common operating picture
Planning	Whole community involvement and cooperation
Public Information and Warning	New communication tools and technologies
Risk and Disaster Resilience Assessment	Obtaining and sharing data
Threats and Hazards Identification	Stakeholder collaboration/coordination

* For core capabilities that cut across two or more mission areas, the 2016 State Preparedness Report did not include separate data requests that were specific to each mission area. Gaps identified for these core capabilities are identical for the different mission areas.
** The top-two functional area gaps for Operational Coordination were tied in terms of how frequently they were selected.

By the Numbers

A new study found that $4.80 in losses was avoided for every $1 spent on certain mitigation activities

A 2016 study by the University of Pennsylvania Wharton School found that every $1 spent on new construction under the Florida Building Code over 10 years saved the state $4.80 in potential losses.

An ASPR and CDC working group issued 16 new preparedness objectives

In May 2016, a working group by ASPR and CDC introduced 16 new preparedness objectives for Healthy People 2020. This initiative provides science-based, 10-year national objectives for improving the health of Americans by establishing benchmarks and monitoring progress. The new objectives use data from various sources, including CDC, FEMA, and Save the Children.

Community Development Block Grant Disaster Recovery Assistance—totaling $2.3 billion—for 2016 disasters includes Mitigation Requirements

In January 2017, the U.S. Department of Housing and Urban Development (HUD) published a Federal Register Notice including additional language requiring long-term recovery and hazard mitigation planning to promote sound and sustainable long-term recovery.

Mitigation Snapshots

San Francisco Sea Level Rise Action Plan

Sea level rise is one of San Francisco's most pressing environmental threats. To address it, a task force comprising local agencies developed a plan for San Francisco to mitigate the impacts. Published in March 2016, the plan outlines goals and objectives, such as conducting a vulnerability and risk assessment. San Francisco intends to build upon the plan and fully develop an adaptation plan for sea level rise by 2018.

USGS Interactive Map

In August 2016, USGS produced an interactive map that allows residents living in and around New Mexico's Jemez Mountains to see where they are located in relation to post-wildfire areas that may present debris-flow hazards (e.g., fast-moving landslides). The map also provides land managers and decision-makers with the ability to pinpoint locations where mitigation activities would minimize both the threat of wildfires and the potential for debris flows.

RainReady Midlothian

Midlothian, Illinois, has faced chronic flooding in recent years. In response, Midlothian and its partners developed a flood plan, RainReady Midlothian, that establishes a common understanding of the village's flood risk, describes methods of reducing flood impacts, and explains how to implement them. In addition, the plan emphasizes using green infrastructure not only to mitigate the negative impacts of floods, but also to preserve natural habitats, create jobs, and beautify neighborhoods.

PREPAREDNESS INDICATORS

Percentage of U.S. population (excluding territories) covered by formal mitigation strategies

Hazard mitigation strategies guide jurisdictional risk reduction efforts. DHS measures the percentage of the Nation's population covered by formal mitigation strategies. Between fiscal years 2011 and 2015, this percentage has risen from 68.7 percent to 80.8 percent—an increase of more than 12 percentage points.

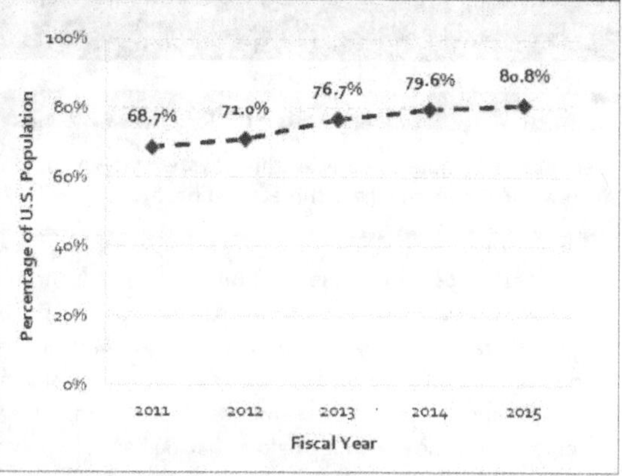

Percentage of communities adopting disaster-resistant building codes

FEMA encourages the adoption and enforcement of disaster-resistant building codes to help communities increase their structural resilience. Adoption rates have shown an upward trend over the past five years. From fiscal year 2011 to fiscal year 2015, the percentage of communities adopting building codes with provisions that adequately address earthquake, flood, and wind hazards rose from 48 percent to 63 percent.

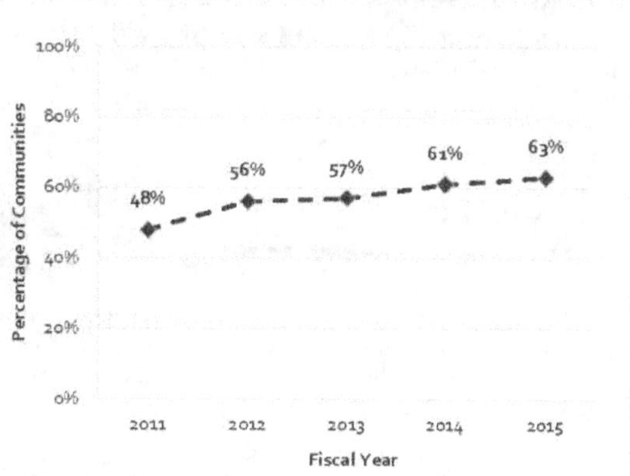

Homeland Security 2017 National Preparedness Report

Recent innovations in early warning systems have the potential to improve the public- and private-sectors' ability to forecast and communicate threats and hazards.

Federal agencies and academic institutions made advancements in earthquake early warning systems in 2016. In February, USGS announced that its prototype earthquake early warning system, "ShakeAlert," entered the next phase of development, in which beta users can receive USGS ShakeAlert warnings on computers or smart devices. ShakeAlert has already detected thousands of earthquakes, including two that caused significant damage. Depending on the location of the earthquake's epicenter and the density of seismic instrumentation, this early warning system provides anywhere from a few seconds to minutes of advanced warning before shaking begins, allowing public safety and key facilities' personnel to take protective actions. In addition, the National Aeronautics and Space Administration (NASA) and Scripps Institute of Oceanography developed improved global positioning system (GPS) technology to estimate more accurate earthquake data, including location, magnitude, depth, and tsunami potential. By combining GPS data on the earth's permanent displacement with seismic data, researchers can determine the magnitude of an earthquake more accurately and predict the likelihood of an ensuing tsunami. NASA started working with NOAA's Tsunami Warning Centers to evaluate the new technology for potential additional application in NOAA's tsunami early warning system.

Becoming familiar with public information and warning systems is an essential activity in advancing mitigation. Receiving alerts ahead of an event enables people to take action to reduce the potential damage to themselves and their homes. Early warning systems also help first responders by giving them additional time to prepare and prioritize before an incident occurs.

The Federal Government has also made progress in developing new technologies for monitoring droughts and floods. In February 2016, NOAA's National Integrated Drought Information System launched new drought early warning systems in the Pacific Northwest and the Midwest. NOAA worked with state, local, and tribal partners in each region to develop these systems, which make climate projections and drought forecasting data readily available to local decision-makers. NOAA also released the Nation's first-ever national water forecast tool, which provides more accurate, detailed, and frequent information on water levels and the potential for areas to flood. The new tool models water movement in the Nation's rivers and streams, improving the ability to predict extreme flooding events. Whereas previous capabilities confined NOAA's water forecasting potential to 4,000 locations every few hours, this model extended that number by nearly seven-hundredfold. The tool provides hourly forecasts for the entire river network at 2.7 million locations. This can especially benefit emergency managers in flash-flood areas by giving them advance warning of at-risk areas to notify or evacuate.

MITIGATION CASE STUDY:
FEMA APP

In 2016, FEMA launched a new feature for the FEMA app that enables users to receive automatic notifications to their devices, reminding them to take steps to prepare their homes and families for disasters. The reminder feature allows users to receive pre-scheduled safety and preparedness tips, including updating emergency kits, testing smoking alarms, and practicing a fire escape plan. Additionally, the FEMA app—available in English and Spanish—provides emergency tips for what to do before, during, and after a disaster; interactive checklists for emergency kits; the ability to store emergency meeting locations; maps to nearby open shelters; and National Weather Service alerts for severe weather, flash flooding, and other hazards.

In October 2016 (the month when Hurricane Matthew made landfall in the United States), Apple users downloaded the FEMA App more than 85,000 times, quadrupling the previous record of 20,000 downloads the week after Hurricane Sandy in 2012. Since its creation in 2011, more than 800,000 downloads of the FEMA app on Android and Apple devices have occurred (as of December 2016). Users have credited FEMA app alerts with helping them avoid flash flooding, as well as actively monitor hazards.

Federal departments, the private sector, and industry groups have launched new efforts to improve understanding of the value of stronger building codes and to increase their adoption.

Throughout 2016, Federal departments and agencies developed new tools and policies to increase the adoption of building codes that lessen the impacts of natural hazard events. The U.S. Army Corps of Engineers (USACE) created a website promoting community resilience through the use of the latest standards, building codes, and climate science. The website is a comprehensive resource for planners and designers to learn how to improve building integrity and resilience. In addition, FEMA issued a new policy in 2016 that requires the use of hazard-resistant building codes as the minimum design standard for building restoration projects under the Public Assistance Program. Requiring recipients of this funding to incorporate hazard-resistant design standards for their building projects will enhance infrastructure resilience in jurisdictions that lack effective building codes. In September 2016, FEMA also issued a new disaster risk reduction policy that requires all FEMA offices and programs to encourage their stakeholders to adopt and enforce hazard-resistant building codes, standards, and provisions.

Building industry stakeholders have also taken steps to encourage the adoption of stronger building codes. For example, as part of its Urban Resilience Program, the Urban Land Institute created Returns on Resilience, an online resource that helps communities build more disaster-resistant homes and buildings. Additionally, the Insurance Institute for Business and Home Safety (IBHS) released a mobile application ("FORTIFIED Home On The Go") to educate homeowners about how to build safer, stronger structures in the face of severe weather events. IBHS also launched incident-specific nationwide programs to help owners implement home improvement projects that increase the resilience of their houses against wind storms and hail storms.

MITIGATION CASE STUDY:
TSUNAMI SAFE HAVEN

After a tsunami devastated Japan's northeast coast in 2011, the Ocosta School District Board of Directors in Westport, Washington, decided to improve their community's tsunami preparedness. In May 2016, the Ocosta School District—with support from Washington State's Project Safe Haven initiative, private-sector partners, and community members—completed construction of a new elementary school that includes a vertical-evacuation safe haven above the gymnasium. This is the first tsunami safe haven of its kind in North America, capable of holding approximately 2,000 people. Since its completion, the school has conducted several tsunami evacuation drills with its students. In addition, as part of a state exercise on June 11, the Washington National Guard demonstrated how they could use helicopters to rescue people from the safe haven.

Key Finding:

FEMA is improving the oversight, accountability, and sustainability of the NFIP to better help insurance policyholders reduce future risk.

In the wake of Hurricane Sandy, residents of affected states expressed concerns that the private insurance companies that implement the NFIP underpaid their claims. In response, FEMA requested that the DHS Office of the Inspector General audit the NFIP's Write Your Own (WYO) program—the cooperative arrangement that allows private insurance companies to write and service NFIP policies under their own names. The DHS Office of the Inspector General published a report in March 2016 concluding that FEMA had not sufficiently monitored the reimbursement or appeals process. Therefore, FEMA could not ensure that WYO companies were properly implementing the NFIP. To address these challenges, FEMA announced several improvements to the program in 2016, including:

- *Removing the NFIP's Financial Assistance/Subsidy Arrangement with WYO companies to provide greater flexibility and governance in the future;*
- *Providing customers in the appeals process with a contact at FEMA (previously, customers could only communicate with their private insurance company); and*
- *Establishing a team within the FEMA Office of Chief Counsel to monitor all lawsuits and oversee all legal bill payments.*

FEMA is also taking new steps to strengthen the NFIP's financial framework. Payouts to claims from major flooding events—including those resulting from Hurricanes Katrina, Ike, and Sandy—have left the NFIP $23 billion in debt (as of December 31, 2016), requiring the program to pay nearly $400 million per year in interest payments to the U.S. Department of the Treasury on the borrowed funds. FEMA is attempting to defray the cost of claims from large and unexpected events and expand its ability to cover these claims by purchasing reinsurance—a form of insurance for insurance providers—from a number of private companies.

In addition, maintaining a balance between the solvency of the NFIP and the affordability of its policies has been an ongoing challenge. Although most NFIP insurance policies have insurance rates that reflect the true flood risk, Congress instituted premium discounts for certain classes of policies. Recent reform legislation directed the NFIP to phase out some of these discounts to increase revenue and improve the program's fiscal stability. However, FEMA still hears concerns about the perceived high cost of flood insurance and about the accuracy of flood maps and insurance rates. As directed by Congress in recent legislation, FEMA is studying flood insurance affordability and providing recommendations for an affordability framework to Congress by September 2017.

Homeland Security 2017 National Preparedness Report

Despite these challenges, the NFIP successfully executed the flood insurance components of FEMA's mission to support several flooding incidents in 2016. In addition to providing WYO companies further guidance through bulletins, FEMA website updates, and public fact sheets associated with each event, NFIP also issued advanced payments to provide expedited relief to survivors, coordinated with State Insurance Commissioners and WYO companies to ensure policyholder needs were being met, deployed staff to support field operations, and provided analytical support to stakeholders making resource decisions. In addition, the NFIP closed over three-quarters of claims resulting from three significant flood events—Hurricane Matthew, Hurricane Hermine, and the August Louisiana floods—within a few months. This demonstrates the progress that NFIP has made in more efficiently helping policyholders impacted by recent events recover.

Federal and state actors are taking steps to address human-induced earthquakes, which are contributing to an overall increase in seismic hazards in the central United States and present threats to infrastructure and people.

Human-induced earthquakes, such as those caused by reinjecting wastewater into the ground during oil and natural gas extraction, are partially responsible for an increase in earthquakes in the central United States. Between 1973 and 2008, the

average number of earthquakes of magnitude 3 or higher each year for this region was 24. In 2015, the number of earthquakes peaked at 1,010. While these induced earthquakes have been of smaller magnitude, they can still create seismic hazards to important structures. Oklahoma, for example, experienced a 5.8 earthquake in 2016, which was the largest earthquake in its history. The structural damage from the 5.8 magnitude earthquake was substantial enough for the state's governor to declare a state of emergency for Pawnee County and for the Oklahoma Corporation Commission, which regulates and supervises activities associated with the production of oil and gas, to shut down all reinjection wells within 725 square miles of the earthquake's epicenter. Earthquakes present a particularly serious threat to oil and natural gas infrastructure in Oklahoma, which contains about five percent of the Nation's pipeline mileage (the third-highest percentage of any individual state).

In 2016, USGS published its first hazard maps to include both natural and human-induced seismic risks. Also for the first time, the maps address earthquake hazards on a one-year timeline—which is unique to induced earthquakes, where changes in policy or industry activity can directly affect their frequency. The new forecasts enable emergency response personnel to better assess risks to people and infrastructure and to issue safety information, if necessary. The maps highlight risks from induced earthquakes for approximately seven million people in areas of the central and eastern United States. Oklahoma and Texas have the largest populations exposed to induced earthquakes.

Kansas has also responded to the threat of human-induced earthquakes. In March 2015, the state commission responsible for regulating oil and gas production issued an order that required oil and gas companies to reduce their saltwater injection rates in counties that had experienced recent increases in seismic activity. During a 180-day period before the commission's order, two counties experienced 107 earthquakes of magnitude 2.5 or greater. This decreased to 65 in the 180 days after the order. Whether the order resulted in the reduced seismic activity remains inconclusive, but in August 2016, the commission issued another order to reduce saltwater injection rates to an expanded geographical area.

Homeland Security 2017 National Preparedness Report

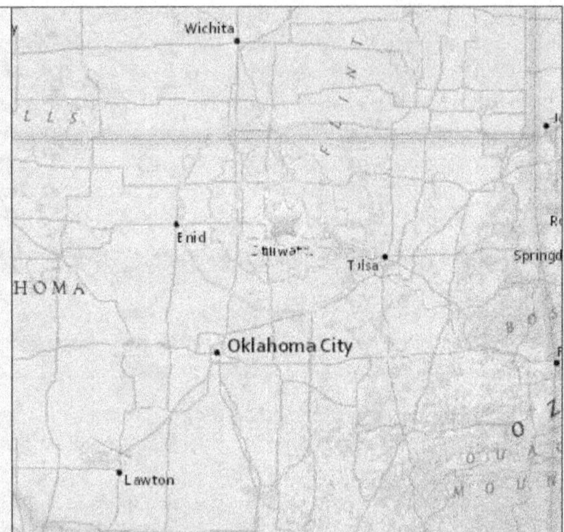

MITIGATION CASE STUDY: REDUCING THE LIKELIHOOD OF HUMAN-INDUCED EARTHQUAKES IN OKLAHOMA

Oklahoma has taken steps to reduce the consequences of human-induced earthquakes. In January 2016, the Governor allocated $1.4 million in state emergency funds to earthquake research and regulation activities by the Oklahoma Geological Survey and the Oklahoma Corporation Commission. The Oklahoma Geological Survey plans to use this funding to improve its ability to collect and analyze earthquake data, while the Oklahoma Corporation Commission used it to direct wells operating in the northwest portion of the state to reduce wastewater reinjection by approximately 40 percent. However, the commission's authority to mandate compliance is unclear, and the state has explored non-regulatory options to mitigate this hazard.

Key Finding:

Coastal communities, including tribal communities, are exploring relocation options to address the growing risks posed by extreme weather events, including sea level rise and coastal erosion.

Increasing sea levels can cause storm surge to push farther inland, leading to more frequent and widespread flooding of coastal areas. Destructive flooding has increased by as much as 900 percent over the past five decades, and a recent study found that 4.2 million people in the continental United States will be at risk of inundation by the year 2100.

For the first time, in 2016 the Federal Government allocated funds to the State of Louisiana to move the entire Isle de Jean community in response to these threats. Louisiana is relocating the entire Isle de Jean Charles community, which is also home to the Band of Biloxi-Chitimacha-Choctaw Indians, to higher ground using a $48 million grant from the National Disaster Resilience Competition. The island has lost 98 percent of its landmass to coastal erosion and sea level rise in the past 60 years. In 1955, the island was five miles wide; in 2016, it was a quarter-of-a-mile wide. The Quinault Indian Nation in Washington State is also developing a master plan to move their main village to higher ground. Taholah, one of the tribal nation's two main population centers, is particularly vulnerable to flooding, coastal erosion, and increasing storm events, since it is located at the confluence of the Pacific Ocean and the Quinault River. In addition, tribal villages in coastal regions of Alaska have begun exploring the option of relocating their communities. The Alaska Division of Community and Regional Affairs established multi-agency planning groups (i.e., Village Planning Groups) with the tribal villages of Shishmaref and Kivalina. Both tribal villages are suffering from land loss due to erosion and increasingly severe coastal flooding.

In 2016, the Community Resilience Working Group, co-chaired by HUD and the U.S. Department of the Interior (DOI), enhanced Federal collaboration to assist these villages. GAO reports have identified 31 villages at risk from coastal erosion and flooding, including those mentioned above.

Key Finding:

As studies predict that drought conditions will persist and intensify, new efforts to fully understand and reduce the long-term consequences of drought have emerged.

Recent research predicts that rising average temperatures will amplify and prolong drought conditions in the future. A March

2016 report from the DOI's Bureau of Reclamation (USBR) estimates that by the end of the 21st century, the United States will experience a temperature increase of five to seven degrees Fahrenheit. Increasing temperatures diminish snowpack, reduce stream flows, and limit the availability of water, further intensifying drought conditions. In addition, the report found that the April to July stream flows of several major river basins in the West will decrease between seven and 27 percent.

The Federal Government has taken the lead on addressing the threat that drought poses to the Nation. In March 2016, *Presidential Memorandum: Building National Capabilities for Long-Term Drought Resilience* formally institutionalized the National Drought Resilience Partnership (NDRP), a Federal partnership of seven departments and agencies tasked with helping communities better prepare for future droughts and reduce the impact of drought events. An accompanying Federal Action Plan identifies specific goals and associated actions for the NDRP to improve resilience to drought. In response, the NDRP completed efforts and launched new ones in 2016 to understand the long-term impacts of drought:

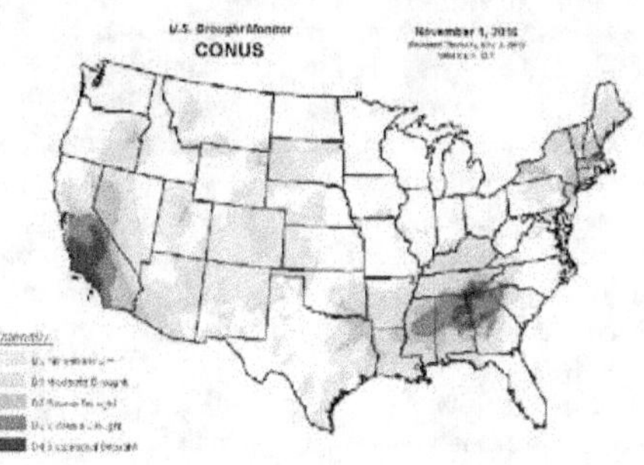

- *NDRP partners are working with The Ohio State University and other private and public partners to develop a national soil moisture monitoring network, which will facilitate more comprehensive and accurate drought impact assessments.*
- *A U.S. Department of Agriculture (USDA) Forest Service (USFS) study on the consequences of drought for forests found that more frequent droughts could lead to larger wildfires, a higher probability of large-scale insect outbreaks, and reduced forest growth. The report also includes data that land managers can use for measuring the effectiveness of and building upon their drought resilience and climate adaptation efforts.*
- *To help states understand the economic impacts of drought, DHS is developing three reports that explain drought's effects on infrastructure operations that are critical to state economies. Two of the reports will identify how California's drought affected data center and manufacturing operations. The third report will focus on how drought has affected thermoelectric power plant operations in California and Texas. DHS plans to develop the reports' findings into decision-support guides for stakeholders making decisions on how to accommodate competing water needs during droughts.*
- *USGS, the Nature Conservancy, and the Wildlife Conservation Society formed the Ecological Drought Working Group to assess the ecological impacts of drought and its implications for human well-being, in order to help communities prepare for and adapt to the effects of drought.*

NDRP members also reported recent activities that aim to strengthen drought resilience over the coming years:

- *The USDA and USBR are investing $47 million to support local water management projects and agricultural water-use efficiency across 11 states in the West.*
- *USDA's Natural Resources Conservation Service (NRCS) allocated $1.1 million towards local drought mitigation projects in the Missouri Headwaters Basin in Montana.*
- *The USBR began five pilot studies exploring how reservoir operations can adapt to the impacts of climate change. The pilots, which will end in December 2017, study water sources in the Great Plains, the Mid-Pacific, the Pacific Northwest, and the Upper and Lower Colorado regions. Based on these pilots, USBR is developing guidance to identify and implement improvements to reservoir operations by considering improved scientific information, enhancing existing operational flexibility, and planning for changes to reservoir operations under drought conditions.*
- *The EPA and Montana's Department of Natural Resources, in partnership with other Federal and state agencies and nongovernmental organizations, launched a three-year demonstration project to enhance long-term drought resiliency in the Missouri headwaters basin by providing tools for drought monitoring, assessing, and forecasting; developing local and regional capacity to plan for drought; and implementing local projects to build regional drought resilience. The results will enhance local drought resilience and demonstrate how communities across the country can also mitigate drought.*

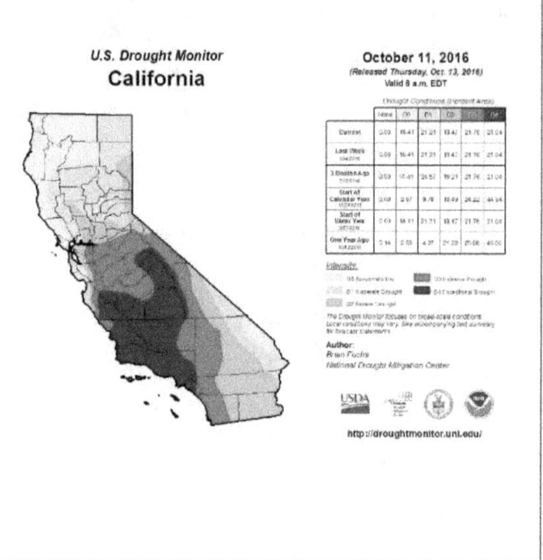

MITIGATION CASE STUDY: THE CALIFORNIA DROUGHT

Entering its sixth consecutive year of drought, California has been in a state of emergency since January 2014. As of October 11, 2016, 84 percent of the state is experiencing drought, and the remaining 16 percent is abnormally dry. However, California's water conservation efforts, such as refraining from hosing off sidewalks and reducing runoff while watering lawns, have shown promising results. Between June 2015 and March 2016, California communities reduced water use by nearly 24 percent, which could provide 6.5 million Californians with enough water to last a year. In May 2016, Governor Brown issued an executive order directing state agencies and the public to use water more wisely, eliminate water waste, strengthen local drought resilience, increase the efficiency of agricultural water use, and improve drought planning. Through these requirements, the order aims to transition drought mitigation in California from temporary to permanent activities.

Wildfire suppression costs have risen rapidly over the past few decades, mainly due to longer and more severe fire seasons. According to USFS, fire seasons are now, on average, approximately 78 days longer than in 1970, and USFS expects this trend of longer fire seasons and increasing fire suppression costs to continue over the next decade. Between fiscal years 2014 and 2015, the USFS suppression budget grew by $115 million and the budget for non-fire programs that reduce the risk of future wildfires—such as forest restoration projects—fell by the same amount.

Forest restoration projects can play an important role in helping to minimize the risk of wildfires by thinning forests and reducing vegetation that fuels them. Private and nonprofit organizations have helped bolster Federal initiatives for wildfire risk reduction projects in 2016. For example:

- *In June 2016, USFS and NRCS announced a partnership with the American Forest Foundation to address wildfire risk across 3.5 million acres of land in the western United States and provided a combined initial investment of $5 million to fund forest restoration projects and public engagement. A portion of the funds will enable the American Forest Foundation to conduct outreach and education to 17,500 landowners in important watersheds. The remainder of the funds will provide cost-share dollars directly to landowners in one of the project landscapes. The partnership's goal in the first two years is to restore more than 11,000 acres of land.*

- *As in 2015, DOI committed $10 million in 2016 to 10 Wildland Fire Resilient Landscapes (WFRL) "Collaboratives," to improve the integrity and wildfire resilience of forests and rangelands nationwide. WFRL Collaboratives consist of partnerships among Federal, tribal, state, and local governments, private landowners, and nonprofit organizations. Employing integrated land management techniques and pooling their resources, WFRL Collaboratives restore native vegetation and modify or remove vegetative fuels to support fire resilience and landscape management objectives. During 2015 and 2016, the WFRL Collaboratives accomplished 930,000 acres of landscape-level treatments.*

- *Blue Forest Conservation—a team of financial and engineering professionals—is working with USFS, other USDA agencies, and nonprofit partners to develop and pilot the Forest Resilience Bond in California. This new investment platform will deploy private capital to accelerate forest restoration projects in watersheds. The bond enables the beneficiaries of these projects (e.g., water utilities) to repay investors over a 10-year period to help defray the financial burden.*

2016 Preparedness Campaigns

FEMA estimates that as of 2016, **less than a quarter of Americans have attended preparedness meetings or trainings.** Eighteen percent of respondents to the 2015 National Household Survey reported attending a meeting on how to become better prepared for a disaster within the last year. This is a decrease of five percentage points from 2012. To improve this trend, both public and private stakeholders used **more accessible media to promote individual and household preparedness** in 2016.

The Oregon Office of Emergency Management worked with a graphic novel publishing company to produce **a comic book touting tsunami preparedness** targeted towards younger audiences.

As part of National Preparedness Month, **the popular video recipe website Tastemade** partnered with FEMA to develop preparedness products designed to leverage the popularity of the online recipe video trend.

20th Century Fox and Blue Sky Studios partnered with Save the Children to launch a new emergency preparedness public service announcement (PSA) campaign featuring characters from the feature film **"Ice Age: Collision Course."**

FEMA's Ready Campaign and the Ad Council demonstrated how **"Being Ready Can Be Scary Simple"** in a series of videos that encourage families to prepare for emergencies by discussing emergency contacts and packing go bags.

The USFS, the Ad Council, and the National Association of State Foresters launched **a new Smokey Bear PSA campaign** to promote awareness about how to avoid accidentally starting a wildfire.

For the first time, the Ready Campaign released their "Don't Wait. Communicate. Make Your Emergency Plan Now" national **PSA in Mandarin Chinese—** the third most-spoken language in the United States.

MITIGATION CASE STUDY: YOUTH PREPAREDNESS

Promoting emergency preparedness at an early age contributes to overall individual preparedness. Examples of age-appropriate programs that engage youth to be better prepared for disasters include:

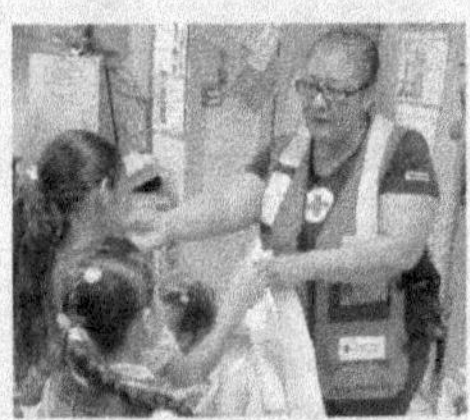

- **The Pillowcase Project:** *In 2013, the American Red Cross partnered with the Walt Disney Company to launch the Pillowcase Project, a nationwide program that teaches elementary school students how to prepare for and stay safe during disasters. As of September 2016, this program has reached more than 500,000 students, teaching 3rd–5th graders how to create their own emergency supply kit by packing essential items in a pillowcase for easy transport during an emergency. Since its inception, the program has helped save at least six lives from house fires. By sharing the information with their families and following what they had learned through the Pillowcase Project, students were able to help save their loved ones and themselves.*

- **FEMA Youth Preparedness Council:** *As children grow older, they have opportunities to improve the resilience of not just their families, but also their communities. The FEMA Youth Preparedness Council consists of high school students who serve as national advocates of youth preparedness. In 2016, a FEMA Region IX council member organized the 2016 Service Learning, Youth and Community Preparedness Summit as part of her ongoing efforts to strengthen community resilience in Guam. During the summit, local students developed emergency plans for a variety of hazards, including earthquakes, typhoons, and tsunamis.*

- **ReadyCampus:** *For college students, experiencing disasters while in school can cause difficulties as they are no longer under the protection of their parents or guardians. To address this vulnerability, FEMA Region VII released an updated version of its ReadyCampus Development Guide in 2016 for institutions of higher education. ReadyCampus is a student-focused program that helps these institutions develop and implement their own actionable, adaptable, and scalable preparedness programs. As of fall 2016, 11 institutes of higher education within Region VII are using the development guide and promoting positive interactions between students, campus and local emergency management, and public safety officials. These activities not only enhance understanding of campus emergency procedures and available resources, but also increase awareness about emergency management as a career path for college students.*

Focused on ensuring that the Nation is able to respond effectively to all types of incidents, including those of catastrophic proportion that require marshalling the capabilities of the entire Nation

CORE CAPABILITIES IN PRACTICE

The Response mission is to save lives, protect property and the environment, and meet basic human needs after an incident. The National Response Framework describes 15 core capabilities, including how they guide the Nation's response to disasters and emergencies.

To effectively respond to an incident, emergency management officials and responders implement tasks, as identified through **Planning** efforts. They use **Operational Coordination** to ensure that tasks are carried out in an organized fashion. Through **Public Information and Warning**, officials deliver clear, actionable, and accessible information about relevant threats and hazards to the community. **Operational Communications** enable emergency managers and responders to exchange critical information promptly and efficiently. Throughout the response, decision-makers use **Situational Assessment** to understand the extent and nature of the hazard, which supports informed decisions.

For those survivors who may be immobilized or trapped, trained personnel conduct **Mass Search and Rescue Operations** to locate and rescue these individuals. For incidents involving fires, **Fire Management and Suppression** efforts may also be necessary to save and protect lives, as well as property and the environment. When a large number of fatalities occur, **Fatality Management Services** recover the deceased and share information to help reunify families.

During the response, **Environmental Response/Health and Safety** operations and **On-scene Security, Protection, and Law Enforcement** protect both response workers and the public. Public, private, and community-based organizations provide **Public Health, Healthcare, and Emergency Medical Services** and **Mass Care Services** to address the needs of survivors, including those with access and functional needs, such as children, individuals with disabilities, older adults, and

CORE CAPABILITIES IN THE RESPONSE MISSION AREA

- Critical Transportation
- Environmental Response/Health and Safety
- Fatality Management Services
- Fire Management and Suppression
- Infrastructure Systems
- Logistics and Supply Chain Management
- Mass Care Services
- Mass Search and Rescue Operations
- On-scene Security, Protection, and Law Enforcement
- Operational Communications
- Operational Coordination
- Planning
- Public Health, Healthcare, and Emergency Medical Services
- Public Information and Warning
- Situational Assessment

persons with limited English proficiency. Moreover, officials use **Critical Transportation** and **Logistics and Supply Chain Management** to ensure that affected communities receive essential commodities and services. This aids owners and operators of **Infrastructure Systems** in restoring and revitalizing systems and services for the community.

The following are examples of actions taken in 2016 to improve preparedness that highlight the relationships among a select number of the 15 core capabilities in the National Response Framework:

❑ Operational Communications and Public Information and Warning

The Integrated Public Alert and Warning System (IPAWS) enables public safety officials to issue alerts and quickly provide the public with life-saving information. From a single interface, officials can access various public alerting systems, such as the Emergency Alert System, Wireless Emergency Alerts, and NOAA's All Hazards Weather Radio. As of December 2016, all 50 states have adopted IPAWS; in total, 851 public safety organizations—including two territories, the District of Columbia, two tribes, and two Federal agencies—have received access.

Additionally, FEMA and the Federal Communications Commission (FCC) conducted the second nationwide test of the Emergency Alert System in September 2016. The test demonstrated the readiness of radio and television broadcast stations, cable operators, and other Emergency Alert System participants to receive and broadcast a national-level emergency message to the public. In the 2016 test, 95 percent of all participating broadcasters, cable operators, and other Emergency Alert System particpants received the national test message, representing a significant improvement over the first national test in 2011 (at 82 percent). Moreover, the 2016 test message was the first time that a national test message was presented in multiple languages, including both English and Spanish.

❑ Planning and Public Health, Healthcare, and Emergency Medical Services

On September 8, 2016, HHS's Centers for Medicare & Medicaid Services finalized a rule requiring healthcare providers and suppliers participating in Medicare and Medicaid to meet four emergency preparedness best practice standards. Affecting more than 72,000 healthcare providers and suppliers, the rule requires them to develop emergency plans and coordinate with Federal, regional, state, local, tribal, and territorial stakeholders. These more comprehensive requirements help ensure that facilities are sufficiently prepared to provide and coordinate patient care during disasters and emergency situations. Providers and suppliers affected by this rule must comply by November 16, 2017.

In addition, CDC has released multiple guidance documents, for Zika and for many other infectious threats. For example, CDC recently released a review of biologic threat preparedness for pregnant women. To help deal with the challenge of Zika, CDC developed nine clinical guidance documents for healthcare providers caring for patients with Zika. CDC and the Centers for Medicare & Medicaid Services also collaborated on Zika healthcare funding and performance metrics.

❑ Environmental Response/Health and Safety and Planning

Few, if any, states have established pre-incident waste management plans (PI-WMPs) to address the potential waste generated from wide-area urban incidents involving chemical, biological, or radiological threat agents. Responding to such incidents without a PI-WMP can increase the overall cost and timeline of response and recovery efforts.

- *EPA—in collaboration with states and local agencies and first responders—is developing a PI-WMP tool, an initial version of which is ready for testing. The tool, which incorporates the latest EPA knowledge and research, assists emergency management planners and others in building their own PI-WMP.*

- *EPA collaborated with New York City's Department of Mental Health and Hygiene and New York state agencies to develop guidance that provides tactical solutions and strategies for responding to a wide-area biological incident taking place in New York City.*

- *EPA worked with Virginia's Departments of Emergency Management and Environmental Quality to develop the first-ever PI-WMP for a subway system, which was used to address waste generated during a field test that evaluated the response to a biological incident.*

SUMMARY OF PROGRESS

The Response mission area continues to be an area of relative strength nationwide. Real-world incidents in 2016 provide validation of capability progress, as captured in several of this section's key findings. In addition, states and territories reported higher-than-average proficiency for eight Response core capabilities, making Response the mission area with the highest levels of proficiency for the fifth consecutive year.[7]

Response efforts during the August Louisiana flooding, the Zika virus outbreak, and Hurricane Matthew highlighted specific strengths in **Mass Search and Rescue; Operational Coordination;** and **Public Health, Healthcare, and Emergency Medical Services,** while revealing challenges in delivering **Mass Care Services.** Training and exercises occurring across the

---

[7] Unless otherwise noted, figures and statements do not include contributions from the three core capabilities common to all mission areas—i.e., Planning, Operational Coordination, and Public Information and Warning.

Nation further demonstrate the extensive preparedness activities underway in this mission area. For example, 84 of the 98 exercises conducted under FEMA's NEP in 2016 addressed one or more Response core capabilities (50 more exercises than the next highest mission area). Five of the 10 capabilities most frequently selected as a high priority were in the Response mission area. Even so, **Fatality Management Services, Infrastructure Systems, Logistics and Supply Chain Management,** and **Mass Care Services** exhibited below-average levels of proficiency in 2016 State Preparedness Report responses (see Figure 10). Though states and territories reported a five percent increase in **Fatality Management Services** from 2015 (the largest increase of all core capabilities), **Infrastructure Systems, Logistics and Supply Chain Management,** and **Mass Care Services** all declined in proficiency from last year.

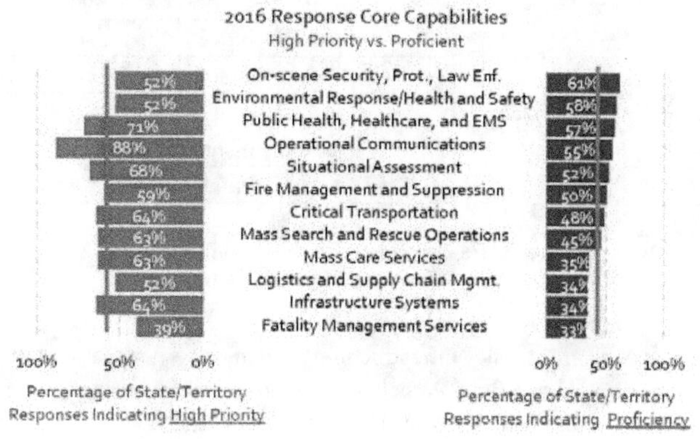

Notes: Vertical red lines (|) indicate the average ratings for all core capabilities. The chart and statements do not include contributions from the three cross-cutting core capabilities— Planning, Operational Coordination, and Public Information and Warning

Figure 10. In their 2016 State Preparedness Report responses, states and territories provided information on their high priority core capabilities, as well as ratings on core capability proficiency.

Table 6 lists the most frequently identified "functional area" gap for each Response core capability, as selected by states and territories in their 2016 State Preparedness Report submissions. Functional areas break down core capabilities into more granular-level functions, which were identified from an analysis of the Goal, the National Response Framework, and other national-level preparedness doctrine.

Table 6. In their 2016 State Preparedness Report responses, states and territories identified remaining gaps in their ability to accomplish various functions associated with each Response core capability.

Most Frequently Identified Functional Area Gap in Each Response Capability	
Core Capability*	Gap
Critical Transportation	Evacuation
Environmental Response/Health and Safety	Health and safety monitoring and assessment
Fatality Management Services	Mortuary services
Fire Management and Suppression	Specialized firefighting
Infrastructure Systems	Infrastructure site assessments
Logistics and Supply Chain Management**	Donations management
	Resource delivery

Most Frequently Identified Functional Area Gap in Each Response Capability	
Core Capability[*]	Gap
Mass Care Services	Sheltering
Mass Search and Rescue Operations	Specialized operations
On-scene Security, Protection, and Law Enforcement	Securing disaster areas
Operational Communications	Interoperable communications between first responders
Operational Coordination[**]	Command, control, and coordination
	Establishing a common operating picture
Planning	Whole community involvement and cooperation
Public Health, Healthcare, and Emergency Medical Services	Medical surge
Public Information and Warning	New communication tools and technologies
Situational Assessment	Analyzing information

[*] For core capabilities that cut across two or more mission areas, the 2016 State Preparedness Report did not include separate data requests that were specific to each mission area. Gaps identified for these core capabilities are identical for the different mission areas.
[**] The top-two functional area gaps were tied in terms of how frequently they were selected.

The 2017 *National Preparedness Report* identifies **Infrastructure Systems** as a national area for improvement (see page 12). Additionally, three core capabilities specific to Response—**Environmental Response/Health and Safety**, **Operational Communications**, and **Situational Assessment**—are capabilities to sustain in this year's report (see page 11).

BY THE NUMBERS

THE FEMA OFFICE OF DISABILITY INTEGRATION AND COORDINATION TRAINED 650 INDIVIDUALS

In 2016, FEMA's Office of Disability Integration and Coordination delivered its two-day course, "Integrating Access and Functional Needs into Emergency Planning," 25 times to a total of approximately 650 individuals, which included emergency planners and managers, as well as disability support, service, and advocacy personnel. The course informs participants on how to use disability-inclusive practices throughout emergency response and recovery.

ASPR IDENTIFIED FOUR CAPABILITIES AND 17 ASSOCIATED OBJECTIVES FOR THE HEALTHCARE DELIVERY SYSTEM

In November 2016, ASPR released *2017–2022 Health Care Preparedness and Response Capabilities*, which identifies four capabilities and 17 associated high-level objectives that the Nation's healthcare delivery system should undertake to prepare for, respond to, and recover from emergencies. Recipients of Hospital Preparedness Program (HPP) funding will implement these capabilities starting with the July 2017 HPP project period.

THE U.S. FIRE ADMINISTRATION DELIVERED 3,466 COURSES

In fiscal year 2016, the U.S. Fire Administration's National Fire Academy delivered 3,466 courses and trained 99,636 students in preparedness subjects, including Incident Management, Hazardous Materials Response, and Mass Casualty Incident Management.

Homeland Security 2017 National Preparedness Report

EMERGENCY PREPAREDNESS IN CHICAGO CHILD CARE CENTERS

In 2016, the City of Chicago, FEMA, HHS, and the American Red Cross of Greater Chicago held a four-part workshop series on emergency preparedness for child care center directors and employees. More than 40 child care directors from Chicago attended the workshops to review ways of better preparing their facilities for emergencies, plan escape routes, and draft action plans to use community resources during an emergency.

COLUMBIA RIVER GORGE INLAND SPILL EXERCISE SERIES

This exercise series consisted of national, regional, and principal-level, discussion-based exercises that addressed a fictional crude oil spill in the Columbia River. An incident similar to the exercise scenario later occurred on June 3 in Mosier, Oregon, in which 16 railcars carrying crude oil derailed along the Columbia River. Participation in the exercise series resulted in enhanced response coordination among state, local, and tribal organizations, as well as the railroad industry, during the actual spill.

WIRELESS NETWORK RESILIENCY COOPERATIVE FRAMEWORK

In April 2016, five wireless service providers and the Cellular Telecommunications Industry Association announced the Wireless Network Resiliency Cooperative Framework, a voluntary initiative that enhances industry collaboration through various actions (e.g., encouraging mutual aid between service providers, coordinating service restoration). After working with wireless service providers to test the framework during the August Louisiana floods and Hurricane Matthew, where it contributed to rapid restoration of wireless communications, FCC adopted the framework in December 2016.

PREPAREDNESS INDICATORS

Cumulative number of PSAPs ready to receive text-to-911 messages

With an estimated 70 percent of 911 calls made from cell phones, FCC encourages 911 emergency call centers to accept text messages from mobile phones or devices in addition to voice calls. Before 2014, none of the Nation's PSAPs (i.e., emergency call centers) were capable of receiving text-to-911 requests. This measure analyzes the cumulative number of new public safety answering points ready to receive text-to-911 requests. As of December 28, 2016, 754 of the Nation's 6,419 public safety answering points are ready to receive text-to-911 messages.

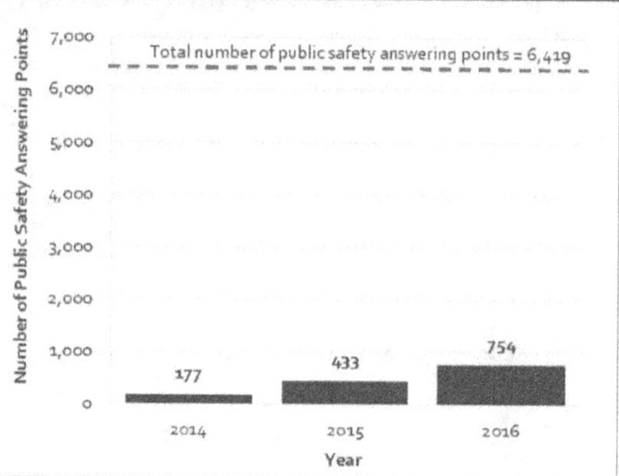

Percentage of people in imminent danger saved in the maritime environment

Each year, FEMA, the Air Force Rescue Coordination Center, the National Park Service, and the U.S. Coast Guard (USCG) collectively assign or carry out tens of thousands of rescue missions in urban, inland, and maritime/coastal environments. In particular, USCG serves as the Federal search and rescue coordinator for the maritime environment. This measure assesses the percentage of people in imminent danger saved each year by USCG. Though factors beyond USCG's control can lead to tragic outcomes, the percentage of people saved in fiscal year 2016 was 79.3 percent.

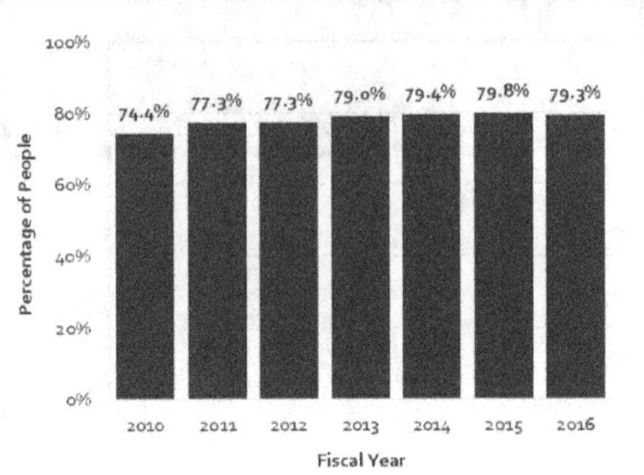

Homeland Security 2017 National Preparedness Report

Public- and private-sector partners are collaborating to advance diagnostics, case monitoring, and case management in response to the Zika virus outbreak.

As of December 28, 2016, CDC reported more than 39,700 cases of Zika virus infections in U.S. states and territories. While infected adults can experience no to mild, flu-like symptoms, Zika virus infection during pregnancy can cause serious birth defects. Federal, state, and local partners have worked to diagnose Zika cases, monitor infections in pregnant women and infants, and expand care for affected infants and families.

Diagnostic Tests: Federal agencies have collaborated with private research companies since the start of the outbreak to advance Zika diagnostic capabilities. Because no commercially available U.S. Food and Drug Administration (FDA)-approved diagnostic tests existed for the Zika virus disease before the current outbreak, FDA issued 14 Emergency Use Authorizations (as of December 12, 2016). These authorizations allow the use of unapproved Zika diagnostic tests during an emergency. To expedite diagnostic development, ASPR and BARDA coordinated the collection and sharing of blood samples from individuals infected with Zika with diagnostic companies to validate test performance. Furthermore, CDC purchased $2.5 million in supplies and equipment for laboratories in every state, the District of Columbia, Puerto Rico, and 16 DoD facilities to expand access to Zika testing. As of September 2016, only two states have not completed the process to be able to use the diagnostic test associated with the purchased materials. Before this purchase, local health departments that could not perform Zika testing had to send samples to CDC.

Safeguarding the U.S. Blood Supply Against Zika Virus

Because most people infected with the Zika virus do not show any symptoms, blood donors may be unaware that they are infected. Although no reported Zika virus transfusion–transmitted cases have occurred in the United States as of January 2017, documented cases of probable Zika virus transfusion–transmitted cases have occurred elsewhere (in Brazil). In addition to supporting diagnostic tests for Zika in individuals, BARDA is working on developing diagnostic tests that enable detection of the Zika virus in the blood supply. Although no FDA-licensed test for the Zika virus exists, FDA Investigational New Drug authorizations are allowing blood centers in all states to use these tests to screen donated blood. In addition, FDA-approved devices that can effectively reduce the amount of Zika virus in blood components (i.e., plasma, platelets) provide an alternative means of ensuring the safety of the U.S. blood supply.

Surveillance: To monitor the number of pregnant women with evidence of Zika virus infection and track infant outcomes, government agencies implemented various surveillance measures. The CDC created the U.S. Zika Pregnancy Registry to collect information from state, local, tribal, and territorial health departments (except for Puerto Rico) on pregnancy and infant outcomes following laboratory evidence of Zika virus infection during pregnancy. As the number of Zika virus cases is significantly higher in Puerto Rico, the Puerto Rico Department of Health worked with CDC to develop a similar Zika surveillance system, the Zika Active Pregnancy Surveillance System. The CDC uses the information from these surveillance systems to update clinical care recommendations, plan services for pregnant women and families affected by Zika virus, and improve prevention of infection during pregnancy.

Case Management: Public health agencies are working to expand awareness about the Zika virus and the issues associated with caring for infants affected by congenital Zika virus infection. Case management is particularly challenging for infants, since knowledge regarding the potential effects of Zika virus infection during pregnancy is limited. Nevertheless, HHS's Health Resources and Services Administration (HRSA) and ASPR both released planning resource guides, such as "Supporting Children with Special Healthcare Needs Planning Resource," which describe Federal and nonprofit services and programs for infants and children with special healthcare needs. These resources can help support the complex health needs of families affected by the Zika virus. CDC released interim guidance for doctors and healthcare providers on evaluating and providing care for pregnant women or infants with possible Zika virus infection, which will be updated as understanding of the virus evolves. CDC continuously engages with professional medical organizations to share any advancements in Zika virus knowledge.

Public- and private-sector partners are also involved in other efforts to improve care for children and families affected by the Zika virus, including:

- In May 2016, ASPR developed *Promoting Stress Management for Pregnant Women during the Zika Virus Disease Outbreak*, which includes strategies that healthcare providers can use to help their pregnant patients manage stress during a Zika virus update. ASPR also partnered with HHS's Office of Minority Health to produce a culturally appropriate, Spanish-language version of the document.

- HRSA awarded grants to Puerto Rico, the U.S. Virgin Islands, and American Samoa health departments to fund healthcare and support services for children and families affected by the Zika virus.

- HHS and the American Academy of Pediatrics are collaborating to provide technical assistance and education, including tele-mentoring and consultation, to clinicians in the United States, including Puerto Rico.

- The Puerto Rico Primary Care Association, in partnership with the Migrant Clinicians Network, is using a telecommunications platform to host monthly meetings with seven clinics across the territory for clinicians to collaborate and discuss how they are addressing problems with Zika diagnosis and treatment in their communities.

- Through a cooperative agreement, CDC has worked with the American Congress of Obstetricians and Gynecologists and the American Academy of Pediatrics to develop tools and resources (e.g., toolkits, videos) for healthcare providers and families.

- CDC has conducted surveys of providers to assess the understanding and uptake of clinical guidance.

- CDC has worked with many organizations during the public health response to Zika, including: the Society for Maternal-Fetal Medicine; the Infectious Diseases Society for Obstetrics and Gynecology; the American Academy of Family Physicians; the American Nurses Association; the Association of Women's Health, Obstetric and Neonatal Nurses; the Association of Maternal and Child Health Programs; the Association of State and Territorial Health Officials; the National Association of County and Health Officials; CityMatCH (the National Organization of Urban Maternal and Child Health Leaders); MotherToBaby; and Family Voices. In addition, CDC is closely working with the Centers for Medicare & Medicaid Services and HRSA.

- CDC has instituted a new local health department program that assigns individuals to local health departments to help with surveillance, outreach, and referral to care.

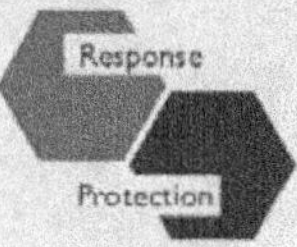

MISSION AREA CONNECTIONS

INFORMATION SHARING

The increasing pace and scale of global human movement is enhancing the potential spread and speed of disease transmission. In 2005, DHS signed a Memorandum of Understanding (MOU) to, among other forms of cooperation, share traveler information with HHS to prevent the introduction, transmission, and spread of serious communicable diseases in the United States. However, the MOU did not fully address the sharing of traveler information from HHS to DHS. During the 2014 Ebola virus epidemic, this became problematic when DHS needed quick information from HHS's CDC on potentially infected persons traveling to or arriving in the United States. To improve information sharing between DHS and HHS, the two departments signed a new MOU in 2017 to allow for the rapid provision of traveler information by HHS's CDC to DHS's CBP, when appropriate.

Evaluation of U.S. Capacities for Public Health Emergencies

In 2016, ASPR led 23 Federal agencies in a comprehensive self-assessment of U.S. capacities to detect, prevent, and respond to public health emergencies. An external, independent evaluation of those capacities by a multinational, multi-sectoral team of experts under the Framework of the International Health Regulations followed, which resulted in a report outlining strengths and areas for improvement. The Office of Policy and Planning within ASPR is coordinating the development of a strategic "roadmap" to address the health security gaps identified in the report; and working with Federal agencies to describe as many as 40 specific action plans that address the highest priority gaps. Over the next two to three years, the Office of Policy and Planning will continue to track progress on the action plans and prepare the U.S. Government to conduct another independent evaluation in 2020.

Key Finding:

Complex incidents that do not fall within the Stafford Act continue to challenge Federal response.

A Stafford Act declaration provides the legal authority for the Federal Government to provide specific forms of supplemental Federal assistance to jurisdictions during an emergency or major disaster that overwhelms state, local, tribal, and territorial governments. Most notably, a Stafford Act declaration triggers specific funding mechanisms, like the Disaster Relief Fund, which are otherwise unavailable to Federal agencies. In incidents that do not receive a Stafford Act declaration, there is no identified mechanism to fund the response, leaving agencies to seek funding solutions on an ad hoc basis. Although the lead Federal agency routinely handles incident response in a non-Stafford incident, the incident's scale, complexity, and implications may require coordinated Federal support across agencies. Examples include the 2012–2013 national drought, the 2014 influx of unaccompanied children across the Southwest border, the 2014 Ebola virus epidemic, the Flint Michigan Water Contamination, and the Zika virus outbreak. The 2015 *National Preparedness Report* detailed interagency coordination challenges in responding to non-Stafford Act events due to uncertainty regarding when, how, and under whose authority national-level coordination structures could be used.

Homeland Security 2017 National Preparedness Report

HHS Public Health Emergency Declaration for Zika Virus Outbreak

In 2016, the vast majority of Zika virus infections in the United States and its territories occurred in Puerto Rico. Consequently, on August 12, 2016, the Secretary of HHS declared a public health emergency for Puerto Rico. The public health emergency declaration allows HHS to award grants, access emergency funds, and temporarily appoint personnel. In a follow up to this declaration, HHS staffed a group of public health experts in Puerto Rico to coordinate Federal, state, and local response activities. Since HHS does not have a designated disaster fund, however, the effectiveness of the response was contingent on receiving additional appropriations from Congress, according to HHS. On November 4, 2016, the Secretary of HHS renewed the public health emergency declaration.

During the Zika virus outbreak, the Nation's early collaboration and application of National Response Framework coordination structures highlighted progress in managing a non-Stafford incident response. To address coordination challenges reported in previous responses, the President declared HHS as the lead Federal agency for managing both response and recovery activities. HHS's leadership role during the Zika virus outbreak, as well as the Flint water contamination crisis (see page 83), highlights its new and evolving responsibility to coordinate Federal efforts in the face of threats to national health security. Despite some initial confusion in response efforts, HHS (with ASPR acting as its lead representative) coordinated Federal agencies early in the Zika virus outbreak to efficiently support state and local response efforts. Beginning January 5, 2016 ASPR convened the Disaster Leadership Group for Zika response; this group brings together senior leaders from across the operating and staff divisions of HHS to discuss major policy decisions, align efforts, and maximize response resources. Since February 2016, a broader group of Federal agencies have coordinated efforts through the ASPR-led Zika Virus Task Force, which developed the *United States Government Zika Virus Disease Contingency Response Plan* to outline Federal agency roles and responsibilities in combatting the spread of Zika virus. In addition, ASPR extended the concept of a Unified Coordination Group—a National Response Framework coordination structure traditionally used in Stafford Act events—to synchronize, augment, and integrate ongoing Zika prevention and response activities. In Puerto Rico, the most severely affected U.S. jurisdiction, ASPR, FEMA, and other Federal agencies established the first-ever Unified Coordination Group in response to a biological incident. Based on lessons learned from the Zika virus outbreak, Federal agencies are refining the requirements and processes for establishing a Unified Coordination Group in non-Stafford incidents to improve future responses.

Lessons Learned from the 2014–2016 Ebola Virus Disease Epidemic

To strengthen the response to future biological incidents, Federal agencies are working to implement lessons learned from the Ebola virus epidemic. In June 2016, *The Report of the Independent Panel on the HHS Ebola Response* found that the United States was not prepared to respond to emergent crises that require a rapid, integrated domestic and international response; did not produce communications with an appreciation for the public's fear; and applied different policies at the Federal, state, and local level. In response to these findings, HHS published the *Ebola Response Improvement Plan* detailing actions the Department plans to take to improve preparedness and response efforts for future public health crises. HHS will release at least two reports in the next year to delineate progress on each active action item described in the plan.

Key Finding:

Some state and local jurisdictions are taking advantage of private-sector and nonprofit delivery mechanisms to address persistent challenges in dispensing medical countermeasures.

During a public health emergency, the Nation's largest supply of potentially life-saving pharmaceuticals and medical supplies for use in a public health emergency, the SNS, can quickly distribute large quantities of medical countermeasures to state, local, tribal, and territorial jurisdictions, which in turn dispense the countermeasures to affected populations. However, state and local authorities have identified challenges in delivering supplies to affected individuals during a public health emergency. These challenges include the public's unwillingness to place themselves at increased risk of exposure by going to a central site to receive countermeasures; potentially large crowds (and increased potential for exposure); and the inability of authorities to staff a more distributed approach to delivery.

To identify tools, plans, and resources that jurisdictions have implemented to address these challenges, ASPR led—in collaboration with CDC, DoD, and FEMA—six Medical Countermeasure Dispensing Planning Regional Summits in 2016. One best practice jurisdictions shared was using public-private partnerships. For example, Washington State developed and signed MOUs with over 400 pharmacies to use their existing infrastructure to dispense medical countermeasures during a public health emergency. In 2016, 83 percent of Washington residents lived within five miles of a participating pharmacy. More broadly, Federal agencies used best practices identified during the summits to inform a national virtual tabletop exercise, as well as to develop "Emerging Best Practices in Medical Countermeasures Dispensing," which is a training course available through the Emergency Management Institute.

Federal, state, and local governments have also begun coordinating with Meals on Wheels America to better assist individuals unable to travel to a pharmacy or dispensing site during future public health emergencies. In 2016, CDC collaborated with Meals on Wheels and state and local jurisdictions to develop standardized protocols and processes that jurisdictions can use to have Meals on Wheels deliver medical countermeasures to its existing clients. Several jurisdictions have already partnered with Meals on Wheels to support medical countermeasures dispensing, including counties in Maryland and North Carolina, and the states of Kansas, Oregon, and Massachusetts.

Federal agencies demonstrated their agility by anticipating and reacting to evolving response needs during Hurricane Matthew.

After Hurricane Matthew made landfall on October 4, 2016, in Haiti, the National Hurricane Center projected that Hurricane Matthew would hit the United States in Florida as a Category 4 storm and cause mass evacuations across the Southeast United States from Florida to South Carolina.

In light of the possible consequences of such an approaching storm, FEMA took numerous steps to ensure rapid support to affected communities. Although FEMA has prepositioned resources ahead of other storms, the agency took a faster approach toward deploying personnel in Hurricane Matthew than in response to previous storms. For example, on the day of the first Matthew-related major disaster declaration, FEMA had deployed 1,390 personnel to Florida, Georgia, North Carolina, and South Carolina, compared to slightly more than 600 staff deployed to potentially impacted states for Hurricane Sandy over a similar time period. In addition, FEMA prepositioned 2.8 million meals, 3 million liters of water, and 48,000 blankets.

Other Federal agencies and organizations mobilized or prepared resources prior to Hurricane Matthew's arrival:

- *USACE worked with FEMA to coordinate mission assignments four days prior to the storm's landfall. A mission assignment for temporary emergency power set ahead of the storm expedited the installation of 26 generators at damaged facilities after the storm.*
- *HHS deployed multiple teams and liaison officers to potentially impacted states. HHS also securely disclosed Federal health data from its emPOWER Initiative to support life-saving outreach efforts to more than 40,000 at-risk individuals with access and functional needs in Florida and North Carolina.*
- *DoD transported more than 120,000 gallons of gasoline and diesel fuel, 236,000 meals, and other commodities to military bases in Georgia and North Carolina, and set prepare-to-deploy orders for 21 search and rescue aircrafts and*

three teams in preparation for response and recovery activities.

- *With assistance from FEMA, the American Red Cross and other voluntary partners deployed 1,400 staff to support anticipated sheltering and feeding operations.*
- *In addition to having more than 100 AmeriCorps Disaster Response Team members on standby, AmeriCorps deployed 45 staff members to Emergency Operations Centers in Florida and 20 staff members to a special-needs shelter ahead of the storm.*

Federal departments and agencies adjusted their response posture and assigned deployment locations as Hurricane Matthew's forecasted track evolved. On October 8, Hurricane Matthew made landfall in South Carolina rather than in Florida, causing severe flooding and coastal damage to South Carolina, Georgia, and North Carolina. One day after Hurricane Matthew's landfall, FEMA and other Federal agencies significantly readjusted staff deployments so that the number of staff deployed to Florida and Georgia decreased to allow a robust deployment of staff to the affected areas of North and South Carolina. During this same period, though deliveries of essential commodities continued to Florida, Georgia, and South Carolina, FEMA increased its deliveries to North Carolina by 93 percent (compared to 68 percent in Florida) to adjust for the location of actual landfall.

NOAA Surveying Efforts Following Hurricane Matthew

In the aftermath of Hurricane Matthew, NOAA mobilized various surveying capabilities to assist in response efforts. NOAA's ship, the *Ferdinand R. Hassler*, and Navigation Response Teams provided rapid response surveys of the ports of Charleston, South Carolina, and Savannah, Georgia, that allowed ships to transit safely in and out of the ports. NOAA Office of Coast Survey staff also assisted USACE in completing surveys between pilot areas and USACE docks.

Additionally, NOAA's National Geodetic Survey (NGS) collected aerial oblique imagery along the East Coast from Key Largo, Florida, to Cape Henry, Virginia, and imagery over inland portions of South Carolina. Compared with traditional imagery, oblique imagery captures a wider area and provides visuals of the sides of buildings (as opposed to only the tops of buildings). In total, NGS collected 5,177 images (covering 1,230 square miles), which were used to assess damage to infrastructure and buildings, coastal hazards to navigation, and flood damage.

RESPONSE CASE STUDY: NORTH CAROLINA'S REAL-TIME FLOOD WARNING SYSTEM

North Carolina's Flood Inundation Mapping and Alert Network System integrates USGS and state-collected data to analyze, map, and communicate flood risks in real-time to emergency responders and the public. During Hurricane Matthew, the system developed detailed flood maps and projections of peak flood levels, based on National Weather Service flood forecast information, that helped local emergency responders plan transportation routes, state troopers identify the hardest-hit areas to support, and two prisons decide whether to evacuate. In total, the system received 3.7 million hits by potential users during this period.

Homeland Security 2017 National Preparedness Report

The whole community supported the response to the August flooding in Louisiana through both traditional and innovative practices, although mass care challenges remain.

In 2016, the United States experienced several severe flooding incidents. According to NOAA, four incidents each resulted in more than $1 billion in damages. In particular, the August flooding in Louisiana was the most damaging U.S. flood since Hurricane Sandy in 2012. Record rainfall amounts hit some areas over a period of less than 48 hours.

The sudden, swift-moving floodwaters trapped Louisiana residents in homes and cars, resulting in thousands needing rescue. In response, government agencies and volunteers conducted search and rescue operations that rescued 30,000 individuals, as well as thousands of pets. For example, the Louisiana National Guard deployed more than 3,800 Guardsmen and rescued more than 19,000 individuals and 2,660 pets. FEMA Urban Search & Rescue deployed 120 personnel and the Texas Urban Search & Rescue Task Force assessed 5,320 buildings and secured 17 caskets. Moreover, groups of local volunteers known as the "Cajun Navy" used their boats to rescue thousands of additional individuals trapped by floodwaters. FEMA Urban Search & Rescue delivered "Just-In-Time" training to volunteers, who had no prior knowledge of search and rescue protocols, and provided essential mapping and GPS equipment from their task force cache to support search squads. Since cache resources were insufficient to support all search squads, volunteers also used smart phones and other alternatives to track and document searches.

In their annual State Preparedness Report submissions, states and territories most frequently indicated Mass Care Services capability gaps in "sheltering" (63 percent of all responses). During the flooding in Louisiana, public- and private-sector partners sought to address the extensive demand for mass care services. However, the Louisiana flooding revealed several challenges in mass care response efforts. For example, Federal and community partners reported difficulty in finding hotel rooms, including accessible hotel rooms, to participate in sheltering; tracking hotel use by survivors; and providing survivor transportation assistance, particularly accessible transportation assistance. In addition, community service organizations described lower volunteer turnout and deficiencies in volunteer housing compared to previous response efforts.

RESPONSE CASE STUDY: MULTI-AGENCY SHELTER TRANSITION TASK FORCE

During the August flooding in Louisiana, FEMA created a Multi-Agency Shelter Transition Task Force to transition survivors from shelters into temporary housing. Task force teams comprised representatives from Federal and nongovernmental organizations, including FEMA, the American Red Cross, and Catholic Charities. Teams reviewed survivor cases as a group, which increased coordination of resources across agencies and organizations to best support the needs of disaster survivors, including maintaining the health, independence, and self-determination of individuals with disabilities.

Homeland Security 2017 National Preparedness Report

CATASTROPHIC PREPAREDNESS

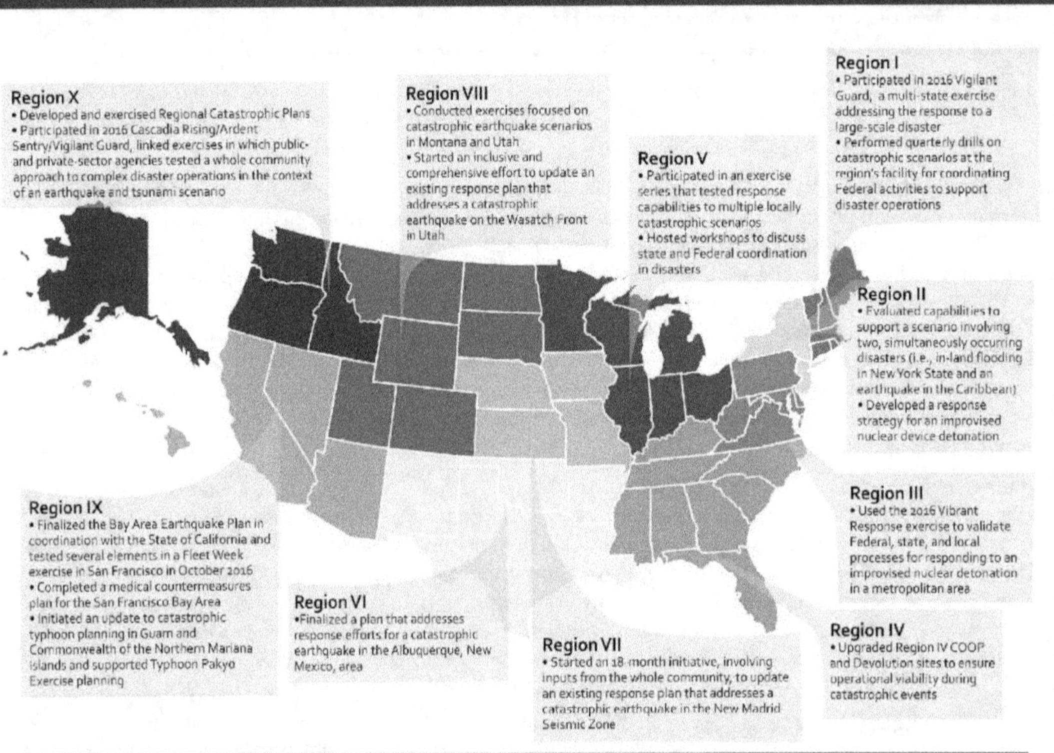

Each year, FEMA conducts various activities nationwide to better prepare for catastrophic incidents. For example, in June 2016, more than 20,000 individuals representing Federal, state, and local governments; tribal nations; private sector businesses; and nongovernmental organizations participated in a four-day exercise addressing a 9.0-magniture earthquake along the Cascadia Subduction Zone—a 700-mile fault line off the coast of the Pacific Northwest. The exercise helped test and validate existing catastrophic plans, uncovering strengths and areas for improvement in coordinating delivery of Response core capabilities, particularly Critical Transportation; Mass Care Services; Operational Communications; Operational Coordination; Public Health, Healthcare, and Emergency Medical Services; and Situational Assessment (see also page 96). For example, while some jurisdictions effectively communicated the status of their transportation infrastructure and ongoing damage assessment efforts, there was an overall failure to quickly prioritize which key transportation routes to restore into and out of the affected region. Updates to existing plans are occurring based on lessons learned and senior leadership guidance from this exercise. As shown in the map above, this exercise was one of several efforts in 2016 to improve catastrophic preparedness.

RESPONSE CASE STUDY: DISTRICT OF COLUMBIA MASS FATALITY EXERCISE

To address areas for improvement highlighted by the Navy Yard shooting in 2013, the District of Columbia Office of the Chief Medical Examiner hosted the District's first-ever Mass Fatality Symposium and full-scale exercise in September 2016. This event brought together stakeholders from across the National Capital Region (including the fire and emergency medical services, police departments, and health departments), as well as international fatality management experts, to share information and to discuss lessons learned from mass fatality incidents. Through the exercise, the District evaluated Homeland Security Grant Program investments it had made to address gaps identified in the Navy Yard shooting after-action report. The investments—which included the *District Wide Fatality Management Plan* and the purchase of a mobile command vehicle, mobile digital x-ray system, and field disaster morgue—significantly improved the District's mass fatality services. The exercise enabled the District to validate its strength in multi-agency leadership and collaboration, as well as the ability to adapt to lead agency protocols and procedures.

Though Federal, state, and local agencies have worked to address challenges in interoperability for first responder emergency communications, progress has been incremental.

Although the ability of Federal, state, and local responders to communicate by voice, data, and video in real-time is critical to an effective response, emergency communication systems often lack interoperability. In their 2016 State Preparedness Report submissions, states and territories most frequently identified Operational Communications capability shortfalls in "interoperable communication between responders" (63 percent of all responses). To address this problem, the Federal Government, in conjunction with public safety organizations and entities, has been working since 2012 to establish a single, nationwide, interoperable network—the Nationwide Public Safety Broadband Network (NPSBN)—for public safety and first responder communications. The FirstNet, the independent government authority established by law to create this network, has continued to make progress toward this goal:

- *In fiscal year 2016, FirstNet held over 400 meetings with states, territories, and tribes to ensure the NPSBN is designed to meet the needs of public safety agencies throughout the Nation.*
- *In November 2016, FirstNet opened a laboratory in Boulder, Colorado, to provide a test environment for validating and verifying future features, devices, and applications before their deployment to the NPSBN.*
- *As of December 2016, FirstNet is evaluating proposals to select a private-sector partner to build and deploy the NPSBN.*[8]

Interoperability challenges often stem from issues of governance, procedures, training, and education, rather than technology. To help address these issues, Federal, state, and local partners continue to use state- and regional-level governance bodies to provide a forum for public safety officials to set standards, share best practices, and conduct joint exercises and training. In addition, the DHS Office of Emergency Communications (OEC) Interoperable Communications Technical Assistance Program provides direct support to state, local, and tribal emergency responders and has helped promulgate best practices and

---

[8] Since the writing of this report, FirstNet has selected a network partner and on March 30, 2017, announced the award of the NPSBN contract.

standards nationwide. In fiscal year 2016, OEC conducted 21 statewide communication interoperability plan workshops and completed 180 requests for technical assistance, including 27 requests for training on broadband technologies. As of December 2016, while all 56 states and territories have a foundational strategic plan that addresses interoperability issues, 54 have revised statewide communication interoperability plans.

Also in fiscal year 2016, OEC developed and implemented the Interoperable Communications Capabilities Analysis Program through a series of six pilot observations during planned events in California, the District of Columbia, Hawaii, Indiana, Los Angeles, and San Antonio. The purpose of these pilots was to observe multi-jurisdictional and multi-disciplined planned events to identify best practices and gaps between the stated communication needs of public safety agencies and their current assets. The program builds on groundwork laid in 2010, when OEC worked with public safety agencies to measure progress made toward interoperability. Additionally, OEC and the National Governors Association hosted workshops in five states to review and identify best practices and strategies to implement in their statewide interoperability plans. Through these workshops, states recognized the need to identify a single entity to oversee all aspects of emergency communications; to secure sustainable funding for that entity to ensure seamless interoperability; and to increase education and outreach to public safety agencies to avoid misconceptions about interoperable communications. OEC is incorporating these lessons learned and best practices into future technical assistance offerings and workshops.

RESPONSE CASE STUDY: DATACASTING PILOT IN HOUSTON, TEXAS

In 2016, the City of Houston piloted DHS's datacasting capabilities during the Republican Primary Debate in February and the NCAA Final Four Basketball Tournament in April. Supported by the DHS Science and Technology Directorate, datacasting technology uses available bandwidth in digital television signals to deliver encrypted data to targeted recipients. During the events, the city was able to securely share emergency operations center displays, surveillance camera footage, and live-stream mobile videos to public safety officials from multiple agencies, increasing situational awareness. By taking advantage of existing television infrastructure (with its pre-existing redundant systems), datacasting provides a relatively inexpensive, highly reliable solution to current interoperability challenges. Datacasting is meant to be complementary to, not competitive with, the NPSBN by providing a supplemental broadband capability to offload bandwidth-intensive content (e.g., video footage). In October 2016, DHS and America's Public Television Stations—a nonprofit organization of 350 public television stations in all 50 states—signed an agreement to make datacasting technology available nationwide.

In 2016, FCC also took steps to improve interoperable communications between U.S. and Canadian responders. First responders on both sides of the U.S.–Canadian border frequently provide cross-border assistance to nearby jurisdictions, but, until recently, faced challenges communicating with one another. For example, in 2007, a Canadian fire truck was delayed at the border while attempting to respond to a fire in New York because it was unable to communicate with the border crossing station or on-scene incident commander. A 2014 letter of intent updated the 1952 treaty between the United States and Canada, which allowed public safety agencies to operate mobile radios across the border, to allow public safety agencies to use portable radios, and to use local or cross-border frequencies to communicate with responding agencies. As a result, in June 2016, FCC released guidance to U.S. public safety agencies seeking to cross into Canada, to communicate with the United States from Canada, to host Canadian responders on U.S. frequencies, and to use Canadian frequencies to communicate with Canadian first responders. The guidance, developed in collaboration with Canada, helps improve communications for first responders on both sides of the border.

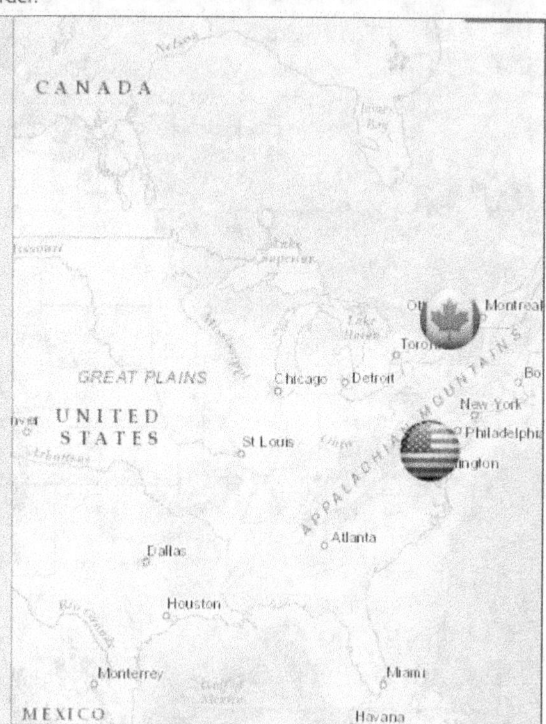

RESPONSE CASE STUDY: CANADA-UNITED STATES ENHANCED (CAUSE) RESILIENCY EXPERIMENT SERIES

In April 2016, the DHS Science and Technology Directorate's First Responders Group, in collaboration with Public Safety Canada and Defense Research and Development Canada's Centre for Security Science, carried out the fourth installment of the CAUSE Resiliency experiment series (i.e., CAUSE IV). The goals for this series are to build and strengthen binational communications interoperability, and to connect, test, and demonstrate emerging operational technologies. CAUSE IV took place at the Blue Water Bridge (on the Michigan-Ontario border), the second-busiest transit point between the United States and Canada, and consisted of two distinct, but connected scenarios. The first tested voice and data communications during cross-border patient transfers, and the second tested alerts and warning during a tornado. Participants found that the interoperable technologies tested facilitated the exchange of cross-border voice, video, and data communications; and supported decision-making processes for local and cross-border response operations. However, the experiment also identified the need to establish formal policies and procedures to guide the appropriate use of these technologies and optimize their benefits.

Key Finding:

New Federal guidance establishes a mechanism to coordinate Federal response to large-scale malicious cyber activity, while cyber threats such as attacks on industrial control systems continue to rise.

Reacting to persistent concerns over cybersecurity, the Federal Government has sought to better coordinate the U.S. response to malicious cyber activity. One such example is Presidential Policy Directive (PPD) 41, which provides a framework for responding to large-scale cyber incidents with national security implications. For significant cyber incidents,[9] PPD 41 directs that a Cyber Unified Coordination Group will be stood up. This approach addresses cyber incidents with the same coordination structure already used to coordinate Federal interagency responses to other types of incidents. In particular, this Cyber Unified Coordination Group identifies three sets of actions to take in response to a cyber incident: threat response, asset response, and intelligence support (see Figure 11). An interagency working group also released a document advising the whole community on how and when to report major cyber incidents to the Federal Government. Additionally, a finalized *National Cyber Incident Response Plan* further clarifies the roles and responsibilities of Federal agencies and state, local, and private-sector partners in the event of a cyber incident, including significant cyber incidents.

---

[9] PPD 41 defines a significant cyber incident as a cyber incident that is (or group of related cyber incidents that together are) likely to result in demonstrable harm to the national security interests, foreign relations, or economy of the United States or to the public confidence, civil liberties, or public health and safety of the American people.

Cyber Unified Coordination Group			
Lead Agency	**Threat Response - FBI**	**Asset Response - DHS**	**Intelligence Support - ODNI**
Role	Addressing law enforcement functions such as gathering evidence, conducting investigations, attributing the attack, identifying patterns or related attacks, and identifying means to pursue and mitigate the immediate threat	Providing technical assistance to affected entities, identifying other sectors that may be vulnerable after an incident, and mitigating broader risks to regions or sectors	Contributing to the building of situational awareness during an incident, promoting information sharing, analyzing threat trends, identifying knowledge gaps, and weakening the capabilities of adversaries

Figure 11. A Cyber Unified Coordination Group, as defined by PPD-41, addresses three sets of activities, each led by a specific Federal entity.

The Federal Government is taking steps to enhance information sharing and responses to cyber incidents. FBI notifications to critical infrastructure sector victims of cyber attacks continued to rise in 2016 (i.e., up more than 450 notifications from 2015, an 11.5 percent increase in notifications recorded in Cyber Guardian). Cyber attacks on industrial control systems are of particular concern, in part because of the potential for costly physical consequences. Industrial control systems include a variety of computerized or automated functions that help operate large facilities such as utilities. Disruptions to these control systems could disable such facilities or create conditions that could result in physical harm or loss of life. In fiscal year 2016, the Industrial Control Systems Cyber Emergency Response Team (ICS-CERT) closed 290 incidents involving critical infrastructure, principally affecting the Critical Manufacturing (63 incidents), Communications (62 incidents), and Energy (59 incidents) sectors. In 2016, DOJ indicted a group of alleged state-sponsored Iranian-based hackers in connection with several cyber incidents, including remote hackers that accessed the control systems of a dam in New York.

 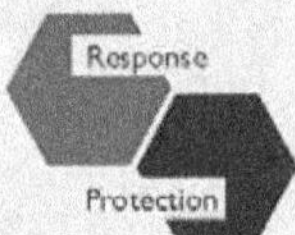

ICS-CERT has also expanded its facilitation of domestic assessments to help operators of privately and municipally owned infrastructure identify and address vulnerabilities to secure their control systems. The team conducted 130 assessments across 12 sectors in fiscal year 2016, up from 112 assessments across eight sectors in fiscal year 2015. The assessments included:

- *Fifty-five Design Architecture Reviews, which provide critical infrastructure operators with a comprehensive technical review and cyber evaluation of their industrial control systems;*
- *Forty-three Network Architecture Verification and Validation assessments, which help owners and operators visualize traffic on their control-system networks; and*
- *Thirty-two Cyber Security Evaluation Tool assessments, which provide organizations with a broader understanding of their cybersecurity posture.*

Key Finding:

First responders have adopted new approaches to combat active shooters; however, recent events illustrated the need for expanded responder medical training.

To maximize lives saved, active shooter response tactics have shifted away from containment efforts to subduing the shooter, accessing the injured quickly, and rapidly providing appropriate medical care to address life-threatening injuries. In 2013, FBI adopted Advanced Law Enforcement Rapid Response Training, which emphasizes immediately engaging and neutralizing the threat, as the national training standard for active shooter response. Since 2002, more than 105,000 law enforcement

Homeland Security 2017 National Preparedness Report

officers received this training. Moreover, the International Association of Chiefs of Police recommended in 2013 that all law enforcement personnel receive tactical emergency medical training, including life-threatening hemorrhaging control. Since then, additional opportunities for law enforcement officers to receive such trainings have emerged. For example, as part of DHS's "Stop the Bleed" campaign, which seeks to raise awareness of basic techniques to stop life-threatening bleeding, trauma surgeons trained more than 80 Tulane University police officers in 2016 on how to use tourniquets. In addition, FEMA supported the Tactical Emergency Casualty Care training—which covers how to stop bleeding, maintain airways, prevent hypothermia, and efficiently move patients—to more than 10,000 first responders.

Recent active shooter incidents have reaffirmed the value in the shift to using such tactics. In the 2015 San Bernardino shooting, responding officers formed a four-man team to immediately engage the shooter based on their active shooter training. Additionally, a fire medic assigned to a SWAT team triaged victims inside the Inland Regional Center where the shooting occurred, which an after-action review found enhanced victim extrication and survival. Similarly, during the 2016 Orlando nightclub shooting, officers began evacuating victims from the dance floor while a potential threat from the shooter still existed.

An after-action review of the San Bernardino shooting, however, found that law enforcement officers were not adequately trained to provide on-scene emergency medical care to shooting victims. In 2016, the Federal Government expanded funding opportunities available to state and local police departments to better support active shooter training, including medical training. Congress passed the *Protecting Our Lives by Initiative COPS Expansion (POLICE) Act of 2016* to allow law enforcement and medical personnel to use Office of Community Oriented Policing Services (COPS) grants—which more than 13,000 of the Nation's 16,000 law enforcement agencies have received since 1994—for active shooter training. Additionally, in December 2016, DHS announced the new Program to Prepare Communities for Complex Coordinated Terrorist Attacks, which will provide nearly $36 million in funding to state, local, tribal, and territorial jurisdictions to improve their ability to prepare for, prevent, and respond to complex coordinated terrorist attacks, such as active shootings.

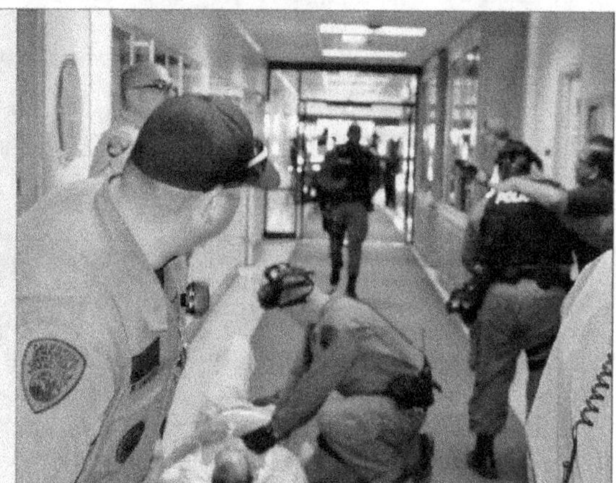

RESPONSE CASE STUDY: ACTIVE SHOOTER/HOSTILE EVENT SUMMIT II

In January 2016, the InterAgency Board, a voluntary panel of emergency preparedness and response practitioners, and its Federal partners brought together over 80 participants from 14 agencies and organizations to the second Active Shooter/Hostile Event summit. The goal of the summit was to develop and publish a set of guidelines for municipalities to use in building their own Active Shooter/Hostile Event plans or modifying existing plans. The resulting *Active Shooter/Hostile Event Guide*, released in July 2016, includes specific procedures for incident command, emergency communications, medical operations, training and exercises, community outreach and engagement, and equipment.

Homeland Security 2017 National Preparedness Report

Focused on a timely restoration, strengthening, and revitalization of the infrastructure; housing; a sustainable economy; and the health, social, cultural, historic, and environmental fabric of communities affected by a catastrophic incident

CORE CAPABILITIES IN PRACTICE

The *National Disaster Recovery Framework* (NDRF) provides a flexible structure and process for jurisdictions affected by disasters to recover quickly and effectively. The NDRF identifies eight core capabilities needed to support the physical, emotional, and financial needs of disaster-affected community members.

Three core capabilities facilitate the effective implementation of disaster recovery activities. Communities use **Operational Coordination** to ensure that multiple levels of government and other recovery partners build successful coalitions. Key stakeholders provide regular input into pre- and post-disaster **Planning** processes to identify recovery objectives and how to best achieve those objectives. Community leaders convey the actions being taken to support recovery efforts and explain what assistance is available to residents and businesses through the **Public Information and Warning** core capability.

The remaining five core capabilities address specific aspects of recovery. Re-establishing the functions and facilities necessary to provide **Health and Social Services**—such as hospital care or healthcare, child care, counseling, and other services—helps address the physical and mental health of disaster survivors. Communities set strategies for **Economic Recovery** to return economic and business activities to a healthy state. The recovery process also involves experts coordinating with the community to preserve, protect, and restore **Natural and Cultural Resources**, including publicly and privately owned cultural assets and historical properties. Public- and private-sector owners and operators of **Infrastructure Systems** must also restore and sustain essential community services. Meanwhile, residents displaced by disasters seek temporary and permanent **Housing** solutions, including affordable and accessible housing.

CORE CAPABILITIES IN THE RECOVERY MISSION AREA

- Economic Recovery
- Health and Social Services
- Housing
- Infrastructure Systems
- Natural and Cultural Resources
- Operational Coordination
- Planning
- Public Information and Warning

The following are examples of actions taken in 2016 to improve preparedness that highlight the relationship among a select number of Recovery core capabilities:

☐ Housing and Public Information and Warning

> Following Louisiana's historic floods in August, state, local, and nongovernmental stakeholders—in coordination with the Federal agencies responsible for supporting disaster housing activities—hosted the first-ever Housing Resource Fairs in different state parishes. The events provided hundreds of Louisiana homeowners and renters with housing resources and information to aid in short- and long-term housing recovery. The fairs covered topics such as temporary and permanent housing solutions, insurance, and home elevation. To address the shortage of available rental units for displaced residents, the fair in East Baton Rouge also provided resources to help transition financially ready families from renting to purchasing a home, with the goal of freeing up rental units for others.

Homeland Security 2017 National Preparedness Report

◻ Planning and Operational Coordination

The Maryland Emergency Management Agency released the "Local Recovery Planning Toolkit," an online collection of materials and guidance to help local jurisdictions with their recovery planning. To assist jurisdictions in developing their own pre-disaster recovery plans, the toolkit provides materials from regional recovery initiatives underway in the state. Ellicott City played a role in developing some of these materials (as part of the Baltimore Urban Area's recovery planning efforts), which better prepared the city for recovering from flash flooding in 2016. The toolkit also includes guidance and case studies on transitioning the management of recovery efforts to a long-term recovery committee. Jurisdictions in Maryland have begun using the toolkit to help develop customized recovery plans.

◻ Health and Social Services

In 2016, ASPR developed behavioral health materials and tools to ensure these considerations are integrated into response and recovery efforts. For example, ASPR updated its "HHS Disaster Behavioral Health: Current Assets and Capabilities" fact sheet, which helps emergency planners understand potential behavioral health resources to take advantage of during emergency response and recovery efforts. ASPR also developed a new fact sheet to assist HHS responders with effectively directing people to appropriate resources during times of extreme stress. In November 2016, ASPR released an update of the *HHS Disaster Behavioral Health Concept of Operations*, adding language to address incidents of mass violence and terrorism, and to further describe behavioral health assets and capabilities. ASPR also convened three interagency meetings with HHS, DOJ, the U.S. Department of Education, and the American Red Cross to enhance collaboration and information sharing in relation to providing behavioral health support after mass violence events, such as school shootings. As a result, ASPR developed internal tools and protocols to ensure a shared understanding of roles, responsibilities, and resources available in the aftermath of these types of incidents.

◻ Natural and Cultural Resources and Economic Recovery

In February, the Deepwater Horizon Natural Resource Damage Assessment Trustee Council—including all five Gulf of Mexico states, NOAA, EPA, DOI, and USDA—released an all-inclusive restoration plan for the Gulf of Mexico as part of a legal settlement with BP stemming from the 2010 *Deepwater Horizon* oil spill. The plan builds on earlier activities and sets the approach for comprehensive restoration in the Gulf, including water quality, wildlife, and recreational activities. The plan also identifies possible effects of proposed actions on communities and their economies, such as employment opportunities or impacts to fishing industries. In addition to payments to address damages to natural resources, BP will provide up to $5.9 billion to the Gulf States and local governments to address economic damage claims resulting from the spill. BP will also pay $5.5 billion in civil penalties under the Clean Water Act, most of which will help restore natural resources, boost economic recovery, and strengthen tourism and seafood industries.

SUMMARY OF PROGRESS

The Recovery mission area continues to face challenges. For the fifth consecutive year, states and territories reported some of their lowest levels of proficiency in Recovery core capabilities. Recovery-specific core capabilities also remain a lower priority for states and territories relative to most other core capabilities. Data does indicate that the Nation is focusing more attention on this mission area than before. Despite progress, five Recovery core capabilities—**Economic Recovery, Health and Social Services, Housing, Infrastructure Systems,** and **Natural and Cultural Resources**—continue to show proficiency levels that are well below average. In particular, the 2017 *National Preparedness Report* identifies four of these core capabilities—**Economic Recovery, Housing, Infrastructure Systems,** and **Natural and Cultural Resources**—as national areas for improvement (see page 12).

As captured in this section's key findings, recovery efforts for the Louisiana floods, Hurricane Matthew, and the Flint water crisis have called attention to specific challenges in **Housing, Health and Social Services,** and **Economic Recovery,** while highlighting improvements in **Operational Coordination.** Moreover, the current NEP cycle of exercises has also emphasized addressing the Recovery mission area. Specifically, 41 percent of NEP exercises addressed one or more core capabilities in the Recovery mission area, compared to 27 percent in the prior cycle. Based on FEMA preparedness grants in fiscal year 2015 (the latest year for which grant data by core capability are available), a smaller portion of funding goes to the Recovery mission area than to any other mission area. Excluding the core capabilities common to all mission areas (i.e., Planning, Operational Coordination, and Public Information and Warning), grant expenditures on Recovery core capabilities represented less than 1.3 percent of all FEMA preparedness grants in fiscal year 2015, with **Health and Social Services, Economic Recovery,**

Housing, and Natural and Cultural **Resources** each receiving less than \$2 million.

States and territories reported the lowest proficiency ratings in the Recovery mission area for the sixth consecutive year (see Figure 12).[10] Moreover, excluding **Natural and Cultural Resources,** the proficiency ratings of all remaining Recovery core capabilities declined in 2016. In their State Preparedness Report submissions, states and territories reported a two percent decrease in proficiency ratings in the Recovery core capabilities between 2015 and 2016. This included a six percent proficiency decrease in **Housing** in 2016—the third-largest decrease of all core capabilities. Moreover, states and territories reported that Recovery core capabilities remain among those in the greatest danger of decline. Twenty-nine percent selected **Economic Recovery** as among those in most danger of decline, as well as 20 percent for **Natural and Cultural Resources, Infrastructure Systems,** and **Housing.**

2016 Recovery Core Capabilities
High Priority vs. Proficient

Notes: Vertical red lines (|) indicate the average ratings for all core capabilities. The chart and statements do not include contributions from the three cross-cutting core capabilities—Planning, Operational Coordination, and Public Information and Warning

Figure 12. In their 2016 State Preparedness Report responses, states and territories provided information on their high priority core capabilities, as well as ratings on core capability proficiency.

Natural and Cultural Resources, Health and Social Services, and **Housing** were among the core capabilities that states and territories most frequently reported as low priorities. In particular, 52 percent reported **Natural and Cultural Resources** as a low priority, the most of any core capability. Conversely, **Infrastructure Systems** has consistently been the Recovery core capability with the highest priority rating—80 percent of states and territories selected it as a high priority in 2015 and 64 percent selected it as a high priority in 2016. Despite the high priority rating, however, states and territories reported a four percent decrease in proficiency in 2016.

Table 7 lists the most frequently identified "functional area" gap for each Recovery core capability, as selected by states and territories in their 2016 State Preparedness Report responses. Functional areas break down core capabilities into more granular-level functions, which were identified from an analysis of the Goal, NDRF, and other national-level preparedness doctrine.

---

[10] Unless otherwise noted, figures and statements do not include contributions from the three core capabilities common to all mission areas—i.e., Planning, Operational Coordination, and Public Information and Warning.

Table 7. In their 2016 State Preparedness Report responses, states and territories identified remaining gaps in their ability to accomplish various functions associated with each Recovery core capability.

Most Frequently Identified Functional Area Gap in Each Recovery Capability	
Core Capability[*]	Gap
Economic Recovery	Economic impact assessments
Health and Social Services	Determining health and social needs
Housing	Addressing housing shortages
Infrastructure Systems	Infrastructure site assessments
Natural and Cultural Resources	Environmental preservation and restoration
Operational Coordination[**]	Command, control, and coordination
	Establishing a common operating picture
Planning	Whole community involvement and cooperation
Public Information and Warning	New communication tools and technologies

[*] For core capabilities that cut across two or more mission areas, the 2016 State Preparedness Report did not include separate data requests that were specific to each mission area. Gaps identified for these core capabilities are identical for the different mission areas.
[**] The top-two functional area gaps for Operational Coordination were tied in terms of how frequently they were selected.

BY THE NUMBERS

SBA APPROVED 25,235 DISASTER ASSISTANCE LOANS

In fiscal year 2016, SBA approved 25,235 Disaster Assistance Loans totaling more than $1.4 billion. Approximately 50 percent of this total stemmed from the August floods in Louisiana. Disaster assistance loans help businesses, nonprofits, homeowners, and renters repair and replace physical losses, and assist nonprofits and small businesses with post-disaster operating expenses.

30 STATES PROVIDED TRAINING ON DISASTER RECOVERY

In 2016, approximately 30 states used the "Recovery from Disaster: The Local Community Role" course to provide instruction to local communities, allowing greater access to the course (beyond solely Federal offerings). The course focuses on the roles and responsibilities of local disaster recovery teams, and provides guidance on developing and implementing pre- and post-disaster recovery plans.

FEMA CONSOLIDATED 15 RECOVERY POLICIES

In September 2016, FEMA published *Individuals and Households Program Unified Guidance*, which provides recovery stakeholders with increased transparency about how the Individuals and Households Program works. The unified guidance consolidates 15 previously disjointed policies (many not publicly available) into a single reference.

Homeland Security 2017 National Preparedness Report

RECOVERY SNAPSHOTS

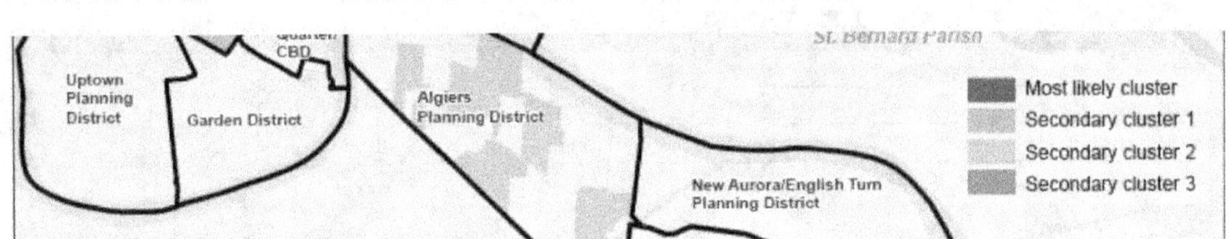

IOWA LEGAL AID APP

In August, Iowa Legal Aid, a nonprofit organization that provides legal services and support to the state's vulnerable and low-income populations, launched a disaster relief mobile app that helps users prepare for, respond to, and recover from disasters. Among its many features, the app allows users to securely store insurance information, learn about post-incident assistance and legal rights, and communicate with Iowa Legal Aid staff following disasters. As of January 2017, more than 200 downloads of the app have occurred.

"HOMES FOR WHITE SULPHUR SPRINGS" PROGRAM

This program—a collaboration between Mennonite Disaster Service (MDS) and private sector partners—assists in the recovery of White Sulphur Springs, West Virginia, which experienced flooding in June 2016. The program buys out properties located in the floodplain and allows their owners to use proceeds from the sale toward purchasing homes in a new housing development (outside the floodplain). As of December 2016, the program had raised over $1.7 million, providing MDS with funds to purchase materials for 20 homes—many of which are already complete and occupied by disaster survivors.

SPATIAL ANALYSIS OF BEHAVIORAL HEALTH

In 2016, CDC published a study using geographic information system (GIS) and spatial analysis to locate at-risk areas and populations following Hurricane Katrina. The analysis indicated that hospitalizations increased from 2004 to 2008 and geographically shifted from flood-exposed areas to more insulated areas over time, with poverty as a central factor. The study demonstrates the potential for GIS tools to locate at-risk populations, which emergency managers can use to improve pre-disaster recovery plans and better allocate resources post-disaster.

PREPAREDNESS INDICATORS

Quality of FEMA Individual Assistance Program services delivered to disaster survivors

FEMA's Individual Assistance Program helps individuals and households affected by disasters to recover as quickly and efficiently as possible. This performance measure demonstrates how well the program delivered services to affected individuals by combining metrics such as how long it took to award assistance funds, how quickly assistance call centers answered survivor calls, and how satisfied survivors were with the program. At 95 percent, fiscal year 2016 results surpassed the target set for the fiscal year (94 percent).

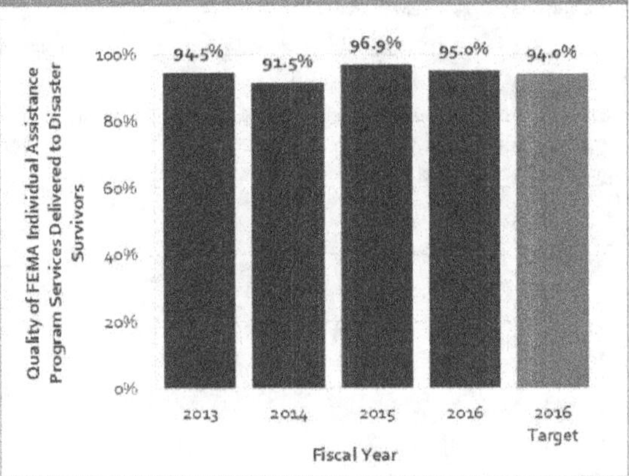

Quality of Public Assistance Program services delivered to communities

FEMA's Public Assistance Program provides grants—averaging $4.7 billion annually over the last 10 years—for infrastructure recovery and debris removal to state, local, and tribal governments so that communities can quickly recover from disasters. This performance measure combines inputs such as how quickly FEMA began addressing requests for assistance and how well tools and processes worked in delivering program services. At 92 percent, results from fiscal year 2016 were unchanged from the previous year. FEMA is implementing a new delivery model for Public Assistance that aims to improve the program's effectiveness and better meet the needs of applicants.

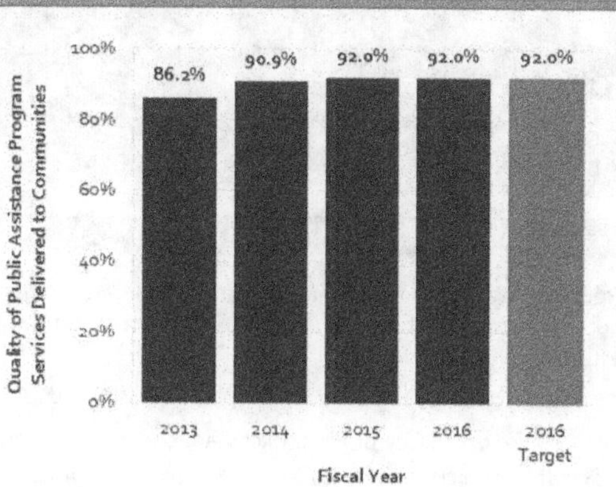

82

Recovery activities following the Flint, Michigan, water crisis demonstrate the adaptability of the private and public sectors in coordinating resources during a non-traditional disaster, despite challenges in addressing the crisis's ongoing effects.

In April 2014, the City of Flint, Michigan, changed its water source from Lake Huron to the Flint River. The river's water corroded municipal pipes, causing lead and other pollutants to leach into the city's drinking water and creating a public health crisis. In January 2016, President Obama signed an emergency declaration under the Stafford Act, authorizing FEMA to provide commodities such as water filters and test kits for the state to distribute. More broadly, he designated HHS as the lead Federal agency to coordinate Federal efforts in support of response and recovery. Public- and private-sector organizations also mobilized, using their own resources to contribute to Flint's recovery.

Private-sector organizations supported Flint's recovery needs in numerous ways:

- *In May 2016, 10 private foundations—including the Ford Foundation and the Robert Wood Johnson Foundation—committed nearly $125 million to the city.*
- *Grants to local businesses from programs such as the Moving Flint Forward Fund are assisting with economic recovery. By June 2016, the fund provided grants to 30 Flint businesses to help them retain jobs, make repairs, and purchase new equipment, among other needs.*
- *Philanthropic dollars helped Flint open a new early childhood learning center with a particular focus on children exposed to lead.*
- *United Way and the American Red Cross supported the establishment of community resilience groups, facilitated information sharing, and provided funding to community organizations that support vulnerable populations.*
- *The Food Bank of Eastern Michigan, with support from Pepsi Co. and the C.S. Mott Foundation, opened two mobile distribution centers that provide bottled water, food, supplies, and physical and mental health support to Flint residents.*
- *AARP also partnered with the City of Flint to send volunteers to inform seniors about FAST Start, a program to replace residential pipelines. The organization conducted a survey of senior residents, developed an action plan, and is planning to launch public service announcements on TV to increase its reach to seniors.*

State and local governments augmented these private-sector activities. In coordination with local partners and residents, state agencies developed a list of short-, intermediate-, and long-term goals to facilitate Flint's recovery. These goals addressed topics such as health and human services, education, water infrastructure, and economic development. The state also created the Flint Water Interagency Coordinating Committee, a group of city and state partners working toward solutions to address recovery issues. As of February 2016, total state funding for the water crisis topped $230 million.

At the Federal level, HHS introduced recovery considerations early in the Federal response and coordinated Federal recovery efforts through non-Stafford Act authorities. Numerous Federal agencies engaged in initial recovery efforts, and continue to work with state and local governments and community organizations to provide health and economic recovery services:

- *HHS coordinated efforts such as health screenings, behavioral health and nutrition programs, as well as long-term health studies to ensure the best health support and outcomes for residents exposed to contaminants. HHS also collaborated with the American Red Cross and the Genesee County Health Department to train behavioral health providers on providing psychological first aid.*

- *Through a National Dislocated Worker Grant, the U.S. Department of Labor is providing up to $15 million toward employment-related projects that include assistance with humanitarian and recovery efforts. The state received an initial $7.5 million award, which it is using to provide Flint residents with temporary employment performing recovery-related activities, as well as additional training and career assistance to help these individuals secure permanent employment.*
- *The USDA is working to ensure that children have increased access to foods rich in nutrients that may help reduce lead absorption. Under the Summer Electronic Benefits Transfer Pilot program, USDA expanded funds toward nutritious food purchases during the summer months for over 15,000 lead-impacted children in affected areas. The USDA also gave funding to several county schools for fresh fruit and vegetables for their students.*

Despite the progress public- and private-sector partners made during the recovery, a number of challenges emerged. For example, the Flint water treatment plant lacked the technical and managerial capacity to ensure that the water purchased from the Great Lakes Water Authority had adequate concentrations of the appropriate chemicals, including a chemical used to optimize treatment within the city's oversized and damaged distribution system. In October 2015, EPA formed the Flint Safe Drinking Water Task Force to provide the city with technical assistance to optimize treatment. Residents low usage of water, however, resulted in reduced flow through the distribution system, hindering the re-coating of pipes with a protective scale.

EPA Intervention in the Flint Michigan Water Contamination

Regarding EPA intervention in Flint, the EPA's Office of Inspector General (OIG) found that EPA had the authority and sufficient information to issue an emergency order months sooner than it did, to require the City of Flint, Michigan, and the Michigan Department of Environmental Quality to take necessary action to protect public health. The EPA OIG concluded that the delay was due to a lack of understanding of how and when EPA can use its emergency authorities to immediately address urgent public drinking water issues. The EPA OIG issued a management alert recommending that EPA update its guidance and provide staff training on issuing emergency orders under Section 1431 of the Safe Drinking Water Act.

Additionally, initial progress was slow in replacing the pipes that led to the contamination. As of late September 2016, Flint only replaced 177 of the several thousand lines with the $27 million in initial funds provided by the state. Moreover, while HHS and EPA announced that filtered water was safe for consumption on June 25, 2016, unfiltered water in Flint remained unsafe to drink throughout 2016. By the end of 2016, the city replaced approximately 800 lines, as well as refined its operational plan to replace 6,000 lines per year over the next three to four years. In January 2017, the Michigan Department of Environmental Quality reported that the most recent compliance period showed that lead in Flint's drinking water is now below the Federal action level established in the Lead and Copper Rule, which is 15 parts per billion. As of February 2017, the lead values in Flint's water remained below the Federal action level. Nevertheless, out of caution, EPA and state officials are advising that Flint residents continue to use filters while lead service lines are being replaced. The State of Michigan plans to continue its program to offer free water sampling for Flint's residents.

Key Finding:

Nongovernmental and private organizations provide critical support during disaster recovery, but their ability to sustain recovery efforts faces challenges.

Nongovernmental and private organizations are providing valuable recovery assistance in the wake of disasters. A 2016 RAND study called attention to the significance of corporate and nonprofit funding in disaster recovery. It noted that the private sector introduces flexible funding methods and strategies, as well as helps develop new technologies and brings them into play. Recent real-world events also demonstrate the opportunities for private organizations to supplement Federal efforts in disaster recovery. Since 2015, the Center for Disaster Philanthropy has awarded grants to approximately 20 organizations through its Midwest Early Recovery Fund to aid low-attention disaster recovery efforts, especially those supporting individuals disproportionately impacted by disasters. During the program's first two years, the Center

Homeland Security 2017 National Preparedness Report

for Disaster Philanthropy made 31 grants totaling $1.6 million. The fund aided the 2016 establishment of the "Bridge to Recovery Coalition," which uses public and private resources to help repair homes owned by vulnerable and at-risk residents and damaged by the December 2015 flooding in Missouri.

In addition, state chapters of Voluntary Organizations Active in Disaster (VOAD) played a significant role in 2016 events, collaborating with the public sector and communities to address long-term recovery needs. In West Virginia, the state's VOAD chapter worked with both public- and private-sector partners on the Bridge Project, which helps families regain access to critical services by rebuilding bridges that were located on private property and destroyed by flooding in 2015. As of June 2016, the project rebuilt 16 bridges.

While the involvement of private organizations is crucial to disaster recovery, their ability to sustain recovery operations remains challenging. Although private organizations receive financial assistance and support from volunteers immediately following a disaster, both forms of support may not be stable over time. In 2016, organizations across the country found it increasingly difficult to attract and sustain volunteers and donors over the long-term recovery process. The number of volunteers assisting West Virginia flood recovery efforts fell rapidly after an initially large turnout. After two major flooding events in Louisiana, volunteers and resources to assist with home cleanup were also in short supply. Moreover, depleted resources and low volunteer turnout adversely impacted state VOAD capability. These challenges are exacerbated when an event receives low media attention, as was the case in Louisiana. Fundraising totals from the public also decreased in 2016, and donations shifted toward smaller organizations—including crowdsourcing websites—as opposed to larger, well-known organizations. These fluctuations and shifting trends can destabilize recovery activity on the part of private organizations.

RECOVERY CASE STUDY: LOUISIANA DISASTER RECOVERY ALLIANCE

After observing limited levels of individual and philanthropic giving following the March 2016 flooding in Louisiana, the Federal Disaster Recovery Coordinator and Philanthropic Liaison team began working to engage the philanthropic community in Louisiana. After the August 2016 floods, this effort gained momentum and led to the establishment of the Louisiana Disaster Recovery Alliance. The purpose of the alliance was to garner support for ongoing recovery efforts by raising awareness about flooding disasters and strengthening cross-sector engagement. This first-of-its-kind consortium also brings together private, nonprofit, and corporate partners together with government stakeholders to improve recovery by fostering dialogue and information sharing. This includes more effectively using public and private resources for recovery efforts by avoiding duplications of effort. The Louisiana Disaster Recovery Alliance will also help philanthropic partners collect recovery funds during non-disaster periods to finance and support lower-scale disasters that do not receive a major disaster declaration.

Re-establishing child care services is an important element in helping families to recover, but most child care centers face severe challenges after a disaster.

Child care services play an important role in recovery by ensuring that children are safe while their parents take part in rebuilding efforts. For example, without adequate child care services, parents may be unable to easily and quickly return to work. Child care providers, however, may face their own challenges following a disaster, preventing them from repairing damages or reopening quickly. After Hurricane Sandy in 2012, both center- and home-based child care providers reported challenges with rebuilding, including lengthy application processes for disaster assistance, and initially paying (or being unable to pay) for repairs out of pocket. More than four years later, the challenges facing child care providers remain. One month after the August 2016 Louisiana floods, 70 child care centers were still closed (10 percent of the state's licensed care capacity), affecting up to 5,000 children and their families.

One major challenge states and localities identify for child care centers in post-disaster recovery is funding. The vast majority of child care facilities are not eligible for financial assistance from FEMA's Public Assistance Program because they are businesses and for-profit entities. Centers may be underinsured, insurance claims processing may take many months, and they may lack funds to pay for repairs out of pocket, leaving the businesses financially vulnerable. Although private nonprofit child care centers are eligible for Public Assistance, many do not apply for undetermined reasons. Of the 70 Louisiana child care centers closed one month after the August floods, at least eight have closed their doors permanently.

Federal and state governments have made efforts to support recovery planning for child care centers in 2016. HHS's Administration for Children and Families published its *Post-Disaster Child Care Needs and Resources*, which outlines Federal and non-Federal resources that address various child care challenges following a disaster. Additionally, FEMA introduced its "Children and Disasters" webpage in April, consolidating information and links to approximately 50 resources related to children's needs in disasters. By the end of 2016, the webpage had received over 14,000 views. Some efforts have faced challenges and made limited progress. The Child Care and Development Block Grant Act of 2014, as amended, required each state to develop and fully implement a comprehensive statewide child care disaster plan—including guidelines for reopening child care facilities following a disaster—by September 30, 2016. However, as of March 2016, only 10 states had met this requirement.

<table>
<tr><td>

RECOVERY CASE STUDY: "HELP KIDS COPE" APP

Following a disaster, children can experience—to a more extreme degree than adults—short- and long-term trauma and behavioral health problems, including post-traumatic stress disorder, depression, anxiety, and social withdrawal. In 2016, the National Child Traumatic Stress Network released its Help Kids Cope app, which is designed to assist parents in talking to their children about different disasters. The app includes sections on explaining disasters to children, as well as preparedness, response, and healing tips. By providing information on disasters before they occur, the app can help parents anticipate and prevent extreme reactions and prepare children for potentially traumatic experiences. Since its release, users have downloaded the app more than 1,500 times.

</td><td>

</td></tr>
</table>

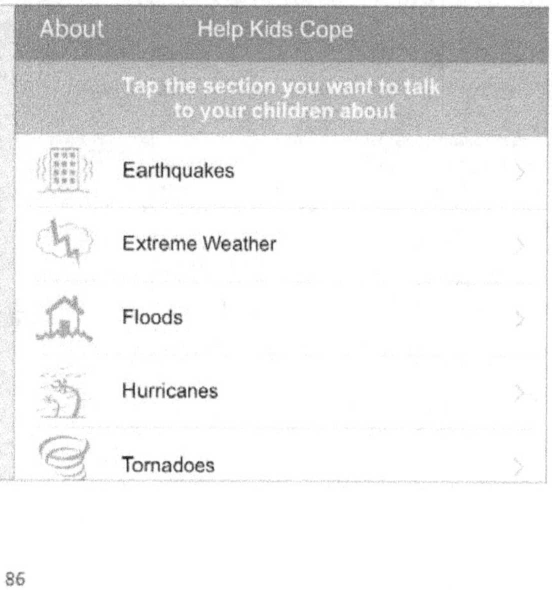

Recent flooding events highlight ongoing gaps in delivering housing solutions efficiently and effectively after disasters.

In their 2016 State Preparedness Report submissions, only 21 percent of states and territories reported proficiency in their Housing capability ratings, the third lowest among all core capabilities. Moreover, 59 percent of states and territories reported that they perceive it to be primarily the responsibility of the Federal Government to address gaps in the Housing core capability. In August 2016, torrential rains in Louisiana caused the flooding of more than 100,000 homes, resulting in significant demand for Federal housing assistance. As of December 2016:

- *FEMA provided more than $745 million to survivors through its Individuals and Households Program, which provides grants that eligible individuals can use to support repair or replacement of their homes, temporary rentals, and other disaster-related expenses.*
- *SBA approved over 15,000 home loans—totaling approximately $1 billion—that disaster survivors can use to replace or rebuild their primary residence.*
- *The USDA Multi-Family Housing program identified 700 available apartments in rural regions across the state to address the housing needs of disaster survivors in rural areas.*

MISSION AREA CONNECTIONS

FLOODPLAIN MANAGEMENT AND HOUSING

Following a disaster, relocating or rebuilding outside of floodplains can enhance a community's flood resilience. However, balancing long-term vulnerability reduction while meeting the permanent housing needs of disaster survivors continues to be a challenge. As 2016 flooding disasters demonstrated, individuals and families may prefer to rebuild in their current locations due to the difficulties in relocating or rebuilding elsewhere.

RECOVERY CASE STUDY: SUSTAINABILITY ADVISOR

The Federal Government officially introduced the position of "Sustainability Advisor" in the 2016 update to the *Recovery Federal Interagency Operational Plan*. The Sustainability Advisor advocates for and guides Federal, state, and local partners in adopting sustainable, green, and resilient principles and practices in recovery operations. Following 2016 flooding in Louisiana, EPA deployed a Sustainability Advisor for the first time. In Louisiana, the Sustainability Advisor is working with FEMA to integrate opportunities to advance sustainable development, mitigation planning, and long-term disaster recovery by leveraging financial and technical resources to support regional and local needs, such as green infrastructure, ecosystem assessment, and grant writing. Additionally, the Sustainability Advisor is partnering with other Federal, state, and local partners to increase education and outreach efforts that promote the incorporation of sustainability practices into land use decisions, housing alternatives, and capacity building efforts.

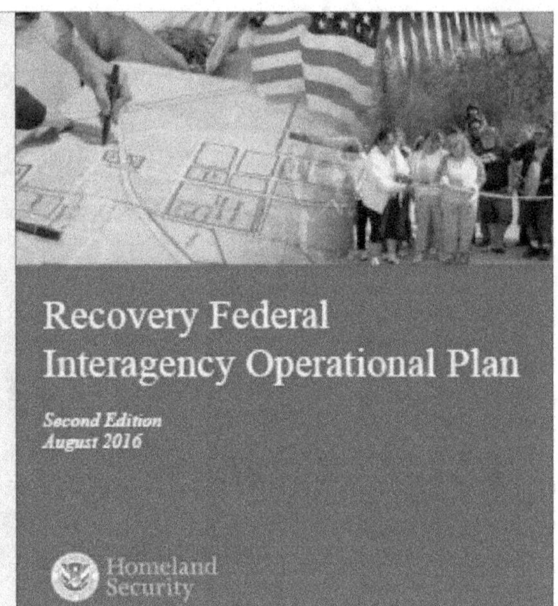

In addition, the flooding led to one of the largest mobilizations in history of FEMA manufactured housing units (second only to Hurricane Katrina), with over 3,000 manufactured housing units in Louisiana as of December 2016. Some are upgraded units that adhere to strict HUD safety standards and feature an innovative sprinkler system to address the risk of fire. In addition, upgraded units are available for eligible disaster survivors with disabilities or other access and functional needs that include improved accessibility features, in accordance with the Uniform Federal Accessibility Standards. Survivors unable to identify other means of housing may depend on manufactured housing units as an alternative temporary housing option.

However, the experiences of displaced residents following the August flooding in Louisiana, as well as other flooding events in 2016, highlighted several challenges in identifying housing solutions:

- ***Assistance for Renters:*** *Although FEMA provides eligible survivors with temporary rental assistance, this benefit can be difficult for survivors to use in rental markets with low availability. Renters within flood-impacted areas faced limited short-term or long-term housing options—with waitlists for apartments as long as five years—due to a rental market still stretched from March flooding. Survivors often preferred to remain in their neighborhoods and school districts, narrowing the pool of practical rental options. To assist with this challenge, the Federal Government increased the amount of rental assistance available to survivors in designated parishes by 25 percent. This increase widened the pool of options that were affordable to survivors who required temporary housing.*

- ***Manufactured Housing Units:*** *Following 2016 floods in Louisiana, FEMA made over 3,000 manufactured housing units available, and individuals and families had occupied approximately 2,500 of these by December 2016. However, FEMA projected that more than 4,000 units were necessary to address needs in Louisiana. Additionally, delivery and installation of these units can be logistically challenging. Understanding these issues, FEMA worked in 2016 to prioritize and improve production efficiency for manufactured housing units.*

- ***Homeowner Verification:*** *Following a disaster, homeowners' absence of paperwork providing proof of ownership (e.g., deed or title) can complicate the receipt of disaster assistance. While much improved since 2005 (i.e., Hurricane Katrina), in the aftermath of the Louisiana flooding, some families whose homes had been passed down from generation to generation were unable to produce the required paperwork to verify home ownership. While FEMA is typically able to work with eligible individuals to identify acceptable alternatives to verify their ownership, these additional steps can complicate a disaster survivor's ability to navigate the FEMA assistance process.*

- ***Rebuilding in Floodplains:*** *Immediately following disasters, homeowners without flood insurance may not have the resources to move or hire contractors, and often complete repairs on their own. Even if owners receive funding assistance, they may have already taken on debt with repairs, motivating them to remain in their homes. Additionally, survivors may often prefer to stay in their current communities and school districts.*

- ***Accessible Housing Options:*** *Prolonged shelter operations following the Louisiana floods highlighted the lack of housing options available and appropriate for individuals with disabilities. Additionally, destroyed or damaged vehicles belonging to these individuals now meant that most would have to rely on public transportation in the interim or permanently, precluding them from housing options in remote geographic areas. Moreover, survivors with disabilities often need to stay in close proximity to their established support system, which further limited the pool of available accessible housing options.*

RECOVERY CASE STUDY: SEVIER COUNTY AND MOUNTAINTOUGH.ORG

In late 2016, a series of wildfires devastated Sevier County, Tennessee. To assist with recovery efforts, Sevier County and its cities created mountaintough.org, a website that links survivors to resources such as food and supplies, job opportunities, and information on applying for disaster assistance. To address housing needs, mountaintough.org includes a form to help survivors identify housing opportunities. The form asks for details such as preferred monthly rent and number of residents to strategically match applicants with appropriate options. Property owners can also fill out a separate form to list any units available for rent.

Key Finding:

Federal departments and agencies are implementing corrective actions to address persistent challenges to core capabilities in the Recovery mission area.

Each year, the *National Preparedness Report* identifies core capabilities that are in need of improvement, requiring sustained attention from leadership and the Nation to address persistent challenges. In the Recovery mission area, previous *National Preparedness Reports* have repeatedly identified five core capabilities as areas for improvement: Economic Recovery, Health and Social Services, Housing, Infrastructure Systems, and Natural and Cultural Resources (see Table 8).

Table 8. Each edition of the *National Preparedness Report* has identified Recovery core capabilities as national areas for improvement.

Core Capability	2012	2013	2014	2015	2016	2017
Economic Recovery	•	•		•	•	•
Health and Social Services	•	•	•			
Housing	•	•	•	•	•	•
Infrastructure Systems	•	•	•	•	•	•
Natural and Cultural Resources	•	•			•	•

In 2016, Federal departments and agencies with responsibilities under these core capabilities took a number of actions to address identified challenges:

- *Economic Recovery: Previous* National Preparedness Reports *have identified that economic development professionals and emergency managers often struggle to communicate effectively and share information, which can impede efforts toward economic recovery. To address these challenges, FEMA launched a compendium of resources on DisasterAssistance.gov to make post-disaster recovery information easily accessible to both disaster survivors and community leaders, including economic development and emergency management professionals. In addition, each U.S. Economic Development Administration (EDA) regional office is conducting outreach to regional partners involved in economic recovery, with the goal of establishing Economic Recovery Support Function Regional Working Groups. The objective of these groups is to build regional capability by helping states identify resources, as well as promoting collaboration and information sharing among stakeholders.*

- *Health and Social Services: Recent studies and real-world events suggest that stakeholders can better integrate health considerations into plans and collaborate more effectively to meet the needs of survivors following disasters. To meet increasing demands for Federal engagement on Health and Social Services post-disaster, ASPR plans to cross-train staff to support field recovery operations. ASPR continues to update recovery planning resources on its website and through its Technical Resources, Assistance Center, and Information Exchange, a healthcare emergency preparedness information gateway, consisting of three complementary domains (i.e., Technical Resources, Assistance Center, and Information Exchange), that ensures the whole community has access to information and resources to improve preparedness efforts. In addition, the National Institutes of Health (NIH) Disaster Research Response (DR2) Program, led by the National Institute of Environmental Health Sciences, is an available resource for all state, local, and municipal health departments, as well as all academia and others interested in performing timely health data collection and vital research in response to disasters. The open access protocols and tools are available on the National Library of Medicine NIH DR2 website. CDC is currently using the DR2 resources to help with disaster preparedness and training for local and state health departments through organizations such as the Council for State and Territorial Epidemiologists.*

- ***Housing:*** *Persistent challenges remain in identifying successful strategies to restore permanent or long-term housing for communities after disasters, including affordable and accessible housing. To address these issues—as well the lack of comprehensive, updated housing doctrine—HUD and FEMA developed and plan to release the Housing Recovery Support Function Concept of Operations. The update comprehensively addresses housing issues ranging from emergency sheltering through permanent housing. With a focus on populations who may be disproportionately impacted by a disaster, HUD also released a toolkit in 2016 that helps recovery stakeholders better consider homeless individuals in pre-disaster planning, response, and long-term recovery. The toolkit includes a "Recovery Action Plan," with strategies for finding transitional or permanent housing solutions for individuals experiencing homelessness after a disaster.*

- ***Infrastructure Systems:*** *Public- and private-sector partners continue to focus on improving infrastructure systems to address vulnerabilities posed by deteriorating critical infrastructure. To facilitate information access and sharing, the National Institute of Standards and Technology's Community Resilience Standards Panel—with cooperation from other Federal partners—created a new section on the "U.S. Climate Resilience Toolkit" website. The new section includes resource compendiums for topics ranging from wastewater and energy systems to disaster planning and social equity. The portal allows easy access to resources that can help communities strengthen their infrastructure resilience. Additionally, DHS is conducting a phased rollout of the Infrastructure Development and Recovery program, an initiative to support the critical infrastructure community with planning expertise, resources, technical assistance, and subject-matter expertise on critical infrastructure protection and recovery. The Infrastructure Development and Recovery program applies a holistic approach to strengthening security and resilience that incorporates resilient strategies, policies, and best practices and informs planning, design, construction, and day-to-day operations of critical infrastructure. DHS piloted the program with local jurisdictions in Alabama, California, and Colorado in December 2016. FEMA is also piloting a new model for reviewing and validating Public Assistance grant applications (see page 92 for additional details).*

- ***Natural and Cultural Resources:*** *While the Natural and Cultural Resources core capability has potentially significant ramifications for disaster recovery—particularly for communities whose economies depend on natural resources—many states and territories do not consider it a priority (see page 14). To bring greater attention to this capability, the National Endowment for the Humanities provided grant funding to organizations such as the Foundation of the American Institute for Conservation of Historic and Artistic Works (FAIC), the Museum of Fine Arts, Houston, and the Bureau of Indian Affairs to launch new forums and webinars in 2016 to provide training and guidance to emergency managers and cultural resources partners. In the FAIC webinar series, for example, cultural-heritage experts shared best practices for topics such as organizing disaster assistance networks, integrating volunteers into recovery efforts, and developing tabletop exercises for training.*

2016 Federal Interagency Recovery Readiness Assessment

The Recovery Support Function Leadership Group (RSFLG) is the senior-level entity that coordinates responsibilities and resolves operational, resource, and preparedness issues relating to interagency recovery activities at the national level. In 2015, the RSFLG created and implemented the Federal Interagency Recovery Readiness Assessment to assess the Federal Government's readiness to support state, local, tribal, and territorial communities in their recovery from disasters and improve resiliency for future incidents. In 2016, the RSFLG refined and reapplied the methodology for this assessment to determine how departments and agencies could perform during multiple, simultaneous, and very large events. Within this scenario, over 25 departments and agencies evaluated their capacity to support recovery efforts, as measured by over 600 Recovery support statements detailing Federal programs or actions implemented during recovery efforts.

During 2016, RSFLG member departments and agencies reflected on experiences since the original publication of the NDRF in 2011 and self-assessed their ability to provide the services, resources, or other support outlined in each support statement. Early analysis of the resulting data indicates that support statements were rated "Perform without challenges" 11 percent of the time (designated "P" in Figure 13) and "Perform with some challenges" 55 percent of the time (designated "S"). Further analysis is underway to identify the causes for ratings of "Perform with major challenges" or "Unable to perform" (designated "M" and "U," respectively). This additional analysis should also reveal how significant the reductions in performance are, including in the "Perform with some challenges" category.

In the self-assessment, Federal departments and agencies most frequently identified "personnel" and "financial" causes behind the challenges inhibiting performance (see Figure 14). For example, personnel constraints may lead some Federal departments and agencies to assign disaster recovery responsibilities as an "additional duty," which can conflict with staff members' primary duties and lead to less support for recovery activities both pre- and post-incident. For other Federal departments and agencies, however, establishing a dedicated recovery cadre may present a financial challenge, as costs associated with developing and maintaining such a cadre are prohibitively large and untenable. Ongoing analysis efforts of the 2016 readiness assessment data, as well as future assessments, will seek to better understand the relationship between these challenges and the appropriateness of possible solutions for individual Federal departments and agencies.

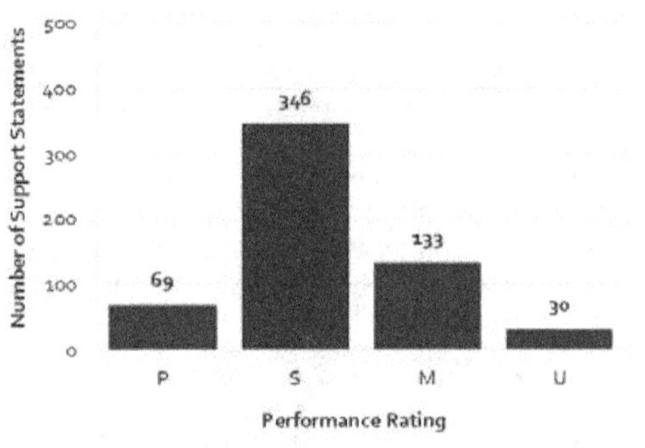

Figure 13. Departments and agencies provided self-assessed performance ratings for Recovery support statements.

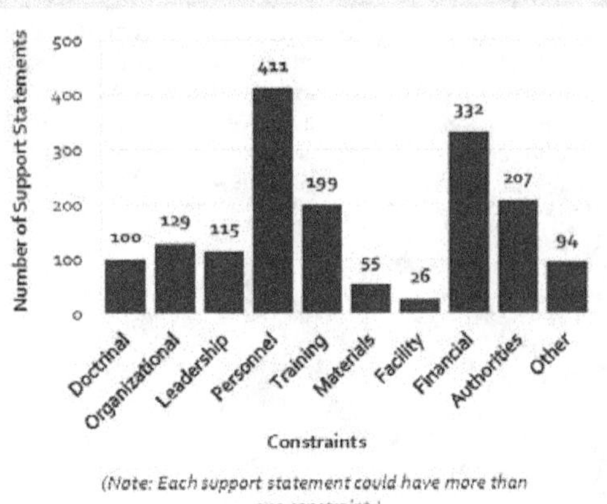

Figure 14. Federal departments and agencies identified one or more constraints inhibiting their performance in Recovery support statements.

Key Finding:

FEMA is applying new methods to provide public assistance for the reimbursement of debris removal, emergency protective measures, and infrastructure projects.

FEMA's Public Assistance Program provides grants to states, tribes, and territories for debris removal, emergency protective measures, and the repair and replacement of public facilities such as roads and bridges following a presidential disaster declaration. Public Assistance Program distributions account for slightly more than half of all FEMA grants and have provided an average of $4.7 billion in disaster assistance annually over the past 10 years. While the program has played an important role in helping communities recover from disasters, a number of challenges in the grant process have hampered the program's timeliness and efficacy.

Jurisdictions seeking support from the Public Assistance Program to support a recovery project must submit an application to FEMA. Historically, FEMA has reviewed and validated the applications without regard to a project's size and complexity, or the changing needs of affected communities. This has resulted in inconsistent and long processing times from application to initial obligation of funds. Moreover, issues arose related to thoroughly reviewing projects, as well as clearly communicating to applicants their eligibility status. This has resulted in instances where applicants funded projects they believed were eligible, only to face a de-obligation of funds or a lack of reimbursement.

To address these challenges, FEMA is piloting a new model for reviewing and validating Public Assistance grant applications. FEMA designed the new model to help affected communities receive funding more quickly by categorizing projects and processing applications according to cost and complexity. This can help prevent large, complex projects from delaying the processing of grants for smaller or already completed projects, which FEMA could otherwise quickly process to speed community recovery. FEMA also developed new positions staffed with subject-matter experts to perform more specialized roles in order to increase consistency during all phases of the application process. Finally, to improve accountability, information sharing, and communication with applicants, the model includes a new web-based tracking system that applicants can use to view and upload required project documentation and track the status of their project applications.

FEMA tested the new delivery model following a late 2015 flooding disaster in Iowa, as well as in 2016 flooding events in Oregon and Georgia. These tests revealed a number of strengths and challenges related to the new delivery model. For example, FEMA found that the new process promoted consistency throughout the grant process. However, both FEMA staff members and applicants reported having insufficient understanding of the new process, as well as many of the tools developed to document damage, work, and costs. Additionally, in Oregon, FEMA had difficulty determining the staffing levels required to implement the new model. FEMA is using the lessons learned from these pilot tests to further update the processes and project-tracking system tools, and FEMA will continuously assess and modify both as needed during future pilots. FEMA is also working to train Public Assistance staff, FEMA Regions, states, and applicants on the new model and its requirements before implementing it nationally.

While *National Preparedness Reports* (of which this is the sixth) describe numerous actions taken to increase national preparedness, they also identify persistent or emerging issues that hinder progress. This section highlights examples of such issues in each of the five mission areas. No easy solutions exist for addressing these complex, national challenges. Instead, each requires innovative ideas and sustained efforts from all preparedness stakeholders to achieve meaningful improvements.

Prevention

Challenge:

Collecting information in an environment of increasingly encrypted communications

The expansion of platforms for encrypted communications, through which terrorists can avoid legal efforts to access and monitor their communications, complicates the IC's ability to prevent and investigate terrorist actions. While encryption services have been available for some time, the seamless integration and default enabling of them on popular devices (e.g., mobile phones) have simplified and facilitated the use of encrypted communications. This change has had the unintended effect of limiting access to a potentially valuable source of intelligence to uncover and interdict terrorist plots. However, weakening encryption so that communications can be readily intercepted increases the cyber risks presented by hackers, criminals, and espionage. More broadly, encrypted communications touch on the conflicting demands for security, privacy, economic competitiveness, and government access to information. Increased engagement between the IC and private-sector companies may provide alternatives to help resolve these conflicting demands.

Challenge:

Detecting and preventing attacks by homegrown violent extremists

Detecting and interdicting plots by homegrown violent extremists (i.e., individuals inspired by foreign terrorist organizations based and primarily radicalized to violence in the United States whose actions are not directed by a foreign terrorist organization) is one of the most difficult challenges law enforcement and intelligence agencies face. Although attacks by this type of individual are historically rare (fewer than 100 such attacks have occurred in the United States since the 1940s), these attacks are becoming increasingly common and deadly. The current decade has already surpassed each prior decade since the 1940s in both the numbers of attacks perpetrated and associated fatalities. Moreover, the June 2016 Orlando Pulse nightclub shooting, which was committed by a homegrown violent extremist, was the deadliest shooting in U.S. history. Homegrown violent extremists are less likely to draw the attention of authorities because their radicalization to violence and planning may be observable only by family or associates who may be hesitant to inform law enforcement, which decreases the likelihood that their terrorist plot will be discovered by law enforcement. Additionally, the growing prevalence of terrorist messaging online increases the number of avenues through which individuals could become radicalized to violence and decide to launch independent attacks. To help prevent radicalization to violence, the Federal Government and private-sector partners have engaged in efforts such as educational outreach, counter-narrative messaging, and suspension of terrorist-linked social media accounts (see page 39 for additional details).

93

Protection

Challenge:

Securing increasingly interconnected systems from cyber attack

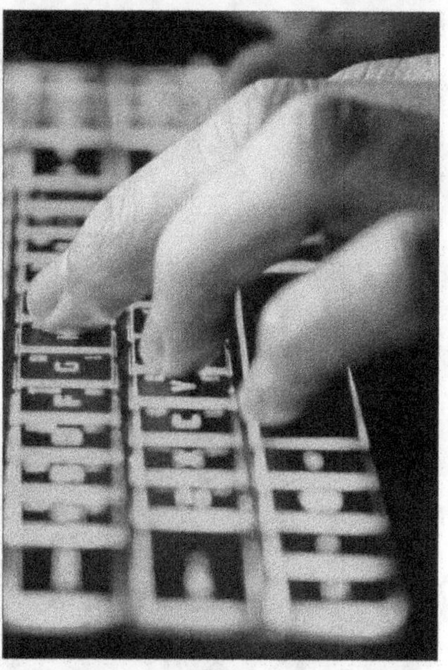

An increasingly connected set of systems and devices, often called the "Internet of Things," controls or monitors everything, from Wi-Fi–enabled home thermostats to industrial control systems in critical infrastructure facilities. Greater connectivity increases efficiency and convenience, but it also increases potential vectors of attack for malicious cyber actors. This expansion in the number of avenues for malicious cyber activity has the potential to degrade the Nation's capacity to protect (and, if need be, restore) electronic communication, information, and service systems. For example, the 2013 hack into Target's payment systems may have originated with a heating, ventilation, and air conditioning vendor who had remote access to Internet-connected devices to monitor temperatures inside stores. More recently, a DDoS attack in October 2016 widely affected Internet access across multiple areas of the United States (see page 9). As more devices are connected every day (one technology research firm estimated a 30-percent growth in Internet-connected devices from 2015 to 2016, up to 6.4 billion devices worldwide), securing individual systems and entire networks will only grow in complexity. In November 2016, DHS released *Strategic Principles for Securing the Internet of Things (IoT)*, which explains the risks presented by the growth in interconnected devices and systems, as well as provides principles and best practices to help ensure their security.

Challenge:

Balancing competing demands between increasing security and minimizing disruptions to travel and commerce

The global movement of people and goods continues to place burdens on balancing steady-state protective operations such as screening, search, and detection operations against minimizing disruptions to travelers and businesses. Over the previous decade, international air travel (measured by distance flown) has grown at an average annual rate of 5.5 percent. As of 2016, TSA screens approximately two million passengers, 4.9 million carry-on items, and 1.3 million checked bags every day. Keeping pace with demand while screening travelers remains a persistent challenge, as exemplified by a springtime surge in airport security wait times in large airports like New York's JFK and concerns over summer delays, and the subsequent expedited hiring of more than 700 TSA officers in May 2016. U.S. seaports handled more than 12.2 million cargo containers in fiscal year 2016 and have experienced a nearly 14 percent increase in units of cargo over the last five years. CBP has taken steps to improve screening efficiency (see page 43). With international travel and commerce increasing, Federal agencies will likely engage in a continual search for ways to help relieve the resulting pressure on screening efforts while maintaining security.

Mitigation

Challenge:

Inspiring individuals to prepare for emergencies

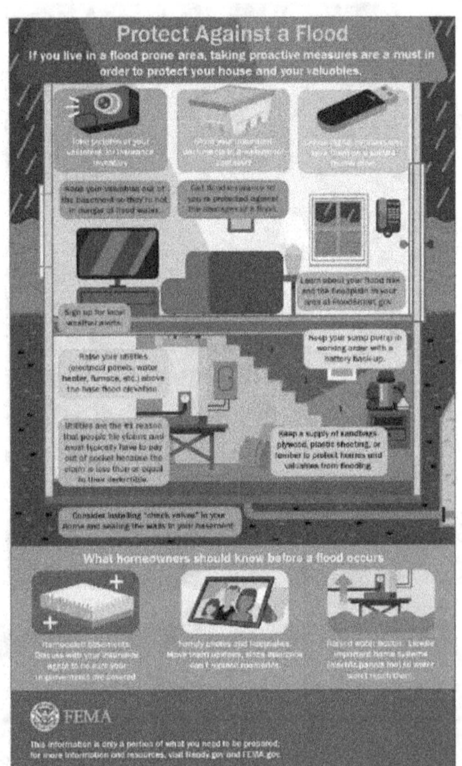

Motivating and empowering individuals to take action prior to an incident is a fundamental pillar for mitigating potential consequences. Through public campaigns such as Ready and America's PrepareAthon!, DHS endeavors to educate individuals on how to prepare for disasters. This includes providing services and auxiliary aids for persons with disabilities and others with access and functional needs, including persons with limited English proficiency. However, increasing the overall level of individual preparedness nationwide proves challenging, as such cultural and behavioral changes require sustained, long-term efforts from the whole community. Although annual National Household Surveys show rising trends in many areas (e.g., having and discussing emergency plans or having supplies), the surveys also identify specific challenges (e.g., variation in awareness by hazard or specific populations) and indicate that the overall level of national preparedness remains low. The varying level of community preparedness education and/or awareness serves as a contributing factor to low levels of national preparedness. For example, in the 2015 *National Household Survey*, FEMA reported that only 34 percent of individuals living in areas with a history of flooding reported having read, seen, or heard information on how to better prepare for a flood. Despite such challenges, results from the same survey reaffirm the positive connection between awareness and taking action. To increase awareness and promote action, Federal agencies and community partners target accessible preparedness messages to whole communities, to include underserved populations, and tie these messages to notable events and popular cultural icons. In addition, stakeholders engage in outreach through websites and social media and support and/or participate in programs that promote awareness and action.

Challenge:

Advancing and communicating cost-benefit analyses to support mitigation decisions

After a disaster, a key component of effective mitigation is the strengthening of resilience against future hazards during rebuilding efforts. Traditionally, FEMA and local governments have examined data on past disasters to project the risk of future disasters and determine whether rebuilding stronger is a worthwhile investment. However, as mitigation stakeholders continue to note, historical meteorological data have not been a good indicator of the growing risk from more frequently occurring natural disasters. In addition, the available data to support cost-benefit analyses are often inconclusive or missing altogether. According to GAO, the lack of comprehensive and reliable data for these analyses may inhibit local governments from investing in mitigation activities. Federal and state stakeholders may be able to improve their cost-benefit analyses and implement better risk management strategies by partnering with private insurance companies, which specialize in identifying, analyzing, and modeling risks.

Response

Challenge:

Ensuring that disaster survivors with disabilities and others with access and functional needs receive equal access to response services

During Hurricane Katrina, many survivors with disabilities and others with access and functional needs experienced difficulties in accessing emergency services, or were stranded while waiting for evacuation assistance or refused shelter by unprepared organizations. Persons with disabilities and others with access and functional needs subsequently experienced a disproportionately high number of fatalities after that hurricane. Since then, emergency managers at all levels of government have placed a greater focus on integrating individuals with disabilities and others with access and functional needs in response efforts. For example, FEMA established the Office of Disability Integration and Coordination in 2010 and added a Disability Integration Advisor position to its deployable disaster workforce in 2012. Challenges remain, however, in providing services for all affected populations during and after a disaster. In 2016, FEMA's National Advisory Council noted that jurisdictions still had limited operational guidance and training on how to incorporate considerations from the *Americans with Disabilities Act* into their emergency management activities. Federal agencies also described difficulty reaching individuals with disabilities and others with access and functional needs with actionable messaging delivered in an accessible format during a disaster. In August 2016, DOJ, HHS, HUD, DHS, and DOT issued joint guidance to ensure that recipients of Federal financial assistance comply with Title VI of 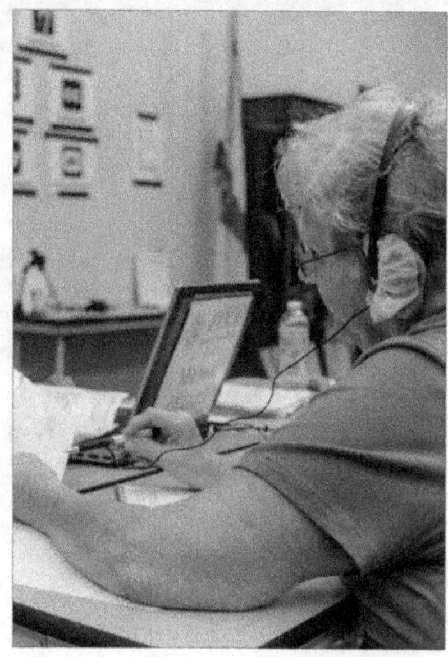 the Civil Rights Act of 1964 and not discriminate against individuals on the basis of race, color, or national origin—including those with limited English proficiency—when providing emergency preparedness, response, and recovery services.

Challenge:

Improving responder capacity and coordination in catastrophic events

Despite progress in preparing for an unprecedented catastrophic event, the Nation remains underprepared to respond to an incident on the scale of a catastrophic earthquake in the Cascadia Subduction Zone or the New Madrid Seismic Zone. Unlike other incidents, these scenarios will likely break existing mechanisms and networks that emergency management employs, with projected consequences (e.g., tens of thousands of survivors requiring immediate medical attention, millions requiring emergency shelter) overwhelming official response and recovery measures for an extended period of time. An after-action report on Cascadia Rising 2016/Ardent Sentry 2016 (see page 71) found that the Nation lacked the capacity to fully respond to an incident of this magnitude, which would present complexities and challenges such as simultaneous requests for limited resources (e.g., access to water) and novel communications and transportation challenges, as well as require adaptive solutions to address life-saving needs. One area that emergency planners at all levels of government have struggled with is incorporating survivors, grassroots organizations, and the general public into response efforts. Historically, these groups have been decisive stabilizing factors in the aftermath of every disaster—even catastrophes—by augmenting response capability (e.g., search and rescue, first aid, radio communications) and serving as important sources for creative and unconventional solutions that catastrophic incidents require. By continuing to promote a culture that empowers these groups, emergency managers can develop additional, much-needed capacity to better address catastrophic events.

Recovery

Challenge:

Comprehensively addressing the housing needs of disaster survivors

Previous *National Preparedness Reports* have cited longstanding issues that impede progress concerning the housing needs of disaster survivors, including accessible and affordable housing. For example, many states and territories expect the Federal Government to take on the responsibility of addressing housing gaps, as states often face gaps in capabilities for housing operations following a large-scale disaster. Resource and logistics challenges in large-scale events may stress Federal capacity as well. Federal agencies also face challenges coordinating their efforts across different phases of housing support (from short-term to long-term housing). Because housing options are constrained by legal, administrative, and logistical requirements, the availability of possible housing solutions is sensitive to decisions made early on in a disaster. HUD is implementing a portal for information access and sharing of FEMA Individual Assistance information to expedite delivery of recovery assistance. It also plans to release the *Housing Recovery Support Function Concept of Operations*, which will address Federal coordination of a variety of housing issues from emergency sheltering to permanent housing.

Challenge:

Developing comprehensive pre-disaster plans to support post-disaster recovery efforts

Under the NDRF, pre-disaster recovery planning provides an opportunity for communities to develop partnerships at all levels of government, establish goals, identify essential resources, and accelerate recovery after a disaster. However, as highlighted in prior *National Preparedness Reports*, strengthened participation from key stakeholders in pre-disaster recovery planning is necessary. For example, a 2015 report from the Institute of Medicine, funded by ASPR, HUD, and the Robert Wood Johnson Foundation, affirms the importance of pre-disaster planning that proactively links emergency management and health leadership at the community level. Moreover, insufficient inclusion of economic development experts in pre-disaster planning continues to hinder post-disaster economic recovery efforts and suggests a similar disconnect between the emergency preparedness community and local economic-development experts. To improve coordination and capabilities for economic recovery efforts, EDA and FEMA are developing training opportunities that bring together officials, emergency managers, and economic development specialists, including the private sector. The EDA is also creating regional working groups with the goal of strengthening planning and information sharing among economic recovery partners across the public and private sectors.

ACF	Administration for Children and Families, U.S. Department of Health and Human Services
AOC	Airport Operations Center
ASPR	Office of the Assistant Secretary for Preparedness and Response, U.S. Department of Health and Human Services
BARDA	Biomedical Advanced Research and Development Authority
BSIR	Biannual Strategy Implementation Report
C2M2	Cybersecurity Capability Maturity Model, U.S. Department of Energy
CAUSE	Canada-United States Enhanced (Resiliency experiment)
CBP	U.S. Customs and Border Protection, U.S. Department of Homeland Security
CDC	Centers for Disease Control and Prevention, U.S. Department of Health and Human Services
COPS	Community Oriented Policing Services
CSI	Container Security Initiative
CVE	Countering violent extremism
DARPA	Defense Advanced Research Projects Agency, U.S. Department of Defense
DDoS	Distributed denial of service
DHS	U.S. Department of Homeland Security
DNDO	Domestic Nuclear Detection Office, U.S. Department of Homeland Security
DoD	U.S. Department of Defense
DOE	U.S. Department of Energy
DOI	U.S. Department of the Interior
DOJ	U.S. Department of Justice
DOT	U.S. Department of Transportation
DR2	Disaster Research Response (Program), National Institutes of Health
E.O.	Executive Order
EDA	U.S. Economic Development Administration
EPA	U.S. Environmental Protection Agency
FAIC	Foundation of the American Institute for Conservation of Historic and Artistic Works
FBI	Federal Bureau of Investigation
FCC	Federal Communications Commission
FDA	U.S. Food and Drug Administration
FEMA	Federal Emergency Management Agency
FESAP	Federal Experts Security Advisory Panel
FIOP	Federal Interagency Operational Plan
FirstNet	First Responder Network Authority
GAO	U.S. Government Accountability Office

GIS	Geographic information system
GPS	Global positioning system
HHS	U.S. Department of Health and Human Services
HPP	Hospital Preparedness Program
HRSA	Health Resources and Services Administration, U.S. Department of Health and Human Services
HSIN	Homeland Security Information Network
HUD	U.S. Department of Housing and Urban Development
I&A	Office of Intelligence and Analysis, U.S. Department of Homeland Security
IBHS	Insurance Institute for Business and Home Safety
IC	Intelligence Community
ICS-CERT	Industrial Control Systems Cyber Emergency Response Team
IED	Improvised explosive device
IIR	Intelligence Information Report
IP	Office of Infrastructure Protection, National Protection and Programs Directorate, U.S. Department of Homeland Security
IPAWS	Integrated Public Alert Warning System
IT	Information technology
JTTF	Joint Terrorism Task Force
MDS	Mennonite Disaster Service
MOU	Memorandum of understanding
NASA	National Aeronautics and Space Administration
NBIB	National Background Investigations Bureau
NCTC	National Counterterorrism Center
NDRF	National Disaster Recovery Framework
NDRP	National Drought Resilience Partnership
NEP	National Exercise Program
NFIP	National Flood Insurance Program
NGS	National Geodetic Survey, National Oceanic and Atmospheric Administration
NIH	National Institutes of Health, U.S. Department of Health and Human Services
NIMS	National Incident Management System
NIST	National Institute of Standards and Technology
NOAA	National Oceanic and Atmospheric Administration
NPSBN	Nationwide Public Safety Broadband Network
NRC	Nuclear Regulatory Commission
NRCS	Natural Resources Conservation Service, U.S. Department of Agriculture
NSA	National Security Agency
OBP	Office for Bombing Prevention, U.S. Department of Homeland Security
ODNI	Office of the Director of National Intelligence
OEC	Office of Emergency Communications, U.S. Department of Homeland Security
OIG	Office of Inspector General
OPM	U.S. Office of Personnel Management
PI-WMP	Pre-Incident Waste Management Plan

PII	Personally identifiable information
POETE	Planning, organization, equipment, training, exercises
PPD	Presidential Policy Directive
PSA	Public service announcement
PSAP	Public safety answering point
RSFLG	Recovery Support Function Leadership Group
SBA	U.S. Small Business Administration
SNS	Strategic National Stockpile
SWAT	Special Weapons and Tactics
TSA	Transportation Security Administration, U.S. Department of Homeland Security
TSC	Terrorist Screening Center
USACE	U.S. Army Corps of Engineers, U.S. Department of Defense
USBR	Bureau of Reclamation, U.S. Department of the Interior
USCG	U.S. Coast Guard
USDA	U.S. Department of Agriculture
USFS	U.S. Forest Service, U.S. Department of Agriculture
USGS	U.S. Geological Survey, U.S. Department of the Interior
VOAD	Voluntary Organizations Active in Disaster
WFRL	Wildland Fire Resilient Landscapes
WMD	Weapon of mass destruction
WYO	Write Your Own program, National Flood Insurance Program
Z-CART	Zika Community Action Response Toolkit

The Federal Emergency Management Agency (FEMA) coordinates the development of the *National Preparedness Report*. To ensure a comprehensive report that reflects progress and challenges occurring nationwide, FEMA takes several actions to collect, analyze, and present information from numerous sources, including:

- *Applying a criteria-based approach in analyzing preparedness assessments, exercises, funding, and long-term trends influencing preparedness to identify national areas for improvement and capabilities to sustain among the 32 core capabilities;*

- *Analyzing 2016 Threat and Hazard Identification and Risk Assessments from 113 states, territories, tribes, and urban areas, as well as 2016 State Preparedness Report submissions from all 56 states and territories, in order to identify national shifts in the threats and hazards that jurisdictions are using to drive their capability requirements, to compare relative performance among all capabilities, and to identify performance trends over time;*

- *Conducting a data call with Federal departments and agencies to solicit their input and identify national preparedness accomplishments and related challenges;*

- *Completing a literature review of open-source material from all levels of government, academia, professional organizations, and the private sector for information on notable progress and challenges related to the 32 core capabilities identified in the Goal;*

- *Coordinating outreach with professional organizations and other non-Federal partners to obtain information, solicit perspectives on preparedness, and identify example case studies;*

- *Examining exercises and real-world events occurring or reported in 2016 to identify preparedness outcomes and lessons learned; and*

- *Engaging Federal departments, agencies, and senior interagency coordination groups to review and supplement report content.*

What is the 2016 Threat and Hazard Identification and Risk Assessment and State Preparedness Report?

The 2017 *National Preparedness Report* includes results from the integrated 2016 Threat and Hazard Identification and Risk Assessment and State Preparedness Report. These programs support the National Preparedness System by helping states, territories, tribes, and urban areas annually assess their preparedness capabilities and identify capability gaps. Jurisdictions use the Threat and Hazard Identification and Risk Assessment process to determine threats and hazards of primary concern, establish capability targets, and analyze the resources required to address anticipated risks. Next, states and territories assess their current capability levels against their assessment targets in the State Preparedness Report. States, territories, and the Federal Government use this information to support decisions to build, validate, deliver, and sustain core capabilities. The Federal Government also uses the results to guide strategic direction for programs that help close preparedness capability gaps.

Homeland Security 2017 National Preparedness Report

These activities provided a wide range of sources and insights, as well as a broader perspective on preparedness. In total, the 2017 *National Preparedness Report* reflects input from more than 600 data sources. Since preparedness is the shared responsibility of the entire Nation, FEMA solicited input not only from 124 Federal agencies, but also 29 non-Federal partners. In particular, non-Federal partners contributed to the report in numerous ways, playing prominent roles in a number of preparedness initiatives; issuing the results of various topically relevant assessments, reports, and surveys; and sponsoring conferences and workshops that address preparedness issues.

SOURCES

FEMA compiled the 2017 *National Preparedness Report* using a combination of qualitative and quantitative preparedness data and contributions from multiple sources.

BY THE NUMBERS

167	**124**	**600+**	**113**	**29**
Inputs Recieved from Formal Data Call	Federal Offices Engaged	Data Sources Referenced	Threat and Hazard Identification and Risk Assessment and State Preparedness Report Submissions	Non-Federal Stakeholders Engaged

NON-FEDERAL COMMUNITY ENGAGEMENT INCLUDED:

- American Society for the Prevention of Cruelty to Animals
- Blue Forest Conservation
- Center for Internet Security
- Iowa Legal Aid
- National Academy of Sciences
- Washington State Military Department
- Other Private-sector Partners

The majority of the 2017 *National Preparedness Report* consists of key findings that assess specific areas of national preparedness. Key findings draw on both quantitative and qualitative sources to document relevant advancements and challenges. Five criteria helped identify key findings from the data sources and inputs:

- **Advancements in or challenges to preparedness programs:** *Whether major initiatives saw progress or difficulties that affected preparedness or resilience nationwide*
- **Consequential increases or decreases in resources:** *The extent to which increases or decreases in resources—such as funding and personnel—meaningfully affected building, sustaining, or delivering a core capability*
- **Broad impact across the public and private sector:** *Whether preparedness activities or assessments addressed multiple levels of government and non-Federal partners, including performance in real-world incidents*
- **Significant increases or decreases in capability:** *The extent to which quantitative data demonstrated increases or decreases in a preparedness capability over time, as well as the underlying drivers for these changes*
- **Relevance to national priorities:** *Whether an activity demonstrated progress in establishing or implementing national-level strategies and policies that set priorities for improving capability performance*

For inclusion in the 2017 *National Preparedness Report*, key findings had to satisfy at least two of these five criteria.

With 2016 marking the 15-year anniversary of the 9/11 tragedy, the 2017 *National Preparedness Report* presents this case study as a means of reflecting on ways the Nation has restructured and retooled its preparedness efforts following 9/11. In the wake of 9/11, Congress and the President established a bipartisan commission to investigate the facts and circumstances surrounding the attacks. In *The 9/11 Commission Report*, published in 2004, commission members identified 41 recommendations to guard against future attacks. This case study highlights some of the Commission's recommendations, noting where the Nation has made substantial progress, as well as where some recommendations remain unfulfilled.

Achieving Greater Unity of Effort

Several of the Commission's recommendations called out the fragmented nature of homeland security efforts at the time of the attacks. For example, commission members determined that structural barriers and concerns about security led to excessive over-classification and compartmentalization of information among agencies, making it impossible for the Intelligence Community to piece together relevant information to uncover and prevent the attacks. They recommended encouraging information sharing to address the observed imbalance between security and shared knowledge.

Since 9/11, various nationwide efforts have enhanced information sharing among Federal, state, and local law enforcement, and the private sector:

- *The Federal Bureau of Investigation (FBI) increased the number of Joint Terrorism Task Forces (JTTFs), which conduct counterterrorism investigations, from 35 in 2001 to more than 100 today. While FBI-led, these task forces integrate other Federal, state, local, tribal, and territorial law enforcement partners and inform intelligence products shared with law enforcement and homeland security agencies.*
- *The Terrorist Screening Center (TSC), created in 2003, consolidated and manages the Terrorist Screening Database (commonly known as the "watchlist") to enable screening for immigration and travel, law enforcement, counterterrorism investigations, and intelligence purposes. The TSC ensures the timely dissemination of terrorist identity information to screening agencies for the appropriate and lawful use of terrorism-related information.*
- *Seventy-eight state and major urban area fusion centers play a complementary role in gathering, analyzing, and sharing information, connecting law enforcement and state and local leadership with the rest of the homeland security enterprise.*
- *Information-sharing platforms (e.g., the Homeland Security Information Network, the Technical Resource for Incident Prevention) facilitate the sharing of sensitive information.*

Information-sharing efforts also now include a more well-defined role for local law enforcement and the public, particularly as it relates to detection. The Nationwide Suspicious Activity Reporting Initiative helps train state and local law enforcement to recognize behaviors and indicators related to terrorism, and standardizes how these observations are documented and shared. Meanwhile, the "If You See Something, Say Something™" campaign has raised public awareness of indicators of terrorism and crime and emphasizes the importance of reporting suspicious activity to the proper authorities.

Several of the aforementioned capabilities were involved in apprehending Faisal Shahzad, a terrorist who attempted to detonate a car bomb in Times Square. On May 1, 2010, two New York City sidewalk vendors—both of whom later referred to the "See something, Say something" mantra—alerted a nearby police officer about a suspicious vehicle. The resulting discovery of a failed car bomb initiated investigations by JTTFs in New York, Connecticut, and Massachusetts, with members from the FBI and New York Police Department playing key roles. The investigations led FBI to nominate Faisal Shahzad to the watchlist. As events unfolded, fusion centers also mobilized to identify and share potential leads with the JTTFs. Two days later, Faisal Shahzad was attempting to leave the country through JFK airport, but was denied boarding due to his inclusion in the watchlist. U.S. Customs and Border Protection (CBP) officers then took Faisal Shahzad into custody.

A second area in which fragmented preparedness efforts proved costly on 9/11 was in coordinating response activities at the World Trade Center. Commission members identified problems with command and control that hampered responders' abilities to work together, and the commission recommended that emergency response agencies adopt the incident command system and unified command. As a result, in 2003, President Bush directed the establishment of a single, comprehensive National Incident Management System (NIMS)—which incorporates the incident command system and unified command as best practices—to enable responders at all jurisdictional levels and across disciplines to work together. This directive required all Federal departments and agencies to adopt NIMS and made NIMS a requirement for receiving Federal preparedness assistance. Since then, millions of individuals nationwide have received training in NIMS. As of 2016, 91 percent of states and territories have incorporated NIMS concepts and principles into all appropriate training. In recent self-assessments, states and territories have consistently rated themselves the most proficient in carrying out Operational Coordination (compared to other core capabilities). The Nation's performances during Hurricane Sandy, and most recently, Hurricane Matthew, while continuing to reveal room for improvement, indicate progress in coordinating large-scale response efforts.

Commission members also identified issues with interoperability. While evacuating civilians from the World Trade Center, first responders struggled with situational awareness of what other responders were doing. Since its inception in 2003, the U.S. Department of Homeland Security (DHS) has awarded billions of dollars in grants to state and local agencies to enhance their communications capabilities. In addition, under the direction of Congress, DHS worked with stakeholders from all levels of government to develop the first National Emergency Communications Plan, which provided a more strategic approach to strengthening emergency communications capabilities nationwide and included three national performance goals to evaluate emergency communications. To measure progress toward these goals, DHS analyzed performance reports from more than 2,800 counties (covering 30,000 public safety agencies). While nearly 75 percent of counties reported consistently being able to provide communications during routine incidents involving multiple jurisdictions, disciplines, and agencies, only 34 percent reported they could do so during a significant event. Despite wide variation in the level of proficiency, the assessments provided evidence of nationwide progress.

Challenges in Implementing National Initiatives

Despite improvements in emergency communications, progress has been slow to address the 9/11 commission's recommendation to free up and assign additional communication frequencies (i.e., frequency spectrum) for public safety use and to support interoperable communications. While Congress included provisions in the *Middle Class Tax Relief and Job Creation Act of 2012* for a new nationwide broadband network for public safety communications, the establishment of this network remains in progress.

Indeed, a few of the commission's unfulfilled recommendations underscore the sweeping nature of the changes called for in the report, as well as the challenges of implementing change on a national scale. For example, while Congress provided seven billion dollars for initial seed funding for the network, experts expect that the cost of deploying the nationwide public safety broadband network will likely exceed this initial funding. FirstNet had to consider this fact in its request for proposal and is why its new partner, AT&T, has committed to about $40 billion in additional funding throughout the life of the 25-year contract. Additionally, five jurisdictions in close coordination with FirstNet have moved forward on five Early Builder broadband projects, which will be reconciled and/or integrated with the FirstNet network, when it is deployed in their jurisdictions.

The *9/11 Commission Report* outlines two other commission recommendations that have encountered significant implementation challenges:

▪ ***Establishing a biometric entry-exit screening system:*** *While CBP has collected biometric entry data on foreign nationals since 2004, it still lacks a comprehensive, nationwide system for collecting biometric exit data. Combined entry-exit data—especially biometric data, which provides greater assurance of a traveler's identity —is essential to identifying foreign nationals who are overstaying their visits and who may pose homeland security risks. Five of the 19 hijackers on 9/11 exceeded their authorized stay periods. Collecting biometric data at points of departure, however, will likely disrupt existing processes and delay travel and commerce. For example, U.S. airports lack the infrastructure and processes to ensure exit control (i.e., that screened passengers actually depart) and accomplish this in a time-sensitive fashion.*

▪ ***Secure Identification:*** *In 2005, Congress passed the REAL ID Act, which sought to enhance national security by preventing the fraudulent issuing and use of state driver's licenses and identification cards. Six of the 9/11 hijackers used state-issued identifications to check in for their flights, of which three were obtained fraudulently. In alignment with the 9/11 Commission's recommendation, the Act establishes minimum security standards for state-issued identification (e.g., driver's licenses) and prohibits Federal agencies from accepting identification that fails to meet these standards, including boarding commercial aircraft and entering Federal buildings. Implementation has encountered resistance and delays, with numerous states enacting laws expressly prohibiting state agencies from complying with the Act, and DHS has provided multiple extensions on its deadlines for compliance. As of January 2016, less than half of states and territories were fully compliant.*

For each of these initiatives, the Nation has encountered multiple barriers to successful implementation, requiring new policies, processes, and legislation; increased awareness and buy-in; supporting infrastructure; and innovative technological solutions. While progress has occurred, it has been incremental in nature, with significant uncertainty regarding timelines for completion.

Conclusion

The effects of the attacks on 9/11 reverberated throughout the homeland and triggered numerous efforts to restructure and retool existing capabilities nationwide to better prepare for all threats and hazards, including the creation of DHS. As highlighted by this case study, the attacks prompted a deep examination of the Nation's state of preparedness and led to sweeping changes, some of which have been challenging to implement. More than 15 years later, however, the Nation is more prepared and resilient as a result.

CAPABILITIES TO SUSTAIN

Selection Methodology - Appendix D

The Federal Emergency Management Agency (FEMA) used a two-part analysis to identify capability to sustain candidates. The first part of the analysis assesses proficiency, and the second part assesses a potential gap between demand and performance. Higher scores indicate that a core capability is a better candidate for being a capability to sustain.

In the first part of the analysis, FEMA scored each core capability against nine preparedness indicators to identify core capabilities that the Nation is proficient in executing (see Table 9). A maximum of 5.5 points was possible.

Table 9. Part one of the capabilities to sustain analysis includes nine preparedness indicators that help identify core capabilities the Nation is proficient in executing.

Criteria	No. of Indicators	Max. Point Contribution
Do the key findings in the 2017 *National Preparedness Report* indicate that this capability is an area of strength?	1	1 point
Do the 2016 State Preparedness Report results indicate proficiency in this core capability nationwide?	1	1 point
Is this core capability exercised frequently?	3	1 point
Do data indicate strong participation in relevant training courses for this core capability?	1	0.5 points
Do various assessments indicate that the core capability is relatively mature?	3	2 points

In the second part of the analysis, FEMA scored each core capability against six additional indicators to identify core capabilities in which a growing gap may be likely between demand for the core capability and its performance (see Table 10). A maximum of 3.5 points was possible.

Table 10. Part two of the capabilities to sustain analysis includes six preparedness indicators that help identify core capabilities in which a growing gap in capability may be likely in the future.

Criteria	No. of Indicators	Max. Point Contribution
Do trends in State Preparedness Report results indicate a decreasing ability to meet performance targets for this core capability nationwide?	3	1.5 points
Has this core capability experienced a significant drop in grant funding that may result in a future decline in capability levels?	1	0.5 points
Do Federal strategic plans indicate that increasing demand for this core capability may exist in the future?	1	1 point
Do various drivers influencing change in emergency management indicate that increasing gaps in this core capability may exist in the future?	1	0.5 points

Homeland Security 2017 National Preparedness Report

AREAS FOR IMPROVEMENT

Selection Methodology - Appendix E

The Federal Emergency Management Agency (FEMA) scored each core capability against nine preparedness indicators to identify area for improvement candidates (see Table 11). Higher scores indicated a likely area for improvement. FEMA scored each core capability against nine preparedness indicators. A maximum of 5.0 points was possible.

Table 11. The areas for improvement analysis consists of nine preparedness indicators that help identify core capabilities in which the Nation is less proficient.

Criteria	No. of Indicators	Max. Point Contribution
Do the key findings in the 2017 *National Preparedness Report* indicate that this capability exhibits major deficiencies in its performance nationally?	1	1 point
Do the 2016 State Preparedness Report results indicate low proficiency in this core capability nationwide?	1	1 point
Is this core capability infrequently exercised?	3	1 point
Do data indicate low numbers of relevant training courses for this core capability?	1	0.5 point
Is there evidence of progress in assessing and validating core capability performance?	1	0.5 points
Has this core capability experienced a significant drop in grant funding that may result in a future decline in capability levels?	1	0.5 points
Do various drivers influencing change in emergency management indicate that increasing gaps in this core capability may exist in the future?	1	0.5 points

FEMA reviewed all scores as part of its final selection process. This review set the threshold for consideration as an area for improvement. If a core capability's score was above the required threshold of 1.5 points with no discrepancies identified, FEMA selected that core capability as an area for improvement.